Paula Jane Rubin

ART
AN INTRODUCTION

ART
AN INTRODUCTION

Dale G. Cleaver
UNIVERSITY OF TENNESSEE

HARCOURT, BRACE & WORLD, INC.
NEW YORK / CHICAGO / BURLINGAME

Preface

For a balanced introduction to art, a dual approach is really needed: (1) a consideration of the elements of form, design, and technique, and (2) a historical survey of art as it reflects the stylistic evolution and development of these elements. This book addresses itself to both needs.

Part I introduces the visual and tactile elements of art and demonstrates their use in painting, sculpture, and architecture. It then takes up the functions of recognizable objects and symbolism, the basic techniques used in the arts, and finally the philosophical and practical problems in making value judgments about art.

Part II presents broad, generally accepted interpretations of the most important periods, stylistic movements, and individual artists in Western culture. Each chapter treats the general stylistic developments within each of the three media and describes representative works of art (for periods through the Middle Ages) or representative artists (from the Renaissance on), selected for their aesthetic and historical importance and for their capacity to demonstrate stylistic trends and important techniques.

The result, it is hoped, is a core text with concise interpretations and a carefully selected group of high quality plates that can serve as a structural basis for courses of varying aims and orientations. The book is intended to be used in conjunction with other material. Selective bibliographies are provided at the end of each chapter, and abbreviations in the margins of Part II guide the reader to books in the bibliographies that contain additional illustrations of each artist's work. The book can also be supplemented by materials on areas such as primitive and oriental art, photography, and various special fields of design. Of necessity, the writing has been highly condensed, and only the most important cultural periods and the major media have been included.

I should like to thank my artist-colleagues in the Art Department of the University of Tennessee for their suggestions about the section on techniques, the staff of the James D. Hoskins Library for courteous assistance, and my mother for her advice as a dedicated teacher.

DALE G. CLEAVER

Contents

Preface   *v*

Part One
THE PRINCIPLES OF ART   *1*

Chapter 1 Visual and Tactile Elements in Art   3
     2 Functions of Design   21
     3 Subject Matter   29
     4 Techniques   35
     5 Problems of Value Judgment   57

Part Two
THE HISTORY OF ART IN WESTERN CULTURE   *61*

Chapter 6 Egypt: 3200–30 B.C.   63
     7 Greece: 1100–100 B.C.   79
     8 Rome: 200 B.C.–330 A.D.   95
     9 Early Christian and Byzantine Art: 100–1453   109
    10 Medieval Art in the North: 400–1400   121
    11 Renaissance Art: 1400–1600   141
    12 Baroque and Neo-Classic Art: 1600–1800   177
    13 Modern Art: 1800 to the Present   217

Index   277

COLOR PLATE 1

GIORGIONE. *The Pastoral Concert*. About 1510. Oil on canvas. About 4′ x 5′. Louvre Museum, Paris. (Photo: Conzett & Huber, Zürich)

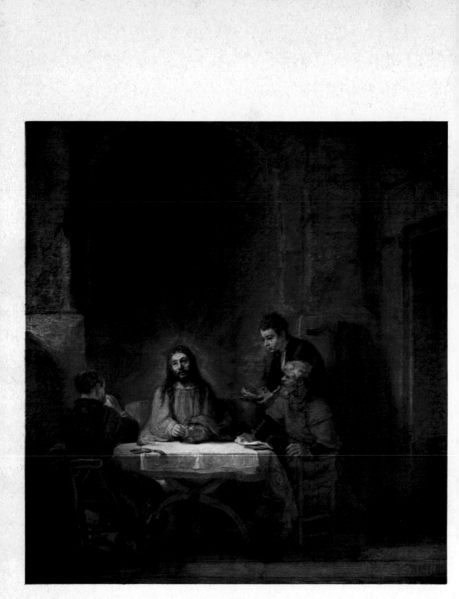

COLOR PLATE 2

REMBRANDT VAN RIJN. *Supper at Emmaus*. 1648. Oil on panel.
27″ x 26″. Louvre Museum, Paris. (Photo: Giraudon, Paris)

COLOR PLATE 3

MONET. *Rouen Cathedral, West Façade Sunlight.* 1894. Oil on canvas
39½″ x 26″. National Gallery, Washington, D.C., Chester Dale Collection.

COLOR PLATE 4

MATISSE. *Decorative Figure on an Ornamental Background.* 1927. Oil on
canvas. About 4′ x 3′. Museum of Modern Art, Paris.
(Photo: Giraudon, Paris)

List of Plates

COLOR PLATE 1
Giorgione, The Pastoral Concert

COLOR PLATE 2
Rembrandt van Rijn, Supper at Emmaus

COLOR PLATE 3
Monet, Rouen Cathedral, West Façade Sunlight

COLOR PLATE 4
Matisse, Decorative Figure on an Ornamental Background

PLATE

1 Menkure and his queen, from Giza
2 Temple of Horus, Edfu
3 Temple of Horus, hypostyle hall from the court
4 Temple of Horus, plan
5 Fowling scene from the tomb of Amenemheb, Thebes
6 Parthenon, Athens
7 Parthenon, plan
8 Artemision statue
9 Lapith fighting with centaur, metope from the Parthenon
10 Exekias, Ajax and Achilles playing draughts, vase painting
11 Praxiteles, Hermes with the infant Dionysus
12 Portrait of a Roman
13 Justinian and attendants, mosaic in S. Vitale, Ravenna
14 Colosseum, Rome
15 Pantheon, Rome
16 Pantheon, plan
17 Pantheon, interior
18 Triumphal Arch of Constantine, Rome
19 Maison Carrée, Nîmes, France

20   Mosaic showing street musicians
21   S. Apollinare in Classe, Ravenna
22   S. Apollinare in Classe, interior
23   S. Apollinare in Classe, plan
24   The Apocalyptic Christ, tympanum, Moissac
25   St. Sernin, Toulouse
26   St. Sernin, interior
27   Amiens Cathedral
28   Amiens Cathedral, nave
29   Amiens Cathedral, choir vaults
30   Last Judgment, from central portal of west façade of Amiens Cathedral
31   Golden Virgin (Vièrge Dorée), from south transept trumeau of Amiens Cathedral
32   Jan van Eyck, Arnolfini and His Bride
33   Giotto, Pietà
34   Ghiberti, Sacrifice of Isaac, Gates of Paradise, Baptistery, Florence
35   Donatello, Young John the Baptist
36   Raphael, Madonna of the Meadow
37   Michelangelo, Tomb of Giuliano de' Medici
38   Masaccio, The Tribute Money
39   Leonardo da Vinci, The Madonna of the Rocks
40   Michelangelo, Creation of Adam, detail from the ceiling of the Sistine Chapel, Vatican
41   Titian, Danaë
42   Brunelleschi, Pazzi Chapel, Florence
43   Brunelleschi, Pazzi Chapel, plan
44   Giuliano da Sangallo, S. Maria delle Carceri, Prato, plan
45   Giuliano da Sangallo, S. Maria delle Carceri
46   Giuliano da Sangallo, S. Maria delle Carceri, interior
47   Palladio, Villa Rotonda, Vicenza
48   Palladio, Villa Rotonda, plan
49   Dürer, The Four Horsemen of the Apocalypse
50   Holbein the Younger, The Ambassadors
51   Bruegel the Elder, The Wedding Feast
52   El Greco, Crucifixion
53   Rubens, Coup de Lance (The Crucifixion)
54   Borromini, S. Carlo alle Quattro Fontane, Rome
55   Borromini, S. Carlo alle Quattro Fontane, plan

56 Borromini, S. Carlo alle Quattro Fontane, interior
57 Bernini, The Ecstasy of St. Teresa, Cornaro Chapel
58 Poussin, Orpheus and Eurydice
59 Watteau, Embarkation for Cythera
60 Mansart and Lemercier, Val-de-Grâce, Paris
61 Mansart and Lemercier, Val-de-Grâce, plan
62 Mansart and Lemercier, Val-de-Grâce, interior
63 Cosmas and Egid Quirin Asam, Assumption of the Virgin
64 Neumann, The Church of the Fourteen Saints (Vierzehn-heiligen), near Banz
65 Neumann, The Church of the Fourteen Saints, plan
66 Neumann, The Church of the Fourteen Saints, interior
67 Goya, May Third, 1808
68 David, The Death of Socrates
69 Constable, The Hay Wain
70 Turner, Rain, Steam, and Speed
71 Canova, Pauline Borghese as Venus
72 Jefferson, Monticello, Charlottesville, Virginia
73 Rodin, The Thinker
74 Barry and Pugin, Houses of Parliament, London
75 Delacroix, The Lion Hunt
76 Ingres, The Apotheosis of Homer
77 Manet, The Luncheon on the Grass
78 Corot, Souvenir de Mortefontaine
79 Degas, The Glass of Absinthe
80 Renoir, The Swing
81 Seurat, Sunday Afternoon on the Island of La Grande Jatte
82 Van Gogh, Wheat Field with Cypresses
83 Cezanne, Mt. S. Victoire from Bibemus Quarry
84 Picasso, Dr. Claribel Cone
85 Beckmann, Self-Portrait with Graver
86 Kandinsky, Improvisation
87 Dali, The Persistence of Memory
88 De Kooning, Woman
89 Kline, Le Gros
90 Mondrian, Composition with Blue and Yellow
91 Davis, Something on the Eight Ball
92 Picasso, The Three Musicians
93 Maillol, Mediterranean
94 Moore, Reclining Figure

95   Gabo, Linear Construction
96   Roszak, Whaler of Nantucket
97   Calder, Under the White Sickle Moon
98   Wright, Robie House, Chicago
99   Wright, Robie House, plan
100 Le Corbusier, Notre-Dame-du-Haut, Ronchamp
101 Le Corbusier, Notre-Dame-du-Haut, interior
102 Le Corbusier, Notre-Dame-du-Haut, plan
103 Mies van der Rohe, Seagram Building, New York

Part One **THE PRINCIPLES OF ART**

To understand the art of our own time or that of other eras, it is necessary first to consider the nature of art and some of the principles by which it operates. For our purposes, a work of art might be defined as an object that has the capacity to express and stimulate experience within a discipline. The experience may range from the pity evoked by the face of a starving child to a revelation of order in architecture. The discipline may vary from the strictest geometrical organization to a spontaneous irregularity that comes perilously close to the accidental; yet discipline provides for order, completeness, and intensity.

The basis for the visual arts is visual and tactile experience, but not all visual and tactile experiences are art; the difference lies in human purpose. The artist arranges an experience for us by manipulating, within the limits of a discipline, such elements as line, shape, mass, light and dark, texture, and color. The painter or sculptor may use these elements to represent well-known objects from our daily world and to suggest feelings about them, or he may create an entirely new world for our contemplation. The architect is equally concerned with these elements, although he is rarely inclined to depict objects in his art and must usually consider utilitarian functions such as shelter and useful space. Whatever his field, the artist creates by composing the basic elements, and the word COMPOSITION *is often used to denote a work of art. The individual*

1

objects or parts within the work of art are frequently called FORMS, *but the word* FORM *is also used for the total character or structure of a composition. Thus we call the study of how visual and tactile elements function in art* FORMAL ANALYSIS.

Chapter One VISUAL AND TACTILE ELEMENTS IN ART

Line

Line may be thought of as the path of a moving point, as the edge of a flat shape, as the axis (dominant direction) of a shape, or as the contour of a solid object. Line may be of even or modulated (varied) thickness; and the range of personality it may express is wide: quick, slow, or still; nervous, majestic, or rigid. It can suggest mass, texture, light, and shadow; it can emphasize form or create mood.

In Picasso's pencil drawing of *Dr. Claribel Cone* (PLATE 84), the lines overlap and are modulated to suggest roundness and heaviness in the body, but they become light and rippling to depict the ruffles of lace. In contrast, the *Self-Portrait with Graver* drypoint by Beckmann (PLATE 85) expresses a nervous, tense personality with its jerky, restless lines and their conflicting angles. Beckmann used *cross-hatching* (superimposed sets of parallel lines) for the shadows that define the mass of the head.

In the painting by Ingres (PLATE 76), line is seen mainly as the distinct contour of objects or as the sweeping folds of clothing. Calculated precision and static equilibrium are expressed by the clear linear definition of parts and the obvious axial balance. Delacroix (PLATE 75) evoked line with short curving brush strokes that occasionally establish the contour of an object but more often blur the separations between parts and heighten the frenzied activity.

Sculptured line may have the calm of Canova's *Pauline Borghese as Venus* (PLATE 71), where the distinct, quiet body contour and the gentle curves in the clothing confirm the static pose. On the other hand, the *Assumption of the Virgin* by Cosmas and Egid Asam (PLATE 63) has a Delacroix-like activity in its twisting, complex contours.

3

In architecture, line may emphasize rigid simplicity and sharply defined edges as in *S. Maria delle Carceri* (PLATE 45). The simple balance of vertical and horizontal lines in this church is sacrificed in *Amiens Cathedral* (PLATE 27) for a lavish upward surge of dominating vertical lines.

MOTION IN LINE

To suggest or emphasize movement, as in the painting by Delacroix or *Amiens Cathedral*, line may be used in at least two ways: it may represent or suggest things that we know are capable of motion, such as rippling waves, or it may imply motion by its form or by its relation to other lines. Our experience of gravity causes us to feel that vertical and horizontal lines are stable, whereas unsupported diagonal lines move in the direction of their leaning (*Fig.* 1). Grouped lines may suggest tensions between each other by the degree to which they seem to require or to provide mutual support (*Fig.* 2). Curving lines tend to move in the direction of their greatest thrust; modulating the thickness of the line can accentuate this effect (*Fig.* 3). Angles often seem to point toward their apex (*Fig.* 4), and a line may suggest motion by drawing our attention toward one end (*Fig.* 5). The dynamic effect of lines upon each other is dramatically illustrated by several classic diagrams. The vertical lines in Figure 6a are actually parallel but appear not to be because of the pushing forces of the diagonals. The horizontal lines in Figure 6b are equal in length but appear different because of the expanding and contracting qualities of the diagonals, whereas the verticals in Figure 6c seem to push the two diagonals out of line. These effects may be exploited deliberately or instinctively by the artist.

LINE AND SPACE

The depth in Masaccio's *Tribute Money* (PLATE 38) is achieved partially by *linear perspective*, one means of creating the illusion of depth on a flat surface. To our eyes, parallel lines in a plane pointing into space appear to converge at a *vanishing point* (V.P.) on the horizon established by our eye level (*Fig.* 7). Frequently, however, intervening objects hide the horizon. In Figure 8, the converging lines of Masaccio's building have been extended until they meet, thus revealing the vanishing point, the hidden horizon, and the eye level chosen for us by the artist. Masaccio used linear perspective also to emphasize the major figure in the composition, Jesus, by placing the vanishing point right behind His head. In choosing the

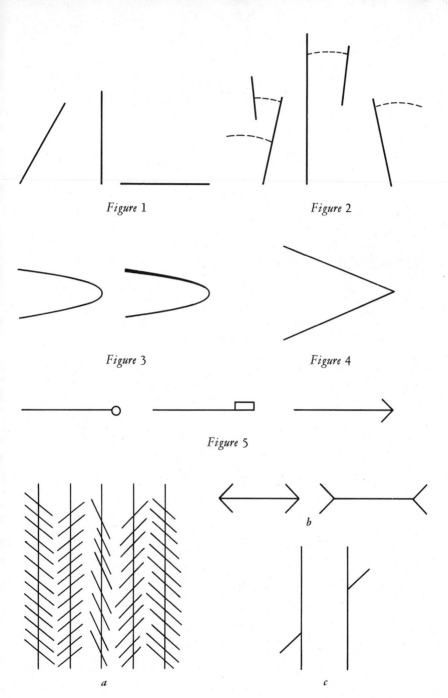

Figure 1

Figure 2

Figure 3

Figure 4

Figure 5

Figure 6

eye level and hence the horizon, the artist may give us an ordinary view (*Fig.* 7) or a worm's-eye view (*Fig.* 9). When all converging lines focus on a single vanishing point, as in the Masaccio, we call it a *one-point perspective* system (*Fig.* 7). Often it is desirable to have more than one vanishing point, as in Figure 9; an appropriate term is *multiple-point perspective*. The artist is not bound to restrict himself to a particular system. The various types of perspective—and there are others not mentioned here—are only devices that the artist may or may not wish to use. He may deliberately use two or more different eye levels in the same painting in order to emphasize certain objects or to create for us an unusual experience of space.

Shape

A *shape* is an area or a plane with distinguishable boundaries. If we think of shape as having length and width only, then it is a more limited term than *form* and is distinguishable from *mass*, which requires depth as a third dimension (although it is possible to ignore the third dimension of a mass and consider it as a shape if we view it one surface at a time or see it in silhouette). Shape, like line, may have many personalities: rigid, flexible, precise, uncertain, calm, active, awkward, or graceful.

Picasso's *Three Musicians* (PLATE 92) has shapes that tip, slide, bend suddenly, break up, and interweave in a staccato fashion; the total effect is one of great activity. In the *Decorative Figure on an Ornamental Background* (COLOR PLATE 4), Matisse placed a massive, rigidly contoured figure in an environment of shapes which blossom expansively within loose-framing lines (*Fig.* 10). It is the room that appears to move, while the woman seems motionless. This unusual effect comes partly from the orientation of the figure along vertical and horizontal lines, which seem stable compared with the diagonals of the floor and the irregular curves on the wall. In contrast, the *mosaic* (composition made from small pieces of colored stone or glass) of *Justinian and Attendants* (PLATE 13) uses rigidly outlined shapes with large, quiet, unbroken areas. Our attention is not pulled suddenly from one shape to another. The equilibrium seems motionless. In Degas's painting *The Glass of Absinthe* (PLATE 79), the shapes of the table tops create depth and lead us to the figures.

To consider shape in sculpture and architecture, as we have seen, it is often necessary to ignore the third dimension. The *Artemision Statue* (PLATE 8), however, was conceived predominantly in two

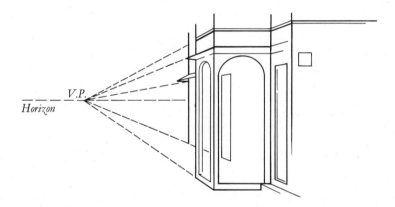

Figure 7

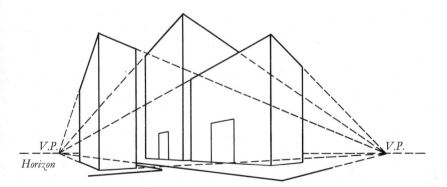

Figure 8

Figure 9

Figure 10

dimensions. It occupies a high and wide, but shallow, space, and the side view is the most satisfactory one. The shape has a simple majestic poise as the horizontal arms balance on the rising curves of the legs and torso. The shapes in Bernini's *Ecstasy of St. Teresa* (PLATE 57) are complex and irregular. Their fluttery activity is emphasized by the contrast of the darker background, and the constant turning and twisting shapes intensify the drama of the subject. The simple rigid shapes, organized by line, of *S. Maria delle Carceri* (PLATE 45) contrast with the restlessly undulating surfaces of *S. Carlo alle Quattro Fontane* (PLATE 54). The façade of the latter is interrupted by many niches or linear elements, and the multiplicity and changes in direction of the shapes create a busy effect.

MOTION IN SHAPES

Static shapes have a stable equilibrium within themselves and with their environment (*Fig.* 11). Shapes become more dynamic as they lead our attention in a specific direction. The triangle in Figure 12 pushes upward more than to the sides. The rectangle is relatively stable, yet because of its width our attention is drawn along a horizontal axis. Even the stability of the square may be disturbed if we move it out of alignment with a stable environment (*Fig.* 13). Less regular shapes can suggest much more activity; Figure 14 shows several of the shapes in Picasso's *Three Musicians* (PLATE 92). Their liveliness comes from irregularly expanding and contracting parts that draw our attention in several directions.

SHAPE AND SPACE

The illusion of depth on a flat surface may be produced simply by overlapping shapes, as in the Picasso painting and the Corot *Souvenir de Mortefontaine* (PLATE 78). Even the position of shapes on the picture surface can be made to suggest space. In Figure 15a we tend to feel that the upper figure is farther away even though the two figures are equal in size. The assumption is that the figures stand on a plane that extends to an unseen horizon outside the picture. Diagonal lines or parallels that do not converge may strengthen the effect of depth (*Fig.* 15b), although the illusion of space is strongest when linear perspective is employed.

Mass

Mass, or three-dimensional solidity, is used directly by architects and sculptors but must be created by illusion in painting and drawing. The artist can produce the effect of thickness or roundness with highlights and shadows, as in Masaccio's *Tribute Money* (PLATE 38); with lines describing some forms pushing in front of others, as in Picasso's drawing of *Dr. Claribel Cone* (PLATE 84); or with lines delineating the various sides of a three-dimensional object, either with linear perspective, as in Masaccio's *The Tribute Money*, or without it, as in Davis' *Something on the Eight Ball* (PLATE 91); and with colors that advance or recede (see p. 18) to pull some parts of an object forward. Mass may express dynamic power, as in Rubens' *Coup de Lance* (*The Crucifixion*, PLATE 53), where the vast bulk, foreground positions, and constant twisting of the forms emphasize the dramatic violence of the subject (*Fig.* 16). Rembrandt reinforced the quiet equilibrium of his *Supper at Emmaus* (COLOR PLATE 2) by aligning and framing the figure masses with the stable architectural forms and the rigid edges of the painting (*Fig.* 17).

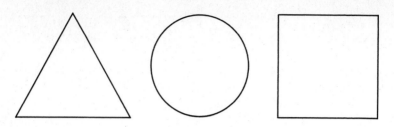

Figure 11

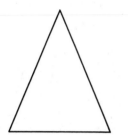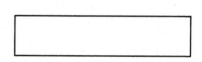

Figure 12

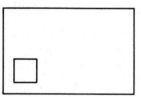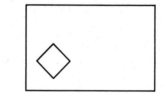

Figure 13

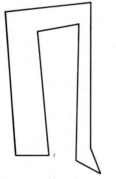

Figure 14

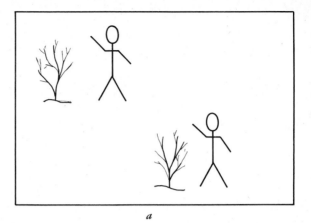

a

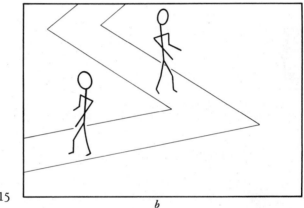

Figure 15

b

Sculpture may emphasize or deny mass. The term *closed form* is used for sculpture, painting, or architecture that stresses impenetrable mass. The figures of *Menkure and His Queen* (PLATE 1) have simplified anatomical forms with broad surfaces of blocklike permanence. The mass is not opened up between the two figures or between their legs or their arms and bodies. For more *open form* and more violent push-pull tensions, look at Roszak's sculpture (PLATE 96). Some sculptors deny the importance of mass. Gabo, for example, prefers transparent plastics that seem to give order to space without displacing it, as in *Linear Construction* (PLATE 95).

Architecture usually employs mass to define interior space, and the character of architectural mass ranges from the quiet symmetry

11

Figure 16

Figure 17

of the *Villa Rotonda* (PLATES 47 and 48) to the swooping, turning liveliness of *Notre-Dame-du-Haut* (PLATES 100–02). In the *Seagram Building* (PLATE 103), glass and steel reduce the mass to thin, transparent, membrane walls.

Value

Variations in lightness and darkness, called variations in *value*, are used to define shapes, to suggest line, to create the illusion of mass and space on a flat surface, to emphasize certain parts, and to express feeling. Value changes define shapes in Picasso's *Three Musicians*

13

(PLATE 92). In his *Coup de Lance* (PLATE 53), Rubens *modeled* (molded) solids with light and shadow, focused attention on Christ by flood-lighting, and reinforced the dramatic quality of the scene with bold contrasts in value. Holbein clarified details and space relations with light and shadow in his *Ambassadors* (PLATE 50); but Rembrandt, in the *Supper at Emmaus* (COLOR PLATE 2), obscured much of the detail in deep shadow, sacrificing clarity for an effect of soft glowing at-mosphere and quiet drama. Bold or soft contrasts of light and deep shadow, such as those in the above works by Rubens and Rem-brandt, are often called by the Italian term *chiaroscuro*.

In sculpture and architecture, value contrasts are produced by different degrees of projection and recession in the masses and by use of different materials and colors as in *The Ecstasy of St. Teresa* (PLATE 57), where the contrasts are dramatically intensified through the floodlighting of the figure group by a hidden window behind the architectural frame. In the *Robie House* (PLATE 98), the elegant hovering horizontals are stressed by the value contrast of brick and concrete and by highlights and shadows of projecting and receding parts.

VALUE RELATIONS

Our perception of the value, as well as of the size and color, of a given form may be affected by its environment through the principle of *simultaneous contrast*. Of the two circles of equal white in Figure 18a, the top one appears lighter because of its strong contrast with its surroundings. In Figure 18b, the top circle tends to appear larger because light areas seem to radiate and expand against darker back-grounds or surroundings. In the *Coup de Lance* (PLATE 53), such effects help create the monumentality of the figure of Jesus, the glowing flesh of Mary Magdalene at the foot of the cross, and the malevolent eye of the warrior who thrusts the lance into the side of Jesus.

VALUE CONTRAST AND SPACE

Value contrast can be used in painting to create the illusion of space by defining mass, which implies the space necessary to contain it; by separating planes or edges; and by sharpening or softening details. The deep space in Corot's landscape (PLATE 78) depends on a carefully adjusted sequence of overlapping foliage masses which are seen as flat planes separated by value contrasts that become softer and softer from foreground to background. The Corot painting

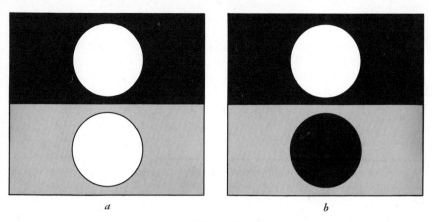

a *b*

Figure 18

achieves the illusion of depth by means of *aerial* or *atmospheric perspective*, where the softening of focus in value contrasts and details and the muting of colors give the effect of distance. Aerial perspective is used by Giorgione in his *Pastoral Concert* (COLOR PLATE 1) and by Masaccio in his *Tribute Money* (PLATE 38). Dali, on the other hand, creates the illusion of deep space in *The Persistence of Memory* (PLATE 87) without aerial perspective and demonstrates that sharp value contrasts can be forced back into deep space if foreground objects are strengthened by color, size contrast, or linear perspective.

Texture

Texture is the quality of a surface: smooth, rough, slick, grainy, soft, or hard. In painting, it may apply both to the texture of the paint itself and to the textures that are depicted. The painter, the sculptor, and the architect frequently use texture for variety, focus, or unity. In Holbein's *Ambassadors* (PLATE 50), the smooth surface of the paint helps give unity to the work even while the painting gives the illusion of a great variety of textures in the different objects depicted. Delacroix was less interested in depicting a variety of textures in his *Lion Hunt* (PLATE 75). He used the rough texture of the paint in undisguised brush strokes to stress the violence of the action and to unify the variety of shapes. In Gabo's *Linear Construction* (PLATE 95), space is molded mainly by nylon string that produces the illusion of grooved—i.e., textured—surfaces. The Bernini *Ecstasy of St. Teresa* (PLATE 57) has a multiplicity of textures that increases the complexity of the composition but also helps to separate the figures from their setting. From a distance, the thousands of sculptured details on the surface of *Amiens Cathedral* (PLATE 27) give the cathedral a bristling roughness of texture that has great variety. The countless perforations in the stone façade accentuate the soaring lightness of the structure. *Notre-Dame-du-Haut* (PLATE 100), with its more asymmetrical form, attains some of its unity and massive strength from its relatively uninterrupted surfaces and the overall texture of concrete.

Textural variation may be used in painting to give the illusion of space. The softening of focus in aerial perspective involves the softening of textural qualities—not only the depicted textures but the actual texture of the paint. In sculpture and architecture, effects of space may be emphasized by using bold textures in the foreground and softer ones for more distant surfaces.

Color

Color is one of the artist's principal means of achieving variety, emphasis, and unity; of creating the effects of mass and space; and of expressing feelings. In Giorgione's *Pastoral Concert* (COLOR PLATE 1), the focal color of the red hat is set against the cool light green of the distant meadow; the contrast of warm and cool colors works with the contrast of values and aerial perspective to create depth, and the total effect of serenity and elegance comes partly from the opulent but quiet colors. Monet was fascinated by the shimmer of light and color on the stone façade of *Rouen Cathedral* (COLOR PLATE 3). Vibrating contrasts of blue and orange dance backward and forward in accord with their brightness and warmth, denying the mass of the stone and producing a luminous vision. The colors in Matisse's *Decorative Figure on an Ornamental Background* (COLOR PLATE 4) are heavier and more earthy, but they provide a rich and lively variety as they change in modulations of reds, browns, blues, yellows, and greens.

Color in sculpture and architecture may come from the natural color of materials or from paint, glaze, or chemical treatment (see Ch. 4). Color may complicate the form, or it may stress the point of central importance and even act as the axis of balance. Color can separate the various parts of a composition or pull the parts together by giving them a common characteristic. Architecture may be united with a landscape through the use of native wood or rock that repeats the colors of the setting, or the building may be separated from its environment by the use of "foreign" colors.

THE NATURE OF COLOR

Sunlight, or white light, contains the elements of all colors in such a mixture that each color is canceled. White light can be broken into its component colors by projection through a prism. An object has a color for our eyes because it absorbs some elements of white light and reflects others. An apple is red when it reflects those elements of light that we have named red and absorbs the others.

The basic color that the artist chooses to give an object is called its *local color*. The artist may emphasize local colors, stress their modifications, or subordinate the local colors to a general effect. The local red of an apple may be modified by reflections from a green tablecloth and by light coming through yellow curtains. By partly subduing local colors, Rembrandt achieved the overall effect of brown-gold light that characterizes many of his works, such as the *Supper at Emmaus* (COLOR PLATE 2). Matisse, in contrast, retains more local colors (COLOR PLATE 4).

The word *color* refers to a combination of *hue*, *saturation*, and *value*. *Hue* is the property that distinguishes one color from another, the property that enables us to name the color. Three hues are especially important because, in theory, they can be mixed to produce all the others. These are called *primary colors*. In pigments, the primary colors are red, yellow, and blue (primary colors are not the same in light because of its greater purity). The convenient arrangement called a color wheel (see back endpaper) places between each two primary colors the color made by mixing them. Thus orange, green, and violet are called *secondary colors*. Mixing of primaries and secondaries produces additional colors; the mixing could go on indefinitely. Colors directly opposite each other on the wheel are called *complementaries*. Complementary colors have the property of dulling or canceling each other when mixed. A small amount of green added to red will dull the red. A larger amount of green will convert the red to brown, and a very careful adding of still more green will usually turn the brown to neutral gray. The proportions required of red and green will depend on the purity of the hues employed; since absolutely pure hues do not exist in pigments, the theoretical relationships described here are flexible in practice.

Complementary colors placed side by side usually intensify each other. This characteristic is basic to the intensity and spatial effect in Monet's blues and oranges (COLOR PLATE 3) and the focal and spatial effects of the red hat in the Giorgione (COLOR PLATE 1).

Saturation refers to the purity or vividness of a color. A strong red is said to be of high saturation. It is possible to lower the saturation of a color by adding its complementary, by diluting it with white, or by darkening it with black (see back endpaper).

The *value* of a color is its darkness or lightness, its position between the extremes of white and black (see back endpaper). As a color is darkened, its value is lowered. Colors with values lighter than a medium gray are called *tints;* colors with a darker value are called *shades.*

THE EFFECTS OF COLOR

For the greatest possible control over his medium, the artist must consider the effects of simultaneous contrast in colors. A neutral gray or a white placed near a strong color will seem to acquire a touch of the complementary of the color. This effect also occurs with combinations of colors; for example, red next to yellow will assume a touch of yellow's complement, violet; the yellow will appear to have a tinge of red's complement, green.

Certain colors (yellow, red, orange, and often violet) are considered *warm*, while others (greens and blues) are considered *cool*. This sensation is largely based on our association of certain colors with light and heat. Contrasts of warm and cool colors can be especially intense. Warm colors tend to make an object seem larger; cool colors tend to diminish its size, although value and saturation differences can be manipulated to reverse this effect. Warm colors tend to advance toward our eyes; cool colors seem to recede. A red shape seems to float in front of a green background of approximately the same saturation. The physiological reason is that the lens of the eye focuses on warm colors in the same way that it focuses on close objects; for cool colors, the lens focuses as though upon distant objects. The attention-getting power of a highly saturated cool color, however, may "push" it ahead of a warm color of much lower saturation.

Suggestions for further study

Birren, Faber. *Color, Form, and Space*. New York: Reinhold Publishing Corporation, 1961.

Itten, Johannes. *The Art of Color*. Trans. by Ernst van Haagen. New York: Reinhold Publishing Corporation, 1961.

Norling, Ernest R. *Perspective Made Easy*. New York: The Macmillan Company, 1939.

Sargent, Walter. *The Enjoyment and Use of Color*. New York: Dover Publications, 1923.

Chapter Two FUNCTIONS OF DESIGN

The satisfaction received from a work of art depends not only on order, which can be monotonous, but also on variety, which stimulates and holds our interest. As he designs, the artist may consciously or unconsciously work with the visual and tactile elements to create variety and order. He may employ *rhythm*, a recurrence of variations—often in the form of accents and intervals—that have enough similarity to establish continuity and a scheme of order. Rhythm may be extended indefinitely; it does not require limits. *Balance*, the equilibrium of opposing or self-completing forces, does involve limits and provides self-sufficiency and unity. Balance may be *axial*, i.e., organized on either side of an actual or implied axis that acts as a fulcrum (*Fig.* 19), or *central*, i.e., radiating from or converging upon an actual or implied central point (*Fig.* 20). Axial balance may be *obvious* (symmetrical), having very similar or identical elements on either side of the axis (*Fig.* 19a, b, c), or it may be *occult* (asymmetrical), having an equilibrium of elements that are dissimilar in size or shape (*Fig.* 19d, e). Central balance may also be obvious (*Fig.* 20a, b), with similar elements in equilibrium around a center, or occult (*Fig.* 20c, d), using dissimilar elements. Axial balance and central balance usually become three-dimensional in sculpture, in architecture, and in painting that contains the illusion of depth.

Different kinds of rhythm and balance, or the lack of them, can evoke strong reactions in the viewer of a work of art. Such reactions are in part due to the process of *empathy*, by which we identify ourselves with an object and tend to respond to it sympathetically. The statue of a man in an unbalanced or awkward pose may cause us twinges of physical discomfort. Empathy is especially strong with images of our own species, but it also occurs in response to designs without human or animal form.

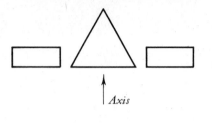

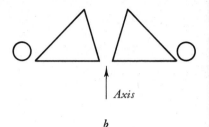

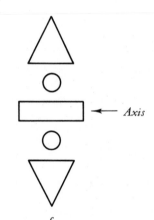

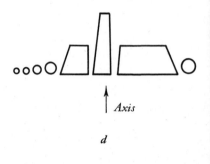

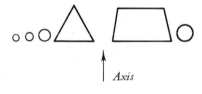

Figure 19   *Types of axial balance. a, b,* and *c are in obvious axial balance; d* and *e are in occult axial balance.*

Both rhythm and balance involve *proportion*, the size relationship of parts. It is partly because of proportion that some schemes of rhythm and balance are more satisfying than others. Throughout history, numerous theories have been proposed as bases for satisfying proportions. One of the most famous is that of the *Golden Mean*, whose mathematical ratio cannot be stated in finite terms though its proportions are easily found by using geometry (*Fig.* 21).

Order and variety in art are dependent upon some basic devices, which we shall examine below.

a   b

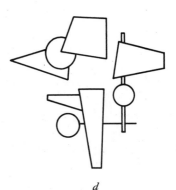

c   d

Figure 20   *Types of central balance*

Repetition and variation on a theme

The most elementary means of order is repetition. We instinctively assume a relationship between similar or identical things. In the visual arts, repetition may appear in line, shape, mass, value, space, color, size, or even directional emphasis. In *The Apotheosis of Homer* (PLATE 76), Ingres used repetition to build a severely symmetrical composition, or, more precisely, one of obvious axial balance. The background columns are a keynote for the repetition of poses and figure groups on either side of Homer, giving him great importance as the axis of the organization. Such formal order was meant to ennoble the subject. In Matisse's *Decorative Figure* (COLOR PLATE 4), the scalloped shapes on the wall are a theme that is repeated with

23

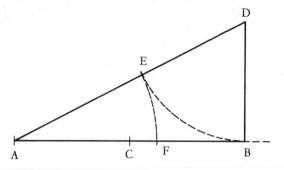

Figure 21   *The Golden Mean. To divide line* AB *by the Golden Mean, first bisect the line (point* C). *At* B, *erect a perpendicular equal in length to* AC. *Complete the triangle* ABD, *and on the hypotenuse* AD *locate point* E *so that* DE *equals* BD. *Then locate point* F *on line* AB *so that* AF *equals* AE. *Line* AB *is divided by point* F *according to the proportions of the Golden Mean.*

variations in the mirror, the plant, and the floor designs. Even the sturdy figure of the woman is *modulated,* or modified, by curved drapery around the hips to conform to the other curved shapes. The rippling alternation of concave-convex shapes gives rhythmic vitality to the scene. Objects are further related by thematic colors, such as the browns, greens, and yellows, that are repeated with variations. Unlike *The Apotheosis of Homer,* Matisse's painting employs an occult axial balance. The figure is opposed by the potted plant and the diagonal floor lines, and the implied axis would be a vertical line running through the knees of the figure to the fore-'ground bowl of fruit.

In the *tympanum* (a framed surface in architecture, here over a door) at the Abbey Church of Moissac (PLATE 24), the twenty-four elders of the church, in variations of the same pose, form an obvious balance and build with increasingly sharper focus toward the axial center of the composition, the Jesus of the Apocalypse. Platelike overlapping curves and angular edges occur repeatedly, often reinforcing the directional emphasis of the forms—as in the rising curve in the body of the eagle (symbol of John the Evangelist) by Christ's shoulder—and giving rhythmic vitality within the ritualistic formality of the strict symmetry. Repetition unifies the parts, suggests motion, and directs our attention. In Michelangelo's *Tomb of Giuliano de'Medici* (PLATE 37), the concave curves of the reclining figures are countered by the convex curve of the sarcophagus (*Fig.* 22). Within the obvious axial balance, symmetrical repetition of alternating curves leads our attention to the figure of Giuliano, who is given added importance by the buildup of repeated architectural forms.

The columns of the *Parthenon* (PLATE 6) create a rhythmic repetition of masses and spaces that adds variety to the rectangular building and enriches its symmetry. Subtle variation in the intercolumnar spaces helps to preclude monotony. The horizontals of the platform on which the temple sits are contrasted with repeated verticals in the columns and echoed by horizontals in the roof, making an almost static balance with very sharply defined limits. In *Amiens Cathedral* (PLATE 27), a profusion of repeated vertical and horizontal elements frames variations on the theme of the pointed arch. The arches, in turn, frame circular or *foliated* (scalloped) openings and occasional standing figures. Complexity makes the compositional limits fuzzy, but order is achieved by repetition and variations on themes within the obvious axial balance.

Contrast

Contrast is basic to variation and important for visual interest. Contrast can be used to clarify or modify form, to create mass and space, to suggest activity, to provide balance, to express feeling, and to focus attention. The lively, aggressive personality of Picasso's *Three Musicians* (PLATE 92) depends on contrasts in color, in value, and in shape. Contrast of direction gives Roszak's *Whaler of Nantucket* (PLATE 96) its tense equilibrium of bristling energy, while contrasts of texture, value, and color emphasize the horizontals of brick and concrete masses in the *Robie House* (PLATE 98).

Gradation and climax

Gradation is smooth or step-by-step development that usually suggests direction and builds to a climax. Any of the visual and tactile elements may be treated in this way. In the *Supper at Emmaus* (COLOR PLATE 2), Rembrandt developed a gentle gradation from shadow toward a climax of light that emphasizes Jesus. In *The Apotheosis of Homer* (PLATE 76), Ingres employed gradation in the lines of the heads to make Homer the climactic apex of at least two triangular arrangements that are echoed in the background temple. The artist may seek variety within unity by using a theme with variations of

Figure 22

gradation; for example, the angles of the heads of the elders in the bottom row of the tympanum of Moissac (PLATE 24) become progressively sharper as they approach Jesus. At *Amiens Cathedral* (PLATE 27), the gradation in the size of the three main doors emphasizes the center one. Each entrance, in turn, is the focus of a funnel-like gradation of arches of decreasing size.

Suggestions for further study

Arnheim, Rudolf. *Art and Visual Perception: A Psychology of the Creative Eye.* Berkeley: University of California Press, 1954.
Kepes, György. *The Language of Vision.* Chicago: Paul Theobald and Company, 1944.

Lowry, Bates. *The Visual Experience: An Introduction to Art*. Englewood Cliffs, N.J.: Prentice-Hall; New York: Harry N. Abrams, 1961.

Moholy-Nagy, László. *Vision in Motion*. Chicago: Paul Theobald and Company, 1947.

Pepper, Stephen C. *Principles of Art Appreciation*. New York: Harcourt, Brace & World, 1949.

Pope, Arthur. *The Language of Drawing and Painting*. Cambridge, Mass.: Harvard University Press, 1949.

Ross, Denman W. *A Theory of Pure Design; Harmony, Balance, Rhythm; with Illustrations and Diagrams*. Boston and New York: Houghton Mifflin Company, 1907.

Scott, Robert G. *Design Fundamentals*. New York, Toronto, and London: McGraw-Hill Book Company, 1951.

Seiberling, Frank. *Looking into Art*. New York: Henry Holt and Company, 1959.

Zevi, Bruno. *Architecture as Space: How to Look at Architecture*. Ed. by Joseph Barry. Trans. by Milton Gendel. New York: Horizon Press, 1957.

Chapter Three   # SUBJECT MATTER

Subject matter is most simply defined as the recognizable objects depicted by the artist; yet subject matter acquires meaning on different levels and can be employed in different degrees.

Levels of meaning in subject matter

Factual meaning in subject matter consists of superficially identifiable objects. Understanding the significance of the subject matter, however, frequently involves more than recognizing the objects. An inventory of the subject matter in Jan van Eyck's portrait of the Arnolfinis (PLATE 32), for example, does not explain why the couple is so formally posed in the privacy of a bedroom; nor does a description of objects in Raphael's *Madonna of the Meadow* (PLATE 36) convey its content to a person unfamiliar with Christian scriptures. Factual meaning is often supplemented or supplanted by meaning on other levels.

CONVENTIONAL MEANING
Certain objects, actions, and even colors acquire special meaning for a particular culture. In our culture, for example, the cross stands for Christianity, red suggests life or danger, and white is associated with purity. Research is often necessary to understand the publicly accepted conventional symbolism in art from other cultures or other times. In the Van Eyck portrait, a number of symbols would be missed by the casual observer today. The painting is a testament to the marriage vow. The lone candle symbolizes the all-seeing Christ; the fruit on the window sill refers to the state of innocence before the Fall of Man; the mirror and the crystal beads are symbols of purity; the wooden shoes recall the command of God to Moses on Mt. Sinai to take off his shoes when he stood on holy ground; the dog stands for marital fidelity; and the back of the chair by the bed

is carved in the image of St. Margaret, the patron saint of childbirth. The study of such conventional symbols is called *iconography*.

Some of the most pervasive symbols in Western art derive from the Christian tradition. The following are only a few of the hundreds of symbols used in Christian art, and for these only the more frequent meanings are included. The iconography of other cultures will be considered in the historical chapters in Part II.

APPLE   Tree of Knowledge in the Garden of Eden, hence evil. An apple held by Jesus or Mary means salvation from sin.

CARNATION   Red means pure love; pink stands for marriage.

CAT   Laziness, lust.

CHALICE   Last Supper. A chalice with serpent identifies St. John the Evangelist. A chalice with wafer identifies St. Barbara. A broken chalice indicates St. Donatus.

COLUMBINE   Holy Ghost.

CROSS   The Latin cross (tall post with short crosspiece) refers to Jesus; the Greek cross (equal arms) stands for the Christian Church; an X-shaped cross refers to St. Andrew the Apostle.

DOVE   Holy Ghost, peace, purity.

EAGLE   St. John the Evangelist. Resurrection. Generosity.

EGG   Resurrection, source of life.

EWER AND BASIN   Purity, cleanliness.

FISH   Christ, since the five letters for the Greek word for *fish* form the initials of the words: "Jesus Christ, God's Son, Saviour."

FOUNTAIN   Mary, seen as the "fountain of living waters" (Song of Solomon 4:12 ff. and Psalms 36:9) because she was the mother of Christ the Saviour.

GARDEN, ENCLOSED   Mary. A symbol of the Immaculate Conception of Mary (Song of Solomon 4:12).

GLOBE   Earthly or spiritual power, depending upon the person holding it.

GRAIN   Body of Jesus (bread in Holy Communion).

GRAPES OR GRAPE VINE   Christ as the "true vine" of which his followers are the branches (John 15:1, 5, 8). Blood of Jesus (wine of Holy Communion).

GRIDIRON   St. Lawrence, who was martyred on a grid over a fire.

HALO   Saintliness. A round halo is most common. A triangular halo reflects the Trinity; a square halo refers to living persons.

HAMMER Instrument of the Passion, used in the Crucifixion.

INRI The initials of the Latin words for *Jesus of Nazareth, King of the Jews*, which appear on the Cross of Jesus.

IRIS Sorrow and purity of Mary. The bladelike leaf is associated with a sword and alludes to the suffering of Mary.

KEY St. Peter, a reference to Christ's charge to Peter of the keys of the kingdom of heaven (Matthew 16:19).

LADDER Instrument of the Passion, used in the Crucifixion.

LAMB Jesus, the sacrificial lamb of God. The sinner saved by Jesus the Good Shepherd. St. John the Baptist. St. Agnes. St. Clement.

LAMP Wisdom.

LIGHT Christ.

LILY Purity, Mary.

LION Jesus. St. Mark the Evangelist. St. Jerome. Courage, majesty.

MANDORLA Almond-shaped radiation of light surrounding the whole body of Jesus or Mary.

MOON Mary, who is identified as the woman with the moon under her feet (Revelations 12:1).

NAILS Instruments of the Passion.

OINTMENT BOX Mary Magdalene, a reference to her anointing of Christ.

OLIVE Peace.

OX OR BULL St. Luke the Evangelist. The Jewish Nation. Patience.

PALM Victory.

PEACOCK Vanity. Immortality, because of the ancient belief that the flesh of the peacock does not decay.

PILLAR Instrument of the Passion (the pillar to which Christ was tied while he was whipped).

RIVERS The four rivers of Paradise, thought to flow from the same rock, symbolize the four Gospels, which had their source in Jesus.

ROSE Red for martyrdom, white for purity.

SCALES Equality and justice. The Archangel Michael is often shown with scales for the weighing of souls.

SCOURGE Instrument of the Passion.

SHIP The Christian Church, referring to the ark of Noah and the Church as means of salvation.

SKULL   The vanity of earthly life (often shown with St. Jerome). A skull at the foot of the Cross refers to Adam and indicates the Cross as a means of salvation from man's original sin.

SPEAR   Instrument of the Passion.

SPONGE   Instrument of the Passion.

STAR   Divine guidance, as in the journey of the Magi. One star is also the symbol of Mary. Twelve stars stand for the Apostles or for the twelve tribes of Israel.

SUN   Mary (Revelations 12:1).

SWORD   A symbol of martyrdom by the sword, often shown with St. Paul, St. Peter, St. Justina, St. Agnes, and many others.

THORNS   Sin, grief. Instrument of the Passion (Christ's crown of thorns).

TOWER   Identifies St. Barbara, who was confined in a tower.

WATER OR A WELL   Purification, baptism, rebirth.

WHALE   A symbol of the Devil or of the story of Jonah.

WHEEL   Identifies St. Catherine, who was tortured on a wheel.

XP   The Greek letters *Chi* and *Rho* are the first two letters in the Greek word for Christ. They are often superimposed: ☧

A society often modifies its iconography according to changes in prevailing tendencies in thought. The study of factors causing changes in iconography and the interpretation of such changes within the history of thought is called *iconology*.

SUBJECTIVE MEANING

The individual artist may consciously or unconsciously employ a private symbolism based on an association of certain objects, actions, or colors with past experiences, a temporary state of mind, or an adopted world view. Likewise, the observer tends to interpret art according to his own associations, and over this interpretive activity the artist never has complete control. In a sense, therefore, a work of art is recreated anew each time it is experienced by an observer. Dali (PLATE 87) paints objects in such a way as to encourage a wide range of individual interpretation. So did Kandinsky (PLATE 86), who felt that painting should approach the art of music. Mondrian (PLATE 90) argued that recognizable objects were impurities that distracted the observer from the essential quality in art: a unique equilibrium of line and color. Thus his work can be described as the most "subjectless," i.e., the least encouraging to associational meaning.

Degrees of subject matter

Writers on art generally employ three terms to classify works according to degree of subject matter. These categories overlap somewhat, but the terms are worthwhile if they are used cautiously. *Representational* art has clearly recognizable objects (PLATE 76); *abstract* art has a basis in identifiable objects (PLATE 92); and *nonobjective* art has no direct reference to such objects, i.e., no subject matter (PLATE 90). These terms may be applied from either the artist's or the observer's standpoint, with possible disagreement. The artist may work so abstractly that the observer finds no apparent subject matter and assumes the painting to be nonobjective; conversely, the artist may work nonobjectively, but the observer may imagine that he sees recognizable objects in the work and consider it to be abstract. It is important to recall that recognizing objects in representational or abstract art is not necessarily grasping its content. Content in representational art, as in abstract art, is an interaction of subject matter with the interpretive qualities of the visual and tactile elements. In fact, subject matter may acquire meaning on different levels if it is present in any degree.

Suggestions for further study

Ferguson, George. *Signs and Symbols in Christian Art*. New York: Oxford University Press (Hesperides Books), 1961.

Ogden, C. K., and I. A. Richards. *The Meaning of Meaning*. New York: Harcourt, Brace & World (Harvest Books), 1959.

Panofsky, Erwin. *Gothic Architecture and Scholasticism*. New York: The World Publishing Company (Meridian Books), 1957.

———. *Meaning in the Visual Arts: Papers in and on Art History*. Garden City, N.Y.: Doubleday & Company (Anchor Books), 1955.

———. *Studies in Iconology: Humanistic Themes in the Art of the Renaissance*. New York: Oxford University Press, 1939.

———, and Dora Panofsky. *Pandora's Box: The Changing Aspects of a Mythical Symbol*. Rev. ed. New York: Pantheon Books, 1962.

Chapter Four **TECHNIQUES**

The content of a work of art depends in varying degrees on its visual and tactile elements, which in turn depend on the materials and techniques used. A particular material, along with the technique appropriate to it, is often called the *medium* (plural: *media*) of expression. We can better understand a composition if we know something of the problems and possibilities inherent in the medium. Today artists often combine many media in one work.

Drawing

Though generally identified with line, drawing is a term used so broadly that it often overlaps the realm of painting. A drawing may be a *study*, an investigation of a certain detail of what may become a more extensive work; it may be a *sketch*, the quick notation of the general organization and effect of a composition; or it may be a *cartoon*, a full-size composition meant to be transferred to another surface for a finished work.

In *pencil drawing*, a wide range of values is possible with *leads* (graphite) of differing hardness. Colored pencils and colored paper provide a range of color. Hard lead on a smooth surface is good for a precise light line, such as that in Picasso's drawing of *Dr. Claribel Cone* (PLATE 84); soft lead applied lightly to a rough surface gives a dark line with grainy texture. If the lead is sharpened to a wedge shape, it can be twisted to create a line with considerable modulation.

In *ink drawing*, great variety is possible through the use of colored inks, colored papers, inks of differing degrees of opacity, and different pen points. Formerly pens were made by splitting quills or reeds; nowadays pen points of many shapes and sizes are available in steel. Modulation in line depends on the width of the point and on the flexibility that governs the spreading of the split point. Today fountain pens with felt points add to the range of possibility.

35

Charcoal varies in hardness; it can be used directly for crisp lines, or it can be rubbed to produce soft grays. Large areas can be covered quickly in a variety of values characteristic of painting. Charcoal does not adhere well. Soft paper with considerable *tooth* (texture) takes it best, and smearing is minimized if the drawing is sprayed with a *fixative* (thin varnish).

Chalk and *pastel* are made of powdered pigments (coloring matter) mixed with glue and formed into sticks. *Crayons* are made with wax, which adheres well but does not lend itself to rubbing for soft gradations. Pastels and chalks are more powdery because of their weak glue binder. They have the advantages and disadvantages of charcoal and require a fixative.

Brush drawing—ink or watercolor applied with a brush—is often used in combination with pen and ink or pencil. In *dry brush drawing*, opaque ink or watercolor is used, permitting great detail and easy correction. In *wash drawing*, watercolor or ink diluted with water is used for flowing transparent washes, and correction is more difficult. In brush drawing of both types, usually only one or two colors are used. The color limitation permits a distinction between brush drawing and watercolor painting.

Printmaking

A *print* is a work of art produced by a duplicating process. It is considered an original rather than a reproduction because the artist works toward the print as the end product. For this reason the print has been called a multiple original. Many artists perform the whole process themselves; some prepare the printing surface and have special printers make the prints; still others create the composition only and have specialists transfer it to a printing surface and make the prints. In any case, the artist must understand the printing process to be used if he is to utilize its possibilities effectively. The total number of prints made is called an *edition*. After the edition is printed, the printing surface is usually destroyed. The edition is thus limited, and the prints are more valuable to collectors. Today the artist frequently signs each print in pencil on the margin and uses a fraction to indicate the place of that particular print in the total edition; the number 6/45 would mean the sixth print in an edition of forty-five. Trial prints made during the preparation of the printing surface are called *artist's proofs*. Different stages of the composition (often indicated by artist's proofs but sometimes carried out even during the printing of the edition) are called *states*. A composition may have one or many states. An artist might make a number of prints of a landscape and then decide to add a cloud in the sky. Prints without the cloud would be first-state; prints with the cloud would be second-state.

The many processes used in printmaking may be grouped in four broad categories, although the contemporary tendency to mix techniques within each of these general groups sometimes makes it difficult for the observer to know how a print was produced.

RELIEF PROCESSES

In a relief process, the artist cuts away parts of the printing surface. The parts of the surface left in relief are inked, and the ink is then transferred to paper in the manner of an ordinary rubber stamp.

For *woodcuts*, a piece of wood is cut or gouged to leave the design in relief. Prints may be made with a press or by placing paper over the inked block and rubbing a backing of cardboard with a spoon. Color woodcut prints traditionally are made with a separate block for each color. Careful *registration* is necessary to ensure that each color is printed exactly in the proper area. Transparent colors may be overlapped to produce additional colors, and colored paper may be used. Woodcut lends itself to bold lines and large areas of light and dark. Sometimes the grain of the wood or the texture of the paper will be evident in the print.

In *wood engraving*, an end-grain (grain at right angles to the surface) block is used, allowing easy cutting in any direction. *Burins* (cutting tools) of various shapes and sizes are employed, and great detail is possible.

For *linoleum cuts*, linoleum mounted on a wood block is cut in the same manner as a woodcut. There is no wood grain to exploit. Like a woodcut, the linoleum cut does not encourage great detail.

In a *metal cut*, metal is cut away with engraving tools or lowered with punches; or the design may be drawn with acid-resistant material and the rest of the plate eaten (etched) with acid, leaving the design in relief.

INTAGLIO PROCESSES

In *intaglio processes*, the low parts, rather than the relief parts, of the printing surface carry the ink. The lines of the design are cut or eaten into a metal plate (usually copper). Ink is forced into these lines, and the surface of the plate is wiped clean. A high-pressure press forces dampened paper against the surface and into the depressed lines. Often the dried ink can be felt standing in relief on the surface of the finished print. Unless the plate is larger than the print paper, the pressure of the press mashes the paper down around the edges of the plate and makes an indented *plate mark*, which may later be cut away. Since the pressure of the press slowly breaks down the edges or ridges between the intaglio lines, the size of an edition is limited (unless the copper plate is electroplated with a firmer metal), and early prints in an edition are generally valued more highly than later ones. As in the relief processes, a separate plate is traditionally employed for each color.

The sunken lines that hold the ink in an intaglio plate may be produced in several ways. In the *drypoint* process, a sharp point is used to scratch lines into the soft copper plate. Tiny ruffles of displaced metal (*burr*) pile up along the sides of each scratch. The ink held by the burr creates slightly fuzzy lines that can be used very effectively by the artist (PLATE 85). The burr quickly wears off, however, and drypoint editions are small.

For *metal engraving*, burins are used to cut out the metal, rather than to push it aside as in drypoint (a drypoint plate with the burr worn off produces the same effect as an engraved plate). Great sharpness and precision are possible. Engraving is often used in combination with etching.

In the process of *etching*, a copper plate is coated with acid-resistant material (*ground*) through which the lines of the design are easily drawn. The plate is immersed in acid, which eats into the metal wherever lines have been scratched through the ground. Thus the artist does not fight the resistance of the metal, and lines are produced more easily than in drypoint or engraving. Some lines may be etched a longer time than others to obtain greater depth; these hold more ink for greater darkness of line in the print. Etched lines are generally softer and freer than engraved lines. For *soft ground etching*, the ground is so soft that lines drawn on a paper placed on the plate will pick up the ground when the paper is pulled away from the plate. The plate is then etched. Fabrics and other materials may be pressed into the soft ground and lifted off. The ground is pulled away where the texture of the material pressed into it, and the texture of the material can then be etched into the plate. *Aquatint etching* produces soft sandy or speckled areas. It is done by sifting resin powder onto a heated plate. The resin melts partially and sticks to the plate. Acid attacks the metal exposed between the resin particles and produces thousands of tiny pits that hold ink and create speckled areas on the print. The evenness and darkness of the aquatint will depend on the amount of resin sifted onto the plate, the size of the resin particles, and the length of time the plate is exposed to acid. Although resin is sifted over the whole plate, the aquatint effect is limited to chosen areas by *stopping out* other areas with acid-resistant varnish.

PLANOGRAPHIC PROCESSES
As the name implies, these methods print with a level rather than a raised or lowered surface.

The *monotype* process produces only a single print. Inks or paints are brushed, dripped, or rubbed on a smooth glass or metal plate. A paper is laid over the plate and rubbed. Wide varieties of super-imposed colors and textures are made possible by this procedure.

For *lithography*, the printing surface is traditionally fine grained limestone, but in commercial lithography metal plates are used. The drawing is done with grease-containing crayons, pencils, or inks, and the surface is then treated chemically to make it reject ink except where the greasy substance has established the drawing. Printing is done with a special press.

STENCIL PROCESSES
One of the most important stencil processes is *silk-screen*, often called *serigraphy*. Many methods are used. Basically, the idea is to fill or cover the pores of the silk (stretched on a frame), leaving them open only in the shape of the design. Colored inks are then rolled or scraped across the silk and penetrate to form a print of the design on paper or cloth underneath.

Painting

Oil paint, watercolor, crayon, and pastel can all be made from the same pigment. The determining factor is the *binder* (the substance that holds the color particles together and makes them adhere to a surface). The word "paint" is normally applied to media that are used in liquid or paste form. The immediate surface which receives the paint is called the *ground* (an entirely different meaning, obviously, from an etching ground). For watercolor, the ground is usually the surface of the paper. For many paints applied to wood or canvas, an intervening substance such as sizing or priming must be applied to limit the absorption of the base material. Then the panel or canvas becomes the *support*, and the preparatory coating becomes the ground. Paint may be applied in a single layer (*alla prima*) or in many layers. Transparent layers are called *washes* in watercolor and *glazes* in oil paint. Opaque color can be rubbed or dragged loosely over previous colors to modify them without obscuring them, a process called *scumbling*. Paint applied very thickly is called *impasto*.

TEMPERA PAINTING

In *tempera painting*, the binder is an emulsion (a mixture of oil and water) that may include casein, glue, gum, egg, or egg and oil. The advantages of tempera are its quick drying ability, its potential for precise detail, its resistance to yellowing and darkening with age, the relative insolubility of dried tempera in water, and—for some types of tempera—the convenience of taking a water thinner. The disadvantages are the brittleness of some tempera formulas, the difficulty in blending it smoothly, some change in color and value between wet and dry tempera, and the impossibility of creating impasto textures.

WATERCOLOR PAINTING

The binder in watercolor is an aqueous solution of gum. For whites, transparent watercolor depends on the whiteness of the paper, and colors are lightened by thinning with water. The quality of the paper is very important because yellowing can spoil the colors as well as the whites. Advantages of watercolor are the cheapness and lightness of the materials, the quickness with which large areas can be covered with washes, the rapid drying time, and the lively sparkle of transparent washes over the white ground. Disadvantages in transparent watercolor are the difficulty of correction, the change in color value during drying, and the necessity of working from light to dark. Opaque watercolor, or *gouache*, sacrifices transparency and quick washes for greater ease of correction and the possibility of using opaque light colors over dark ones.

OIL PAINTING

The most common binder in oil paints is linseed oil. Most supports (wood, canvas, or synthetic materials) require a ground of oil or synthetic primer. For glazing purposes, complex thinning mixtures are used to increase transparency, to add flexibility, or to speed drying. The advantages of oil paint are its permanence and durability, its range of textural effects from transparency to impasto, the ease with which it can be manipulated and corrected, and the fact that colors do not change in drying.

FRESCO PAINTING

True fresco, or *buon fresco*, is done with pigments combined with just a water binder. The ground is wet lime plaster, usually on a wall. The paint becomes part of the ground and is very permanent. The mat surface of fresco allows the painting to be seen easily from all angles without disturbing reflections. *Fresco-secco* is painting on a dry plaster surface, and a variety of media—tempera is common— may be used.

ENCAUSTIC PAINTING

The binder used in *encaustic painting* is refined beeswax with additives. Paints are mixed on a heated *palette* (mixing surface) and applied quickly to a rigid surface, usually a wood panel. A heat source (today, an electric coil) is then passed over the surface to "burn in" the wax. The inconvenience of heating is compensated for by the extraordinary range of effects from transparency to impasto, the quick drying time, and the permanence of the colors.

OTHER MEDIA

Casein paints, with a casein glue binder, harden to a water-resistant but brittle surface, requiring a rigid support. They have the conveniences of taking a water thinner, drying rapidly, and producing a *mat* or dull finish, which does not create annoying light reflections as does a shiny surface. Modern science has developed synthetic binders such as acrylic resin and polyvinyl acetate that are also fast-drying and have a mat finish. With some such paints, water can be used for thinning and the dried surface is water-resistant. Heavy impasto is not possible with many of these paints unless they are combined with pastes or paints that have been specifically developed for impasto effects.

Sculpture

Sculpture may be freestanding or in relief (projecting from a background). Relief sculpture may be *high relief*, such as Ghiberti's *Sacrifice of Isaac* (PLATE 34), with high projections from its background, or *low relief*, with forms projecting only slightly.

MODELING AND CASTING

Modeling is an additive process of building up a sculpture from plastic material such as clay or wax. A wire, pipe, or wood *armature* (frame) can be used inside the work to prevent sagging (*Fig.* 23). No tools are necessary for modeling, although wooden spatulas with wire loops at one end are convenient for shaping and cutting. For permanence, natural clay can be *fired* (baked) in a *kiln* (oven), but it then cannot contain an armature, since shrinkage of the clay during firing would cause cracking, nor can it be of vastly different thicknesses. *Ceramic glazes* (a fine clay or glass coating) may be fired on the clay work, making possible a variety of textures and transparent or opaque colors. All fired clay may be called *terra cotta*, but the term refers more precisely to a brown-red unglazed clay.

Another way that clay sculpture may be given permanence is to cast it in plaster. A plaster mold is made while the clay is still wet. The mold is removed and oiled, soaped, or treated in some other way so that new plaster will not stick to it. After the mold has been reassembled and sealed, it is filled with plaster. Small sculptures may be cast solid; larger ones should be hollow. After the plaster has set, the mold is pulled or chipped away. This type of mold is called a *waste mold* because it is usually destroyed to free the cast within; for more than one cast a rubber or gelatin mold may be used. Plaster may be colored to imitate metal or stone.

Both cast plaster and fired clay are breakable, however; and for the greatest permanence in sculpture, the traditional rivals are stone and bronze. In the *sand mold* process of bronze casting, *French sand* (a mixture of clay, silica, and alumina) is pressed around a plaster cast of the work to form a mold. The parts of the sand mold are fitted into a *flask* (iron holder), and a core of French sand is made to fill the sand mold except for a one-eighth to one-quarter inch air space all the way around. The core is suspended inside the sand mold and flask by metal rods. Holes are made in the mold so that air can escape as molten bronze is poured into the air space between

42

Figure 23   *An armature*

the core and mold. After the bronze has cooled, the mold is removed and the core is dug out. The hollow bronze cast needs much cleaning up before special workers (*patinières*) can give the cast its *patina* (color) by acid baths and heat treatment. In the *lost wax method* (*cire perdue*) of bronze casting, the following procedure is one of several. A gelatin mold and a plaster shell to support it are made from the sculptor's plaster cast of the original clay work. On the inside of the gelatin mold, layers of wax are built up to the desired thickness of the bronze. The gelatin is removed, and the hollow wax replica is filled with a core of heat-resistant material. This material is also used to form a mold around the outside of the wax. Metal rods hold the core inside the mold, and vents are made to allow the melted wax to drain away when the assembly is heated. The air space left between the core and the mold by the removal of the wax is filled with bronze. The mold and core are taken away, and the finishing process begins.

Today the sculptor may do *direct sand casting* by working negatively, that is, creating the mold directly in a special sand mixture. Iron and aluminum are frequently used for the cast.

43

Another material common today is *cast stone*. A heavy reinforced plaster or gelatin mold is made from the original clay work, and a mixture of stone dust, color, sand, and cement is poured or packed into the mold. Sometimes an armature is included to reinforce the cement. After several days of "curing," the mold is pulled or chipped away, and the cast can be finished by filing or carving.

CARVING

The carver must have foresight, since the subtractive process does not allow for addition if too much is cut away. The most common materials, stone and wood, have different kinds of texture and grain that have aesthetic potential for the sculptor. The stone carver uses hammers, picks, drills, and toothed chisels to rough out the form. Chisels and abrasives are used for finishing. The wood carver works with chisels, gouges, files, and sandpaper. Frequently the sculptor does the final work from a smaller preliminary model. A *pointing machine* may be used to transfer the proportions of the model to the larger block.

CONSTRUCTION

Constructed sculpture, of which Gabo's *Linear Construction* (PLATE 95) and Roszak's *Whaler of Nantucket* (PLATE 96) are examples, has become increasingly important during the twentieth century. The sculptor uses any materials or ready-made objects to build his composition, often soldering or welding them. The strength of metals and plastics has made possible very open form. Different colors are obtained by the use of different metals, by painting, or by controlled oxidation. *Kinetic sculpture*, or mobile sculpture, utilizes air currents or motors to bring actual movement into the composition.

Architecture

The basic diagrams of architectural design are *perspective views*, *plans*, and *elevations*. Perspective views show how the building will appear in three dimensions. A plan shows the two-dimensional distribution of interior spaces, walls, windows, and doors. An elevation shows the side of a room or a building without perspective distortion.

Traditional architectural materials are wood, mud brick, plaster, concrete, stucco, and masonry of fired brick or stone. More recent materials are iron, steel, aluminum, glass, reinforced concrete (ferro-concrete), plywood, and plastics. The strength of reinforced concrete has made possible very open form. Prestressed concrete is particularly strong; here the concrete is allowed to harden around stretched steel cables, or cables are run through the concrete in tubes and anchored under tension at each end. The result is a built-in compression that offsets the weakness of concrete under tension.

POST AND LINTEL

The simplest type of structure is post and lintel, a combination of uprights (*posts*) supporting a crosspiece (*lintel*). Columns, such as those of the *Parthenon* (PLATE 6), often serve as posts. The span between posts is severely limited by the strength of the material in the lintel. In our century, steel, reinforced concrete, and prestressed concrete have made possible very wide spans (*Fig.* 24). A lintel that extends beyond its supports (*Fig.* 24b) is called a *cantilever*. Lintels are frequently made in the form of *trusses*. A truss is a very strong

Figure 24   *Post and lintel construction*

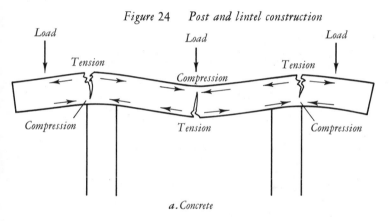

a. Concrete

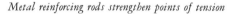

Metal reinforcing rods strengthen points of tension

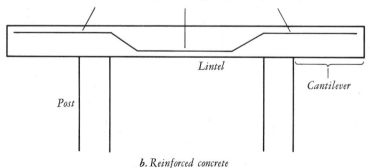

b. Reinforced concrete

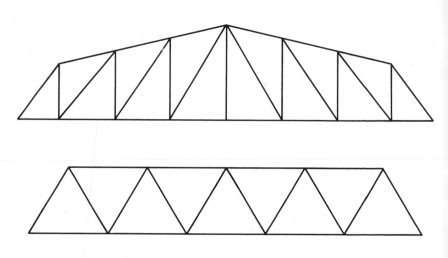

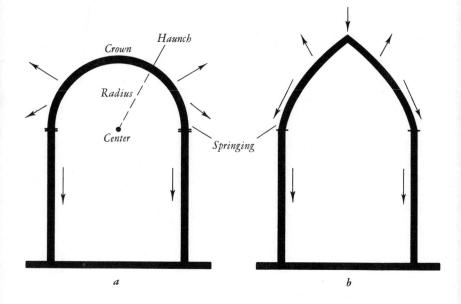

Figure 25   Trusses

Crown   Haunch

Radius

Center

Springing

a

b

Figure 26   The dynamics of arches

but light framework made of small pieces fastened together in such a way that they brace each other (*Fig.* 25).

ARCH

An arch diverts the load—the weight sustained—to the sides as well as down toward the vertical, making possible wider spans than does a post and lintel system in the same material; the arrows in Figure 26 show the forces exerted by weight and the tendencies of the arch to fall in and the walls to buckle out. Until the nineteenth century and the development of steel and ferroconcrete, the most common arch was the masonry arch, a structure of wedge-shaped blocks spanning an opening. True arches have several forms. One, the flat masonry arch (*Fig.* 27c), resembles the post and lintel. The steep sides of a pointed arch divert the load more directly toward the ground (*Fig.* 26b) and require less outside *buttressing* (bracing) than the round arch (*Fig.* 27a). A *corbeled arch* (*Fig.* 27d) is not a true masonry arch; it sacrifices strength to avoid the more precise cutting required in the wedge-shaped blocks of the true arch (*Fig.* 27a, b, c). A masonry arch is supported during the course of its construction by a wooden scaffolding called *centering*.

VAULT AND DOME

Vaulting is arched roofing of stone, brick, or concrete. The *tunnel*, *barrel*, or *wagon vault* is an extension of a round arch (*Fig.* 28). It requires continuous buttressing along the sides. In medieval masonry, the common solution to the buttressing problem was thick walls, and windows were kept below the level of the *springing* (the beginning of the curve of the arch) to avoid weakening the vault (*Fig.* 29). The interior view of *St. Sernin* (PLATE 26) shows how medieval vaults were often divided into *bays* (sections) by *transverse arches* (arches at right angles to the length of the vault that have the appearance and sometimes the function of reinforcements). The bay division was often continued all the way down to the floor by *engaged columns* (columns partially buried in the wall). In medieval architecture, vaulting is so important that it is often indicated on floor plans. The plan of *St. Sernin* (*Fig.* 50, p. 128) shows the transverse arches in dotted lines.

Greater strength and flexibility are obtained if two vaults are crossed at right angles (*Fig.* 30). The *cross vault*, or *groin vault*, focuses the load on four legs and allows the sides to be opened up.

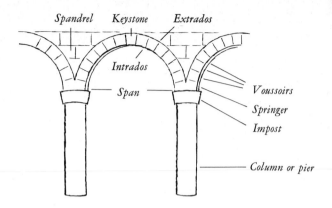

a. Round

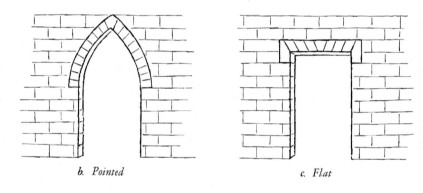

b. Pointed

c. Flat

d. Corbeled arches

Figure 27   Types of masonry arches

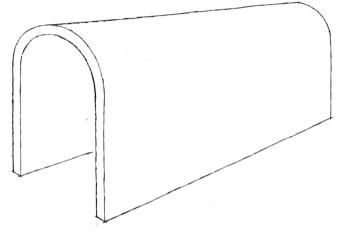

Figure 28   *Tunnel vault*

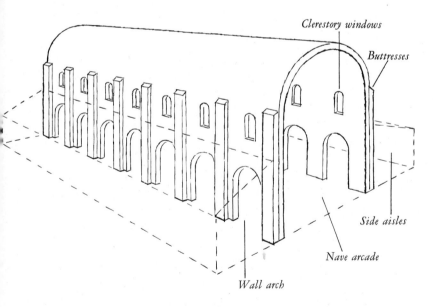

Clerestory windows

Buttresses

Side aisles

Nave arcade

Wall arch

Figure 29   *Tunnel vault on a Romanesque church*

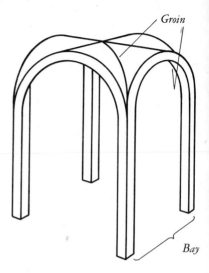

Groin

Figure 30   Cross vault

Bay

The exterior indentations where the vaults meet are the *groins*. On the interior the groins project as ridges. From directly above or below, the groins form an X-shape between the transverse arches and are so indicated on the plans (*Fig.* 31). When the groins are emphasized by moldings or *ribs* on the interior, the vault is called a *ribbed cross vault*, a series of which can be seen over the nave of *Amiens Cathedral* (PLATE 29). It is thought that in medieval architecture the ribs were often built first, as a skeleton to shape the vault, and panels of stone were filled in between ribs and side arches. Since the X formed by the ribs divides the vault into four parts, it is called a four-part or *quadripartite* vault. Sometimes an additional transverse arch was added in the center of the X creating a six-part or *sexpartite* ribbed cross vault (*Fig.* 32). When tunnel vaults are crossed, the semicircular ribs are higher than the wall arches and the transverse arches because the ribs cover a greater distance (*Fig.* 33a). The vaults therefore acquire a domical form that makes a segmented visual effect when they are used in a series. The crowns of the vaults can be made more even by depressing the ribs (and often the transverse arches) to less than semicircles (*Fig.* 33b), but depressed arches are weaker than semicircular ones. A level effect can be achieved without sacrificing strength if the principle of the pointed arch is applied to the vaulting. The pointed ribs and arches are easily ad-

50

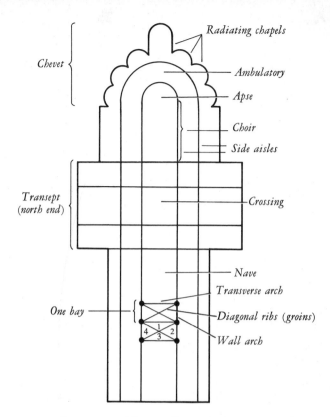

Figure 31   Plan of Amiens Cathedral

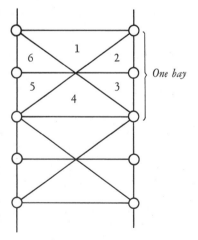

Figure 32   Plan of a sexpartite vault

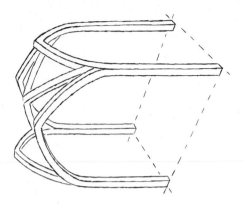

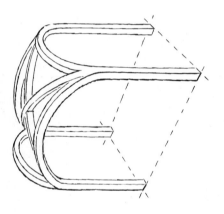

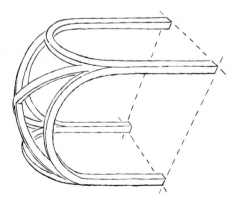

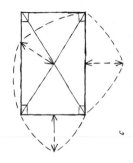

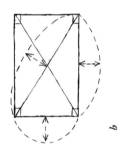

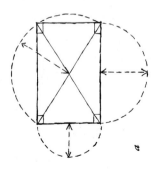

Figure 33   Ribbed cross vaults

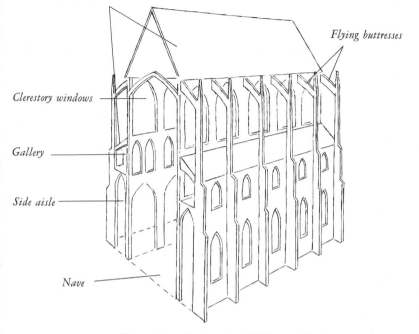

Wooden roof to protect masonry vaults

Flying buttresses

Clerestory windows

Gallery

Side aisle

Nave

Figure 34   Section of a Gothic cathedral

justed to different heights by varying the degree of pointedness (*Fig.* 33c), as was done at *Amiens Cathedral* (PLATE 28). The pointed ribbed cross vault, like the pointed arch, can be built higher with less buttressing. As the height of medieval vaults increased, *flying buttresses* were developed to help bear the load (*Fig.* 34).

Domes may be hemispherical, less than hemispherical (like the depressed arch), or pointed. The problem of buttressing varies accordingly. To hold in the outward buckling tendency, large domes may be made of massive thickness or have circling bands of chain or wood buried in the masonry or concrete (modern domes may be made of ferroconcrete). Unlike the arch, the dome is not weakened by an opening in the crown, because the inward leaning only wedges the circular form more tightly together, and the load forces pushing inward are converted to an outward buckling tendency (*Fig.* 35). Openings in the sides of a dome, however, tend to destroy the circular system of self-support and require special buttressing. The use of a dome over a square room requires a transition to the round

53

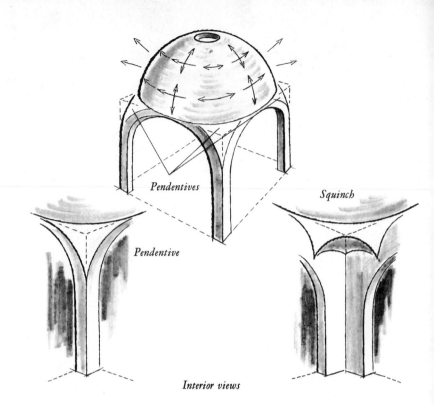

Pendentives

Pendentive

Squinch

Interior views

Figure 35   The dome and its supports

Figure 36   Geodesic dome

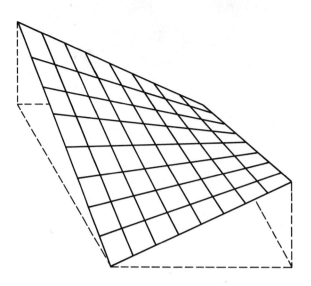

Figure 37   *Hyperbolic paraboloid*

base of the dome. Two solutions have been widely used: the *pendentive* and the *squinch*. The pendentive cuts off or fills in the corners of the square with curved triangular fillets (*Fig.* 35). The squinch is a more abrupt transition made by arching over the corners to form an octagonal base which is easily accommodated to the circular dome (*Fig.* 35).

Two of the more striking forms developed in recent years are the *geodesic dome* and the *hyperbolic paraboloid*. The geodesic dome utilizes the geometry of the tetrahedron to create a light structure of enormous strength (*Fig.* 36). Buoyant spacious effects are possible with the hyperbolic paraboloid, where straight members can be used to construct a curved surface of great strength (*Fig.* 37).

Suggestions for further study

DRAWING

Moskowitz, Ira, ed. *Great Drawings of All Time*. New York: Shorewood Publishers, 1962. 4 vols.

Nicolaïdes, Kimon. *The Natural Way to Draw*. Boston: Houghton Mifflin Company, 1941.

PRINTMAKING

Biegeleisen, J. I., and M. A. Cohn. *Silk Screen Techniques*. New York: Dover Publications, 1958.

Hayter, S. W. *About Prints*. London: Oxford University Press, 1962.

Heller, Jules. *Printmaking Today; An Introduction to the Graphic Arts*. New York: Henry Holt and Company, 1958.

Ivins, William M., Jr. *How Prints Look: Photographs with a Commentary*. Boston: Beacon Press, 1958.

PAINTING

Doerner, Max. *The Materials of the Artist and Their Use in Painting*. Trans. by Eugen Neuhaus. Rev. ed. New York: Harcourt, Brace & World, 1949.

Mayer, Ralph. *The Artist's Handbook of Materials and Techniques*. Rev. ed. New York: The Viking Press, 1957.

SCULPTURE

Lynch, John. *Metal Sculpture; New Forms, New Techniques*. New York: The Viking Press (Studio Books), 1957.

Rich, J. C. *The Materials and Methods of Sculpture*. New York: Oxford University Press, 1947.

Struppeck, Jules. *The Creation of Sculpture*. New York: Henry Holt and Company, 1952.

ARCHITECTURE

Collins, Peter. *Concrete: The Vision of a New Architecture*. London: Faber & Faber, 1959.

Giedion, Sigfried. *Space, Time, and Architecture*. 4th ed. Cambridge, Mass.: Harvard University Press, 1962.

Gropius, Walter. *Scope of Total Architecture* (World Perspectives, Vol. 3). Ed. by Ruth N. Anshen. New York: Harper & Brothers, 1955.

Hamlin, Talbot. *Forms and Functions of Twentieth-Century Architecture*. New York: Columbia University Press, 1952. 4 vols.

Wright, Frank Lloyd. *Frank Lloyd Wright: Writings and Buildings*. Ed. by Edgar Kaufmann and Ben Raeburn. New York: The World Publishing Company (Meridian Books), 1960.

Chapter Five # PROBLEMS OF VALUE JUDGMENT

Problems of objectivity and subjectivity

Value judgment in art involves both objective and subjective factors. Perhaps the most clearly objective factor is the artist's skill in the use of his chosen medium to produce a work of art that does not fall to pieces because of poor structure or change color because of chemical reactions. It is possible to consider objectively the artist's skill in depicting recognizable objects when to do so seems relevant to the work of art, but complexities arise with nonobjective and abstract work. We can also judge with some objectivity the extent to which the artist has exploited the expressive possibilities of his medium; yet he may have deliberately limited the range of colors in his painting, the modulation of line in his drawing, or the variety of texture and color in his architecture. Furthermore, limitations may have been imposed upon him by his time and place. The artist of ancient Egypt did not have the technical knowledge available to the artist of the nineteenth century, but we do not assume that, for this reason, any work produced by a competent nineteenth-century artist is superior to the best work of the older culture. Clearly, quality means more than technical virtuosity. Art goes beyond the skillful description of facts and feelings to the more subtle and subjective realms of expression and evocation, where the artist needs not just an imitative facility but a special sensitivity to the visual and tactile elements. He may also need sensitivity to human experience, a capacity for empathy, an agile imagination, and an understanding of the symbols or iconography that will be meaningful to his fellow men. Such things would be hard enough to measure even if they were not colored by the interpretation of individual observers, whose capacities to respond may vary widely.

The individual's sensitivity to the visual and tactile elements depends partly on the natural sensitivity of his sensory perceptions and partly on his training. Variations among individuals may therefore lead to disagreement about the total effect of a work of art. The breadth of the observer's experience is important. A person accustomed only to the flowing harmonies of paintings like Raphael's *Madonna of the Meadow* (PLATE 36) might find the relative dissonance and liveliness of Picasso's *Three Musicians* (PLATE 92) lacking in unity. The same might be said of the color harmonies in a comparison of Rembrandt and Matisse (COLOR PLATES 2 and 4). The observer's response also rests on his sensitivity and understanding in regard to human experience. A child might respond with great sensitivity to Rubens' *Coup de Lance* (PLATE 53), but more mature experience added to the same sensitivity would deepen the content for him. The observer's response may be very limited if he has no understanding of relevant iconography.

Because of the tremendous stylistic variety encountered in examining even one medium, such as painting, and because of the many subjective factors we have described, the major problem in art criticism and the judgment of quality is to find workable standards. Most critical statements might be subsumed under the broad demands for *unity*, *variety*, and *intensity of experience*, qualities we value because they enable us to experience life more completely by developing the sensitivity and subtlety of our perception, imagination, and understanding. Yet it is obvious that no fixed proportion of these three qualities would make an ideal formula for more than one work of art; nor is it easy to agree upon a measurement for such things in a given work of art.

Aesthetic theories of value judgment

Aesthetics, the branch of philosophy that deals with the nature of beauty, has described many different attitudes toward value judgments. These attitudes, which may be conscious or unconscious, may be classed broadly in three overlapping areas.

OBJECTIVISM

The most extreme objective attitude assumes unchanging standards by which absolute judgments can be made for the art of any time and place. An example is the "neo-classic" art theory of the eighteenth and nineteenth centuries, which held that painting, sculpture, and architecture of any culture should be measured against Greek or Roman art. Such an attitude tends to reject the art of many cultures and to deny variability in concepts of aesthetic value. A more flexible objective position argues that such qualities as unity, variety, and intensity—developed in varying degrees and proportions according to the nature of the art object—give the object aesthetic value not only for its own culture but also for others. The capacity of an observer to judge will vary with his sensitivity and understanding. Changes in the history of taste therefore do not prove changes in value but only in preference, and preference is not the same as evaluation; a person may prefer one work over another but concede that the second has a higher aesthetic value.

SUBJECTIVISM

Subjective theories consider the judgment of art to be purely personal; each individual uses different criteria or different interpretations of criteria, and all criteria are equally valid. The aesthetic value of an art object rests not in the object but in the response of the observer, who may grant or deny such value to any object.

RELATIVISM

Relativist views hold that there are objective standards which can be valid for the members of a particular culture but that each culture forms its own standards. When an observer judges art from a culture other than his own, he should attempt to escape the prejudices of his own culture and judge it on the basis of the criteria of the culture that produced the work. Historical perspective or cultural differences may enable the outsider to comprehend the standards of a foreign culture more objectively than would its own members. Relativist views make value judgments between art objects from different cultures difficult or undesirable, or they force a comparative judgment of different cultures with their own sets of values. One aspect of relativism is the frequent attempt to understand the artist's intention and then judge to what extent he achieved his aim. One may use *internal* evidence (evidence within the art object or other works by the same artist) and *external* evidence (such as statements by the artist about his own work). However, it is conceivable that the work of art might have high aesthetic value even if the artist did not achieve his intent; conversely, if the intent was achieved, we are left with a decision about the aesthetic value of the intent. Which is better, a superficial success or a magnificent failure?

Suggestions for further study

Beardsley, Monroe C. *Aesthetics: Problems in the Philosophy of Criticism.* New York: Harcourt, Brace & World, 1958.

Bell, Clive. *Art.* Reprint. New York: G. P. Putnam's Sons (Capricorn Books), 1958.

Berenson, Bernard. *Aesthetics and History.* New York: Doubleday & Company (Anchor Books), 1954.

Boas, George. *Wingless Pegasus: A Handbook for Critics.* Baltimore: The Johns Hopkins Press, 1950.

Fry, Roger. *Vision and Design.* Reprint. New York: The World Publishing Company (Meridian Books), 1956.

Heyl, Bernard. *New Bearings in Esthetics and Art Criticism.* New Haven, Conn.: Yale University Press; London: Oxford University Press, 1943.

Langer, Suzanne. *Feeling and Form: A Theory of Art.* New York: Charles Scribner's Sons, 1953.

Read, Herbert. *Icon and Idea: The Function of Art in the Development of Human Consciousness.* Cambridge, Mass.: Harvard University Press, 1955.

———. *The Meaning of Art.* 6th ed. rev. Baltimore: Penguin Books (Pelican Books), 1959.

Venturi, Lionello. *History of Art Criticism.* Trans. by Charles Marriott. New York: E. P. Dutton & Company, 1936.

Worringer, Wilhelm. *Abstraction and Empathy: A Contribution to the Psychology of Style.* Trans. by Michael Bullock. London: Routledge & Kegan Paul, 1953.

Part Two # THE HISTORY OF ART IN WESTERN CULTURE

The beginnings of art precede written records. The most prolific time for prehistoric art was the LATE PALEOLITHIC *or* LATE OLD STONE AGE, *which lasted approximately from 30,000 years ago to 10,000 years ago. Particularly in the period between 15,000 and 10,000 years ago, men painted and scratched animals, hunting scenes, and geometric designs on the walls of caves and rock shelters. The artist sometimes painted with charcoal and colored earths with a binder of animal grease, and sometimes spread the grease on the wall and blew powdered colors against it from a hollow bone tube. Many cave paintings have been found in France and northern Spain; some of the most remarkable are in the caves of Altamira in Spain and Lascaux in France. In these paintings, modulated contours and modeling in light and dark create the illusion of mass in the bodies of bison, horses, and cows, and a keen understanding of anatomy is combined with a sensitive expression of an animal's speed, ferocity, or gentleness. Paleolithic artists did not include landscape backgrounds, and each image or group of images is an isolated episode rather than one scene within the time sequence of a story; human figures were shown infrequently and often simplified, with single lines for torso and limbs. The frequent representation of animals pierced by arrows or spears, the casual overlapping of images, and the frequent location of paintings in almost inaccessible parts of caves all suggest that the making of pictures was a magic ritual to ensure success*

61

t. A purely aesthetic impulse might be *y the geometric designs, but these too could* *motivated or rationalized by the need of* *aleolithic artists not only painted but also* *n soft earth and carved bone, tusk, and antler.* *, animals and the hunt were the preferred sub-* *ject . . ., it we have found female statuettes that may have been meant to increase the fertility of the clan. Some of the characteristics of these paintings and carvings are found in the art of primitive societies today. While early discoveries of prehistoric art were difficult to authenticate, it is now possible to be more certain. One method used for dating objects relies on* STRATIGRAPHY; *an object is dated according to the age of the earth stratum in which it is found. A more precise method is that of* CARBON 14 *measurement. While it is living, each organic substance maintains a known amount of radioactive carbon 14. After the substance ceases to live, the carbon 14 begins to lose its radioactivity at a constant rate. Thus the amount of radioactivity allows us to determine the age of the organic substance.*

The concept of STYLE *is fundamental to an understanding of both prehistoric and historic art, for the subtle differences in style reveal man's changing ideas of the beautiful or the significant. Style is a characteristic manner of expression and the kind of content that goes with it. It exists on several levels.* PERIOD STYLE *is the style that unites work from different areas at a given time; we speak of the style of the Middle Ages or of the Renaissance. The characteristics of a period style are very general and are overlaid with local and individual variations.* REGIONAL STYLE *can be detected in the work of various artists working in the same country or area, if there has not been too much influence from other regions.* INDIVIDUAL STYLE *is seen in the work of a particular artist, whose style may change several times in the course of his career.*

Chapter Six   **EGYPT: 3200-30 B.C.**

Ancient Egyptian history falls into three major periods, which are further divided into dynasties (ages during which a single family provided the succession of rulers). The *Archaic* period and the *Old Kingdom* may be considered together as the first major period, one that began with the unification of northern and southern Egypt, saw the establishment of Memphis as a cultural center, and ended with the decline of central power and an era of confusion and civil war. Order was restored during the *Middle Kingdom,* but in a feudal system that weakened the authority of the *pharaoh* (king). This kingdom eventually collapsed under the burdens of civil war and invasion by the Hyksos (probably Canaanites and Anatolians), who exacted tribute from much of Egypt until they were expelled by princes from Thebes. Thebes became a major center for the *New Kingdom* or *Empire,* the period that brought Egypt to its greatest power. We may group the Empire with the less important periods that followed and with the age of defeats that ended Egypt's leading role in ancient history. She was invaded by Assyrians in the seventh century B.C., by the Persians in the sixth century B.C., and by the Macedonians in 332 B.C.; finally, in 30 B.C. Egypt became a Roman province.

Egyptian civilization began as a series of independent city-states, each with its own patron god. The unity of these parts was always precarious, as Egyptian literature and art reveal; for example, the pharaoh is sometimes depicted wearing the crown (with a flat top and a raised portion at the rear) of northern or Lower Egypt, sometimes with the crown (shaped like a bowling pin) of southern or Upper Egypt, and occasionally with a combination of both crowns. Life depended on the rhythmic cycles of the Nile River, whose floods enriched the bottom lands but necessitated the frequent re-surveying of fields; hence the Egyptians quickly developed a practical mathematics as well as astronomy and a rational calendar.

Egyptian society consisted of the nobility, which owned much of the land; the middle class, which consisted of merchants, artists, civil servants, and—in the Empire—soldiers; and the serfs, who formed the bulk of the population. By the end of the Empire, the power of the nobility had been partially taken over by the growing priesthood and by the increasing number of civil servants.

All Egyptian culture was pervaded by a complex religion that stressed a life after death; therefore, most of the painting, sculpture, and architecture was religious and sepulchral. Egyptian art presents a bewildering variety of gods—male and female human figures and combination animal-human creatures such as the sphinx. Some of the more important gods were Osiris, lord of the underworld (often shown as a swathed mummy); Anubis, the jackal-god of embalment; Nut, the sky goddess (a human form arched over the earth); Hathor, the goddess of love and joy (usually shown with cow's horns); Horus, one aspect of the sun god (often shown as a hawk); and Re or Ra, the sun god who traveled across the sky in his sun-ship during the day and through the underworld during the night. The pharaoh himself was believed to be a god. Many of the gods assumed each other's forms or evolved in form and name during the course of Egyptian history. The most striking development in this history was the effort of the XVIIIth-dynasty king Akhenaten to establish a monotheistic religion founded on the worship of the sun god.

Archaic period: 3200–2680 B.C., dynasties I through III and Old Kingdom: 2680–2258 B.C., dynasties IV through VI

ARCHITECTURE

The palaces of the nobility and the homes of the wealthy were built either of wood frames with walls of colored reed mats or of mud brick with plaster or stucco surfacing decorated with paintings; more modest dwellings were probably of reed mats plastered with mud. Such impermanent materials have left few remains. The Egyptians concentrated their efforts on tombs and temples, built to serve the deceased or the gods and to defy time and the destructive power of nature. Stone and brick were used for this more permanent architecture, but because the stone and brick sometimes encased only a rubble filling the wall was not always as permanent as it might have been. The arch was known but rarely used; the basic structural system was post and lintel.

Egyptian architecture emphasizes mass and employs rigid simple contours. Interior spaces are usually small in proportion to the masses enclosing them and placed in a mazelike succession, with dead ends or roundabout connections. One of the basic tomb types is the *mastaba* (*Fig.* 38), originally a rectangular block with *battered* (sloping) sides and more mass than enclosed space, though later mastabas are less regular in form and enclose more space. The basic parts are (1) the burial chamber, reached by a vertical or sloping shaft; (2) the statue chamber, a walled-up room containing a statue substitute for the body; (3) a mortuary chapel, where offerings could be left for the deceased; and (4) a false door through which the spirit of the dead was to have access to the offerings. Often the statue chamber has a peephole leading to the chapel. The statue chamber and burial chamber with its entry shaft are often encased in hard stone, meant to improve durability and to discourage tomb-robbers, who were attracted by the treasures buried with the dead. The mastaba was thought of as a house for the dead, and groups of mastabas formed cities of the dead. It is conjectured that the *pyramid* tomb may have evolved from stacked-up mastabas of decreasing size, as in the tomb of King Zoser (*Fig.* 39).

Such a step-pyramid could have led to the true pyramid form, which protects its burial chamber and treasures under a mountain of stone (*Fig.* 40). The basic parts of an Old Kingdom pyramid complex are: (1) the pyramid, (2) a mortuary chapel or temple beside or against the pyramid, (3) a causeway leading from the mortuary temple to (4) a valley temple close to the Nile (*Fig.* 41). The huge pyramids only inspired greater efforts by tomb-robbers, however, and in later periods smaller tombs were built. For their post and lintel structures, the Egyptians derived column designs from plants and from construction methods; some columns suggest bundles of saplings or reeds tied together for strength, while others are polygonal with grooved sides like the later Doric column of Greece. Capitals atop the columns resemble lotus buds, papyrus blossoms, palm leaves, or leafy blossoms (*Fig.* 42).

Step-pyramid of Zoser (Saqqara, dyn. III).   The first large Egyptian architecture in stone, this 195-foot-high mass seems to have developed from an original mastaba by added stages. Around the pyramid, a wall originally enclosed a funerary community with

Fig. 39
JAN.
L. & H.
W. S. S.
U. & S.

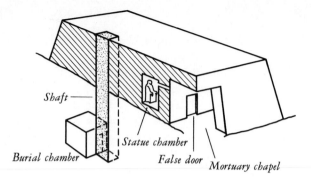

Shaft

Burial chamber

Statue chamber

False door

Mortuary chapel

Figure 38   Cross section of a mastaba

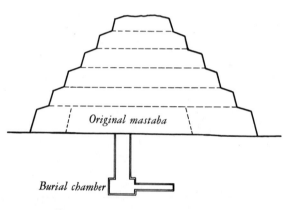

Original mastaba

Burial chamber

Figure 39   Step-pyramid of Zoser

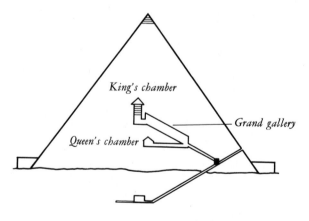

King's chamber

Grand gallery

Queen's chamber

Figure 40   Cross section of the Pyramid of Khufu

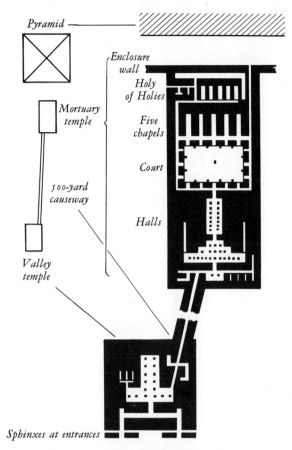

Pyramid

Enclosure wall

Holy of Holies

Mortuary temple

Five chapels

Court

500-yard causeway

Halls

Valley temple

Sphinxes at entrances

Figure 41   *Pyramid of Khafre, Giza*

chapels, palaces, and temples. Bundle, fluted (grooved), and papyrus blossom columns are used. The architect was Imhotep.

Pyramids of Khufu, Khafre, and Menkure (Giza, dyn. IV).   These
largest of Egyptian tombs are in true pyramid form and were originally encased in polished limestone. The largest of the three, that
of Khufu, has a base about 750 feet square and was originally about
475 feet high. The method of construction is not known with certainty; the mammoth stones may have been pulled on sledges up
ramps of earth that were raised with each level of the structure.
The massive, stable geometric form and the simple surfaces are
characteristic of monumental architecture in Egypt.

Figs. 40
and 41
JAN.
L. & H.
W. S. S.
U. & S.

67

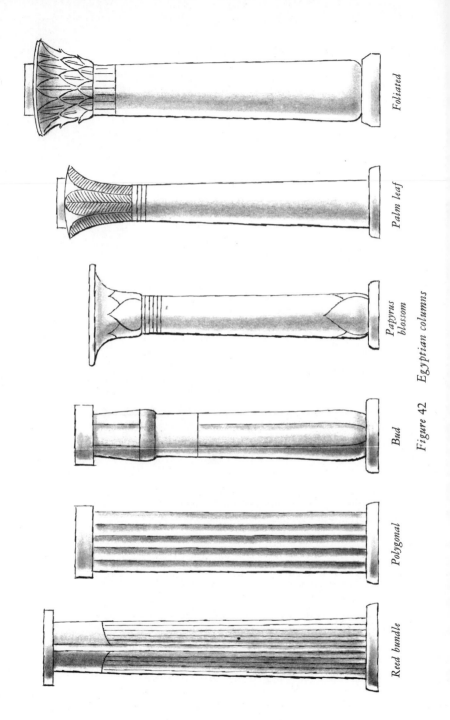

Foliated

Palm leaf

Papyrus blossom

Bud

Polygonal

Reed bundle

Figure 42   Egyptian columns

Mastaba of Ti (Saqqara, dyns. V).   This mastaba is L-shaped and measures about 110 feet by 143 feet. It consists of two statue chambers, a pillared hall, a corridor, and an offering chapel and contains fine examples of painted relief sculpture.

SCULPTURE

Egyptian sculpture ranges from colossal statues to delicate goldsmith's work. The most significant pieces were done for tombs or temples. For large work, hard stones such as granite, diorite, or basalt were preferred. Softer alabaster was exploited for its translucence, and sandstone, limestone, or wood sculpture was often surfaced with plaster and painted. Small sculpture, or inlay work in large sculpture, might consist of gold, silver, electrum (an alloy of gold and silver), lapis lazuli (a semiprecious azure-colored stone), and enamel.

Relief sculpture, generally low relief consisting of sharp-edged, relatively flat forms, has some of the abstract symbolic character of Egyptian hieroglyphic writing. The human body is portrayed by conventionalized forms developed early in Egyptian history. A frontally seen eye is combined with a profile face, frontal shoulders, and profile hips and legs; the artist seems to have thought through an action step by step and shown these steps as in a diagram. The standardized bodies occasionally admit the depiction of age, but otherwise the passage of time is excluded, for the sharp edges and angular poses tend to freeze any suggestion of motion. Motion implies time as mass implies space; neither is typical of Old Kingdom relief. Some overlapping of flat shapes suggests a very shallow space, but massive forms and a perspective illusion of space are not found. As a result, the reliefs do not weaken the mass of the wall or the *stele* (an upright marker) which carries them.

In freestanding sculpture, the standard poses are free from the wall, but they may be attached to a supporting back-slab (PLATE 1). Much Egyptian sculpture retains the massive four-sidedness of the block from which it was carved, and mass aids the impression of durability. Closed form is typical. Anatomy is simplified in the direction of geometric shapes, so that the figure assumes the rigidity and static permanence of Egyptian architecture. Individuality is concentrated in the face, which is often alert in expression but motionless. It should be noted, however, that the art of the different areas of Egypt varies in its adherence to the conventional forms.

The functions of the various statues, as votive images to the gods or as images of servants meant to serve the deceased in his afterlife, also influenced the style of the work.

<table>
<tr><td>

JAN.
L. & H.
W. S. S.
U. & S.

</td><td>

Victory palette of Narmer (Egyptian Museum, Cairo, dyn. I, slate, 25″). An elaborate version of the palettes used for mixing eye paints commemorates the subjection of northern Egypt by the South. On one side, King Narmer, wearing the tall crown of the South, is about to strike a northerner. A hawk holds captive a plant with a human head, probably the papyrus symbol of the delta region. Above, the symbol for Narmer is framed by a small palace. On either side of this is a human head with cow's horns, the symbol for Hathor. On the other side of the palette, Narmer, wearing the crown of northern Egypt, surveys decapitated enemies. At the bottom, he is seen as a bull knocking down the walls of a city. Typically, the artist shows the figures in "elevation" standing on base lines, until a different point of view is needed to convey the information he is giving. Then the artist changes to an aerial view to show the number of slain enemies.

</td></tr>
<tr><td>

JAN.
L. & H.
W. S. S.
U. & S.

</td><td>

Prince Rahotep and his wife Nofret (Egyptian Museum, Cairo, dyn. IV, painted limestone with inlaid quartz eyes, about 4′). Traditionally, brown was used for the skin of men and yellow for that of women. The equal size of the figures here suggests that the wife had equal importance, but such equality of scale is not typical in Egyptian art. Rahotep was a prince, a high priest, and an army commander; his wife was a member of the court.

</td></tr>
<tr><td>

JAN.
L. & H.
W. S. S.
U. & S.

</td><td>

Seated King Khafre, sometimes called Chephren (Egyptian Museum, Cairo, dyn. IV, diorite, 66″). The statue was one of many in Khafre's valley temple. The pose is typical in its rigid formality and closed form. The god Horus sits behind the king's head, and the unity of northern and southern Egypt is symbolized by the intertwined plants on the sides of the throne.

</td></tr>
<tr><td>

PLATE 1

</td><td>

Menkure and his queen (Museum of Fine Arts, Boston, dyn. IV, slate, 56″). The king wears a ceremonial false beard; the queen wears a wig. The individual facial features are somewhat simplified, and yet they contrast with the more generalized treatment of the bodies. The pose is typical for standing figures. Closed form and anatomy reduced to geometric rigidity give a timeless dignity to the couple.

</td></tr>
</table>

PAINTING

Papyrus was occasionally used by the Egyptians for painting, as well as for writing, but the most important paintings are on the walls of tombs and temples. Paint was also used often to enhance relief or freestanding sculpture. Grounds are smoothed stone or a coating of stucco, plaster, or mud and straw. Pigments made from powdered natural substances, such as soot, copper compounds, or earth colors, were mixed with a binder of water and gum and were applied to a dry ground.

Old Kingdom painting, like the sculpture and architecture, shows a preference for rigidly imposed rectilinear order and a limited number of standard forms. During the millennia of Egyptian history, the striking quality of all the arts is not the subtle change or occasional rebellion against the standard forms but rather their continuity. Old Kingdom painting was often applied to relief sculpture; it was left to later ages to stress painting as an independent art. Like relief, painting stresses sharp-edged flat shapes, and the diagrammatic poses symbolize activity rather than expressing it. Spaces between figures are often filled with hieroglyphics, which counter any slight illusion of depth that might come from overlapping shapes. Typical forms and actions of animals are keenly observed, yet the repetition of shapes and details within shapes imposes a regimented order upon the variety of nature. In Old Kingdom painting, as well as that of later periods, scale is conceptual rather than perceptual; i.e., more important figures are usually larger. Subject matter comes from mythology, ritual, biography, or daily activities. Symbolism is pervasive. Many of the activities, such as sowing, reaping, and offering prayers and food, were apparently intended to "serve" the deceased in his afterlife. As in the reliefs, scenes are organized in *registers* (strips placed one above the other). While overall symmetry was valued, each picture seems to function as an isolated unit, and the accretion of these units gives the painting some of the additive character of the architecture.

Geese from the mastaba of Itet at Medum (Egyptian Museum, Cairo, dyn. III, about 1' x 6'). This is one section from one register in a large wall painting. Yet the composition works effectively as an isolated unit. The colors and the poised strutting of the geese are quite natural, but a typically severe order is evident in the symmetry of the poses and in the crisp patterns of the feathers.

w. s. s.
u. & s.

Middle Kingdom: 2134–1786 B.C., dynasties XI and XII

ARCHITECTURE

The Middle Kingdom produced smaller tombs and tomb-temple combinations. In part, this resulted from less concentration of wealth; it may also be explained by the growth of the Osiris cult, which stressed an afterlife in the underworld rather than in the tomb. Many small stone-faced brick pyramids and mastabas have crumbled away, but more permanent tombs, cut into the rock of the cliffs along the Nile Valley at places like Beni Hasan, still remain.

w. s. s.   *Rock-cut tomb of Amenemhat* (Beni Hasan, dyn. XII).   Here typical features of the rock-cut tombs are seen in the modest size, courtyard, pillared portico, main room supported by fluted columns (sometimes called Proto-Doric because of their resemblance to later Greek Doric columns), and shrine. Such tombs generally contained a simple grave pit for the body. The walls are painted with subjects in the tradition of the Old Kingdom, and the ceiling is decorated with geometric designs that probably imitate textile roofing.

SCULPTURE

Much Middle Kingdom sculpture was destroyed by the Hyksos or by New Kingdom rulers. What remains varies from crude to highly finished carving. The growing middle-class patronage and the dispersal of wealth among the nobles seem in many works to have resulted in the sacrifice of quality for quantity. Frequent use was made of the cheaper method of *sunken relief*, in which the outlines of objects are cut into the wall and the form within the outlines is carved so that most of it is below the surface of the untouched background. In style it owes much to the Old Kingdom, although poses are often more affected. Freestanding sculpture developed even simpler bodies than in the Old Kingdom. Forms are either sleek and flowing or heavy, brutal, and blocky. Many seated figures have arms folded over drawn-up knees; such a statue was simply a modified block surmounted by a head and therefore involved a minimum of carving. The most distinctive feature of Middle Kingdom sculpture is the cynicism and careworn weariness in many of the faces, a quality that is echoed in Middle Kingdom writings. This detailed realism is often in striking contrast to the simplified bodies. Middle Kingdom servant statues tend to be of cheaper materials and cruder execution than earlier examples.

72

King Mentuhotep (Egyptian Museum, Cairo, dyn. XI, painted sand- stone, 6'). The statue was found wrapped in mummy bindings in a shaft under the king's mortuary temple at Deir el-Bahari. The king, wearing the crown of northern Egypt, is seated in the tradi- tional pose. The work exemplifies the heavy-handed carving of much Middle Kingdom sculpture. L. & H. W. S. S.

Relief on the sarcophagus of Mentuhotep's wife, Kawit (Egyptian Mu- seum, Cairo, dyn. XI, limestone, originally painted). Quite unlike the preceding work, this sunken relief exemplifies the sleek, suave contours and rather precious poses characteristic of some Middle Kingdom sculpture. L. & H. W. S. S.

Sesostris III or Amenemhat III—identity uncertain (National Gallery of Art, Washington, D.C., dyn. XII, obsidian, 4''). The tired, lined face illustrates a Middle Kingdom tendency toward greater detail and more distinctly individualistic portrait features. The small scale and hard stone demanded considerable skill. L. & H.

PAINTING

The Middle Kingdom employed painting extensively, perhaps partly because painting was cheaper than relief. One of the chief sites for Middle Kingdom painting is the rock-cut tombs of Beni Hasan. The paintings are typically done in soft, subtle colors, ap- plied to broad simple shapes which sometimes contrast with areas of fussy detail.

Dancing girls from the tomb of Antefoker (Thebes, dyn. XII, about 37'' x 67''). The mild value contrasts, bland colors, simple shapes, and wirelike outlines are typical of much Middle Kingdom painting. MEK.

Prince Sirenpowet, son of Satet-hotep, from his tomb (Aswan, dyn. XII). The prince sits on a chair with lion's legs, typical of the period, and faces a table piled high with offerings, to which his son is about to add a flower. Outlines are used infrequently, but the simple shapes have knife-sharp edges. The lack of depth and the flat shapes are characteristic of Egyptian painting in all three of the major periods. L. & H.

New Kingdom (Empire) and later periods: 1570–30 B.C. dynasties XVIII through XXXI

ARCHITECTURE

Thebes is the center for the important remains of New Kingdom architecture. In the cliffs on the western side of the river are two desolate rock-strewn valleys: the Valley of the Tombs of the Kings and the Valley of the Tombs of the Queens. Here many of the New Kingdom rulers had themselves buried in hidden mineshaft-like tombs. While these cannot really be considered as architecture, they were lavishly decorated with paintings and sculpture. When the tombs became secret, the mortuary temples occupied more convenient locations near the city. Mortuary temples and temples to the gods became especially large during the New Kingdom and later periods (PLATES 2–4). Both kinds were built in the same general plan: (1) entry through a massive battered façade called a *pylon*, (2) an open *courtyard*, (3) a *hypostyle* (colonnaded) *hall*, and (4) a sacred *inner sanctum*. The basic parts could be multiplied, and temples to more than one god might have several sanctums. From entry to inner sanctum, the progression is from larger to smaller spaces, the plan being essentially an elaboration of the Middle Kingdom rock-cut tomb. The temples were often enlarged by a process of accretion over the centuries, and the resulting labyrinthine complexity, which does not lend itself to an easy comprehension of the whole interior, provided effective settings for the processionals so important in Egyptian worship.

w. s. s.   Our knowledge of New Kingdom domestic architecture would be greater had not later generations carried away much of the stone from Akhenaten's new capital at Amarna. His North Palace has an extensive symmetrical plan organized around a large pool and tightly enclosed behind thick walls. Typical materials for such architecture were mud brick and stone.

jan.   *Temple of Hatshepsut* (Deir el-Bahari, dyn. XVIII).   This is a mor-
w. s. s.   tuary temple for the queen and her parents. Parts of it are dedicated to various gods. Two colonnaded terraces, connected by ramps, lead to an open court and finally to a small sanctum carved into the cliff behind the temple. Reliefs depict the divine birth of the queen and the story of an expedition which she sent to acquire incense and myrrh from the land of Punt.

74

Temple of Amun-Mut-Khôns (Luxor, mainly dyns. XVIII· and XIX). The enormous temple was not for mortuary offerings but for the glory of the god Amun (whose identity merged with that of Re), his wife Mut, and their son Khôns. The basic temple parts have been multiplied. From the great pylon and the first court, built under Rameses II (XIXth dyn.), one enters the XVIIIth-dynasty parts of the building: a double row of 52-foot-high papyrus blossom columns, a second court (bud columns), a hypostyle hall, smaller halls, and two sanctums. Originally, two *obelisks* (tapered shafts with pointed tips) stood in front of the temple. One remains; the other now adorns the Place de la Concorde in Paris. The total length of the structure is about 835 feet.

JAN.
L. & H.
W. S. S.

Temple of Amun (Karnak, mainly dyns. XVIII–XX, with additions up to Roman occupation).   The Karnak temple, a prime example of additive building, reached a length of about 1220 feet; four additional pylons (making a total of ten) were added to one side. The gigantic hypostyle hall, occupying about 5,800 square yards, has 140 bud and blossom columns covered with reliefs. Originally, paint and inlays of gold, silver, and electrum enriched its surfaces. Whole cities, as well as vast amounts of land, cattle, and slaves, were given as endowments for the support of such temples and their priesthood.

W. S. S.
U. & S.

Temple of Horus (Edfu, largely 237–212 B.C.).   The building comes from the Ptolemaic era, which followed the Macedonian conquest. It is notable for its good state of preservation and its exemplification of the basic Egyptian temple unobscured by proliferation. The pylon (145′ x 250′) and massive exterior walls enclose court, vestibule, hypostyle hall, storage rooms, and inner sanctum. The plan indicates a characteristic progression to smaller and darker spaces. The columns typify the late period in the use of a variety of palm and foliated capitals.

PLATES
2–4
L. & H.
U. & S.

SCULPTURE
Increasing prosperity during the Empire greatly encouraged artistic activity. Tomb statues were often carved in the living rock of the shaft tombs, and quantities of votive statues and reliefs decorated the temples. Sunken relief is common. Middle Kingdom style continued for a time, but the expansion of empire brought increased

awareness of other peoples, and conventional forms soon relaxed to allow more representation of different racial types. The reign of Akhenaten marked a stylistic change toward more action, greater casualness in pose, increasing complexity in costume and accessory detail, a softening of body forms, and more indication of age. The king's heavy lips, pendulous jaw, long neck, and sagging stomach were stressed to the point of caricature in portraits that he must have encouraged. The royal features soon set the style, and portraits of other people acquired his "ideal" form. The old conventions were modified rather than abolished. Soon after the death of Akhenaten, the old canons returned, but with slightly softer contours in some works and more open form.

L. & H.
W. S. S.

Akhenaten or Amenhotep IV (Egyptian Museum, Cairo, dyn. XVIII, sandstone with coloring, 13'). Although the traditional pose is taken, the features of face and body make a striking contrast to Old Kingdom statues like the *Seated King Khafre*.

JAN.
L. & H.
W. S. S.
U. & S.

Nefertiti, wife of Akhenaten (Staatliches Museum, Berlin, dyn. XVIII, painted limestone with eyes—one missing—of inlaid rock crystal, about 20"). This bust, found in the remains of a sculptor's studio, served as a model. Suggestions of fleshy softness under the chin and around the eyes and mouth lend a flesh-and-blood reality to the regal poise of the queen.

L. & H.

Procession of prisoners from the tomb of Haremhab (Leiden Museum, Holland, dyn. XVIII). In the late XVIIIth dynasty, the influence of Akhenaten can still be seen in the sunken reliefs from the tomb of Haremhab, a general who became king. The procession of prisoners includes figures of different ages and facial types, portrayed with a marked softness of contour.

PAINTING

The best-preserved examples of Egyptian painting come from the highly decorated walls of the New Kingdom. Those from the beginning of the period are characterized by stiff poses and vivid opaque colors, with wide use of blue backgrounds. Later came a change to more graceful poses and more delicate transparent colors applied with brushwork that is occasionally loose and sketchy. The reign of Akhenaten produced startling changes in painting, as in sculpture. When he moved the capital from Thebes to Tell el 'Amarna, he had his palace there decorated with paintings of landscapes and animal life, all done with a new concern for the continuity of all the parts. The direct visual experience of nature breaks through the old symbolic concepts. Human forms acquire the casual poses, soft bodies, and elongated faces common to the sculpture of the period. This so-called *Amarna style* died shortly after Akhenaten, but its influence is seen in the occasional flashes of individuality and naturalism that lighten the official manner of later art. Later painting tends to be repetitious, garish in color, and technically mediocre even though it answered the demands for ostentatious elegance.

Fowling scene from the tomb of Amenemheb, Thebes (fragment in the British Museum, London, dyn. XVIII, 2' 10'').   The artist gives us considerable information about types of fishes, birds, and plants, as well as methods of hunting (note the hunting cat); the compositional arrangement of figures, boat, and papyrus is an ancient one for hunting scenes. The small scale of the hunter's companions indicates their lesser importance. The object on the head of the standing woman is a lump of perfumed ointment.   PLATE 5

Wall paintings in the tomb of Nakht (Thebes, dyn. XVIII).   Nakht was a priest of Amun. The paintings describe offerings made at the painted false door of the chapel, the procedures of farming, and dancers and musicians entertaining guests at a feast. Here also the style indicates the period before Akhenaten, but the freedom of brushwork and the delicate color indicate the period just after the tomb of Amenemheb. The small but well-preserved chapel shows the typically sparkling decorative effect of the many flat shapes used in Egyptian painting.   MEK. U. & S.

References for representative works

Janson, H. W., with D. J. Janson, eds. *Key Monuments of the History of Art: A Visual Survey.* Englewood Cliffs, N.J.: Prentice-Hall; New York: Harry N. Abrams, 1959.   JAN.

Lange, Kurt, and Max Hirmer. *Egypt: Architecture, Sculpture, Painting in Three Thousand Years.* Trans. by R. H. Boothroyd. 2nd ed. rev. London: Phaidon Press, 1957.   L. & H.

Mekhitarian, Arpag. *Egyptian Painting* (Great Centuries of Painting). Trans. by Stuart Gilbert. Geneva: Skira, 1954.   MEK.

w. s. s.　Smith, William Stevenson. *The Art and Architecture of Ancient Egypt* (Pelican History of Art). Baltimore: Penguin Books, 1958.

u. & s.　Upjohn, Everard M., and J. P. Sedgwick, Jr. *Highlights: An Illustrated History of Art*. New York: Holt, Rinehart and Winston, 1963.

Suggestions for further study

Aldred, Cyril. *The Development of Ancient Egyptian Art from 3200–1315* B.C. London: Alec Tiranti, 1952.

Breasted, James Henry. *A History of Egypt from the Earliest Times to the Persian Conquest*. 2nd ed. rev. New York: Charles Scribner's Sons, 1912.

Desroches-Noblecourt, Christine. *Ancient Egypt: The New Kingdom and the Amarna Period*. Greenwich, Conn.: New York Graphic Society, 1960.

Edwards, I. E. S. *Pyramids of Egypt*. Rev. ed. Baltimore: Penguin Books (Pelican Books), 1963.

Frankfort, H. A. G. *Arrest and Movement*. Chicago: University of Chicago Press, 1951.

Smith, E. Baldwin. *Egyptian Architecture as Cultural Expression*. New York: Appleton-Century-Crofts, 1938.

Chapter Seven # GREECE: 1100-100 B.C.

About 1100 B.C., the invasions of the Dorians seem to have added the last major ingredient for the amalgamation of peoples that was the basis for Greek culture. By 100 B.C., Greece was part of the Roman Empire. For Greek culture between these dates, the underlying theme was man and his rational faculty for understanding and perfecting himself and nature. The mild climate favored outdoor activity, influencing architecture directly and painting and sculpture indirectly. The periodic Olympic games (first noted in 776 B.C.) reflect the Greek interest in the physical life and in the human body. Yet the Greeks grew even more interested in the development of the mind, especially the power of reason, and in the conception of ideal forms for all things. Perfection was sought within carefully chosen limits or rules. The conviction that man is the measure of all things was basic to this culture, and even the gods were seen in the image of man, with few combinations of man and animal like those of the Egyptian religion. For art the most important Greek gods are (1) Zeus (Jupiter to the Romans), lord of the sky and supreme ruler, who wielded thunderbolts; (2) Hera (the Roman Juno), wife and sister of Zeus and goddess of marriage; (3) Poseidon (the Roman Neptune), god of the sea, recognized by his trident spear; (4) Athena (the Roman Minerva), originally a goddess of war but more commonly the patron of civilized life and wisdom; (5) Artemis (the Roman Diana), huntress and patron of wild life and the young, often shown with bow and arrows; (6) Apollo (known by the same name to the Romans), god of poetry, music, truth, prophecy, and—in later mythology—god of the sun (sometimes shown with a lyre or with bow and arrows); (7) Aphrodite (the Roman Venus), goddess of love and beauty; (8) Hermes (the Roman Mercury), messenger of the gods and patron of commerce (shown with winged sandals and a wand with entwined serpents); (9) Dionysus (the Roman Bacchus), a latecomer to Greek mythology, god of wine and feasting; (10) Pan (reflected in the Roman god Faunus), god of shepherds and flocks, a mischievous creature largely in human form but with horns and goat's legs; (11) satyrs (also in Roman mythology), who look like Pan and seek all sensual pleasures; and (12) centaurs, who are half man, half horse and are considered (with the exception of Chiron) to be savage creatures. The most common idea of life after death was that of a gray world of drifting spirits, and in contrast to the Egyptians, the Greeks emphasized life, an earthly life of balanced attainments, based on the idea that the complete man is one governed by reason and enlightened by wide interests. Consequently Greek tombs and burial customs were simple.

Geometric (1100–700 B.C.) *and Archaic (700–500* B.C.) *periods*

SCULPTURE

Greek sculpture was mainly religious. Of the works preserved from the Geometric period, many are small bronze votive statuettes dedicated to the gods. During this period, copper and fired clay were also common materials, and it is probable that there were large-scale wooden statues that have disappeared. Some of the metal statuettes were made of sheet metal riveted together; others were cast using a sand mold or the lost-wax process. Greek art was still conceptual in approach; that is, the figures seem to be composed from memory of individual parts of the body rather than from direct visual experience with a model. Divisions between the parts of the body tend to be exaggerated, and some parts are modified according to the sculptor's instinct for design. The result is usually a rigid schematic form that resembles Egyptian art. This strict geometric order is the basis for the name given to the period. The stylistic change during the Geometric period is toward more flowing transitions between the parts and more natural human form.

After the middle of the seventh century B.C., life-size stone sculpture became more common, and the geometric rigidity of the earlier period slowly softened. Nudity, so rare in Egyptian art, occurs early in Greek sculptures of the male body. We have found many statues of young men (*kouroi* sing., *kouros*) sculpted in the seventh and early sixth centuries B.C.; their frontal poses, stiff joints, and symmetry of hair and musculature recall Egyptian sculpture. It is rarely clear whether they were meant to be gods or mortals. A few works are signed, but little is known of sculptors from the Archaic period. A number of standing maidens (*korai* sing., *kore*) have also been discovered. Their pose and clothing (female nudity was not represented until much later) have the same strict order as that of the male figures. On many kouroi and korai the corners of the mouth are turned up in the so-called Archaic smile.

Apollo (Museum of Fine Arts, Boston, 7th cen. B.C., bronze, 8″).   LU. & H.
This Archaic work remains Geometric in style and has an inscription on the thighs dedicating the image to Apollo. The words ("Mantiklos dedicated me to . . .") reveal that the Greeks assigned an independent life to each work of art.

Standing youth, from Attica (Metropolitan Museum of Art, New York,   LU. & H.
late 7th cen. B.C., marble, 78″).   This Archaic kouros statue reveals its ancestry in the Geometric style. The frontal pose and the insistent symmetry are similar to Egyptian work, but there is no back-slab, and the arms are separated from the body, slightly opening up the form.

PAINTING

Greek painting of the Geometric and Archaic periods is known to us only through vase decoration, but vase painting was treated as an important medium until the fourth century B.C. Early Geometric painting consists of geometric shapes in registers. When the human body began to be depicted, it was reduced to sharply divided and simplified parts. The basic colors were provided by painting with a thinned mixture of brown-black clay on the body of red-brown clay, but other colors and white were sometimes added. The technique employing black shapes on the lighter reddish background is called *black-figure* vase painting.

Black-figure painting continued through most of the Archaic period and into the third quarter of the sixth century B.C., when it began to give way to *red-figure* painting, a technique in which the background is filled in with brown-black, leaving a base color of red-orange or warm tan for the figures. During the Archaic period, the figures became more lifelike, and geometric ornament was reduced. Scenes depict events from mythology, and ornament includes animals and floral motifs. Anatomy acquired more flexibility and naturalness of shape and proportion, but conventional formulas still dominated the forms. Beginning in the second quarter of the sixth century B.C., Athens was the center of great activity in vase painting. Both potters and painters (sometimes one man did both vase and painting) began to sign their work.

ROB.

Athenian grave vase (No. 804, National Museum, Athens, 9th cen. B.C., 61"). The geometry of the figures in this funeral scene allows it to fit easily into the large expanse of purely geometric decoration. One of the most common geometric patterns looks like a row of key ends standing upright; this is called the *Greek key* or *fret* and is still in use today. Many such grave vases have been found in the Dipylon Cemetery in Athens. They are often from five to six feet high, and some have perforated bottoms through which liquid offerings could drip onto the grave.

PLATE 10

Ajax and Achilles playing draughts (Vatican Museum, Rome, 550–525 B.C., height of vase: 24").   The black-figured scene decorates an *amphora* (tall vase with two handles) and was done by Exekias, one of the outstanding archaic vase painters. Geometric ornament is sparse. The frontally seen eye is still used with the long-nosed profile of earlier work, and taut flat shapes seem to bend stiffly at the joints (compare this with Archaic sculpture). Figures are anchored to a common base line; there is no effort to suggest round mass or deep space. The painter made the curve of the men's backs repeat the curve of the vase. The diagonals of the spears intensify the focus of attention on the game—the center of the obvious axial balance—and relate the composition to the handles of the vase, which seem to continue the lines of the spears.

ARCHITECTURE

Our knowledge of architecture from the Geometric and Archaic periods is incomplete. The most important buildings seem to have been temples to the gods and treasuries to hold offerings. Prior to 650 B.C., the Greeks built with wood and sun-dried brick; hence we have few remains that date from before that time. As the use of stone increased, some of the wooden structural forms were imitated in stone and became decorative rather than structural. Limestone was the usual material, and it was sometimes covered with a white stucco made of marble dust. Roofs were tile, with colored clay ornaments along the top and edges. The basic structural system was post and lintel. The dominant plan for temples and treasuries was rectangular; from a stepped base, windowless walls rose to enclose one to three rooms, called *cellae* (*Fig.* 43a, b, c, e, f). A *peristyle* (a covered colonnade that surrounds a building or a court) was common. A second type of temple was the *tholos*, which was circular in shape and usually had a peristyle (*Fig.* 43d). The rhythmic alternation of columns and spaces gives the exterior of most Greek temples a lighter, more open form than that of Egyptian architecture. The modest scale, simplicity, and clearly defined limits of a Greek building focus attention upon the proportions and the relationship of the parts to the whole form. Two of the three basic types of Greek columns were developed during the Archaic period: the Doric and the Ionic, the latter being more prevalent in Ionia in Asia Minor. These columns each had a special *entablature* to match. The combination of column and entablature is called an *order* (*Fig.* 44).

Temple of Ceres (Paestum, late 6th cen. B.C., limestone, approximately 48′ x 108′).   Only the peristyle remains from this Doric temple built by the Greek colony at Paestum on the Italian peninsula. The ponderous proportions of the pediment and the abrupt mushrooming of the capitals are typical of Archaic temples and indicate some awkwardness on the part of the provincial builders.   LAW.

Fifth century B.C.

ARCHITECTURE

In spite of the wars with Persia, the Athenian struggle for empire, and the Peloponnesian War, the fifth century B.C. showed remarkable activity in the arts. Of the many types of architecture, temples and treasuries continued to be most important. These are often found in sacred precincts such as Delphi, Aegina, Olympia, and the Acropolis at Athens. Although systematic city planning appeared in the fifth century, vast schemes of axial planning with space and mass were not developed until much later by the Romans; the sacred precincts of the Greeks are, by comparison, more freely arranged. The Athenian Acropolis presents some alignment of parts, however, and contains the most celebrated examples of fifth-century architecture. The major buildings, which owe their beginnings to the statesman

a. *Temple* in antis
(columns set within the antae)

b. *Prostyle temple (columns*
in front of antae)

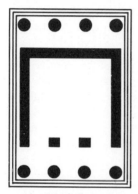

c. *Amphiprostyle temple*
(prostyle at both ends)

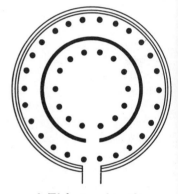

d. *Tholos (round temple)*

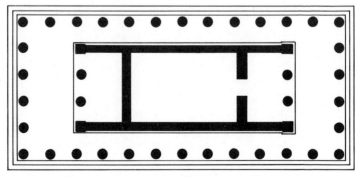

e. *Peripteral temple (surrounded by colonnade) with cella* in antis *at both ends*

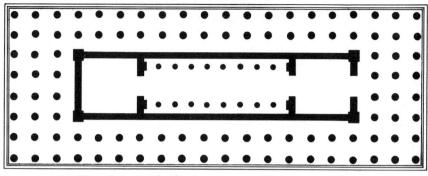

f. Dipteral temple *(double colonnade) with cella prostyle at both ends*

Figure 43 *Types of Greek temples* *a. Athenian Treasury, Delphi* *b. Temple B, Selinus, Sicily* *c. Temple of Athena Nike, Athens* *d. Tholos, Epidauros* *e. Temple of Hephaistos, Athens* *f. Temple of Zeus Olympios, Athens*

Pericles, date from the second half of the century. Marble was used instead of the more economical limestone, and extraordinary efforts were made to achieve the most satisfying proportions and the highest quality of stone carving in both Ionic and Doric temples. The Doric order (*Fig.* 44) received a subtler *entasis* (the slight outward curving of the shaft) than in both the previous and the succeeding centuries, and the capital became a smoother transition between the vertical shaft and the horizontal entablature. In the most refined Doric temples, the temple platform is slightly domed and all columns lean inward imperceptibly, giving the building a more compact, self-contained unity that reinforces the stable equilibrium of vertical and horizontal lines. Unlike the Doric, the Ionic order employed a very slender shaft (sometimes with very slight entasis), a base between shaft and stylobate, a three-part architrave, and usually a continuous frieze instead of the Doric metopes and triglyphs (*Fig.* 44). The third Greek order, the Corinthian, appeared in the second half of the century. It differed from the Ionic only in its leafy capital. The use of two or three orders in the same building became common toward the end of the fifth century. Temples were richly decorated with sculpted moldings (*Fig.* 45) and figure sculpture. Major sculptural compositions were placed in the *pediments* (the triangular gables at the ends of the building), in the frieze area, and sometimes on the outside of the cella walls. As with sculpture, parts of Greek architecture were painted. Blue was common for the pediment background and for an Ionic frieze; red was often used as a background for metope sculpture and for capitals and architraves.

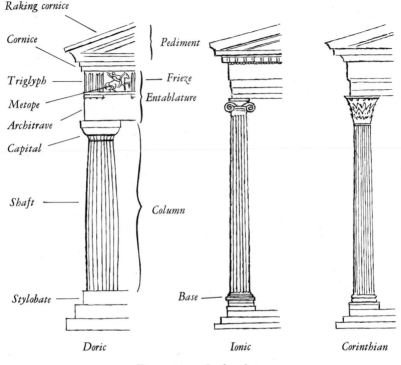

Raking cornice

Cornice

Pediment

Triglyph — Frieze

Metope — Entablature

Architrave

Capital

Shaft

Column

Stylobate

Base

Doric   Ionic   Corinthian

Figure 44   *Greek orders*

PLATES 6
and 7
JAN.
LAW.
U. & S. *Parthenon*, built by Ictinos and Callicrates (Acropolis, Athens, between 447 and 432 B.C., marble, approximately 228′ x 104′ with columns about 34′ high). The Parthenon has the most subtle proportions of all Greek Doric temples and has long been considered the high point of Greek architecture. It is the major building on the Acropolis, was dedicated to Athena, patron of Athens, and formerly sheltered a colossal statue of the goddess in gold and ivory. Originally, the Parthenon had sculpture in the pediments, in the metopes (PLATE 9), and in a frieze around the outside of the cella wall.

JAN.
LAW.
U. & S. *Erechtheum*, built by Mnesicles (Acropolis, Athens, between 420 and 409 B.C., marble). This irregularly shaped temple is famous for the subtle proportions and precise carving of its Ionic order and for a porch with *caryatids* (human figures that serve as columns).

SCULPTURE

For sculpture, as for architecture, the fifth century was a time of brilliant activity. Sculpture was present in public places, in sacred

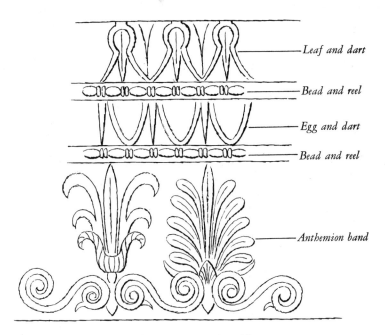

————Leaf and dart

————Bead and reel

————Egg and dart

————Bead and reel

————Anthemion band

Figure 45   *Greek moldings*

precincts, and on temples. Bronze and marble were the main materials. Subjects were usually taken from mythology, although there are occasional portraits, figures of athletes or heroes, and representations of animals; rather than depicting specific historical events, the Greeks used allegory that borrowed its themes from mythology. Early fifth-century sculpture represents youthful ideal bodies with symmetrical, simplified anatomy. Proportions are more natural than in previous work, but action is still slightly stiff, and the musculature is hard. Toward the middle of the century, the work of the great sculptor Myron shows a slight softening and increased flexibility in pose. After mid-century, Phidias started a trend toward more active, flexible poses and more expression of emotion, only to change in his later work to more restrained action and a calmer, poised equilibrium of pose. His rival, Polyclitus, also concerned himself with ideal form, monumental dignity, and the rhythmic grace of the *contrapposto* pose (in which the body relaxes with the weight on one leg, and the tilt of the hips is countered by the tilt of the shoulders). Late fifth-century sculpture worked toward the suggestion of softer flesh and more flexible poses.

Throughout the century, however, space remains strictly limited. In reliefs, a blank background restricts action to a shallow layer of depth; in freestanding statues, the form opens predominantly in two dimensions—shallow crates would suffice for packing the works—and there is almost no spiral twisting of the torso.

JAN.
LU. & H.
U. & S.

Pediment sculptures from Aegina (Glyptothek, Munich, marble with traces of paint, slightly less than life-size). Three sets of pedimental sculpture were found in debris at the base of the temple, apparently dating from 510 to 490 B.C. Scenes of the Trojan War are depicted, but the exact composition of the pediments is not certain. The poses are more open and active than in archaic work, and the anatomy shows more observation of nature, but considerable stiffness of pose and hardness of flesh remain.

PLATE 8
JAN.

Artemision statue (National Museum, Athens, about 460–450 B.C., bronze, eyes formerly inlaid, 6′ 10″). One of the finest of the votive statues which have been found, this work was discovered in the sea off Cape Artemision. The right hand originally held an object that has been lost, possibly a thunderbolt (indicating Zeus) or a trident (for Poseidon). The musculature and pose show the degree of flexibility, vitality, and poise characteristic of work just before mid-century. The composition opens mainly in two dimensions, with severely limited depth.

JAN.
LU. & H.
U. & S.

Pediment sculpture from the Temple of Zeus at Olympia (Olympia Museum, Olympia, Greece, and Louvre, Paris, 465–457 B.C., marble, central figures about 10′ high). The eastern pediment showed the preparation for the chariot race between Oenomaus and Pelops; the western pediment depicted the battle between the Lapiths and the centaurs. Stylistically, the work is close to the Artemision statue.

JAN.
U. & S.

Discus-thrower by Myron (Terme Museum, Rome, about 450 B.C., reconstruction of a Roman copy, 4′ 6″). Myron chose to depict the moment of equilibrium before the forward swing of the thrower. The symmetry of the musculature continues to suggest ideal form and the composition is very limited in depth, but the pose is more complex than that of the Artemision statue.

Spear-bearer by Polyclitus (National Museum, Naples, 450–440 B.C., marble Roman copy, 6′ 6″).   Polyclitus was known for his theories about ideal proportions. The muscular figure attains flexibility through its contrapposto pose, but the hips and shoulders are aligned in the same shallow space, and the only strong three-dimensional extension is the forward-reaching arm. The hair is organized in groups of wavy lines, and the face is simplified in broad planes. The musculature is still quite firm in the torso, but increasing softness and detail are evident in the arms, hands, and knees.

JAN.
U. & S.

Lapith fighting with centaur (British Museum, London, between 447 and 432 B.C., marble, 3′ 11″ x 4′ 2″).   The Parthenon metopes, of which this is an example, were probably carved under the direction of Phidias. Here the rhythmic curves of the cloak unite and soften the divergent forces of the bodies. The blank background, which limits spatial extension, is typical of Greek reliefs. Despite the weathering of the stone, the carving still suggests the softness of skin overlying the bone structure of the ribs and the muscles of the abdomen.

PLATE 9

PAINTING
We must turn again to vases, for the celebrated wall paintings of Polygnotus and Zeuxis are lost. Descriptions by ancient writers indicate that the wall paintings contained some illusion of depth and that theories of perspective had been formulated. The growing interest in depth may have contributed to the decline, after the fifth century, of the importance of vase painting, for depth in vase painting works against the form of the vase by denying its surface. Although red-figure painting continued, there was an increasing demand for delicate colors and light linear drawings on vases with white grounds. Figures became rounder, softer, and more flexible as contours overlapped to indicate folds in the flesh. Objects were drawn with *foreshortening* (as though diagonally extending into space); the eye even appears in profile.

Athenian mixing bowl from Orvieto (No. G 341, Louvre, Paris, 475–450 B.C.).   This work is traditional in its red-figure technique, but demonstrates the increasing interest in natural anatomy, mass, and space. It depicts warrior heroes (perhaps the Argonauts) in casual

ROB.

poses freed from a common base line; the figures are placed at various levels suggesting different degrees of depth. Overlapping contours and foreshortening imply mass in space.

Fourth century B.C.

ARCHITECTURE

Defeat in the Peloponnesian War put an end to Athens' leadership in architecture. During the fourth century, many important buildings were produced in cities like Delphi, Tegea, Epidauros, and—in Asia Minor—at Priene, Ephesus, and Halicarnassus. Efforts spread to a wider variety of types of buildings, many of them secular: *stoas* (colonnaded, open-fronted sheds used in city centers as promenades and shop areas), theaters, council halls, and tombs all received special attention, although they had prototypes in earlier centuries. All types of architecture used one or more of the three orders. The Corinthian capital graduated from interior to exterior use, and there was widespread development of the Ionic temple, particularly in Asia Minor. Theaters usually consisted of a slightly more than semicircular area of tiered seats set into a hillside, a round central space (orchestra), and a structure consisting of a raised stage and a building that provided an architectural background and housed dressing rooms and properties. Council halls were oval, square, or rectangular, often with tiered seats around a central altar. The tholos temple reached a height of subtlety and richness of design, and tomb architecture acquired monumental scale.

JAN.
LU. & H.
U. & S.

Mausoleum (Halicarnassus, 360–350 B.C., 136′).   The building is no longer extant, and its exact form is uncertain. Standing on a rectangular base, it had an Ionic peristyle and was topped by a stepped pyramid and a *quadriga* (chariot pulled by four horses). The structure served as a tomb for Mausolus, a satrap of the Persian kings, and, in antiquity, it was considered one of the Seven Wonders of the World.

JAN.
U. & S.

Choragic monument of Lysicrates (Athens, 334 B.C., limestone and marble, 54′).   This monument, developed from the tholos form, was built to commemorate a victory in a choral contest. It seems to be the earliest example of the exterior use of Corinthian columns. The small size recalls the decrease in monumental building in Athens after the defeat in the Peloponnesian War in 404 B.C.

SCULPTURE

Trends that began in the late fifth century grew more evident during the fourth century. Stone and bronze took on the softness of flesh, contrapposto poses became more pronounced, and poses opened up three-dimensionally, with more spiral twisting in the torso. Stone surfaces were polished until the details grew soft, as though seen through a veil. The famous Praxiteles led these developments in the mid-fourth century. In some work, the serene poise of earlier Greek art gave way to violent motivity, and deep-set eyes and bee-tling brows created an expression of suffering or consternation.

Statue of a young man, found in the sea off Anticythera (National Museum, Athens, about 340 B.C., bronze, eyes inlaid, 6′ 5″).　The young man stands in a twisting contrapposto pose that indicates he has just thrown some object, with the throwing arm extended into space. The three-dimensional extension heralds an important trend in later sculpture. Soft modeling veils the considerable anatomical detail.

LU. & H.

Hermes with the infant Dionysus (Olympia Museum, Olympia, Greece, about 350 B.C., marble, 6′ 11″).　The group may be an original by Praxiteles. Hermes, whose divine powers were of a particularly intellectual bent, was symbolically shown teasing the young god of wine, who often represented human passions, by holding some grapes beyond the child's reach. The cloudlike softness of modeling, the three-dimensional extension of the arms, the spiral twist of the body, and the relaxed contrapposto pose are typical of later work.

PLATE 11

Battle of Greeks and Amazons, from the east frieze of the Mausoleum at Halicarnassus (British Museum, London, about 350 B.C., marble, 35″).　Ancient writers say that the east frieze of the Mausoleum was carved by Scopas, one of the most famous sculptors of the time. In the surviving fragments of the frieze, tense poses and contorted faces express a physical and emotional violence quite unlike the characteristic poise and equilibrium of earlier work. Scopas reveals an interest in depicting the inner man; his style is characterized by deep-set eyes and expressions of anguish.

JAN.
LU. & H.
U. & S.

Hellenistic period: 323–100 B.C.

The Greeks called themselves Hellenes, and their culture is often called *Hellenic*. With the conquests of Alexander the Great, Greek culture, modified by local cultures, spread over the civilized world. This international Greek-inspired culture is called *Hellenistic*. Various dates are used for the Hellenistic period, but 323 B.C., the year of Alexander's early death, and 100 B.C., a year well after Rome had conquered Greece and had begun to transform Hellenistic art into Roman art, can be considered the approximate beginning and end dates.

ARCHITECTURE

The Hellenistic period saw the rise of important art centers in places far from Greece, such as Pergamon, Rhodes, Tralles, and Alexandria. An increase in the wealth of many cities led to larger *agoras* (city centers) with more elegant surrounding stoas. A grid plan of rectangular blocks and intersecting streets gave order to some cities. As in the fourth century B.C., there was a wide variety of types of buildings. Town houses often had two stories built around a central court, and, in better houses, the court eventually acquired a peristyle. Stone, mud brick, and wood were relieved by stucco and painted walls. In temple building, the Doric order became less popular. When it was used, columns were more slender and wall surfaces more ornate; semicircular extensions (*apses*) sometimes emphasized one end of the cella interior. Ionic and Corinthian temples were occasionally raised on high platforms, anticipating later Roman temples. Some of the Ionic temples were *pseudo-dipteral* in plan; that is, the inner peristyle of the *dipteral* plan (*Fig.* 43f) was omitted, leaving a deep porch around the cella.

JAN.
LU. & H.
U. & S.

Altar of Zeus and Athena at Pergamon (no longer extant except in reconstruction, 180–150 B.C., marble). The altar was a U-shaped *peripteral* building (one surrounded by columns, as in *Fig.* 43e) on a base 17′ 6″ high and about 112′ x 120′ wide. The order was Ionic, and the base was heavily decorated with sculpture, typifying the increasing complexity and variety of architectural shapes and the tendency to cover more of the surfaces with decoration.

Fig. 43f
LAW.

Temple of Zeus Olympios (Athens, marble, planned about 170 B.C. but finished 300 years later under direction of Roman Emperor Hadrian). The unusually thick columns are over 55 feet high. The temple, which measures 135 feet by 354 feet, demonstrates the increasing interest in the ornate Corinthian order.

SCULPTURE

Hellenistic sculpture, like Hellenistic architecture, was produced at creative centers far from the Greek mainland. Artists moved from one center to another, and it is hard to assign local styles to the different areas. Most sculpture by that time was not architectural but set in open spaces, in freestanding figures or groups. Specific historical subjects and portraiture were common and encouraged a detailed realism, as did the developing taste for *genre* subjects (scenes from common everyday activity) which were sometimes humorous, undignified, or pathetic, and often revealing of human character. Figures became taller and more slender in proportions, poses were restless and required more three-dimensional space, and surfaces were treated with great refinement.

Apoxyomenos by Lysippos (Vatican Museum, Rome, original probably done between 325 and 300 B.C., Roman marble copy, 81″). Lysippos, court sculptor to Alexander the Great, preferred slender proportions and poses that expand in all three dimensions and consume a comparatively great volume of space. The *Apoxyomenos* is an athlete scraping the sand of the arena from his body. He is in the process of shifting his weight from one leg to the other, creating a more dynamic version of the contrapposto pose.

JAN.
U. & S.

Winged Victory from Samothrace (Louvre, Paris, between 250 and 180 B.C., marble, about 8′). The goddess is of the "nike" type, i.e., she commemorates a military victory. The "wet drapery" effect reveals the Greek interest in the body, and the delicate carving of drapery details reveals an interest in the refinement of surfaces. Although the weight is supported by both legs, the body twists in space. The lines of the wind-whipped costume break the large masses into a restless complexity of lights and shadows.

JAN.
LU. & H.
U. & S.

Aphrodite from Melos (Louvre, Paris, late 3rd or early 2nd cen. B.C., marble, 6′ 8″). Popularly known as the Venus de Milo. After the fifth century, Greek sculpture includes more female nudes. In the extreme softness of modeling, the proportions of small head, narrow shoulders, and wide hips, and the pose with contrasting diagonals or spiral axes, this is one of the finest examples of Hellenistic work.

LU. & H.
U. & S.

Laocoön and his sons (Vatican Museum, Rome, 1st cen. B.C., marble, 8′). Laocoön, with his sons, is being slain by serpents for his dis-

JAN.
LU. & H
U. & S.

obedience to the gods. The present restoration is probably incorrect; the right hand of Laocoön should be closer to the head, thus completing the oval outline of the group. Although the composition has shallow depth, the intricate, restless, open form, the emphasis on anatomical detail, and the portrayal of mental and physical anguish are typical of late Hellenistic sculpture.

References for representative works

JAN.   Janson, H. W., with D. J. Janson, eds. *Key Monuments of the History of Art: A Visual Survey.* Englewood Cliffs, N.J.: Prentice-Hall; New York: Harry N. Abrams, 1959.

LAW.   Lawrence, Arnold W. *Greek Architecture* (Pelican History of Art). Baltimore: Penguin Books, 1957.

LU. & H.   Lullies, Reinhard, and Max Hirmer. *Greek Sculpture.* Trans. by Michael Bullock. Rev. ed. New York: Harry N. Abrams, 1957.

ROB.   Robertson, Martin. *Greek Painting* (Great Centuries of Painting). Geneva: Skira, 1959.

U. & S.   Upjohn, Everard M., and J. P. Sedgwick, Jr. *Highlights: An Illustrated History of Art.* New York: Holt, Rinehart and Winston, 1963.

Suggestions for further study

Bieber, Margarete. *The Sculpture of the Hellenistic Age.* Rev. ed. New York: Columbia University Press, 1961.

Blümel, Carl. *Greek Sculptors at Work.* Trans. by Lydia Holland. London: Phaidon Press, 1955.

Buschor, Ernst. *Greek Vase Painting.* Trans. by G. C. Richards. London: Chatto & Windus, 1921.

Dinsmoor, William B. *The Architecture of Ancient Greece.* Rev. and enl. ed. based on *The Architecture of Greece and Rome* by W. J. Anderson and R. P. Spiers. London: B. T. Batsford, 1950.

Pfuhl, Ernst. *Masterpieces of Greek Drawing and Painting.* Trans. by J. D. Beazley. New York: The Macmillan Company, 1955.

Richter, Gisela M. A. *Archaic Greek Art Against Its Historical Background: A Survey.* New York: Oxford University Press, 1949.

———. *Attic Red-figured Vases: A Survey.* Rev. ed. New Haven, Conn.: Yale University Press, 1958.

———. *A Handbook of Greek Art.* 2nd ed. rev. London: Phaidon Press, 1959.

———. *The Sculpture and Sculptors of the Greeks.* New rev. ed. New Haven, Conn.: Yale University Press, 1950.

———. *Three Critical Periods in Greek Sculpture.* Oxford: Clarendon Press, 1951.

Chapter Eight # ROME: 200 B.C.-330 A.D.

Roman art emerged as a distinct personality during the last two centuries before Christ. In style it persisted until perhaps 500 A.D., but its subject matter was reoriented by Christianity long before then. The year 330 A.D., when Constantinople was dedicated as the new capital of the Roman Empire, can thus be considered the end of the Roman period.

The major sources of Roman culture are the Greek and Etruscan civilizations. Like the Greeks, the Romans had little interest in an afterlife; they focused their attention upon the organization and exploitation of the physical world, and this is evident in their art. But the Romans considered the manual arts of painting and sculpture less dignified than the arts of music and poetry. Roman art and literature took Greek work for their models, and Greek gods reappear in Roman culture with Latin names. The Romans were more concerned with historical documentation than were the Greeks, however; Roman historical writings are paralleled by Roman history-recording art.

Second and first centuries B.C.

ARCHITECTURE

Remarkable engineering skill was applied by the Romans to a variety of building types, most of which received their basic forms in this period. Materials were wood, mud brick and fired brick, stone, stucco, and concrete. The Romans were the first to use concrete extensively; they reinforced it with rubble and often concealed it behind a veneer of stucco, brick, marble, or travertine (a hard, light-colored limestone). The Romans did not limit themselves to the post and lintel system but went far beyond their predecessors in the development of the arch, the vault, and the dome. The semi-circular *Roman arch* (*Fig.* 26a, p. 46) could be extended in depth to

95

form a *tunnel vault* (*Fig.* 28, p. 49). From this, the Romans created *cross vaults* (*Fig.* 30, p. 50) as early as the beginning of the second century B.C. Roman architecture used elaborated and modified basic Greek forms, including the three orders. Whereas the Greeks used columns as structural members, the Romans frequently added them as decoration without structural function. Greek column shafts are made with drums (cylindrical sections) placed one on top of the other and fastened with interior metal clamps; Roman shafts are generally monolithic.

Round Roman temples were inspired by the Greek tholos. Rectangular temples have the high base, frontal steps, and deep porch of pre-Roman Etruscan temples, but the Romans used Greek columns and modified Greek proportions in the entablature and pediment (PLATE 19). The wider Roman cella often has engaged columns, a device used less frequently by the Greeks. The most common form of Roman monument was a *triumphal arch* (PLATE 18 shows a late example), a freestanding structure with inscriptions and relief sculpture describing the event commemorated. One of the types of Roman buildings most influential for later architecture is the *basilica*, a rectangular structure with an apse at one or both ends and entrances in the sides or at one end (see the basilica part of *Fig.* 47). Columns divided the interior into center and side aisles. The roof (usually wooden) of the center aisle is higher than that of the sides so that *clerestory* windows (windows looking out over a lower roof) provide direct lighting for the center. Basilicas functioned as law courts, public halls, and audience chambers for rulers. The masses of the urban population lived in multistory tenements, usually built of mud brick and wood, but private city houses were also built, simple or complex according to the builder's financial means (*Fig.* 46). Larger houses occupy the center of a block and are insulated from the street by shops around the perimeter; therefore, all efforts at impressive architecture were concentrated on the interior of the home. The front door opens into a vestibule that leads to the *atrium*, a receiving hall. In the center of this room is a pool into which water drains from an opening in the roof. The atrium ends in the *tablinium*, where family statues were kept. One then enters the peristyle, a colonnaded walkway around an open court (adapted from Hellenistic houses). Typically, a strong axis from front to back gives order to the progression of interior spaces.

An outstanding example of Roman engineering is provided by

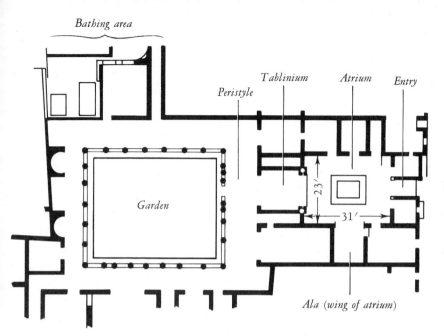

Figure 46   *Plan of House of Menander, Pompeii. Only the central portion
is shown.*

the *aqueducts*, which brought water from the hills to Roman towns.
The aqueducts were probably considered merely engineering projects
by their builders; yet the portions raised above ground on high
masonry arcades are so monumental and satisfying in their proportions as to merit inclusion in architectural history.

House of Menander (Pompeii).   The plan is typical in allowing a   *Fig.* 46
spatial vista down the major axis and in its alternation of small and
large spaces. The high ceilings and the free passage of air from
garden to front door helped to cool the house.

Maison Carrée (Nîmes, France, completed in 16 B.C., 59′ x 117′).   PLATE 19
JAN.
U. & S.
This small provincial temple is very well preserved. It exemplifies
the Roman love of the Corinthian order and the high base, frontal
steps, and deep porch inherited from the Etruscans. It is one of the
few Roman temples having some of the refinements of proportions
found in the best Greek work. The *rinceau* (band of scroll-like vine
ornament) in the entablature frieze was widely used in Roman
architecture.

SCULPTURE

Roman sculpture owes much to the preceding Etruscans and to the Hellenistic Greeks. In spite of extensive importation of Greek sculpture and the demand for copies of famous Greek originals, the Romans developed certain types of sculpture that are distinctly expressive of Roman culture. The Roman interest in the physical world is reflected in the rise of portraiture as a major field. The harsh individualism of Etruscan portraits, the custom of making wax images of dead ancestors, the love of factual documentation, and the late Hellenistic tendency toward realism in portraiture all helped to mold the Roman desire for merciless fidelity to physical appearance. Such realism was countered, however, by occasional periods of interest in the idealism of earlier Greek sculpture. Particularly in certain portraits of Augustus as Emperor, the idealistic simplification and strengthening of basic features can be seen. The other kind of sculpture that became important for the Romans is historical relief. Roman sculpture went much further than Hellenistic sculpture in depicting specific events with specific details in face, costume, and environment. In place of the blank background of earlier Greek relief, the Romans tried for the illusion of infinite space by graduating the relief from high projection in the foreground to fainter projection for distant objects, and by using diagonally receding forms. When occasional allegorical scenes make broader reference to Roman history, more general features reminiscent of earlier Greek art appear. Basic materials of Roman sculpture are wax, terra cotta, stone, and bronze. Parts of stone sculpture were sometimes painted.

JAN.
U. & S.

Statue of Augustus, from Primaporta (Vatican Museum, Rome, about 20 B.C., marble, 6′ 8″).   Individualism is veiled by the interest in ideal form; much detail was omitted in the face, and the large planes are emphasized (note the brows). The visionary stare of the softly carved pupils contrasts with heroic body proportions, a pose of authority, and allegorical scenes on the breastplate referring to the exploits of Augustus. The Cupid and dolphin beside the right leg symbolize the divine source of the Julian family, Aeneas, the half brother of Cupid. The statue thus presents the Emperor as a divinity.

JAN.

Ara Pacis or Altar of Peace (Rome, completed in 9 B.C., marble, height of processional panels: 63″).   The relief sculpture decorates a walled enclosure for the altar. On two walls, a procession of Augustus, his family, and retinue is depicted. An end wall shows an allegorical scene in which *Tellus* (Mother Earth) is surrounded by symbols of the abundance that Augustus brought to the Empire. There is marked contrast between the detailed portraiture of the procession and the ideal figures of the allegory, although the latter has specific details in plants and animals. The illusion of infinite space is present throughout. The lower part of the walls is covered with crisply carved symmetrical vine ornament.

Portrait of a Roman (Museum of Fine Arts, Boston, 1st cen. B.C.,   PLATE 12
terra cotta).   Suffering and disillusion are nakedly revealed by the sagging muscles of the eyes and mouth. The lifeless hair plastered over the wrinkled forehead gives an added feeling of dejection to the figure.

PAINTING AND MOSAICS

Our knowledge of Roman painting depends largely on wall paintings found in three cities buried by an eruption of Mt. Vesuvius in 79 A.D.: Pompeii, Stabiae, and Herculaneum. On such a limited basis, generalization must be tentative. We may assume probable influence of the lost paintings of the Hellenistic age, however, because imported Greek artists were responsible for some of the Roman paintings, as is evidenced by Greek signatures and inscriptions. The wall painting of the second century B.C. consisted of rectangular panels of color, often imitating marble. This *First Style* was succeeded around 100 B.C. by a *Second Style* depicting landscapes, figures, and architectural vistas. For the illusion of deep space, a makeshift system of linear perspective was devised. Effects of light and shadow, aerial perspective, and convincing anatomy were achieved. The wall paintings seem to have been done in tempera with a binder of lime emulsion. Encaustic was used for a few colors. The ground was made with three coats of sand mortar and three of fine-grained plaster, often mixed with marble dust. The plaster was polished before the painting was applied. The permanence of such work has been remarkable. Sometimes wood panels were given the plaster ground and utilized as supports for paintings, but most of these panels have perished. Mosaics were used widely, both on floors and on walls. In both mosaics and painting, the style indicates a strong interest in the visual experience of the physical world.

MAI.   *First Style wall painting from Samnite House* (Herculaneum).   The simple rectangles of various sizes are raised in relief and painted. Some imitate the marble veneer of more elegant buildings. The decoration has no illusion of depth and thus preserves the impression of the wall's solidity.

JAN.   *Villa of the Mysteries* (Pompeii).   A whole room is painted in
MAI.   Second Style with scenes of the ritual from the Dionysiac Mysteries. In an unbroken sequence, the different stages of the initiation unfold along the wall: the neophyte listening to the liturgy, the purification ceremony, the fearful initiate, the unveiling of the mysteries, the flagellation, and the mystic marriage with the god. Anatomy is rendered with easy competence, and the portrait-like faces convey a wide range of feelings.

MAI.   *Odyssey landscapes* (Vatican Library, Rome).   These Second Style paintings were discovered in the ruins of a house on the Esquiline Hill, Rome. Eight episodes from Books X and XI of the *Odyssey* are shown in a continuous landscape (44' x 5') divided only by a painted architectural framework. Lively figures are placed in a world of shimmering light and space. Shadows are used to define the ground plane and to locate objects upon it. Aerial perspective creates depth. The breathtaking effects of color and light seem to be achieved without effort.

MAI.   *Alexander mosaic* (National Museum, Naples).   This depiction of the Battle of Issus between Alexander and Darius was discovered in the pavement of a Pompeian house. It is thought to be a copy of a Greek painting from the fourth century B.C. and may have been brought to Pompeii from a center like Alexandria in Egypt during the period of the Second Style. Shadows are used to define the ground plane, and depth is created by overlapping masses and forms that lead back diagonally. The small size of the *tesserae* (pieces of stone or glass used to form the mosaic) permit subtle gradations in color and shadow.

PLATE 20   *Mosaic showing street musicians* (National Museum, Naples).   The Greek Dioskourides of Samos signed this work, probably during the period of the Second Style. The everyday subject, the characterization in faces and gestures, and the factual treatment of light

and shadow—qualities first developed in late Hellenistic painting—
are typical of much Roman painting. The handling of color is particularly subtle, and shadow areas are enlivened with reflected
lights (highlights made by light reflected from nearby objects).

First century to 330 A.D.

ARCHITECTURE

The Roman Empire reached its height in the second century A.D.,
and its power and wealth are reflected in architectural design. Vast
size and lavish decoration are typical of the period from the first
to the fourth centuries. Roman architects tended to impose a scheme
of order upon the whole site, arranging landscape as well as spaces
and masses to achieve effects of gradation and climax. Plans often
use obvious axial balance. Examples may be found in the *forums*
(civic centers for Roman towns), where temples, government buildings, and commercial houses are organized around an open space
(*Fig.* 47). The forum has its sources in pre-Roman Etruscan town
plans and in the Greek agora. Of the three Greek orders, the Romans
preferred the most ornate, the Corinthian. From this they derived
the *composite* capital by adding Ionic *volutes* (spirals) to the Corinthian capital. In addition they developed the *Tuscan order*, using a
base, an unfluted shaft, a derivation of the Doric capital, and an
entablature without frieze ornament. It was Roman architecture
that established the system of superposed orders for buildings of
several stories. Doric or Tuscan was used on the ground floor, Ionic
on the next, and Corinthian above. These post and lintel forms were
often combined with the arch, as in the *Roman arch order*, an arched
opening framed by engaged columns or *pilasters* (flattened column
shapes that project as planes from the wall) and an entablature. The
Romans also adopted and elaborated Greek architectural moldings
(*Fig.* 45, p. 87).

For an understanding of Roman culture, it is significant to note
that wealth was spent not just on temples but on monuments to
Roman leaders, palaces, and places of public entertainment such as
baths and amphitheaters. For the late period, public entertainment
was very important to Roman politics. The amphitheaters (as distinct from theaters, which followed the Greek form) were built for
athletic or gladiatorial contests. The tiered seats surround an elliptical arena, and the exterior may be banked earth or arcaded galleries.

Some of the largest Roman buildings were the public baths (*thermae*), which served as community centers with lecture halls, libraries, lounges, and outdoor playing fields in addition to bathing pools of various temperatures. All was planned around dramatic axes of interior and exterior spaces. Statues and mosaics decorated the interior; walls and mammoth cross vaults were veneered with sumptuous marble. The populace enjoyed these elegant public facilities and found that they made it easier to return to the apartments (mostly of concrete by the first century A.D.) in which many Romans led crowded lives.

JAN.
U. & S.

Pont du Gard (Nîmes, France, early first century A.D.).   The aqueduct consists here of three arcades rising 160 feet to carry water in a conduit at the top. The first level serves as a bridge. The proportions and permanence of the work testify to the ability of Roman engineers.

PLATE 14
JAN.
U. & S.

Colosseum (Rome, finished about 80 A.D. and frequently restored, elliptical, about 620' x 513').   This vast area seated 50,000 spectators. Tunnel and cross vaults were used in corridors and stairways. The core is concrete, and the façade is faced with travertine. The arcades of the façade employ the Roman arch order with engaged columns in the following sequence: Doric, Ionic, and Corinthian. The fourth level has Corinthian pilasters.

Fig. 47

Forum of Trajan, designed by Apollodorus of Damascus (Rome, completed about 113 A.D., central square about 300' x 350').   The Roman preference for grand organizations of spaces and masses is exemplified here. The symmetrical order moves along the axis from the front gate, through the main forum space, into the basilica, past the column dedicated to Trajan's wars, to the climactic temple of the deified Emperor.

PLATES
15–17
JAN.
U. & S.

Pantheon (Rome, mainly built between 118 and 126 A.D.).   The concrete and brick core formerly had marble and stucco veneer. The dome (diameter of 142") was the most celebrated in ancient architecture. The concrete ranges in thickness from six to twenty feet, and the interior of the dome has *coffering* (an excavated grid effect), a device often used in vaulting by the Romans to lighten the structure without weakening it. Aside from the main door, the only

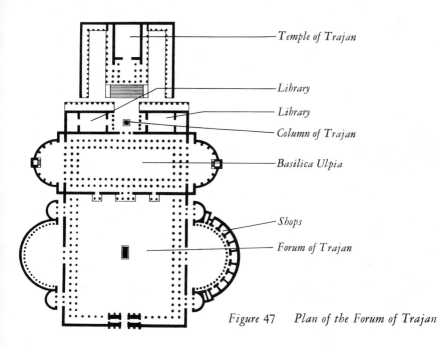

Figure 47   Plan of the Forum of Trajan

light source in the Pantheon is the *oculus* (round opening in the center of the dome). The dramatic lighting and the vast scale make the much-copied Pantheon one of the supreme examples of effective interior space.

Temple of Bacchus (Baalbek, 2nd cen. A.D., 110' x 214').   The   _{JAN.}
Temple of Bacchus is the best preserved though not the largest in the grand temple complex in the former Roman colony at Baalbek, not far from Damascus. A high *podium* (base) raises the rectangular building and its Corinthian peristyle. The ornate interior provides a raised platform for the altar at the end farthest from the entrance, thus employing the full length of the cella for an effect of gradation and climax. A similar focus was provided later in early Christian basilicas, buildings which owed much to the temples and basilicas of the Romans.

Basilica of Constantine (Rome, finished about 320 A.D., after having   _{JAN.}
been started by Emperor Maxentius in 310, 265' x 195').   Most basilicas had wooden roofs, but vast concrete tunnel and cross vaults were used here in one of the largest vaulted interiors of the ancient

world. Formerly huge columns were part of the decorative veneer. The effect was more like that of the great hall of a Roman bath than the hall of a basilica. The building provided a grandiose setting for the ritual of Roman government.

PLATE 18
JAN.
U. & S.

Triumphal Arch of Constantine (Rome, about 312 A.D.). The three arches, the quantity of sculpture (some of it borrowed from earlier monuments), and the decorative Corinthian columns all break up the surfaces and create a sumptuous and dramatic play of light and shadow on the structure.

SCULPTURE

During this period the other-worldly interests of Christianity began to undermine the Roman world of fact, flesh, and blood. In portrait sculpture, the third century brought increased animation in the twist of the head and the turn of the eyes, and the bust-type portrait came to include the shoulders and often one or both arms, but by the fourth century, the eyes had become large and preoccupied, the carving crude or summary, and the forms more stereotyped. Historical and mythological reliefs, used on arches of triumph, commemorative columns, altars, and sarcophagi, became, during the course of the late second and third centuries, more compressed into shallow foreground space, more complex in parts, and less definite about the climactic centers of the composition. By the fourth century, specific events acquired the effect of scenes staged with dolls; the episode became ritual. The figure functioned somewhat abstractly as a symbol for man and for his role in a social or divine order. Heads were shown disproportionately large, without much variety in features or expression; costume folds were indicated by quickly carved grooves, poses were more rigid, and abrupt modeling caused sudden dark shadows that tended to isolate the many parts.

JAN.

Reliefs on the Arch of Titus (Rome, 81 A.D., marble). The arch was built to celebrate the subduing of Jerusalem by Titus. The reliefs depict a triumphal procession carrying booty (note the seven-branched candelabrum). Diagonal masses and increasingly faint relief suggest deep space. The factual detail expresses the disorder of the event without the theme and variations of line and shape that would lend subtle harmony to a Greek interpretation of a similar subject.

Column of Trajan (Rome, finished about 113 A.D., marble, 125'). JAN. The column is divorced from its structural role to become a monument. A spiral relief 656 feet long and 50 inches high winds from bottom to top depicting Trajan's Dacian Wars. Architecture and landscape are reduced to undersized stage settings in order for the figures to present clearly the historical narrative.

Julia Domna, wife of Septimius Severus (Metropolitan Museum, New RIC. York, early 3rd cen., marble, 26″). The animated turn of head and eyes and the inclusion of the body almost to the waist are typical of much third-century portraiture.

Colossal head of Constantine (Capitoline Museums, Rome, early 4th JAN. cen., marble, 8'). Stereotyped forms have begun to erase individuality, and the large meditative eyes stress the role of an exalted and inspired leader.

Constantine addressing the Senate, frieze of the Arch of Constantine (Rome, JAN. early 4th cen.). The style reflects the development of late Roman sculpture, in which the depicted object was becoming an abbreviated symbol. The roughly carved doll-like figures are shown with enlarged heads and repetitive poses; they provide a striking stylistic contrast with the relief medallions right above, which are from the second century.

PAINTING AND MOSAICS
In wall painting a *Third Style* seems to have prevailed between 1 and 50 A.D. Here, the wall was treated more flatly but illusional paintings of columns and moldings of delicate proportions were used. Monochrome landscapes were often added to suggest panel paintings hung on the walls. A *Fourth Style*, between about 50 and 79 A.D. in Pompeii, again opened up the wall with palatial, theatrical architecture, landscapes, cityscapes, and mythological scenes. It pushes illusionism even further than before. From Lower Egypt, during the period of Roman occupation, come a number of portraits on panels which have been preserved by the dry climate. These were attached to mummies. The technique is encaustic, and the style is similar to that of some miniature portraits painted on glass medallions during the third century A.D., probably in Italy. There is some evidence that painters (particularly those working for Chris-

tians), like sculptors, became less interested in physical appearance by the fourth century and turned increasingly to flat, schematic shapes whose power lay in their symbolic content rather than in their imitation of physical reality.

MAI.   *Third Style wall painting with monochrome landscape* (National Museum, Naples). Illusionistic space is kept shallow, and the painted columns and moldings are delicate and slender, decorated with plant ornament. The landscape is presented as a monochrome panel, emphasizing the flat surface of the wall.

MAI.   *Fourth Style wall painting from Herculaneum* (National Museum, Naples). Delicate motifs from the Third Style are combined with bold architecture and deep space. Curtains and an actor's mask stress the effect of stage decoration.

JAN.   *Portrait of a boy, from the Faiyum, Upper Egypt* (Metropolitan Museum, New York, 13″ x 7¼″). Encaustic on wood was used here for the type of portrait that was attached to mummies. Individual features are rendered in somewhat stereotyped forms by an artist accustomed to working quickly and producing in quantity.

References for representative works

JAN.   Janson, H. W., with D. J. Janson, eds. *Key Monuments of the History of Art: A Visual Survey.* Englewood Cliffs, N.J.: Prentice-Hall; New York: Harry N. Abrams, 1959.

MAI.   Maiuri, Amedeo. *Roman Painting* (Great Centuries of Painting). Trans. by Stuart Gilbert. Geneva: Skira, 1953.

RIC.   Richter, Gisela M. A. *Roman Portraits.* New York: The Metropolian Museum of Art, 1948.

U. & S.   Upjohn, Everard M., and J. P. Sedgwick, Jr. *Highlights: An Illustrated History of Art.* New York: Holt, Rinehart and Winston, 1963.

Suggestions for further study

Anderson, William J., and R. P. Spiers. *The Architecture of Ancient Rome* (Part II of *The Architecture of Greece and Rome*). Rev. and rewritten by Thomas Ashby. London: B. T. Batsford, 1927.

Bloch, Raymond. *Etruscan Art.* Greenwich, Conn.: New York Graphic Society, 1959.

Boethius, Axel. *The Golden House of Nero: Some Aspects of Roman Architecture.* Ann Arbor: The University of Michigan Press, 1960.

Brown, Frank E. *Roman Architecture* (Great Ages of World Architecture). New York: George Braziller, 1961.

Hanfmann, George M. A. *Roman Art: A Modern Survey of the Art of Imperial Rome.* Greenwich, Conn.: New York Graphic Society, 1964.

Nash, Ernest. *Pictorial Dictionary of Ancient Rome.* New York: Frederick A. Praeger, 1961–62. 2 vols.

————. *Roman Towns.* Locust Valley, N.Y.: J. J. Augustin, 1944.

Pallottino, Massimo. *The Etruscans.* Trans. by J. Cremona. Baltimore: Penguin Books (Pelican Books), 1955.

Richter, Gisela M. A. *Three Critical Periods in Greek Sculpture.* Oxford: Clarendon Press, 1951.

Rivoira, Giovanni T. *Roman Architecture and its Principles of Construction under the Empire.* Oxford: Clarendon Press, 1925.

Robertson, Donald S. *A Handbook of Greek and Roman Architecture.* New York: Cambridge University Press, 1954.

Strong, Mrs. Arthur. *Roman Sculpture from Augustus to Constantine.* New York: Charles Scribner's Sons, 1907.

Wickhoff, Franz. *Roman Art: Some of its Principles and Their Application to Early Christian Painting.* Trans. by Mrs. S. A. Strong. New York: The Macmillan Company, 1900.

Chapter Nine # EARLY CHRISTIAN AND BYZANTINE ART: 100-1453

One of the most far-reaching changes in western thought came through the impact of Christianity upon the Roman world. Late Roman history reveals an increasing interest in foreign religions, such as the worship of Isis (Egypt) or of Mithras (Persia), but Christianity won out and provided the basis for a new world view. For the Christian, reality was the drama within, the struggle of good against evil, the salvation of the soul, and the attainment of life after death; the physical world was inimical or irrelevant. As reality became less tangible in the minds of men, the role of art became more complex.

Long before the legalization of Christianity by Constantine in 313, painting with Christian subject matter was done on the walls of *catacombs* (underground passageways with niches used for burial by Christians). Thus the period of Early Christian art overlaps that of Roman art. The term *Early Christian art* refers not so much to a certain style as to a period, from about 100 to 500, and to art with Christian subject matter within that period. The term *Byzantine* refers not only to the geographical area of the Eastern Roman Empire, with its capital at Constantinople (the ancient Byzantium), but also to particular stylistic features common to much art of that region from about 500 until the fall of Constantinople to the Turks in 1453. There is, however, no sharp dividing line between Early Christian and Byzantine art. Important art centers were Rome, Constantinople, Antioch, and Alexandria. Much of the Byzantine painting and sculpture was destroyed and its stylistic development affected by *iconoclasm*, a controversy between *iconophiles*, who wanted religious images, and the *iconoclasts*, who felt that images were idols and that religious art should present symbols rather than images of sacred persons. The battle began with an edict from the eastern emperor in 726 prohibiting figurative images and ended with the victory of the iconophiles in 843.

Early Christian period: 100–500

ARCHITECTURE

Early Christian architecture inherited the techniques and the forms of Roman building, but aims had changed and form was modified accordingly. Early Christian builders concentrated on churches, *martyria* (buildings marking the tomb of a martyr or the site of his death, or containing a sacred relic), and baptisteries. They did not seek the earthly grandeur of Roman temples but stressed instead a withdrawal from the physical world and a mystical experience of salvation for the worshiper. Exteriors were left starkly simple; in interiors glittering mosaics and Greco-Roman colonnades, arcades, or masonry piers (often of columns taken from the ruins of Roman temples) were arranged for effects of gradation and climax that focus on the altar. Plans stem from two types, the *longitudinal* and the *central*, both having roots in Roman architecture. The longitudinal type was a modified Roman basilica plan and is therefore called a basilica (*Fig.* 48a). From an entry gate, one passes through an open court (*atrium*) into the *narthex* (vestibule), where one can see the altar at the far end of the nave. By means of these spaces, which provide progressive degrees of withdrawal from the outside world, the altar gains significance. The longitudinal axis, which lends itself so well to dignified processionals, is sacrificed in the central type of building. In the fourth century, the central plan was generally used for martyria, but it soon appeared in churches as well. Although the central space receives the major emphasis, a slight axis may be suggested by placing the altar just off center against an apse (*Fig.* 48c). The central plan may have many forms such as the Greek cross (which has arms of equal length) within a square (*Fig.* 48c) or a circle (*Fig.* 48b); other variations were developed in the Byzantine period (*Fig.* 48d). Central churches often had vaulting or domes of stone or brick. Large basilicas were usually roofed with timber, although tunnel vaults were frequently used over side aisles; smaller basilicas, particularly in Syria and Asia Minor, used stone and brick vaulting.

Fig. 48a
JAN.
Old Basilica of St. Peter (Rome).   This old basilica was destroyed to make room for the Renaissance structure, but the original is

known through drawings and descriptions. Built over the tomb of St. Peter between 324 and 354 by order of Constantine, it exemplifies an early but fully developed basilica plan. The nave was roofed with timber and the outer side aisles with tunnel vaults. Although in later Christian churches the main entrance was traditionally placed at the west, Old St. Peter's had its entrance at the east end.

Sta. Costanza (Rome).   The central building was ordered by Constantine in 324, possibly as a mausoleum for a member of his family, and was converted to a church in the thirteenth century. The central space, about forty feet in diameter, is covered by a dome on a drum which rests upon arcades carried by twelve pairs of columns. Around the central space is a circular side aisle with a tunnel vault. The building was originally peripteral. It is an important source for later central churches.

Fig. 48b
JAN.
U. & S.

PAINTING AND MOSAICS

Painting was done on walls and panels and in book illustrations. Tempera, encaustic, and fresco-secco were employed. The earliest Christian painting is found in the catacombs in Rome. These fresco-secco works depict praying figures and episodes of miraculous salvation taken from the New and Old Testaments. The scenes are reduced to the minimum essentials; the figures are sketchily painted and have large heads, staring eyes, and doll-like bodies. There is little interest in landscape or depth, but the abbreviated episodes are sometimes set into painted geometric designs. The effect is that of brief pictorial prayers. Few catacomb paintings were done after the fifth century.

Until the development of the printing press during the Renaissance, books were copied and illustrated by hand. These *illuminated manuscripts* were at first in the *rotulus* form, following the Roman scroll books; rather than separate pages bound at one side, the text was written on a continuous band held on two rollers, and the reader unrolled one side as he rolled up the other. Between the first and the fourth centuries, the rotulus type was slowly replaced by the *codex* form that we use today. Parchment (made from animal skin) was common for centuries; paper was not used until after the eleventh century. The painted illustrations in the Early Christian manuscripts showed varying degrees of naturalness, modified by a tendency to harden into conventional shapes that were repeated without direct observation of nature. They are often characterized by

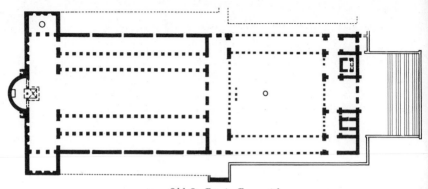

a. Old St. Peter's, Rome, 4th cen.

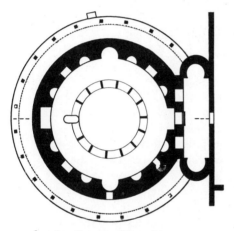

b. Sta. Costanza, Rome, 4th cen.

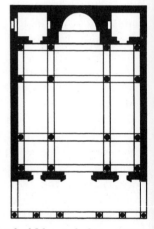

c. Church of Musmiyeh, Syria, 160-400.

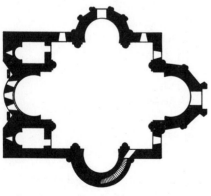

d. Artik Cathedral, Armenia, 7th cen.

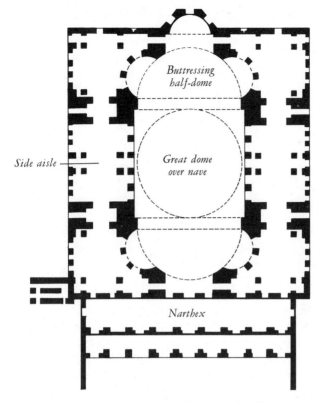

Buttressing
half-dome

Side aisle

Great dome
over nave

Narthex

e.   Hagia Sophia, Constantinople, 6th cen.

Figure 48   *Types of Early Christian and Byzantine Churches*

flat figures, abrupt modeling, and fanciful colors; the rigid boldness
and intensity of these partially abstract and highly symbolic works
made them an effective expression of Early Christian theology. A
similar stylistic tension between nature and symbol is evident in
the mosaics. Generally, it is felt that, like Christianity itself, the
tendency toward flat symbolic forms had its origin in the Near East.

The Good Shepherd and the story of Jonah (Rome, 3rd cen.). The paint-   JAN.
ing is on a ceiling in the catacomb of SS. Pietro and Marcellino.
Within a simple geometrical design, Christ as the Good Shepherd
is shown in a landscape with two sketchily painted trees and several
sheep. From the central scene radiate episodes from the story of
Jonah done in a quick, abbreviated manner. Between the episodes,

praying men hold out their hands to heaven. Some of the contrapposto poses echo pre-Christian Roman art, but the sketchiness and the disregard of scale relationships between Jonah, the ship, and the whale reveal a declining interest in the observation of the physical world.

JAN. *Dome mosaic from St. George* (Salonika).   Estimates of date range from the fourth to the sixth centuries. Many of the mosaics have been lost. The lowest circle of scenes remains largely intact and consists of eight panels; each depicts the figures of saints and bears inscriptions of their names and months of commemoration. The backgrounds are filled with elaborate architecture that recalls the fourth style in Pompeian painting. However, the limited space in the St. George mosaics and the artist's interest in areas of rich linear design forecast Byzantine art.

SCULPTURE

Sculpture showed a remarkable decline in importance, partly because of the Biblical injunction against idols and partly in reaction to the widespread use of idols in Roman temples. It was generally confined to small-scale work, such as sarcophagi, metal plates and chalices, *reliquaries* (elaborate containers for sacred relics), and ivory carvings. What portraits there were showed less and less interest in specific details of physical appearance. Christian sarcophagi of the fourth and fifth centuries are *frieze-type*, with episodes carved in an unbroken frieze along the sides, or *columnar-type*, with scenes divided by engaged columns. Sometimes double registers were used. As in the catacomb paintings, favorite subjects included such miracles of salvation as Jonah and the Whale, the Raising of Lazarus, the Sacrifice of Isaac, Daniel in the Den of Lions, the Healing of the Blind, and Moses Striking Water from the Rock.

During the fourth century, sculptural style moved closer to that of the doll-like figures and repetitious poses on the Arch of Constantine. The decay of interest in the physical world, the increasing love of flat geometric or floral decoration, and the inclination toward abstract symbols—such as the Cross instead of the figure of Jesus, or the monogram made by superimposing X and P (Chi and Rho), the first letters of Christ's name in Greek—grew from the other-worldly emphasis and the symbolic character of eastern thought and art. Long before the time of Jesus, Persian art stressed flat patterns and nonfigurative designs. In Constantinople, Christian-Roman culture had been transplanted into the midst of ancient eastern culture. Thus the more abstract sarcophagi generally come from Constantinople and other eastern centers or from artists trained in those areas. The same might be said for the style of the ivory carvings. *Consular diptychs* (two-part ivory plaques celebrating election to the office of consul) from Rome show more interest in anatomy and natural drapery than those carved in Constantinople, even though the Roman work reflects the changes seen in the sculpture on the Arch of Constantine.

Sarcophagus of Junius Bassus from St. Peter's (Rome, about 359, marble, 46½″ x 95″).   This fine double-register columnar sarcophagus mixes Old and New Testament episodes without regard for chronology. Each episode was an abbreviated symbol for the initiate. In the center of the top register, the enthroned Jesus is giving missions to Peter and Paul. At his feet is the head and wind-blown canopy of Cailus, a Roman sky god. Directly below, the Entry into Jerusalem is flanked by Adam and Eve and Daniel in the Den of Lions. In the spandrels of the lower colonnade, lambs are used to represent episodes ranging from Moses Striking the Rock to the Raising of Lazarus. Much natural detail is retained in faces, poses, and costumes, but legs are shortened and heads are enlarged. Compared with earlier sarcophagi, the architecture here is smaller in scale and has acquired more surface decoration.

JAN.

Byzantine period: 500–1453

ARCHITECTURE

Long before the time of Christ, the dome had been used as a symbol of the heavens and as a covering for sacred places or objects. The domed central plan is particularly characteristic of Byzantine churches; in Constantinople and surrounding regions, however, the central and longitudinal plans are often fused in the form of short, wide, domed basilicas. Domes, usually over square spaces, are supported by pendentives, which were probably developed in Syria, or squinches, which may have originated in Armenia (*Fig.* 35, p. 54). Domes were sometimes constructed with porous stone or hollow pottery in order to reduce weight and avoid the necessity of heavy buttressing. Byzantine architecture tends to conceal structural masses with flat mosaic decoration and multicolored marble veneer. Domes and walls appear eggshell thin, and supporting columns have capitals perforated in basket-like designs that make them look hollow and delicate. The supernatural qualities of the sacred place are expressed in the seeming weightlessness and the shimmering color of walls and domes.

PLATES
21–23

S. Apollinare in Classe (Ravenna, 530–549).   The three-aisled basilica has a characteristically plain exterior with one of the earliest *campanili* (bell towers). Inside, the raised altar receives additional focal emphasis from mosaics. Byzantine patronage is evident not only in the mosaics but also in the nave columns; the soft, spongy-appearing capitals are an abstraction from the crisp, leafy, Corinthian form.

Fig. 48c
JAN.
U. & S.

Hagia Sophia (Constantinople, 532–537).   Emperor Justinian commissioned this domed basilica during the first golden age of Byzantine art. A short basilica plan, similar to that of the Basilica of Constantine, is combined with a central dome inspired by the Pantheon; but the dome (180' high) on pendentives has a much different effect from that of its prototype. The blossoming of light from windows around its base makes the Byzantine dome seem to be a hovering canopy. The delicately perforated capitals, the flat shapes in the mosaics, the concealment of the massive supports in the architecture, and the location of the windows all deny the physical weight of the structure and create the effect of a glittering vision, an expressive symbol of heaven.

JAN.
U. & S.

S. Vitale (Ravenna, 526–547).   This polygonal central church, built under the patronage of Justinian, shows both the direct influence of Constantinople and more distant ancestry in buildings like Sta. Costanza. The central space is scalloped by semicircular niches in the side aisles and gallery. The lightweight dome is constructed of pottery and mortar, allowing large clerestory windows in the drum. Mosaics cover the interior walls, and the capitals have intricate Byzantine basketwork weaving.

PAINTING AND MOSAICS

By the sixth century, a fusion of western (Roman) and eastern qualities had developed in much art produced in and around Constantinople. The resulting style combines frozen figure poses, a disregard for natural scale relationships, and a love of sumptuously decorated flat surfaces. Thus rigid formality is joined with sensuous luxury of design. This style, called Byzantine (after the Byzantine Empire of Constantinople), was not a stable formula, however. Periodic revivals of interest in Greco-Roman art, particularly during the tenth and twelfth centuries, complicate the stylistic development between 500 and 1453. Wall paintings and mosaics in Italian churches range from the worldly interests of ancient Roman painting to the symbolism of Byzantine art. Eastern influence is especially strong in the mosaics at Ravenna, one of the main outposts of the Byzantine Empire on Italian soil during the sixth century. The iconoclasm of the eighth and ninth centuries brought to Rome the talents of displaced Byzantine artists. Christian painting in Syria and Egypt (except for Alexandria) shows much Byzantine character, although Christian art was interrupted in these areas by Muslim conquests in the seventh century. After the iconoclast period, the second golden age of Byzantine art, lasting roughly from the ninth to the twelfth centuries, brought a number of stylistic phases. More expression of emotion, more massiveness, and more natural anatomy appear, but the formal order of Byzantine art never relinquishes its hold on movement, costume, and figure.

In the decoration of Byzantine churches, subjects tend to be located according to order of importance. The dome was reserved for Christ as Judge, the drum and pendentives for angels and Evangelists, the vault of the apse for the Virgin, and the other regions of the walls for the Twelve Feasts of the Church (Annunciation, Nativity, Presentation, Baptism, Transfiguration, Raising of Lazarus, Entry into Jerusalem, Crucifixion, Harrowing of Hell, Ascension, Pentecost, and Death of the Virgin) and other scenes from the lives of Jesus and Mary. The west wall often showed the Last Judgment.

In manuscript illumination, as in other painting, the anthropomorphic symbolism, landscape interest, mass, space, and natural poses of the old Roman style—it has been called the Latin style— were affected in varying degrees by the eastern influence. The stylistic heritage of a painting is sometimes revealed by details; a bearded Christ or one riding sidesaddle into Jerusalem denotes an eastern background, while a beardless Christ or one riding astride the donkey denotes a Latin source.

Apse mosaic from S. Apollinare in Classe (Ravenna, 533–549). This   PLATE 22
is one of the most striking examples of Byzantine art on the Italian

peninsula. St. Apollinaris, who was martyred in Ravenna, is shown as an imitator of Christ's martyrdom. Above the saint, the Transfiguration of Christ is symbolized by the vision of the Cross between Moses, Elias, and three lambs representing disciples. The severe symmetry of the flat shapes and their exotic colors emphasize the symbolic nature of the content.

PLATE 13
JAN.
U. & S.

Justinian and attendants, mosaic in S. Vitale (Ravenna, about 547). The Emperor, accompanied by his representative in Ravenna, Maximianus, carries an offering to Christ. The solid, individually detailed portrait heads contrast with the flat shapes of the costumes, and depth is further negated by the brilliant warmth of the gold background. The artist's indifference to weight and space left him free to allow the feet of several figures to stand upon each other. The ritualistic formality of the staring, symmetrically placed images conveys the hypnotic fascination of Byzantine art. The wall on the opposite side of the altar carries a similar composition depicting Justinian's wife, Theodora, with attendants.

GRA.

Crossing the Red Sea, a page from the Paris Psalter (Bibliothèque Nationale, Paris). The *Paris Psalter* (Psalm book) contains fourteen full page illuminations on parchment. The distortions in scale and anatomy and the schematic treatment of costume reveal Byzantine interests. The modeled roundness of some forms, the relatively natural musculature of the nude male and female sea gods, and the landscape setting are debts to earlier Roman art. The use of human figures for nature divinities, such as the sea gods and the figure of night (in upper left with canopy), is also characteristic of earlier Roman art. The date of the *Paris Psalter* is uncertain; it may come from the tenth century.

JAN.

Madonna enthroned (National Gallery of Art, Washington, D.C., 13th-cen. panel painting, 32″ x 19½″). Standard forms are used in the costume folds and in the flat modeling of the faces. Mass, depth, and natural effects in proportion and drapery are sacrificed for the sake of stern order and elegant formality. The result is a symbolic image that stands outside the realm of the everyday world.

SCULPTURE

There was very little monumental sculpture in the Byzantine Empire during the Byzantine period; the story is quite different in northern

Italy and in Europe, as we shall see in the next chapter. Sarcophagi produced in Constantinople or in its spheres of influence show variations of the Byzantine style. Most of the ivory consular diptychs in the Byzantine style seem to come from the area of Constantinople and to date from the sixth century. Icons or reliquaries combine small scale relief sculpture, often in gold, with enamel painting. Their portability helped to spread the influence of Byzantine art.

Sarcophagus of Theodorus from S. Apollinare in Classe (Ravenna, 6th   JAN.
cen., marble, $39\frac{1}{2}''$ x $81''$).   The Byzantine tendency to use symbols rather than literal description is well illustrated here. The peacocks were symbols of immortality; the grapevines referred to the wine of the Eucharist. In the center and on the lid, the Chi-Rho symbol is hung with Alpha and Omega, the first and last letters of the Greek alphabet, standing for the all-inclusiveness of Christ. The symbols are framed by wreaths of victory. There is little interest in natural detail of vines or animals and no illusion of depth. The forms have little modeling and appear as shallow layers applied to a flat surface.

Diptych of Anastasius (Bibliothèque Nationale, Paris, dated 517,   JAN.
ivory, each leaf $14''$ x $5''$).   The two halves of a diptych frequently carried approximately the same scene. Here the newly elected consul Anastasius is shown in the official act of throwing down the *mappa* (a piece of cloth used as a signal to start the games in an arena). He is surrounded by winged goddesses of victory. The disregard for natural scale relationships between the figures, the preference for flat ornate surfaces rather than mass and the illusion of deep space, the stiff frontal pose, and the masklike faces are all characteristic of Byzantine art.

References for representative works

Grabar, André. *Byzantine Painting* (Great Centuries of Painting). Trans.   GRA.
by Stuart Gilbert. Geneva: Skira, 1953.

Janson, H. W., with D. J. Janson, eds. *Key Monuments of the History of Art:*   JAN.
A Visual Survey. Englewood Cliffs, N.J.: Prentice-Hall; New York:
Harry N. Abrams, 1959.

Upjohn, Everard M., and J. P. Sedgwick, Jr. *Highlights: An Illustrated His-*   U. & S.
tory of Art. New York: Holt, Rinehart and Winston, 1963.

Suggestions for further study

Ainalov, D. V. *Hellenistic Origins of Byzantine Art*. Trans. by E. Sobolevitch and S. Sobolevitch. New Brunswick, N.J.: Rutgers University Press, 1961.

Beckwith, John. *The Art of Constantinople: An Introduction to Byzantine Art, 330–1453*. London: Phaidon Press, 1961.

Dalton, O. M. *Byzantine Art and Archaeology*. New York: Oxford University Press, 1911.

Davies, J. G. *The Origin and Development of Early Christian Church Architecture*. London: Student Christian Movement Press, 1952.

Demus, Otto. *Byzantine Mosaic Decoration*. London: Kegan Paul, Trench, Trubner & Co., 1941.

Lowrie, Walter. *Art in the Early Church*. New York: Pantheon Books, 1947.

MacDonald, William L. *Early Christian and Byzantine Architecture* (Great Ages of World Architecture). New York: George Braziller, 1962.

Morey, Charles R. *Early Christian Art*. 2nd ed. rev. Princeton, N.J.: Princeton University Press, 1953.

Rice, David Talbot, and Max Hirmer. *The Art of Byzantium*. New York: Harry N. Abrams, 1959.

Strzygowski, J. *Origin of Christian Church Art*. Trans. by O. M. Dalton and H. H. Braunholtz. Oxford: Clarendon Press, 1923.

Swift, Emerson H. *Roman Sources of Christian Art*. New York: Columbia University Press, 1951.

Volbach, W. F., and M. Hirmer. *Early Christian Art*. Trans. by Christopher Ligota. New York: Harry N. Abrams, 1962.

Von Simson, Otto G. *The Sacred Fortress: Byzantine Art and Statecraft in Ravenna*. Chicago: University of Chicago Press, 1948.

Weitzmann, Kurt. *Illustrations in Roll and Codex: A Study of the Origin and Method of Text Illustration*. Princeton, N.J.: Princeton University Press, 1947.

Chapter Ten # MEDIEVAL ART IN THE NORTH: 400-1400

Early Christian and Byzantine art is often considered the Mediterranean branch of Medieval art. *Medieval* and *Middle Ages* are both vague and unsympathetic labels invented by scholars who thought of the years between the decline of Rome and the beginning of the Renaissance as a barren transitional period. Today we are more appreciative of the age, but the labels remain standard terms. The beginning and end dates of the Medieval period vary with different interpretations. This text will follow one widespread practice in using the term Medieval with particular emphasis on Europe north of Rome during the period 400–1400.

While Early Christian and Byzantine culture was developing in the Mediterranean area, significant advances were being made by the peoples to the north in areas which now include France, Germany, Scandinavia, the Netherlands, Belgium, and the British Isles. These peoples, called Barbarians by the Greeks and Romans, had an indigenous art before their widespread conversion to Christianity during the third to the tenth centuries. *Barbarian art* slowly changed through the influence of the Early Christian and Byzantine art brought north by missionaries. Art in the northern countries may be divided into at least four periods: *Barbarian art* (400–800), *Carolingian art* (750–987), *Romanesque art* (mainly eleventh and twelfth centuries) and *Gothic art* (overlapping the Romanesque in the twelfth century and extending into the sixteenth century in some areas). The terms Romanesque and Gothic are also misleading, retained only because of entrenched usage. Romanesque, or Roman-like, is an inadequate description of eleventh- and twelfth-century art, just as Gothic, originally meant to imply the barbarism of the Gothic tribes, is a pathetic misnomer for such things as the thirteenth-century French cathedrals.

The greatest efforts of Medieval art were in the service of Christianity, the unifying element in a very divided Europe. The modern distinction between artist and craftsman did not exist; the best talent was often employed to design liturgical equipment, furniture, or jewelry. And since individual identity and originality were not so highly valued as they are today, many works were unsigned and stylistic change was generally gradual. The spread of stylistic influences can be traced along trade routes, the Crusade routes, and the pilgrimage routes. From the sixth century on, pilgrims traveled from northwest Europe to three major goals: Rome, the Shrine of St. James at Santiago de Compostela in Spain, and the Holy Land.

The art of the first three periods developed mainly in the monasteries. Gothic art was more urban and came from the cathedral centers developed by the *secular clergy* (clergy who did not withdraw from lay society to live by rigid rules, as did the regular or monastic clergy). The word *cathedral* comes from the cathedra, the throne of the bishop, placed in the main church of the bishop's diocese.

Barbarian and Carolingian art: 400–987

METALWORK

From the Barbarian period, many of the earliest remains are metalwork of bronze or gold decorated with enamel. Bracelets, brooches, arm bands, swords, and purse covers are typical. The style combines lively, intricate, geometric designs with fantastic animal and human forms. Constantly expanding and contracting shapes, sudden changes of direction, and amazing intricacy account for the vitality and richness of the work. There is no illusion of mass or space.

JAN. *Purse cover from the Sutton Hoo ship-burial* (British Museum, London). This enamel and gold purse cover came from the grave of an East Anglian king who died in 654. It is a fine example of early Barbarian metalwork. The style may have been brought to western Europe in the late Roman period by wandering tribes who had contact with ancient Persian art.

PAINTING

The most significant painting of the Barbarian period that has been preserved from northwestern Europe is in illuminated manuscripts from the British Isles; it is called *Hiberno-Saxon* art or *Celtic* art after the Celts of ancient Ireland. Monasteries became centers of learning where the manuscripts, mainly scriptures, were copied and illuminated. Colors with gum, glue, or gelatin binders were used on *parchment* (sheepskin) or *vellum* (calfskin or kidskin). Like the metalwork, the illuminations employ intricate spiral designs, inter-laced shapes in *strapwork* (flat bands resembling cut leather), and fantastic animals. The Barbarian style was characteristic of Hiberno-Saxon painting until the ninth century; the style slowly changed under the influence of Byzantine paintings and ivories brought from the south by Christian missionaries, however, and the Hiberno-Saxon illuminations developed various mixtures of abstract Bar-barian design and the relatively more static and representational Early Christian and Byzantine art. During the Carolingian era (750–987), important centers of manuscript illumination were es-tablished on the Continent under the patronage of Charlemagne, and different geographic areas evolved different styles. In the Caro-lingian Empire, as in the British Isles, Barbarian stylistic traits were increasingly modified by the influence of Early Christian and Byzantine art. In addition, Carolingian painting shows contact with older Roman art; poses, drapery, and landscape sometimes are closer to Roman art than to the Early Christian and Byzantine styles that intervened.

Initial page (XPI) from the Book of Kells (Trinity College Library, Dublin, 8th cen., $12\frac{5}{8}''$ x $9\frac{1}{2}''$). The manuscript was probably made at the monastery of Kells in Ireland or at that of Iona in Scot-land. It contains tables of references, prefaces and summaries, the Gospels, and part of a glossary of Hebrew names. Here Barbarian art serves Christianity. Intermingled with the interlaces and spiral designs are human heads and animals. Other pages in the book depict more of the human figure, but this illumination of the sacred initials of Christ illustrates the typical shapes and the swirling dynamism of line that modified Roman, Early Christian, and Byzantine ele-ments to form Medieval art.

G. & N.
JAN.
U. & S.

St. Luke from the Gospel Book of Ebbo of Reims (Épernay, 9th cen., $6\frac{7}{8}''$ x $5\frac{9}{16}''$). The so-called Reims School (a regional style) of Carolingian illumination had classicizing tendencies; that is, the pose, costume, massiveness, facial type, and sketchy brush strokes all reflect ancient Roman art. The Carolingian painter intensified

G. & N.

the nervous activity of the lines here to give the image considerable dramatic vitality. The winged bull in the upper left is the symbol for St. Luke.

ARCHITECTURE

Barbarian and Carolingian architecture made extensive use of wood. *Half-timber* construction consisted of a carefully joined wood frame filled in with mud or plaster on reed mats (called wattle and daub). Sometimes walls were *palisades* (logs planted vertically side by side as in a stake fence). Norsemen built frame houses around a central pole, like the mast of a ship. Such *mast construction* was often covered with vertical wood sheathing. Carolingian builders used stone for important buildings only. What little remains of their architecture reveals a strong interest in longitudinal plans. The basilica plan was elaborated to create more space for altars, reliquaries, and worshipers. An *ambulatory* (aisle around the outside of the apse) was added (for a Gothic example, see *Fig.* 31, p. 51); secondary chapels were provided by *radiating apses* around the outside of the ambulatory or by *apses in echelon* (apses placed beside the main apse or on the arms of the transept); and the main apse was separated from the transept by a nave extension called the *choir* (see *Fig.* 31), which allowed space for the clergy choirs. Under the raised choir and apse, a *crypt* provided space for special tombs of local saints and founders of the church or for relics. A Carolingian basilica might be a *double-ender*—that is, it might have an apse at the west end as well as at the east—or it might have a *westwork*, a high, blocklike enlargement giving the effect of a west transept and containing a narthex on the ground level and a chapel above. Carolingian basilicas had timber roofs and many towers; a tower over a westwork and flanking towers at the sides would be echoed by a tower over the *crossing* (where the transept crosses the nave) with flanking towers at the sides. Central-form churches might be octagonal, with tunnel and cross vaults, or a combination of the apse-buttressed square and cross-in-square, four-column type. Such central churches show Byzantine influence in their form and in the rich, flat patterns of decorative details, which were sometimes imported from Italy.

CON.
U. & S.

The Chapel of Charlemagne (Aachen, *Fr.* Aix-la-Chapelle). The major extant example of Carolingian architecture is this central church designed by Odo of Metz and dedicated in 805. It reveals

Charlemagne's admiration for Byzantine culture in that the polygonal plan and the general form come from S. Vitale in Ravenna.
Marble columns, a mosaic, and bronze fittings were sent from Italy.
The central octagonal space is covered by a domical vault, instead
of a true dome, and is surrounded by a cross-vaulted side aisle and
a gallery with special tunnel vaults. Originally, the chapel, which
also served as a tomb for Charlemagne, was part of a palace complex
and contained a throne in its westwork.

Romanesque art: 1000–1200

ARCHITECTURE

Romanesque architecture produced more buildings, greater variety,
and more advanced masonry techniques than the Barbarian and
Carolingian period. The wooden roofing used over the naves of
many basilicas from Early Christian through Carolingian times—a
roofing that invited disastrous fires—was slowly replaced by fire-
proof stone vaulting. Ancient Roman features, such as massive
walls, vaults, engaged columns, and pilasters, were designed with
significant changes. Unlike Roman concrete construction, Romanesque building is of masonry, and Romanesque cross vaults have ribs
(see p. 52). The leading construction of ribbed cross vaults over the
nave occurred in the early twelfth century in Durham Cathedral
(Anglo-Norman England), in St. Étienne at Caen (Normandy), and
in S. Ambrogio in Milan (Lombardy).

Despite its variety, much Romanesque architecture is characterized by: (1) fortress-like massiveness; (2) Roman arches; (3) two
or more towers; (4) *splayed openings*, doorways or windows formed
by layers of increasingly smaller arches producing a funnel effect
(for a Gothic example, see PLATE 27); (5) *blind arcades*, arcades attached to a wall for decoration or for buttressing rather than to
create openings; (6) *corbel tables* (*Fig. 49*)—a *stringcourse* (horizontal
band or molding) supported in the Lombard type by a row of continuous small, blind arches, and in the French type by small brackets
projecting from the wall; and (7) *wheel windows*, round windows
divided into sections by stone dividers radiating from the center
like the spokes of a wheel. The use of *Lombard pilaster strips* (slender
pilasters) spread along the trade routes north to Germany, as did
the exterior arcaded galleries developed in Tuscany and Lombardy,
while the Lombard porch, supported by two columns resting on the

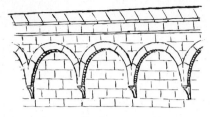

Lombard

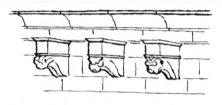

French

Figure 49   *Types of corbel tables*

backs of lions, did not find wide acceptance elsewhere. Tuscan churches employed the Early Christian basilica plan, with entrance at the west end and apse at the east; they were often decorated with patterns of different colors in stone veneer. In Germany the double-ender plan was often employed, while in France, in addition to the pilgrimage church type (see p. 127), some basilicas were built in the form of *hall churches*, where the side aisles are as high as the nave, and the nave arcade rises to the springing of the vaults. Some of the most unusual examples of French Romanesque architecture are the domed churches in Aquitania; their source would seem to be Byzantine architecture, perhaps by way of St. Mark's in Venice. The pointed arches that occur occasionally in Romanesque buildings and become typical of later Gothic work appear to have their source in Mohammedan architecture.

CON.
JAN.
U. & S. *Church of St. Michael* (Hildesheim).   This church was built under the leadership of Bishop Bernward and completed in 1033, during the period of the Ottonian emperors in Germany. It is a double-ender with a second transept, a choir, an apse, a crypt, and a crypt ambulatory in the west end. The nave roof is of wood. Carolingian architecture had provided all the basic elements. The entrances are at the sides of the nave, partly sacrificing the axial emphasis of a basilican plan. Towers over the crossings of both transepts and

at their ends produced an almost equal exterior balance of east and west. The church was severely damaged in the Second World War.

St. Sernin (Toulouse). The church was begun in the eleventh century and finished in the twelfth, with the exception of the upper part of the crossing tower (thirteenth century) and the west façade, which was never completed. The twelfth-century architect was Raymond Gayrard. St. Sernin is a pilgrimage church and one of the largest surviving Romanesque churches in France. It illustrates the elaboration of the basilica plan by means of choir, ambulatory, apses in echelon, radiating apses, double side aisles, and aisles around the transept. The high nave arcade rests on *compound piers* (piers of several parts, here having the form of superimposed pilasters and engaged columns) and is topped by a gallery, which provided more room for the congregation. There is no clerestory, for the heavy tunnel vault needs the abutment of the gallery vaults to sustain it. The bays are clearly marked by the transverse arches resting on engaged columns rising all the way from the floor. The columns break through the horizontal lines to establish a vertical emphasis that suggests the Gothic architecture to come. The exterior exhibits round-arched windows, French and Lombard corbel tables, and blind arcades.

PLATES 25 and 26 *Fig*. 50 JAN. U. & S.

St. Étienne (Caen, 11th and 12th cens.). The west façade of the Norman basilica has a strong relationship to the interior. The three divisions on the horizontal plane reflect the interior divisions into nave and side aisles; the three divisions from the bottom to the base of the towers echo the three-part elevation of the nave within. The Gothic steeples must be ignored; the towers were originally flat. An eleventh-century wood roof over the nave was replaced in the twelfth century by six-part ribbed cross vaults (*Fig*. 32, p. 51). To avoid a domical effect, the diagonal ribs were depressed to less than a semicircle (*Fig*. 33b, p. 52). Every other compound pier was given extra engaged elements that rise to support the ribs and transverse arches. This creates an *alternating system* of supports in the nave arcade. The vaulting of St. Étienne places its Norman builders among the pioneers of Romanesque architecture. The *chevet* (the apse, ambulatory, and radiating chapels) is thirteenth-century Gothic.

JAN. U. & S.

S. Ambrogio (Milan). Construction on the cathedral extended from the ninth to the twelfth century, the ribbed four-part cross

CON. JAN. U. & S.

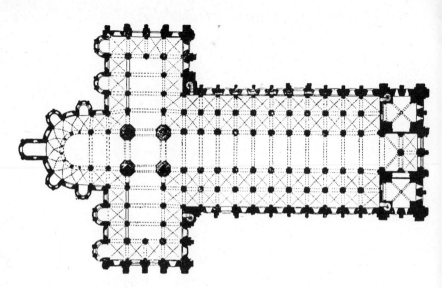

Figure 50   *Plan of St. Sernin, Toulouse*

vaults dating from the early twelfth century. The exterior is massive and simply decorated with pilaster strips and Lombard corbel tables. There are two towers of unequal height beside the narthex and a low polygonal tower over the octagonal domed vault at the crossing. From the atrium, one passes through the narthex to a nave of three low dark bays. A domical effect comes from the cross vaults because the bays are square, and the ribs and transverse arches are semi-circular (*Fig.* 33a, p. 52). An alternating system of piers divides each bay into two nave arches and two gallery arches. The gallery vaults buttress the nave vaults and leave no room for a clerestory. The side aisles terminate in apses in echelon beside the main apse. There is no ambulatory and only the suggestion of a choir. The nave vaults of this Lombard church place Lombardy beside Normandy in France and Durham in England (built under Norman occupation) as a leader in Romanesque vaulting.

Fig. 51
CON.
JAN.
U. & S.

Durham Cathedral (England, 11th and 12th cens., but with later additions such as 13th- and 15th-cen. towers).   Durham Cathedral is a basilica 469 feet long with a large crossing tower and a square east end. An alternating system of supports is used in the nave, and the heavy round columns which constitute the secondary supports are carved with bold geometric decoration. Some authorities believe

128

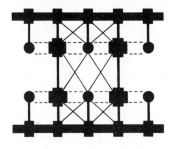

Figure 51   *Plan of vaulting in Durham Cathedral*

that Durham was more important than *St. Étienne* in Caen or *S. Ambrogio* in Milan for the development of ribbed cross vaults. Norman craftsmen were imported for the construction of Durham, however, so its inspiration came from Normandy, which, in turn, may have owed much to the Lombard builders of *S. Ambrogio*. The somber darkness of the Italian church is avoided at Durham, where clerestory windows flood the vaults with light. The segmented domical effect of the bay vaults in *S. Ambrogio* gives way to a level roof ridge formed by the *crowns* (the highest point in an arch or vault) of the vaults in the English church (height of Durham vaults: 73'). The level vaulting is achieved by employing pointed arches in the transverse and side arches so that they may reach the height of the semicircular diagonal ribs (*Fig.* 33c, p. 52, shows how this can be done with the exclusive use of pointed arches). Durham's nave vaults are distinctive in their use of two sets of diagonal ribs for each bay (*Fig.* 51). Like the church of *La Trinité* in Caen (the sister church to *St. Étienne*), Durham has flying buttresses that support the wall at clerestory level, although these buttresses are hidden under a shed roof. Both in vaulting and buttressing, Durham provided an important basis for Gothic architecture.

SCULPTURE

The basic sources for Romanesque sculpture are Barbarian art, Roman art, and Early Christian and Byzantine art. The Carolingian period had shared the Byzantine preference for miniature sculpture. The revival of monumental sculpture came with the Romanesque period, although even then many large sculptural compositions were based on small ivory carvings or on manuscript illuminations. Romanesque sculpture is generally found around the entrances to a church, that is, on the *jambs* (layers of the splayed opening) of the door, in the tympanum over the door, and on the *trumeau* (center post) of a double door; on columns, piers, and capitals; on altars and baptismal fonts; and on tombs. Subjects came from the Old and New Testaments, the Apocrypha, the lives of the saints, the labors of the months (a visual calendar of man's duties in the husbandry of the land), allegorical figures representing the Virtues and the Vices or the liberal arts, and the signs of the zodiac. There are also fantastic animals, which may have personified evil, and geometric or floral designs. Such things suggest the influence of Barbarian art or the art of ancient Persia, by way of Byzantium. The capitals of columns may have modified Greco-Roman forms, geometric ornament, or narrative relief. A number of pre-Christian Roman symbols are woven into the Christian subjects, as in Byzantine art. Romanesque sculpture has considerable regional variation ranging from angular, jerky, stick figures in crowded linear designs (PLATE 24) to relatively massive calm forms. The more massive work is found in southern France and in Italy, where the tradition of ancient Roman art was strong. The beginnings of individual artists' styles can be seen in the work of some of the sculptors whose names have been preserved for us, such as Gislebertus (Cathedral at Autun) of France, Antelami (Fidenza Cathedral) of Italy, and Renier of Huy (Baptismal Font at St. Barthélemy, Liège) of Belgium.

JAN.
U. & S.

Adam and Eve reproached by the Lord, panel from the doors of Hildesheim Cathedral (bronze, panel size: 23″ x 43″). This example of Ottonian bronze casting, done about 1015, was probably inspired by sculptured doors that Bishop Bernward had seen in Rome and was originally made for the Church of St. Michael. Each of the two doors is divided into eight panels. The subjects depict the advent of sin and the means of salvation; the left door deals with the Fall of Man and the Murder of Abel, and the right door tells the story of Christ from the Annunciation to the Ascension. As in Ottonian manuscripts, the abrupt angularity of the figures, active poses, and severely simple backgrounds create dramatic intensity.

JAN.

Christ in glory from St. Sernin (Toulouse, marble). The enthroned Christ is shown within a *mandorla* (elliptical nimbus including the whole figure) which is stabilized at the four corners by the symbols for the four Evangelists: a man for Matthew, a lion for Mark, a bull for Luke, and an eagle for John. Although the lively linear curves contrast with the rigid poses, consistency is maintained by repetition and thematic variation. The work is typical of much early French Romanesque sculpture and is closely related to manu-script painting.

The Apocalyptic Christ (Moissac, 12th cen., width: 18′ 8″).   St.   PLATE 24
John's vision in Revelations and an illumination in the *Beatus Com-mentary on the Apocalypse* were the sources for this tympanum composi-tion depicting Christ surrounded by the symbols of the Evangelists, angels, and the Elders. The overlapping layers of *plate drapery* are characteristic of the Languedoc region. The sharp edges of the plate folds make linear patterns of repeated and varied shapes that turn and twist with jerky vitality. The scene is framed at the sides by a twisted ribbon design and at the bottom by a lintel carved in delicate *rosettes* (round flower shapes), all having ancestry in Greco-Roman architectural ornament.

Sculpture from the west entrances of Chartres Cathedral (1145–70).   The   JAN.
U. & S.
twelfth-century façade is attached to a thirteenth-century church because a fire destroyed all but the façade of the twelfth-century structure. The center tympanum shows Christ and the symbols of the Evangelists, while the surrounding arches are carved to represent the Elders. The Apostles are represented on the lintel. The right tympanum contains the Madonna and Child, and the lintel, in two registers, shows the Nativity and the Presentation in the Temple. The arches personify the liberal arts. The left tympanum depicts the Ascension; the lintel contains angels and Apostles. The arches carry the signs of the zodiac and the labors of the months. The jambs beside all three doors carry large figures that seem to portray the kings, queens, and prophets of the Bible. The capitals of the engaged columns have reliefs depicting the lives of Christ and Mary. The sculpture of Chartres-west is sometimes called early Gothic; how-ever, it is much easier to understand as late Romanesque. A new clarity of parts is combined with the rigid poses and linear design of previous work.

King David from west façade of Fidenza Cathedral, probably done by   JAN.
Benedetto Antelami (about 1180–90).   This Italian Romanesque sculpture is more massive than most French work of the period.

Italy developed an interest in three-dimensional mass along with the revival of monumental sculpture during the Romanesque period. The linear designs in the drapery are related to Byzantine art in that they tend to flatten rather than amplify the mass of the figure.

PAINTING

During the eleventh and twelfth centuries, Romanesque painting, like Romanesque sculpture, proliferated in many regional styles, but its geographical bases were more widespread and its subject matter more varied. The term Romanesque was invented with architecture in mind, and it would be unrealistic to attempt a sharp distinction between Carolingian and Romanesque painting. In the north during this period, the general tendency was toward flat shapes and more insistence on line, line that is more active in its twisting and looping than the line in Byzantine art. Later twelfth-century work becomes more sculptural but often less lively. Byzantine influence is often evident in geometric drapery panels. Italian painting has Byzantine qualities but often loosens up Byzantine formality by means of more natural poses and more sculpturesque form.

G. & N.   *St. Peter receiving the keys, from the Book of Pericopes of Henry II* (Staatsbibliothek, Munich, $10\frac{3}{8}''$ x $7\frac{1}{2}''$). This eleventh-century work is from Reichenau, a school known for illuminations depicting figures with large, dark, staring eyes, bold gestures, and slightly modeled but strongly outlined forms. The bodies here are crowded into spaceless groups and placed against a simple flat background; nothing detracts from the powerful focus on the central action.

JAN.   *Sections from an Ascension scene, stained glass in Le Mans Cathedral* (about 1150, 75'' x 45''). Originally, this Romanesque window depicted Mary and the twelve Apostles watching the Ascension of Jesus; however, the figure of Christ has been lost, and the proper arrangement of the surviving panels is uncertain. The colors are blue, red, yellow, purple, green, and white. The pieces of stained glass were cut to the shapes of the various objects depicted, then the pieces were joined together with strips of black lead, and finally the details were painted on with a brush. The thin figures and the linear drapery designs link the style to that of sculpture and manuscript illumination of the period.

Gothic art: 1150–1400

ARCHITECTURE

In the mid-twelfth century, the first churches that are called Gothic appeared in the Île-de-France region—north-central France, with Paris as its center. From France the Gothic style spread to other countries, where it acquired regional characteristics. The major features of Gothic architecture are height, open walls, and complex linear design, all of which are integrated into a vast system of theological symbolism. The basilica plan attained grand proportions. To its longitudinal focus was added a vertical emphasis achieved with ever higher nave vaults, the pointed arch, and dominating vertical lines in the design of interior and exterior. The trend toward greater height, complexity, and openness in walls is illustrated by a sequence of major French cathedrals such as St. Denis, Noyon, Laon, Paris, Chartres, Reims, Amiens, and Beauvais. Late Gothic work of the fifteenth and sixteenth centuries elaborated the pointed arch and the *tracery* (intricate stone carving within a window) in flame-like curves and is therefore known as *flamboyant Gothic*. Examples may be found in the Cathedral and the small church of St. Maclou in Rouen. As Gothic architecture developed, Romanesque massiveness disappeared (*Fig.* 31 and PLATES 27–29); walls became perforated screens for the glowing colored light from stained glass. In medieval theology, this light was an effective symbol for God. As walls became more open, mass was further denied by an increase in delicate sculptural detail, which gave a total effect of line rather than mass. On the interior, the stone vaults floated like canopies anchored by engaged columns and thin ribs over the clerestory windows. On the exterior, the openness of the forms, the vertical lines, and the fragile silhouette suggest a weightless vision of soaring splendor. During the Gothic period, the French cathedral became a complex symbol for the City of God; this was expressed not only by architectural form but by the extensive iconography presented in sculpture and stained glass windows.

Early English Gothic stressed length in plan and elevation, the major exception being an occasional tall spire or tower over the crossing. Few flying buttresses were needed. Late English Gothic emphasized height and opened the walls for more glass. Thus it is called the *Perpendicular period*. Typically English is the multiplication of vault ribs into an intricate network. The basilica plan in England

133

tends to be rambling, with several transepts and frequently a square east end.

Germany was slow to turn to Gothic architecture but eventually was much influenced by the French style. German Gothic made effective use of the hall church.

JAN.
U. & S.

Cathedral of Notre Dame (Paris, 1163–1250). The Gothic façade here has more openings in the masses, more elaborately carved splayed openings, and more consistent use of the pointed arch than does earlier architecture. Open arcades and delicate detail soften the limits of the forms. The rose window shows the evolution from the wheel window as the sections became petal-like. Verticality is more insistent, although the three-part division from side to side and from bottom to the base of the towers is still evident, as it was at Caen. The west towers are woven into an intricate geometric organization that integrates the sculpture and the architecture. Over the crossing, the tower used in earlier churches has been replaced by a tall, thin spire. The six-part ribbed and pointed cross vaults reach a height of $108\frac{1}{2}$ feet and are supported on the outside by flying buttresses. The pointed arch allows the necessary flexibility for level crowns in the vaults (*Fig.* 33c, p. 52). Because of the six-part vaults, a typical bay of the nave elevation would include two arches of the nave arcade, two sets of gallery arches, and two sets of clerestory windows, each set consisting of two *lancets* (bullet-shaped windows) and a rose. The plan has a long choir, double side aisles, and a double ambulatory.

PLATES
27–29
Fig. 33c
U. & S.

Amiens Cathedral, by Robert de Luzarches (13th cen., with later additions, such as 14th- and 15th-cen. towers and 16th-cen. rose window in west façade). The façade shows a further dissolution of solid wall into superimposed layers of meshlike openings and sculpture. The splayed openings no longer seem to be cut out of the wall; they are extended in the form of porches. Again we find the three-part divisions of the façade, but these have become more complex. The increased perforation and lightness of the walls match the ever more insistent vertical emphasis. The interior vaults reach 139 feet above the floor. From compound columns with leafy capitals, the soaring engaged columns rise through a foliage stringcourse and a plain stringcourse to the four-part vaults above. A typical bay elevation consists of one arch in the nave arcade, two compound arches (each with three arches and a trefoil) at the gallery, which has now become a shallow passage, and a clerestory of four lancets and three roses. There is some variation, however, in the elevation in different parts of the church. A forest of flying buttresses provides support on the exterior. Although Amiens no longer has its original stained glass, the celebration of light and the double directional emphasis—toward the altar and toward the heavens—are dramatically evident.

Salisbury Cathedral (begun in 1220).   Verticality is stressed only in the tower and spire over the crossing. The façade, heavily sculpted but with many horizontal lines, does not have the lightness and openness or the three-dimensional complexity of French Gothic. The length is the same as that of *Amiens* (450′), but Salisbury's interior seems much longer because of the narrower nave, lower vaults (about 81′), and emphatic horizontal lines. Few flying buttresses are needed. The cathedral has a three-level nave elevation and four-part ribbed and pointed cross vaults. The crossing has an elaborate star vault (multiple ribs suggesting superimposed star shapes). The plan is typical in its square east end and secondary transept.

JAN.
U. & S.

Liebfrauenkirche (Trier, 1227–43).   The central plan is an exception to the predominance of the basilica in German Gothic architecture. Radiating chapels fill in the corners of a Greek cross plan that has an extended choir and apse for some longitudinal emphasis. The exterior illustrates the German reluctance to leave Romanesque forms; round arches and fortress towers are mixed with large pointed windows. Inside, the arms of the cross have high ribbed and pointed four-part vaults. The elevation is in two levels: a high arcade and a clerestory of two lancets and a rose. Because the clerestory area is partly covered by the roofing of the outside chapels, however, the lancets had to be filled in until only curved triangular windows remained.

JAN.

Choir of Gloucester Cathedral (1332–77).   In English Perpendicular style, the choir stresses verticality; it contains elaborate ribbed vaults and one of the largest English Gothic windows. The tendency toward open walls and verticality developed much earlier in France.

JAN.
U. & S.

SCULPTURE

The beginnings of Gothic sculpture may be placed in the second half of the twelfth century. At this time, drapery and poses became calmer, and there was somewhat less entangling of forms. Figures began to pull away from their architectural backgrounds. In the early thirteenth century, bodies acquired more three-dimensional mass, more flexibility, more natural poses and drapery, and more individual faces. However, faces and figures retained some simplification and emphasis on large planes. Considerable stoniness and restraint of emotional expression are found in the important figures, lending them a more-than-human dignity and permanence. Later thirteenth-century sculpture gave up this monumental power for more specific anatomy, actions, and emotions; the development produces the effect of the superhuman descending to the human level (PLATE 31). Plants and animals were also depicted more naturally and less imaginatively. Late fourteenth-century work continued in the direction of greater mass and more portrait detail in faces. Stylistic development was quite uneven, and considerable variety may often be seen in the sculpture of one church because it was done by traveling sculptors from different regions or in different periods over a wide time span. In Italy, the remains of ancient Roman sculpture fostered an interest not only in mass but in certain facial types, poses, and methods of draping costumes. These classical tendencies may be seen in the work of men like Nicola Pisano.

By the thirteenth century, France had organized the involved subject matter of earlier sculpture into a complete theological world view including the hierarchy of heavenly beings, the role and duties of man, and the history of the world from events in the Old Testament to the Last Judgment (PLATE 30). So equipped with sculpture (and stained glass), the French Gothic cathedral is a remarkable monument to its age. Other countries did not develop such extensive programs of sculpture.

JAN.

St. Theodore, from south transept portal of Chartres Cathedral (1215–20). The figure, holding a spear and sheltered under a stone canopy, is quite distinct from its supporting column. The more human presentation is carried through in the contrapposto pose, the turning head, and the textures of chain mail and cloth. The earthly reality of the image is qualified by simplification which lends strength to the planes of the face and underlies the order of the drapery folds.

Last Judgment, from central portal of west façade of Amiens Cathedral   PLATE 30
(about 1220–30).   In the lower register, the dead arise from their
tombs to be judged in the scales of St. Michael. Above, the Damned
and the Elect are going to their respective rewards; and, at the top,
Christ is surrounded by Mary, John, and angels bearing the instruments of the Passion. The splayed arches that frame the tympanum
depict the Elect with angels, Martyrs and Confessors, the Wise and
Foolish Virgins, the Elders, the Tree of Jesse (genealogy of Christ),
and the Patriarchs of the Old Law. On the jambs below are larger-
than-life-size figures of the Prophets and Apostles, each identified
by some attribute indicating the instrument of his martyrdom or
symbolizing his role. Below these statues are quatrefoil medallions
with relief sculpture depicting prophecies, Virtues, and Vices. The
trumeau statue is Christ. The size of the figures in the tympanum
and surrounding arches varies with their importance in the hierarchy. The large scale of the jamb statues gives them special grandeur in their nearness to entering worshipers and visually strengthens
the supporting columns for the whole portal. Anatomy in faces and
nude figures still has austere simplicity, and drapery is arranged in
orderly cascades or pleated folds; yet the total effect is so natural
that the turning and twisting Apostles and Prophets seem to con-
verse with each other.

Golden Virgin (Vièrge Dorée), from south transept trumeau of Amiens   PLATE 31
Cathedral (between 1250 and 1270).   This popular statue took its
name from the gilt paint formerly used in the costume. The austere
strength of earlier work is here replaced by extreme gracefulness
and very human emotion. Although the bulky garment obscures the
lower body, the three-dimensional folds seem convincingly activated
by a contrapposto pose.

Crucifix (Pestkreuz), from St. Marie im Kapitol (Cologne, 1304, wood,   JAN.
57″).   The emaciated body is shown with harsh angularity and
much detail in the bleeding wounds and the sores that suggest that
Jesus has suffered from disease and will be sympathetic to the pleas
of the sick. The symmetry and orderly repetition of forms in the
crown of thorns and the ribs make the wounds and the convulsed
hands more shocking by contrast. The hands and arms indicate the
increasing study of nature that characterizes much Gothic sculpture.

JAN.
U. & S.

The Well of Moses, from former Monastery of the Chartreuse de Champmol (Dijon, France, 1395–1406, stone, height of Prophets: about 72").
This is the sculpture of Claus Sluter, who came from Holland to the court of the Dukes of Burgundy at Dijon. The well is surmounted by a badly preserved crucifix placed on a base containing the figures of six Prophets from the Old Testament. In accord with a medieval passion play, the Prophets are depicted as judges who decide that Jesus must be crucified for the sake of mankind. Each Prophet holds a scroll which foretells the sacrifice by a quotation from the Old Testament. The massive forms with their deeply cut depressions, the realism of costume detail, and the individualized faces of Sluter's style forecast the Renaissance, but the slightly exaggerated rhythmic curves in some sections of the drapery relate it to the late Medieval period.

PAINTING

Gothic painters in the north had less wall surface on which to work as walls became more open. Their talents were employed in designing stained glass, which in turn affected style in manuscript illumination. Thirteenth-century illuminations often depict slender, willowy figures in gracefully curving costume folds, all within the architectural frame of a cathedral window. The modeling of the objects is counteracted by strong flattening contours. Space around objects is often denied by the use of flat gold backgrounds. By the fourteenth century, illuminations make less use of the window framework and close observation of nature is evident. Jean Pucelle, in Paris, placed paintings at the top and bottom of a page and surrounded the intervening text with elaborate decorative plants, animals, and geometry. The most pioneering Gothic painting was done by the Italian Giotto di Bondone (1267?–1337). Under the influence of thirteenth-century sculpture, Giotto broke with Byzantine traditions to obtain massive bodies and more natural drapery. Landscape, architecture, and figures are severely simple. The directional movements of all his forms give ponderous dignity to the restrained gestures and facial expressions. The massiveness, the more individual faces, the more natural poses, and the convincing but underplayed emotions all bring a new humanism to Medieval art. Yet Giotto's painting was not fully appreciated by his immediate successors, and it was only with the Renaissance that his interests were developed further. Duccio de Buoninsegna of Siena (about 1255–1319) made a more gentle break with Byzantine style.

Illuminated page from the Psalter of St. Louis (Bibliothèque Nationale, JAN.
Paris, around 1260, about 5″ x 4″).   The illumination depicts
Nahash the Ammonite threatening the Jews at Jabesh. Compared
with most Romanesque work, the human figures here are natural
in proportion and flexible in pose; but less important items, such as
the horses (or architecture in other scenes), are given a diminished
scale. Light and shadow are used sparingly to create a roundness
that is countered by strong outlines. Depth is canceled by the gilt
background. Shapes are filled with strong, relatively unmodulated
colors, with blues and reds predominating. In each illumination in
the *Psalter*, the upper area is treated like a set of stained glass windows set into a Gothic building.

Lamentation or Pietà by Giotto, *from the Arena Chapel* (Padua, fresco, PLATE 33
part of a series of paintings done in 1305-06).   The significance of
the event is expressed not in awe-inspiring otherworldly images,
but in massive human forms whose actions have solemn dignity.
The drapery is simplified and used not to reveal the body but to
emphasize the major movement of each figure. As the figures focus
on Christ, so does the diagonally descending landscape.

Christ entering Jerusalem by Duccio, *a detail from the Maestà Altar of Si-* JAN.
ena Cathedral (1308-11, tempera on wood, size of detail: 40″ x 21″).
The great altarpiece depicts, on the front, a Madonna enthroned
and, on the back, scenes from the life of Christ. Compared with
Giotto's work, Duccio's figures seem doll-like and mashed into flat
groups, but there is delicate expressiveness in the gestures and faces
and the tender details observed from nature. Rigid Byzantine drapery
patterns appear in certain instances, particularly when Duccio shows
Christ in less natural states—during the Transfiguration, for in-
stance, or after the Resurrection. Duccio did not use a consistent
system of linear perspective. The architecture is toylike in scale and
may have been influenced by stage sets for religious dramas.

References for representative works

Conant, Kenneth J. *Carolingian and Romanesque Architecture: 800–1200* (Pelican CON.
    History of Art). Baltimore: Penguin Books, 1959.
Grabar, Arthur, and Carl Nordenfalk. *Early Medieval Painting from the Fourth* G. & N.
    to the Eleventh Century (Great Centuries of Painting). Trans. by Stuart
    Gilbert. Geneva: Skira, 1957.

JAN. Janson, H. W., with D. J. Janson, eds. *Key Monuments of the History of Art: A Visual Survey.* Englewood Cliffs, N.J.: Prentice-Hall; New York: Harry N. Abrams, 1959.

U. & S. Upjohn, Everard M., and J. P. Sedgwick, Jr. *Highlights: An Illustrated History of Art.* New York: Holt, Rinehart and Winston, 1963.

Suggestions for further study

Arnold, Hugh. *Stained Glass of the Middle Ages in England and France.* New ed. London: Adam and Charles Black, 1939.

Crichton, George H. *Romanesque Sculpture in Italy.* London: Routledge & Kegan Paul, 1954.

Decker, Hans. *Romanesque Art in Italy.* Trans. by James Cleugh. New York: Harry N. Abrams, 1959.

Dupont, Jacques, and Cesare Gnudi. *Gothic Painting* (Great Centuries of Painting). Trans. by Stuart Gilbert. Geneva: Skira, 1954.

Frankl, Paul. *Gothic Architecture* (Pelican History of Art). Trans. by Dieter Pevsner. Baltimore: Penguin Books, 1962.

Gardner, Arthur. *Medieval Sculpture in France.* New York: The Macmillan Company, 1931.

Grabar, Arthur, and Carl Nordenfalk. *Romanesque Painting* (Great Centuries of Painting). Trans. by Stuart Gilbert. Geneva: Skira, 1958.

Katzenellenbogen, Adolf. *The Sculptural Programs of Chartres Cathedral: Christ, Mary, Ecclesia.* Baltimore: The Johns Hopkins Press, 1959.

Mâle, Emile. *The Gothic Image: Religious Art in France in the Thirteenth Century.* Trans. by Dora Nussey. New York: Harper & Brothers (Torchbooks), 1958.

Morey, Charles R. *Medieval Art.* New York: W. W. Norton & Company, 1942.

Pope-Hennessy, John. *An Introduction to Italian Sculpture.* New York and London: Phaidon Publishers, 1955–62. Vol 1.

Saalman, Howard. *Medieval Architecture; European Architecture, 600–1200* (Great Ages of World Architecture). New York: George Braziller, 1962.

Von Simson, Otto G. *The Gothic Cathedral: Origins of Gothic Architecture and the Medieval Concept of Order.* New York: Pantheon Books, 1956.

Webb, Geoffrey. *Architecture in Britain: The Middle Ages* (Pelican History of Art). Baltimore: Penguin Books, 1956.

Chapter Eleven   RENAISSANCE ART: 1400-1600

The term *Renaissance* implies a rebirth, and the period is often thought of as a rebirth of the former glory of Greek and Roman culture; yet the Renaissance involved much more than imitation of the past. It was a time of emphasis on the importance of the individual, of interest in the physical characteristics of man and nature, and of search for rational order and ideal form in the arts. The period saw widespread geographical exploration, much activity in scholarship, a rapid growth in the sciences, reformation in religion, and broad changes in the arts. These trends had been gathering momentum since the twelfth century, however, with the exchange of ideas fostered by the Crusades, the emergence of free cities, the rise of the universities, and the developing interests in nature and antique art during the Gothic period. Furthermore, some of the climactic effects of Renaissance trends occurred only afterwards, in the seventeenth century. Thus the beginning and end dates for the period are rather arbitrary markers in the continuous stream of history.

Our concepts of Renaissance art are based primarily on Italy, for it was here that the trends were most distinct. The period from 1400 to 1500 in Italy is called the *Early Renaissance*, the years from about 1500 to 1520 are considered to be the *High Renaissance*, and the remainder of the sixteenth century may be termed *Late Renaissance*. The urbanization of the Gothic period made the cities important centers for the growth of Renaissance ideas and the patronage of art. Artists often joined the courts of nobles and received sustenance and salary in return for painting, sculpture, and design ranging from architecture to theatrical costumes. Florence played the major role in the fifteenth century but was superseded in the sixteenth century by Rome and Venice. Outside Italy, the most productive geographical area for the arts in the fifteenth century was the region

141

of present-day Belgium, the major centers being Tournai, Bruges, Ghent, Brussels, Louvain, and Antwerp. In Burgundian France, Dijon was an important art center until 1420, when the court of the Dukes of Burgundy was moved to Flanders. Paris continued to be important, along with Fontainebleau in the sixteenth century. In the Germanic areas, Cologne, Nuremberg, Vienna, and Basel were especially significant. London was the center of a tardy development of the Renaissance in England.

During the Renaissance, the Church continued to be an important patron of the arts, but the aristocracy and the growing merchant class commissioned art for themselves as well as for the Church. The Visconti and Sforza families in Milan, the Gonzaga family in Mantua, the Este family in Ferrara, and the Medici family in Florence, all powerful families, earned places in history through their patronage. The new individualism stimulated the quest for renown—for accomplishments in the earthly life—and architecture, painting, and sculpture could be seen as permanent monuments to the patron's importance. The desire to live fully was expressed in the concept of the universal man, the man of many abilities and interests as inspired by Greek thought and described in Baldassare Castiglione's sixteenth-century book, *The Courtier*. Breadth of interests affected not only the patronage of art but also the attitude of the artist; Michelangelo was poet, painter, architect, and sculptor, and Leonardo da Vinci was artist, scientist, and engineer. The social status of the artist rose during the fifteenth and sixteenth centuries. By the sixteenth century, the craftsman-artist, trained in a *bottega* (shop) under the apprentice system and the strict rules of a guild, had become the artist-genius, trained in an academy; he was a scholar and a fit companion for princes, a person emancipated from the regulations of the guilds.

During the fifteenth century, the development of the graphic arts in Germany made art in the form of prints available to a larger segment of the population, extending patronage and broadening the artist's audience. Woodcut, wood engraving, and metal engraving were the important media.

The fifteenth century

PAINTING IN THE NORTH
In the countries north of Italy, fifteenth-century painting is sometimes considered to be late Medieval instead of Renaissance because

it shows little interest in ancient Greco-Roman art and does not portray man so heroically in scale, proportions, and action as does the painting of fifteenth-century Italy. Northern painting does intensify the late Gothic study of nature by adding deeper space, more convincing illusion of mass, more flesh-and-blood anatomy, and precise details and textures. Nevertheless, body proportions and drapery effects were conventional. The persistently thin bodies, large heads, narrow shoulders, angular drapery lines, and crowded landscape or architectural settings give much northern painting of the fifteenth century the total effect of a miniature, no matter how large the actual work (PLATE 32). The intricate physical detail was frequently transcended and given spiritual meaning by the elaborate symbolism inherited from the Middle Ages. Painters obtained transparent color through the increased use of oil glazes employed alone or in combination with the more traditional egg tempera.

Robert Campin, probably identical with the Master of Flémalle (Flanders, 1378?–1444). Campin, one of the first painters to use oil paint extensively, had his studio in Tournai. The new realism of his style combines deep space created by means of exaggerated linear perspective, crowded objects, the typically rich color and angular drapery of fifteenth-century northern art, and both private and conventional Medieval symbolism. His *Virgin and Child before a Fire Screen* (c. 1425, National Gallery, London), one of the earliest paintings to show a city view outside the window, presents the Madonna in a comfortable contemporary Flemish house. The fire screen suggests the shape of a halo behind her head, and the chalice (probably a later addition) by her elbow suggests the celebration of the Mass and hints at the future sacrifice of Christ.

JAN. U. & S.

Jan van Eyck (Flanders, about 1390–1441). This pioneer in northern painting worked for Count John of Holland and Philip the Good of Burgundy and finally died in Bruges. He was honored by the rulers and sent on a diplomatic mission to Portugal. The portrait of *Arnolfini and His Bride* (PLATE 32) has typically northern features, such as the fragile bodies, angular drapery, miniature quality, and pervasive symbolism (see p. 29). The converging lines of the architecture are effective in establishing depth, but they are instinctive rather than systematic, for they meet at several different horizon levels. Two natural light sources admit a crossing light that shortens the shadows cast so that even the grain of the floorboards at Arnol-

PLATE 32 JAN. U. & S.

fini's feet is not hidden. Although the woman's face has the smooth wide oval form and tiny mouth found in much northern painting of the period, the striking individuality of Arnolfini's face is undeniable. The entire painting demonstrates remarkably careful observation, from the stubble on Arnolfini's chin to the transparent beads on the wall. The round mirror reveals the artist's interest in optical problems: it shows a wide-angle view of the room, the backs of the couple, and two spectators (perhaps including the artist) in the doorway. The mirror frame contains tiny round scenes of Christ's Passion. The most famous work by Van Eyck is the *Ghent Altarpiece* (1432, St. Bavo, Ghent), which carries the names of Jan and his brother Hubert. There is uncertainty about which parts were done by each and whether or not we have any other paintings by Hubert.

JAN.
U. & S.

Roger van der Weyden (Flanders, about 1400–64).   Roger probably studied under Robert Campin at Tournai. He became the official painter of Brussels and traveled to Italy about 1450. His painting tends to be simpler than that of Van Eyck, with the major figures located in a shallow foreground layer of space, and he was less concerned with leading our attention smoothly from foreground to background; the latter often serves more as backdrop. The faces in Roger's paintings convey more intense feeling than do the faces painted by Jan van Eyck. Roger's major works include *The Descent from the Cross* (c. 1440, Prado, Madrid), *The Last Judgment* (1440's, Hôtel Dieu, Beaune), and *The Virgin and Child* (date uncertain, Kunsthistorisches Museum, Vienna).

JAN.
U. & S.

Jean Fouquet (France, about 1420–81).   Fouquet was born at Tours, and it is thought that he may have attended the University of Paris, since Parisian buildings often appear in his later book illustrations. If so, he undoubtedly saw there the work of Flemish artists, but his paintings contain the Italianate elements that are best explained by a trip to Rome in 1445. Fouquet established himself as painter to the king in Tours, which became the residence of Louis XI. His best-known paintings are the illuminations for the *Book of Hours of Étienne Chevalier* (c. 1450, Musée Condé, Chantilly), the panel painting called the *Virgin and Child from Melun* (c. 1450, Musée Royal des Beaux Arts, Antwerp), the panel portrait of *Charles VII* (1450–60, Louvre, Paris), and the *Pietà of Nouans* (1450's, Nouans).

Hugo van der Goes (Flanders, 1440–82).   Van der Goes died in a JAN.
monastery near Brussels after spending most of his life in Ghent. U. & S.
His work often has a strange tenseness derived from sharp contrasts
in directional forces and between spacious and crowded areas, passive
and active attitudes, and concentrated and distracted attention. His
major work is the *Portinari Altarpiece* (1476, Uffizi Gallery, Florence),
done for the Italian representative of the Medici banking interests
in Bruges. The central panel of this *triptych* (three-part altarpiece)
shows the Adoration of the Shepherds. The disparity between the
size of the Madonna and that of the angels echoes the Medieval
lack of concern for physical reality, while the deep space and realistic detail are characteristically Renaissance. The perspective lines
of the architecture converge toward a vanishing point behind the
head of the Madonna and serve to stress her importance. The foreground symbols include a cast-off shoe as a sign of a holy event,
wheat as a reference to the bread of the Eucharist, scattered anem-
ones as a symbol of sorrow and sacrifice, an iris (sword lily) as a
symbol of the Madonna's suffering during the Passion of Christ,
a lily as a symbol of sacrifice and chastity, and columbine as a symbol
of the Holy Ghost. On the basis of the Portinari painting, a number
of other works have been attributed to Van der Goes through
stylistic similarity.

Hieronymus Bosch (Holland, about 1450–1516).   The extraordinary JAN.
fantasies of Bosch seem closer to the grotesqueries of the Middle U. & S.
Ages than to the rational order of the Renaissance; yet even the
Greeks had their Dionysiac Mysteries, and Bosch painted his visions
with a control of deep space that is one hallmark of the Renaissance.
His religious scenes and representations of proverbs or fables, which
often contain moral lessons, are portrayed through strange combinations of men, plants, and animals, and interpretation is sometimes difficult. Bosch is often cited as an ancestor of twentieth-
century Surrealism. His works include *The Garden of Earthly Delights*
(c. 1500, Prado, Madrid) and the *Hay Wain* (c. 1485–90, Escorial,
Madrid).

PAINTING IN ITALY
While conservative Italian painting continued the traditions of
Byzantine or late Gothic art, the new painting was molded by the
major Renaissance interests: individual man, nature, and ancient

Greco-Roman art. The scattered remains of antique sculpture had encouraged the love of mass in Medieval Italian sculpture. It was Medieval sculpture that helped shape the art of Giotto, which, in turn, became a source for the new fifteenth-century painting (PLATES 38 and 39). Increased efforts were made to duplicate the visual experience of the physical world: linear and aerial perspective was used to create space; natural light (from direct sources and from reflecting surfaces) was studied as a means of suggesting mass; land forms, plant life, and animal and human anatomy were observed in detail; and natural posture as well as convincingly natural movement became important to the new concept of the "real." For all of this, clarity was considered to be essential, but, at the same time, it was conducive to conflicts. Clarity called for sharply outlined edges that contradicted the roundness of the form, and the insistence upon mass sometimes made a painted face seem more like stone than flesh. Only late in the century were deep shadows allowed to obscure parts of the composition in the interests of strong focus (PLATE 39). Portraiture, nature study, Greco-Roman architecture and mythology, and traditional Christian subject matter were often mixed; an Adoration of the Christ Child might be depicted with ancient ruins or with Roman sarcophagi adorned with mythological reliefs, while portraits of the artist's contemporary patrons might be found among the Three Kings and their retinue. The confidence in the importance and capabilities of man was expressed by some artists in dignity of pose, emotional restraint, and boldness of masses (PLATE 38), all producing a kind of monumentality. Much fifteenth-century Italian painting has a breadth of form and a largeness of scale quite unlike the miniature quality of most northern work. Flemish painting was admired by Italians, however, and its landscape backgrounds had some effect upon Italian art. The major media for the period were fresco, tempera, and occasional oil glazing.

DE W.
GOULD
JAN.
U. & S.

Fra Angelico (Florence, 1387–1455). Guido da Vicchio probably studied under Lorenzo Monaco before joining the Dominican Order and taking the name of Fra Angelico. His early style, which lasted from 1418 until the 1430's and is illustrated by such works as the *Coronation of the Virgin* (Uffizi Gallery, Florence), was Gothic in its slender figures, delicate textile patterns, and paradisiac settings. From 1435 to 1445, in such works as the frescoes in S. Marco in Florence, his figures became more solid and the settings more earthbound. His late painting, such as the Nicholas Chapel (Vatican, Rome), has simpler, more massive bodies and deep perspective vistas framed by grand architecture.

Masaccio (Florence, 1401–28).   *The Tribute Money* (PLATE 38) reveals Masaccio's use of aerial and linear perspective (see p. 4) and his modeling with light and shadow to create the illusion of mass. The linear perspective used systematically here was apparently invented by his architect-painter friend Filippo Brunelleschi, who was also an admirer of ancient Roman architecture. Brunelleschi probably encouraged Masaccio to use Roman architecture as a setting for his painting of *The Trinity* (c. 1425, S. Maria Novella, Florence). The massiveness of Masaccio's figures owes much to the painting of Giotto, and the poses indicate the influence of the sculptor Donatello. The greatness of Masaccio lies in the gravity, poise, and depth —the monumentality—which he gave to his humanistic vision of man. These qualities stem from his combination of eloquent but restrained facial expressions, a stately rhythmic accord between the lines of poses and drapery, and the suppression of detail where necessary to strengthen the masses. Certainly the grandeur of scale and mass in the ruins of Roman architecture and sculpture was a formative influence.

PLATE 38
DE W.
GOULD
JAN.
U. & S.

Fra Filippo Lippi (Florence, about 1406–69).   Filippo, a member of the Carmelite Order, acquired some of the massive solids of Masaccio's art but sacrificed the monumentality of the forms by the addition of more detail. A preference for linear accents may have come from Donatello's sculpture. Examples of Filippo's works are *The Madonna Adoring the Child* (c. 1453, Uffizi Gallery, Florence) and *The Annunciation* (c. 1437, S. Lorenzo, Florence). Filippo's style is distinguished from that of his son, Filippino Lippi, by the latter's use of more restless activity and more lavish architectural ornament.

DE W.
GOULD
JAN.
U. & S.

Piero della Francesca (Central Italy, 1415/20–92).   Piero was primarily a painter, but he was also a Renaissance humanist scholar who wrote on perspective and was active as a poet, cosmographer, mathematician, and architect. In painting, his major technical interest seems to have been the effect of light on color and three-dimensional form. His painting often has the quality of bright diffused luminosity. He brought simple massive figures into alignment

DE W.
GOULD
JAN.
U. & S.

with their architectural settings to produce an architectonic stability that reinforces the dignity of the persons portrayed. He owed much to Masaccio's painting and to Donatello's sculpture. Important works by Piero are the frescoes depicting the *Legend of the Holy Cross* (c. 1458–66, S. Francesco, Arezzo) and the *Resurrection* (1460, Town Hall, Borgo S. Sepolcro). His panel paintings of the *Duke and Duchess of Urbino* (1465, Uffizi Gallery, Florence) are fine examples of fifteenth-century profile portraiture stressing individual features and meticulous detail.

Giovanni Bellini (Venice, 1430?–1516).   Probably the most significant fifteenth-century Venetian painter, Giovanni was one of three famous painters bearing the Bellini name. He received his early training from his father, Jacopo, and from Andrea Mantegna. His early style is represented by the *St. Francis Receiving the Stigmata* (Frick Collection, New York), done about 1480. Sharp intricate details reveal a kind of microscopic appreciation of nature. Later, his style changed to softer light, the subordination of detail to large masses, and more emphasis on a general color effect rather than on local color. The late style, which established the characteristic elements of sixteenth-century Venetian painting, is evident in the *Madonna and Saints* (1505, S. Zaccaria, Venice).

Andrea Mantegna (northern Italy, 1431–1506).   Mantegna was apprenticed to Francesco Squarcione in Padua, but it was Donatello's sculpture in Padua that influenced Mantegna's love of statuesque figures with brittle clinging drapery and highlights of stony or metallic character. Precise detail and settings with architectural reliefs and deep rocky landscapes are typical. In 1459, Mantegna became court painter to the Gonzaga family at Mantua, where he painted wall and ceiling frescoes in the palace. Other examples of his art are the frescoes in the Ovetari Chapel in Padua (now destroyed) and the *S. Zeno Altarpiece* (1456–59, S. Zeno, Verona). The *Dead Christ* (c. 1501, Brera Gallery, Milan) is a dramatic example of Mantegna's interest in spatial illusion; the body is daringly *foreshortened* (the effect of spatial recession obtained by drawing the object as a series of overlapping or successive masses). Mantegna's statuesque figures, his use of Roman architecture and sculpture, and his interest in illusionistic space had a wide influence in northern Italy.

Sandro Botticelli (Florence, 1444–1510). From his teacher Fra Filippo Lippi, Botticelli formed a style of knobby, jointed figures and rippling, linear drapery folds. He was patronized by the Medici family, and his *Adoration of the Magi* (1476–78, Uffizi Gallery, Florence) portrays members of the family as the Magi and their followers. His best-known paintings are the *Birth of Venus* (c. 1485) and the *Birth of Spring* (c. 1478), both in the Uffizi Gallery. The obscure symbolism in the latter painting probably came from the romantic allegorical poems of the humanist circle sponsored by the Medici. In 1481, Botticelli was called to Rome to do one of the frescoes on the walls of the Sistine Chapel, the *Moses and the Daughters of Jethro*. In his late work, Botticelli turned increasingly to religious subject matter, and it is thought that his work was influenced by the emotional preaching of Savonarola. The *Pietà* (c. 1496, Alte Pinakothek, Munich) has only traces of the former delicacy of line, imprisoned within harsh angular forms, and the expressions of the participants convey desperate anguish.

DE W.
GOULD
JAN.
U. & S.

Pietro Vannucci, called Perugino (central Italy, 1445?–1523). Perugino worked in Perugia in the region of Umbria except for his trip to Rome in the 1480's to paint the *Handing of the Keys to St. Peter* in the Sistine Chapel. He simplified the parts and the action in his compositions, employing serene landscapes, figures and drapery with gently curving rhythmic lines, and passive faces with small button eyes and delicate mouths. Typical works are the *Crucifixion* fresco in S. Maria Maddalena dei Pazzi in Florence and the *Pietà* panel painting (Uffizi Gallery, Florence), both done in the 1490's. Perugino was the teacher of Raphael.

DE W.
GOULD
JAN.

Leonardo da Vinci (Florence, Milan, and Amboise, 1452–1519). Leonardo was born near Florence and sent at an early age to be trained in the studio of Andrea del Verrocchio. The breadth of Leonardo's Renaissance mind ranged from engineering problems to botanical study, and his notebooks are famous as records of a many-sided genius. *The Madonna of the Rocks* (PLATE 39) reveals not only his interest in anatomy, geology, and botany but qualities that forecast the sixteenth century: a conscious effort to perfect nature through concepts of ideal form and a desire to go beyond surface appearances to express the working of the mind or a condition of the spirit. While Leonardo was not unprecedented in these concerns,

PLATE 39
DE W.
GOULD
JAN.
U. & S.

he faced them more deliberately than his contemporaries did and went further in seeking pictorial means for their expression. Sixteenth-century painting was influenced by his triangular figure groupings and his ideal facial type—the softly modeled oval with slender nose and delicately curved mouth. Unlike most fifteenth-century painters, he no longer felt the need for clarity in all parts. In *The Madonna of the Rocks* (Louvre version), he subordinated local colors to a total color effect and used strong chiaroscuro, leaving parts of the painting in obscurity but providing powerful focus. The highlighted fingers of the Madonna's outstretched hand create a startling illusion of depth; they hover over the head of Jesus and suggest a halo or a crown of thorns. The angel's hand points to the other child, who will become John the Baptist and recognize Jesus as the Christ. The tense concentration of attention between the two children is softened by the meditative gaze of the Madonna, while the angel seems more aware of the spectator. The jagged rocks and delicate plants do not seem to be included merely to demonstrate technical virtuosity or to establish physical reality, as they do in much fifteenth-century work. Instead, the powerful contrasts of light with shadow, of wild nature with soft flesh create the dramatic intensity of a mystery play or a sacred ritual. From 1483 until 1500, Leonardo worked in Milan for the Sforza family and painted, in addition to *The Madonna of the Rocks*, *The Last Supper* in S. Maria delle Grazie, where again the total composition is expressive of mental drama. In Florence once more from 1503 to 1506, he painted the *Mona Lisa* (Louvre, Paris). After a trip to Rome in 1513 and more time in Milan, he accepted the invitation of Francis I to come to Amboise in France, where he died. The variety of Leonardo's interests and his tendency to leave projects unfinished have left us few paintings; his drawings and notebooks contain anatomical and botanical studies and inventions ranging from hydraulic engineering to flying machines. His late painting of *John the Baptist* (Louvre, Paris) has decided Manneristic traits and influenced the Mannerist painter Parmigianino.

SCULPTURE IN ITALY

Florentine sculpture led the movement toward the wedding of mass, contrapposto poses, studied anatomical detail, naturalistic drapery, and portraiture, all inspired by the growing interest in Roman art, the physical world, and man. The first freestanding nude figures since Roman times were produced, and relief sculpture exploited the illusion of depth. As in painting, the desire for clarity often resulted in a linear inscribing of detail on the masses. The range of sculpture widened in subject matter and in function. Human heroes, both contemporary and Biblical, were frequently chosen as subjects, and Greco-Roman mythology and secular allegory appeared more often than before. Enthusiasm for small bronze antique statuettes led Renaissance sculptors to take up this art, often borrowing subjects from mythology. Sculptures of Madonnas and saints acquired portrait-like individuality. Relief sculpture functioned to emphasize focal points in the church, such as pulpits, *cantorias* (singing galleries), and bronze doors. The relief on *tabernacles* (devotional centers ranging in size from a small plaque to a large wall niche) employed striking single-point perspective views surrounded by elaborate architectural frames using variations of ancient Greco-Roman moldings (*Fig.* 45, p. 87). The Renaissance appreciation of the individual is evidenced in the increasing number of portrait busts after the middle of the century. Like old Roman portraits, they contained much detail, yet the sculptor was capable of ennobling the subject by dignity of pose or alertness of expression. The ancient Roman equestrian statue of Marcus Aurelius in Rome inspired similar monuments for fifteenth-century Italians. The desire to perpetuate a name also asserted itself in the Renaissance wall tomb, built into the side of a church. The tombs present Roman pediments, columns, pilasters, moldings, and Roman figure types such as *putti* (Cupids or cherubs) and Greco-Roman winged victory goddesses.

Lorenzo Ghiberti (Florence, 1378?–1455).   Ghiberti's two sets of bronze *doors for the Florentine Baptistery* show the transition from late Gothic to early Renaissance style. The *Sacrifice of Isaac* panel done for the competition for the first set of doors (1401–02) is crowded and shallow in space. The same subject done for the second set of doors (PLATE 34), the so-called *Gates of Paradise* (1425–52), is set in a spacious landscape with deep space created by a suggestion of linear perspective in the lines of trees and an effect of aerial perspective in the contrast of high relief in the foreground and faint relief in the background. Typical of the age are the drapery folds that emphasize the flexible poses of the bodies. Ghiberti's freestanding statue of *St. Matthew* (1420) for Or San Michele adopts the mass, pose, and drapery forms of ancient Greco-Roman statues of

PLATE 34
JAN.
P.-H.
U. & S.

orators. In his *Commentaries*, Ghiberti wrote about the lives of great artists and the theory of art, seeking in this way to establish his own place in the history of art.

PLATE 35
JAN.
P.-H.
U. & S.
Donatello (Florence, 1386–1466).   The most significant figure in fifteenth-century Italian sculpture was Donatello, who learned bronze casting under Ghiberti and traveled to Rome with Brunelleschi the architect to study ancient art. Donatello worked in marble, bronze, and occasionally wood and *stucco* (a fine plaster or cement). His first bronze statue of *David* (1430–32, Bargello, Florence) appears to have been the first freestanding nude since Roman times. Donatello also did relief sculpture, advancing its illusionistic possibilities by suggesting deep space and a variety of spatial relationships without using high relief for the foreground. He often combined his subtle low relief, called *schiacciato*, with architectural settings in single-point perspective; the effect is much like that of a drawing. Poses are active, and drapery breaks into a complexity of nervously rippling linear folds. Major reliefs are those on the *Baptismal Font at Siena* (1423–34), the *Altar of S. Antonio in Padua* (1444–53), the *doors of the Old Sacristy at S. Lorenzo in Florence* (1430's), and the two *pulpits in S. Lorenzo* (c. 1460–70). Donatello's art reflects the growing importance of the individual not only in the use of specific features and expressions but also in the choice of human heroes such as David, Judith, and Gattamelata (a Renaissance general) as frequent subjects. Most amazing is his ability to express convincingly a wide range of human emotions, from the brutal confidence of *Gattamelata* (1445–50, Padua) to the contemplative aloofness of *Young John the Baptist* (PLATE 35) or the tragic suffering of *Mary Magdalene* (c. 1454–55, Florentine Baptistery). Realism of the flesh is accompanied by the realism of bared feelings. Strangely enough, Donatello did not show great interest in the portrait bust, though other sculptors did.

Luca della Robbia (Florence, 1400–82).   The *marble cantoria for the Florence Cathedral* established Luca's reputation as a sculptor in the 1430's. Soon afterward, he began to specialize in glazed terra cotta reliefs, perhaps to answer Brunelleschi's demand for such colorful focal points in his architecture. Luca preferred white figures against blue backgrounds; additional colors, if any, were saved for the flowered frames. After his death, the family workshop, led by

Andrea della Robbia, adopted more flamboyant color schemes and stressed quantity at the expense of quality.

Andrea del Verrocchio (Florence, 1435–88).   Verrocchio was first trained as a goldsmith and then may have worked with Desiderio da Settignano. Only one painting, the *Baptism of Christ* (c. 1472, Uffizi Gallery, Florence), is given with certainty to Verrocchio; his main interest was sculpture. He worked in terra cotta, stone, and bronze, with subjects ranging from the *David* (Bargello, Florence) and the *Christ and St. Thomas* (c. 1465–83, Or San Michele, Florence) to the *Tomb of Piero and Giovanni de' Medici* (completed in 1472, S. Lorenzo, Florence), the equestrian statue of *Colleoni* (1485–88, Venice), and the terra cotta busts of *Giuliano* and *Lorenzo de' Medici* (dates uncertain, National Gallery, Washington, D.C.). His style is characterized by much hard-edged detail, bulbous anatomy, and distinct individuality in the faces. Verrocchio taught Leonardo da Vinci.

DE W.
GOULD
JAN.
U. & S.

ARCHITECTURE IN ITALY

The Renaissance man saw a sharp contrast between Gothic architecture, with its soaring verticals, irregular expansion, and complex geometric proportions veiled by lavish surface detail, and the remains of ancient Roman architecture. The Roman work, long since shorn of its decorative veneer, revealed a basic symmetry and a logical clarity in its proportioning that were simple enough to be quickly felt and comprehended, and the Renaissance scholar eagerly noted the static balance of vertical columns and horizontal architraves, the simple curve of the round arch, and the massive permanence of the walls that related to the rational structure of Greco-Roman literature and philosophy. Some fifteenth-century architects merely applied Roman pilasters, columns, and moldings in Gothic profusion, but the leaders sought to understand principles rather than to imitate details, and significant early Renaissance buildings, such as the *Pazzi Chapel* in Florence (PLATES 42 and 43) and *S. Maria delle Carceri* in Prato (PLATES 44–46), display a severe clarity of plan and elevation. The calculated simplicity and the linear outlining of each part call attention to the proportion of the parts to the whole, and the resulting diagrammatic effect is reminiscent of the linear insistence upon clarity in much fifteenth-century Italian painting and sculpture. Studies of proportion in Roman architecture were intensified by the discovery, in a Swiss monastery in 1414, of the writings of Pollio Vitruvius, a Roman architectural theorist of the first century A.D., although difficulties in translating the work somewhat restricted its influence until the sixteenth century.

Florence sheltered the first early Renaissance architecture, the *Foundlings' Hospital* and the *Pazzi Chapel*. Other northern Italian cities, such as Rimini and Mantua, also became important. In Venice, the Renaissance came late and was mixed with strong Gothic and Byzantine traditions. Balconies and arcades kept walls light and open; Venetian politics were less violent than those of Florence, and the massive, fortress-like character of Florentine palaces was less necessary in the city of canals. Rome was also slow in developing the new style, partly because few buildings were completed during the century. When Renaissance elements appear, as in the *Cancelleria* (begun in 1486), the most evident source of inspiration is the architecture of Leon Battista Alberti.

PLATES 42 and 43 JAN. U. & S. *Filippo Brunelleschi* (Florence, 1377–1446).   Brunelleschi's aspirations as a sculptor may have been crushed by his loss to Ghiberti in the competition for the reliefs on the Florentine Baptistery doors. Brunelleschi turned to architecture, made a prolonged study of Roman ruins, and gained fame by designing a dome for the unfinished *Cathedral of Florence*. His most important surviving buildings are the *Church of S. Lorenzo* (designed in 1418), the *Foundlings' Hospital* (designed in 1419), the *Pazzi Chapel* (c. 1420–29), and the *Church of S. Spirito* (designed in 1436), all in Florence. In the small *Pazzi Chapel* (PLATES 42 and 43), the altar is set into a niche opposite the entry and across the short axis of a simple rectangular plan. Walls and vaults are divided by dark stone pilasters and moldings into distinct geometric areas. The low relief of these details gives the effect of a linear diagram. A Roman dome covers the center of the space, and the unfinished porch employs the Corinthian order and a *broken architrave* (architrave interrupted by an arch) in the Roman manner. Roman moldings, pilasters, and columns organize mass, planes, and spaces with the self-contained stability and dignity that Renaissance men associated with ancient Roman architecture.

JAN. U. & S. *Michelozzo di Bartolommeo* (Florence, 1396–1472).   To his contemporaries, Michelozzo was second only to Brunelleschi as a pioneer in the new architecture. Michelozzo became a favorite of Cosimo de' Medici, and the *Medici-Riccardi Palace* (1444–59, Florence) is the best-known work by the prolific architect. Roman details compose the arches, moldings, and *cornice* (terminating molding that projects at the top of a wall or building), but the windows of the palace are connected by only a stringcourse, and no attempt was made to proportion the floors with vertical dividers in the form of pilasters or columns. The linear quality of the design is modified by heavy *rustication* (rough stonework) on the ground floor, which changes to boldly jointed but finished stone above and finally to smooth masonry in the top floor. The design is powerful but less subtle and less completely integrated in all its parts than works by Brunelleschi. Michelozzo did restoring and additional building for *S. Marco* and the *Palazzo Vecchio* in Florence, and he designed the *Medici Bank* and probably did the drawings for the *Portinari Chapel* (S. Eustorgio), both in Milan. After the death of Brunelleschi, Michelozzo was put in charge of the Cathedral Workshop in Florence. Although occasional Gothic arches link his work to the past, Michelozzo helped to spread the basic elements of early Renaissance architecture to Milan and even to Dalmatia.

Leon Battista Alberti (Florence, 1404–72). Alberti was born in Genoa to an exiled Florentine family and was educated at the universities of Padua and Bologna. He became a universal man of the Renaissance—a humanist scholar, painter, sculptor, mathematician, poet, and architect. His scholarly treatises on architecture, like those of Vitruvius, had a wide influence, and he succeeded Brunelleschi as the leader in Renaissance architecture. For the *Rucellai Palace* (1446–51, Florence), Alberti used Roman arches and moldings and applied pilasters in the Roman sequence, that is, the Doric order at the ground level, the Ionic on the next floor, and the Corinthian above that. As in much fifteenth-century architecture, a linear effect comes from the way in which pilasters, stringcourses, and mortared joints are treated as though cut into the flatness of the wall. Other important buildings by Alberti are *S. Andrea* (1470, Mantua) and the remodeling of *S. Francesco* (1446, Rimini). The latter church took its façade from the form of Roman triumphal arches. [JAN. U. & S.]

Giuliano da Sangallo (Florence, 1445–1516). Giuliano came from a family of celebrated artists and was trained as sculptor, engineer, and architect. His activity extended from Naples to Milan and into [PLATES 44–46 JAN.]

southern France, where he served Cardinal Giuliano delle Rovere in Lyons. Giuliano's *S. Maria delle Carceri* in Prato (PLATES 44–46) came late in the fifteenth century; its central Greek cross plan accords with Alberti's argument that the four-sided symmetry of a central plan expressed divine reason in its unity and harmony. Both Sangallo and Alberti forecast the sixteenth-century interest in central plans. The dome over the crossing of Sangallo's church, the linear framing of dark against light, and the low relief of pilasters and moldings all reveal the influence of Brunelleschi. The pilasters and dark bands on the exterior emphasize the proportions and suggest structural framing without destroying the flatness of the wall surface, while the nature of the interior spaces is clearly revealed by the flatness and simplicity of the enclosing walls. Giuliano's career extended into the sixteenth century; and, in later life, he was appointed to serve with Fra Giaconda and Raphael in carrying on the construction of *St. Peter's* in Rome.

The sixteenth century

PAINTING IN ITALY

Italian painting of the High Renaissance period (1500–20) developed different aims from those of fifteenth-century art and should therefore not be thought of simply as a culmination of less successful fifteenth-century efforts. The earlier emphasis on the exploration of the physical world was superseded by a general effort to transform and transcend surface appearance without sacrificing its physical qualities. The artist sought to perfect nature according to preconceived ideal forms; faces were generalized to present types of humans, and there was less depiction of contemporary costume and more simplification of drapery folds for broad, sweeping, directional emphasis. The linear clarity of fifteenth-century work gave way to fuller masses; softer lighting and softer edges produced a "thick" atmospheric effect (called *sfumato*) that contrasted with the sharp airless space of much fifteenth-century painting. Individual actions conformed to a more flowing, all-inclusive, rhythmic harmony, and bold chiaroscuro provided dramatic focus. All this was part of a concept of the Grand Manner, by which the artist transformed nature and made it expressive of ideal form and inner experience, a concept only possible with the increased tendency for the artist to be considered a divine genius rather than a mere craftsman. In the second half of the fifteenth century, many of the High Renaissance qualities had been developed in the art of Leonardo da Vinci. His work was a formative influence, and he is often considered a High Renaissance painter, even though most of his pioneering works were done in the fifteenth century. It is more helpful to see him as a bridge between the two centuries.

Florence must receive credit as the seedbed for High Renaissance painting, not only because of Leonardo's background there (although some of his major works were done in Milan) but because Raphael painted his first mature works in Florence. However, the blossoming occurred in Rome with the work of Raphael and Michelangelo. In northern Italy, Venetian painting moved away from the sharp detail of the early Renaissance toward softer light, fuller and less detailed masses, and the suppression of local colors for an overall color effect (COLOR PLATE 1). Soft atmospheric effects were made easier to achieve with oil paint, and in the sixteenth century the technique of oil on canvas supplanted the traditional tempera on wood panels that had been used for easel paintings (portable works). Fresco techniques continued to be used for mural painting, although during the sixteenth century use was made of oil on canvas applied to the wall. Venetian painters used oil paint opaquely and in glazes for textural and color effects of great richness.

Italian painting in the Late Renaissance (1520–1600) manifested several stylistic trends, sometimes within the work of a single artist. While High Renaissance concepts continued to shape the art of some leaders, a second trend, known as *Mannerism*, rejected the clear underlying order of High Renaissance painting and replaced it with ambiguity in spatial relations, mood, and even subject matter. Elongated figures with narrow shoulders, wide hips, tapering hands and feet, and self-conscious affected poses were composed with a lack of central focus and deliberately inconsistent scale in crowded spaces. A third trend may be called *Proto-Baroque* because it forecasts the violent activity, dramatic lighting, great complexity, and breathtaking illusionism that became important devices in seventeenth-century Baroque art.

Michelangelo Buonarroti (Florence and Rome, 1475–1564). As a youth, Michelangelo was taken from his birthplace, Caprese, to Florence, where he studied painting with Domenico Ghirlandaio and sculpture with Giovanni Bertoldo. Although his real love was

PLATE 40
DE W.
GOULD
JAN.
U. & S.

sculpture, Michelangelo was forced by papal and financial pressures to do painting and architecture as well. The only easel painting that is known with certainty to be his is *The Holy Family* (1504–06, Uffizi Gallery, Florence); the rest of his painting is mural work done in fresco. One of the greatest monuments of the High Renaissance is his series of frescoes on the ceiling of the Sistine Chapel in the Vatican, done between 1508 and 1512 at the insistence of Pope Julius II. Between 1536 and 1541, he painted the *Last Judgment* on the end wall of the Sistine Chapel, and from 1542 until his death he worked in the Pauline Chapel in the Vatican. Michelangelo concentrated on the human figure, often to the near exclusion of setting, and his concept of ideal form led him to paint figures of awesome bulk and musculature in active or restless poses. The Sistine ceiling boils with writhing giants enacting the creation of the world, the creation and fall of man, the story of Noah, and numerous secondary stories and allegories, all organized within a painted architectural framework. One of the few relaxed figures is that of Adam as he receives life from the outstretched hand of God whose body ripples with energy. Typically, the *Creation of Adam* (PLATE 40) is divided into only two large groupings: that of Adam with the vaguely suggested mound of earth and that of God and surrounding angels framed by the billowing cloak. The two groupings focus on the almost touching fingers of God and Adam. In many other scenes, the extraordinary physical power of the bodies is countered by expressions of mental attitudes ranging from contemplation to consternation and anguish. Michelangelo's art and poetry indicate an increasing disillusionment with the search for physical beauty. The overpowering scale and activity in his painting forecast the Baroque art of the seventeenth century.

PLATE 41
DE W.

Tiziano Vecelli, called Titian (Venice, 1477/90–1576).   As a pupil of Giovanni Bellini, Titian acquired a love of soft, light, warm color effects that subordinated local colors and massive simplified forms. He enjoyed the lavish textiles and elegant costumes of the wealthy Venetian society and incorporated these into his painting. His ideal for the female figure is admirably presented in the Naples *Danaë* (PLATE 41). The breadth of the forms, the division of the composition into a few large parts, the subordination of details to large areas of light and dark, and the preference for spiral torsion in the poses probably owe something to the art of Michelangelo, but Titian's color is richer and his forms are softer. Titian achieved depth and a variety of subtle textures by building up oil glazes of warm and cool colors along with areas of impasto. His preference for dynamic grouping and powerful chiaroscuro manifests itself in early works such as *The Assumption of the Virgin* (1516–18) and *The Pesaro Madonna* (1519–26, both in S. Maria dei Frari, Venice), where figures and areas of contrasting value are grouped as counterbalancing diagonals. His late work, such as the *Pietà* (1573–76, Accademia, Venice), developed even greater dramatic contrast in the chiaroscuro and heavier impasto. Titian's fame spread, and his energies were prodigious; in addition to religious subjects and mythological themes, he painted many portraits, including those of Pope Paul III and the Emperor Charles V.

Giorgione da Castelfranco (Venice, 1478–1510).   The plague cut short the brilliant career of Giorgione, one of Titian's fellow apprentices in the studio of Giovanni Bellini. Scanty documentation has resulted in much discussion about the identification and dating of authentic paintings by Giorgione. Generally accepted works are the *Castelfranco Madonna* (Castelfranco), *The Tempest* or *The Soldier and the Gipsy* (Accademia, Venice), *The Sleeping Venus* (Dresden Gallery), and *The Pastoral Concert*, although the latter has sometimes been questioned. In *The Pastoral Concert* (COLOR PLATE 1) the nude women may personify the subject of the music played by the young men. The nude bodies are painted as heavy three-dimensional forms with soft edges, generalized anatomy, and delicate nuances of light and color. The foliage masses and the lavish costumes have equally full forms and subtle textures. The painting is organized in alternating areas of light and dark that move back step by step from foreground to background; and the colors become cooler and less saturated as they move from the red hat of the central youth into the distance. The forms complement each other in graceful consonance; for example, the tree trunk on the left flows into the vertical arm of the standing woman and also bends to meet the curve of her back, while the leaning position and the rounded forms of the seated woman are echoed in the foliage of the central tree. With his use of soft light, graceful quiet masses, bold simplification of light and dark areas, and glowing color, Giorgione represents the High Renaissance in Venice. His style may be seen as a bridge between the late work of Giovanni Bellini and the painting of Titian.

COLOR
PLATE 1
DE W.
GOULD
JAN.
U. & S.

PLATE 36
DE W.
GOULD
JAN.
U. & S.

Raphael Sanzio (Florence and Rome, 1483–1520). After studying with Perugino in Umbria and revealing his precocious talent in works such as *The Marriage of the Virgin* (1504, Brera Gallery, Milan), Raphael went to Florence (1504–08), where he painted portraits and Madonnas. The *Madonna of the Meadow* (PLATE 36) is typical. The feeling of gentle, sweet serenity is expressed not only through faces and gestures but through the whole compositional structure. The stable triangular group of figures works with the quiet landscape to form an obvious axial balance. The large triangle provides an effect of gradation and climax at the head of the Madonna, while the head of Jesus receives similar emphasis through the triangular shape formed by his body and the cross. The triangular groupings are softened by a modification of bodies and garments to produce variations on ovoid curves. Every part joins the gentle curvilinear harmony and fits into the underlying geometric structure. The face of the Madonna, the triangular grouping, and the sfumato effect owe much to Leonardo. In 1509, Pope Julius II called Raphael to Rome to fresco a series of rooms in the Vatican. *The School of Athens*, in the Stanze delle Segnatura, combines Roman architecture on a vast scale, an ideal concept of human form, and individual portraits of the great minds of various ages. The many figures are organized in large symmetrically balanced groups by geometric systems of sweeping curves, triangles, and vertical and horizontal lines. Restrained emotions, clear serene order, and exhilarating breadth dignify the grand symbolic program. We seem to witness the apotheosis of man. Some of the bodies in the Vatican paintings suggest the physique and poses of the figures in Michelangelo's contemporary frescoes in the Sistine Chapel. Raphael's earlier Vatican works are the epitome of High Renaissance art; the later ones reveal Manneristic qualities. Other important works from his Roman period are the frescoes in the *Villa Farnesina*, the portrait of *Pope Leo X and His Nephews* (c. 1518, Uffizi Gallery, Florence), *The Alba Madonna* (c. 1509, National Gallery, Washington, D.C.), *The Sistine Madonna* (c. 1514, Dresden Gallery), the cartoons for the *Vatican Tapestries* (1515–16, Victoria and Albert Museum, London), and *The Transfiguration* (1519–20, Vatican Gallery).

DE W.
GOULD
JAN.
U. & S.

Antonio Allegri, called Correggio (Parma, 1494–1534). Correggio's art indicates an acquaintance with the painting of Leonardo, Michelangelo, and the Venetians. His *Virgin and Child with St.*

Sebastian (1525, Dresden Gallery), like his frescoes in the *Parma Cathedral* (1526–30), has the spiral poses, fluttering drapery, bold dark and light contrasts, and avoidance of stable verticals and horizontals that forecast much seventeenth-century painting; yet Correggio held the activity within large areas, and the compositions do not figuratively break through their architectural frame. His late work, such as the *Virgin and Child with St. George* (1531, Dresden Gallery), combines saccharine smiles and sensual fleshiness with Manneristic poses.

Francesco Mazzola, called Il Parmigianino (Parma, 1503–40). Parmigianino, a representative of Mannerism, was influenced by Correggio before coming to Rome (1524–27), where he attempted to achieve the dramatic lighting effects of Leonardo, the restless poses of Michelangelo, the rhythmic grace of Raphael, and the sensuality of Correggio. Parmigianino's *Madonna del Collo Lungo* (c. 1535, Uffizi Gallery, Florence) shows the sinuous elongation and the ambiguity in space, scale, and emotions that are typical of the Mannerist aesthetic.

DE W.
GOULD
JAN.
U. & S.

Jacopo Robusti, called Tintoretto (Venice, 1518–94). Tintoretto, one of the giants of Venetian painting, was an admirer of Titian and Michelangelo. His paintings include scenes from the life of St. Mark done for the School of St. Mark (1547–66), scenes from the life of Christ done for the School of S. Rocco (1560–87), and religious and mythological subjects for the Doge's Palace (1577–78), all in Venice. Tintoretto's series were often elaborate in concept and grand in scale. His powers are summarized in the late painting of the *Last Supper* (1594) in S. Giorgio Maggiore, which makes a startling contrast with the same subject treated by Leonardo. Tintoretto grouped the active disciples along a table that pushes diagonally back into space. Halfway down the length of the table, the dazzling *nimbus* (glowing halo) around the head of Jesus provides the major light source in the dark shadows of the room. Small nimbuses glow around the heads of all the disciples except Judas, who is placed on the opposite side of the table from the rest; a foreground lamp seems to radiate sparks, and transparent angels swoop down toward Jesus. This remarkably dramatic interpretation did much to inspire seventeenth-century art.

DE W.
GOULD
JAN.
U. & S.

Paolo Veronese (Venice, 1528–88).   At the age of twenty-seven, Veronese came from Verona to establish himself as a portrayer of the material wealth of Venice. His selection and interpretation of Biblical subjects was governed by his love of lavish costumes, ornate architecture, and elegant table settings. *The Feast in the House of Levi* (1573, Accademia, Venice) is typical in its grand scale. Though Veronese's interest in decorative details sometimes weakened the expressive power of the figures, his technical facility, his use of silvery color, and the exuberance of his composition are very impressive.

SCULPTURE IN ITALY

High Renaissance sculpture, like the painting of the period, sought ideal form, the Grand Manner that involved nobility of action and scale, ideal shapes and proportions, and depth of feeling. Some sculptors employed the serene equilibrium and smooth transitions seen in much of Raphael's painting; others chose the twisting poses and more tense vitality of Michelangelo's painting and sculpture. Both these facets of High Renaissance style contributed to the Late Renaissance trends: Mannerism and the Proto-Baroque. The serpentine curves and self-conscious elegance of a Mannerist figure might reveal the paternity of Raphael's suave harmonies or a softened version of the torsion and heroic musculature in Michelangelo's art. The bold contrast, dramatic action, and powerful focus of Proto-Baroque sculpture were inspired particularly by Michelangelo.

Portrait sculpture tended throughout the sixteenth century to express social position and physical or mental types rather than the sharply individual traits seen in fifteenth-century works. Sixteenth-century wall tombs were often larger and more complex than their fifteenth-century forerunners. The architectural frame developed greater spatial variety in different planes of projecting and receding parts. High Renaissance tombs usually have a smooth integration of figures and architecture, while Late Renaissance tombs may combine Manneristic figures with the lavish materials and bold contrasts that forecast the Baroque. The love of contrast sometimes led the designer to set figures and architecture sharply apart through changes in values, colors, shapes, or scale. The most important source for Late Renaissance tombs was Michelangelo's design for the *Tombs of the Medici* (PLATE 37). Only in the Late Renaissance was the fountain developed as a public monument, one that could combine freestanding sculpture, relief sculpture, and water in movement. Fountains tended to become more complex, and relief sculpture gave way to more and more sculpture in the round (freestanding). Mass became more open, and dark and light contrasts became more extreme.

The major centers for the development of sixteenth-century sculptural style were Florence and Rome; Venice, Milan, and Naples were secondary. The sculptors, like the painters, often were active in several cities in the course of their careers.

Michelangelo Buonarroti.   Michelangelo's early sculpture, such as the *Battle of the Centaurs* done under the patronage of the Medici family in Florence, already showed the artist's preference for the nude, muscular body and active intertwining masses. His first major religious commission was the *Pietà* in St. Peter's (1498). Here cascades of deeply undercut drapery produce strong contrasts of light and shadow within the triangular group. The body of the Madonna is larger than that of her son so that she holds Jesus easily across her lap. Michelangelo's life was constantly upset by the conflicting demands of various patrons, and many of his sculptural projects remained unfinished or were finished in a compromise with original plans. This is the case with the *Tombs of Giuliano and Lorenzo de' Medici* (1524–34) in S. Lorenzo in Florence, which underwent many changes and were left unfinished by Michelangelo's departure for Rome. For the tomb of Giuliano, the wall emphasizes the climactic figure of Giuliano seated in a niche above the sarcophagus. Value contrasts stress the framing effect of the architecture, and the triangular grouping of the figures (*Fig.* 22, p. 26) integrates them with the geometry of the wall in spite of their restless poses and precarious positions; they were obviously designed to rest on horizontal surfaces. As in his painting, Michelangelo created muscular giants; he admitted that the central figure bore little resemblance to the face or body of Giuliano. Michelangelo saw his task not as the portraiture of physical appearance but as the creation of a monument expressive of leadership. The female figure of *Night* and the unfinished male figure of *Day* seem to be grieving for Giuliano. The torso of *Day* reveals the influence of the *Belvedere Torso*, a fragment of a Roman copy of a Hellenistic Greek work that was known to Michelangelo. In view of his style, it is not hard to understand that

PLATE 37
JAN.
P.-H.
U. & S.

Michelangelo's favorite ancient sculpture was the then newly discovered (1506) *Laocoön*, whose muscular power and dynamic pose
suggest the source of Michelangelo's concept of ideal form. The
artist's grandest tomb design, that for *Pope Julius II*, suffered endless
changes during forty years of struggle for funds and conflict with
other projects. The result, in S. Pietro in Vincoli, is a sadly hetero-
geneous collection of parts. Michelangelo's final sculptural work
was an unfinished and defaced *Deposition* (Cathedral of Florence)
meant for his own tomb.

JAN.
P.-H.

Jacopo Sansovino (Florence, Rome, and Venice, 1486–1570).   Jacopo
studied under Andrea Sansovino in Florence and acquired Andrea's
admiration for Raphael. Jacopo's *St. James* (1518), done for the
Cathedral of Florence, has a gentle contrapposto pose with a slight
torsion; the gracefully flowing drapery follows and elaborates the
long S-curve of the body. After two periods in Rome (1505–11 and
1518–27), Jacopo settled in Venice, where he found little competition
to challenge his leadership. He added architecture to his activities
and was responsible for both architecture and sculpture on the
Loggetta (1540) in the Square of St. Mark. He also did the richly
sculpted bronze door for the *Sacristry of St. Mark's* (1546–69). Jacopo
represented the Raphaelesque facet of High Renaissance style
and carried this into the Late Renaissance period; however, his
pupils turned to Proto-Baroque qualities inspired by the art of
Michelangelo.

JAN.
P.-H.

Benvenuto Cellini (Florence, Rome, and France, 1500–71).   Cellini
was trained as a goldsmith and worked mainly in Rome from 1519
to 1540 as a medalist, that is, doing metal medallions with portraits
in low relief. His skill is evident in the gold *Saltcellar of Francis I*
(Kunsthistorisches Museum, Vienna), finished during a sojourn in
France from 1540 to 1545. It was then that Cellini produced his first
large-scale sculpture, a bronze relief known as *The Nymph of Fontainebleau* (Louvre, Paris), using Mannerist proportions that suggest the
influence of Francesco Primaticcio, Cellini's rival at the court of
Francis I. Cellini's masterpiece was the *Perseus* (1545–54, Loggia dei
Lanzi, Florence), done after his return to Florence. The body of
Perseus is posed without twisting or violent action and shows more
sympathy with Raphael than with Michelangelo. The intricate
details reveal the goldsmith's art, and the only Manneristic elements

are in the sculpture on the base. Cellini's autobiography is a fascinating sourcebook for the Renaissance.

Giovanni da Bologna (Florence, 1529–1608). Giovanni da Bologna grew up in Flanders, traveled to Rome, and settled in Florence about 1556. His *Medici Mercury* (1580, Museo Nazionale, Florence) and *Apollo* (1573–75, Palazzo Vecchio, Florence) are Manneristic in their soft anatomy and effeminate poses. The complex outline of the open forms, the intertwining organization, and the dramatic action forecast seventeenth-century art. Much of Giovanni's work, such as *The Rape of the Sabine Women* (1583, Loggia dei Lanzi, Florence) is more Proto-Baroque than Manneristic. He was the first sculptor since the fifteenth century to produce equestrian statues, but his work in this area is very restrained in style and close to its fifteenth-century prototypes. His activity was restricted to the area of Florence, but his influence was widespread.

JAN.
P.-H.
U. & S.

ARCHITECTURE IN ITALY

The High Renaissance in Italy saw the creation of more effects derived specifically from Roman art. Closer attention was paid to Roman proportions, and walls were treated more as sculpted mass, resulting in stronger contrasts of light and shadow. Further study of Roman art revealed a concern for shaping not only mass but space, and High Renaissance architects turned to the possibilities of using mass to shape space not only inside but outside, between buildings in a group, for more comprehensive schemes of order. Architecture, like painting, strove for the effects of equilibrium and monumental scale that were so evident in the ruins of Roman architecture. Details were used with restraint, to stress the largeness of the forms.

Late Renaissance architecture is often characterized by features comparable to Mannerism in painting and sculpture: unexpected contrasts, deliberately crowded forms, fantastic shapes that suggest plants, animals, or men, and ambiguity in structural functions; a column might be robbed of its supporting role by undercutting its base, and an arch might be designed with its keystone slipping precariously out of place. Proto-Baroque tendencies also began to grow in architecture after 1520. Quiet equilibrium and clarity of parts were sacrificed for powerful focal effects, dramatic contrasts, and dynamic forms, such as concave-convex walls and expanding-contracting spaces. Surfaces were broken up with decorative elements in a great variety of depths.

Donato Bramante (Milan and Rome, 1444–1514).   Bramante turned to architecture only after a beginning in painting. His early buildings are in Milan and include the remodeling of *S. Maria presso S. Satiro* (begun c. 1479), where he used illusionistic perspective relief to make the choir seem deeper, and the choir and dome of *S. Maria delle Grazie* (begun in 1492). The early work often shows a typically northern Italian tendency toward rich surface decoration, but there is already some subordination of details to large framing elements, the sign of bolder, grander systems of proportions. Bramante's mature style developed in Rome after 1500, where he was the leader of High Renaissance architecture. The *Tempietto* at S. Pietro in Montorio (1500–1502), based on the Greco-Roman tholos temple, typifies the High Renaissance interest in central buildings. The peristyle employs the Roman Doric order with triglyphs and metopes from the Greeks (*Fig.* 29, p. 49), and the dome is a heightened version of the low Roman saucer dome seen on the Pantheon (PLATE 15). The wall was treated as a sculptural mass with projecting and receding parts; the light, delicate precision of earlier work has given way to a new monumentality. For the new church of *St. Peter's*, Bramante aimed at the magnificence of mass and space that still could be seen in the ruins of Roman baths. He turned back to the old Roman material, concrete, and drew a plan based on a Greek cross within a square. The arms of the cross were to terminate in apses and be roofed with barrel vaults. The crossing would be covered with a great dome inspired by the Pantheon. Bramante's death put the construction into the hands of a succession of architects, and the present church (*Fig.* 52b) owes its form mainly to three men: Michelangelo, who planned a Greek cross as Bramante had but made the masses bolder and more active; Carlo Maderna, who lengthened one arm to create a basilica plan and designed the façade; and Gianlorenzo Bernini, who planned the frontal square and its enclosing colonnades. Since Maderna and Bernini did their work in the seventeenth century, *St. Peter's* can hardly be considered simply as a Renaissance building. Bramante's plan for the *Belvedere Court*, in the Vatican, was realized somewhat more fully. Here he used massive walls and grand scale to mold the courtyard space into a focal apse. The boldness of mass, space, and scale set the key for High Renaissance architecture.

Fig. 52
JAN.
U. & S. *Michelangelo Buonarroti.*   Michelangelo's first major architectural design, the *Laurentian Library* in Florence (1524), sacrificed the quiet equilibrium and logical clarity favored by Bramante. In the vesti-

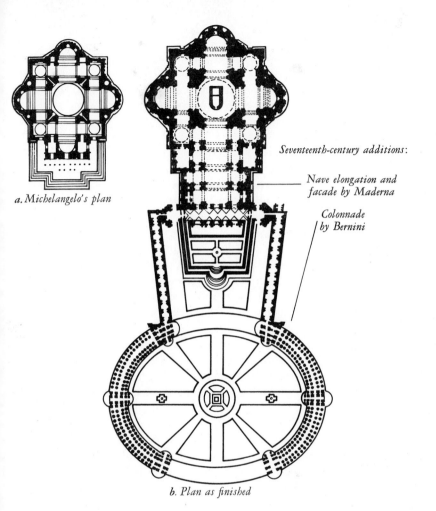

a. Michelangelo's plan

Seventeenth-century additions:

Nave elongation and
facade by Maderna

Colonnade
by Bernini

b. Plan as finished

Figure 52   St. Peter's, Rome

bule of the library, the pilasters have an inverted taper, from small
base to wide top, and engaged columns are denied their supporting
role by being placed on console brackets extending from the wall.
The pilasters, columns, and windows are crowded close together,
and a staircase of expansive curved steps threatens to fill the room
like a flood tide. This dramatic intensity disturbed some of Michelangelo's contemporaries, but it is considered today to be a Manneristic quality. In the 1530's, Michelangelo redesigned the *Campidoglio*,
the Capitoline Hill in Rome. A trapezoidal piazza flanked by two
palaces focuses on the *Palace of the Senators* at the narrow end. The

piazza is filled by an oval pavement that radiates from the ancient equestrian statue of Marcus Aurelius. This dynamic space is enclosed by façades of strongly three-dimensional design, bold value contrasts, and *colossal orders* (columns or pilasters more than one floor high). Michelangelo's plan for *St. Peter's* provided walls of alternating angular and curved projections (*Fig.* 52a), making the form complex to understand, somewhat restless in its undulating movement, and powerful in value contrasts. To avoid weakening and cluttering the great masses of the building, Michelangelo used colossal orders to pull together the levels between base and attic. Such complexity, restlessness, and contrast may be seen as Proto-Baroque elements.

JAN.
U. & S.

Baldassare Peruzzi (Siena and Rome, 1481-1536). Peruzzi was trained in Siena as a painter, but after his arrival in Rome in 1503, he added architectural design to his activities. His reputation eventually gained him the chance to collaborate with Raphael, Jacopo Sansovino, and Michelangelo in planning the church of *S. Giovanni dei Fiorantini*. After 1527, he served as city architect for Siena. Peruzzi's major work, however, is the *Palazzo Massimi* in Rome (begun in 1535), usually cited as an example of Manneristic architecture. The façade bows out in a curve that is gentle at the sides and pronounced in the center. This curving plane is broken dramatically by a deep porch with Doric columns used singly and in pairs to produce complex intervals. The ground floor is sharply divided from the rest of the façade by a projecting molding; the other floors have no horizontal divisions, but the windows of the first floor (above the ground floor) are vertical rectangles that contrast abruptly with the horizontal rectangles of the second- and third-floor windows. The façade contains a number of sudden changes with no smooth transitions or connections between the parts. While the total effect is not disunified, it is strikingly dissonant. Peruzzi succeeded Raphael as architect to *St. Peter's*, but the plans of both men were superseded by others.

JAN.

Raphael Sanzio. Raphael's few architectural designs indicate a debt to Bramante. The façade of Raphael's *Vidoni Palace* (1515-20, Rome) has strong divisions between the floors and a wall design with depth such as we find in Bramante's mature work. Raphael's house in Rome, known to us mainly through a drawing by Palladio, is thought to have been designed by Raphael and built by Bramante, although we are uncertain about the extent of Bramante's contribution to the design. Raphael was one of the architects who succeeded Bramante in the designing of *St. Peter's*, but no significant portions of the finished building are traceable to Raphael's plans. His other designs include the unfinished and defaced *Villa Madama* (1516, Rome), where a treasure of delicate painted ornament and stucco relief is contained within a system of grandly scaled Roman domes, arches, and pilasters. The effect of monumentality and sculpted mass recalls the Roman baths.

Andrea Palladio (Vicenza, 1518–80).   The most influential architect of the second half of the century was Palladio, an admirer of Vitruvius as well as of Alberti, a student of Roman ruins, and a writer on architectural theory. Palladio built in the region of his native Vicenza, but his influence was international, partly because of his *Four Books of Architecture* published in 1570. Many of Palladio's designs seem very conservative in comparison with those of Michelangelo or Peruzzi. A Roman dome and identical Ionic porches grace the simple square block of the *Villa Rotonda* (PLATES 47 and 48). From any one of the façades, designed in obvious axial balance, one quickly comprehends the whole exterior form. Each part has a beginning, a middle, and an end—that is, a base, a main part, and a termination. Minor parts, such as pediments over windows and doors, build toward focal points like the pediments on the porches. Proportions are clearly marked by simple moldings. Inside, an equally severe clarity is felt in the obvious central balance of the plan. Such design fits the concepts of High Renaissance architecture. Touches of Manneristic enigma are found in his *Palazzo Thiene*, however, where windows are framed by columns imprisoned in large blocks and topped by flat arches, the keystones of which break onto a pediment above. And his *Loggia del Capitanio* bristles with crowded surfaces and complex three-dimensional variations, all heralding the Baroque age to come, as does the illusionistic architecture in his *Olympic Theater*, which makes the stage appear deeper than it actually is. One of Palladio's favorite devices, often called the *Palladian motive* (*Fig.* 53), was used frequently in the architecture of the seventeenth and eighteenth centuries.

PLATES 47
and 48
Fig. 53
JAN.
U. & S.

PAINTING IN THE NORTH

By 1520, Manneristic Italian elements had infiltrated the work of many northern artists. We find imaginative constructions of antique

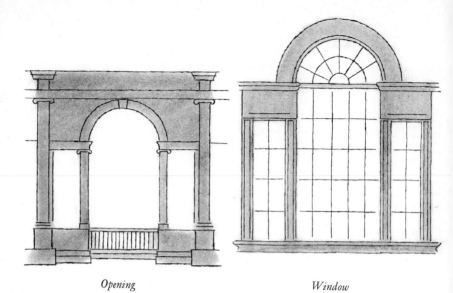

Opening   Window

Figure 53   *The Palladian motive*

architecture, heroic proportions, broad, full masses, and the occasional use of chiaroscuro and sfumato. In Flanders, Antwerp became
a prolific center for paintings in an exaggerated Michelangelesque
style imported from Rome. The intricacy of fifteenth-century work
was retained in another type of Antwerp painting, done for export
to other European countries: small religious scenes containing weird
combinations of Italianate architectural parts and elongated figures
in self-conscious poses and fantastic costumes. The term *Antwerp
Mannerism* is sometimes applied to both trends. Antwerp and Brussels
were both important for landscape and *genre* (scenes from everyday
life) painting. Landscapes were panoramic, with delicate detail and
subtle color; genre subjects, often including still life, tended to have
sharply defined shapes in complex compositions.

In Germany, Austria, and Switzerland, the Medieval love of intricate active line, on the one hand, and flat patterns of clearly
edged shapes, on the other, qualified the ideas that came from Italy.
While religious, mythological, and portrait subjects predominated,
landscape painting was developed by painters working in the vicin-
ity of the Danube River. Their so-called *Danube Style* created visions
of icy peaks, winding valleys, and feathery evergreens or clawlike
branches, all in delicate detail.

Sixteenth-century French painting centered around the Palace of Fontainebleau, where Francis I, Henry II, and Henry IV gathered native and foreign artists. The leaders were Italian Mannerists.

In sixteenth-century England, portraiture was the major interest, and leadership came from foreigners such as Hans Eworth of Flanders and Hans Holbein the Younger of Switzerland. Typical stylistic features are brilliant detail in costume and accessories and containment of details within larger areas with sharply defined edges.

Grünewald (Germany, about 1470/80–1528).   Matthias Neithardt-Gothardt, called Grünewald, may have been born in Würzburg; little is known of his life. Between 1508 and 1514, he was court painter to the Archbishop-Elector and then to the Elector of Mainz. Grünewald's major work is the large, many-paneled *Isenheim Altarpiece* (1509–11, Unterlinden Museum, Colmar, France), commissioned for a church at Isenheim. The central panel depicts the torn body of Jesus on the Cross, flanked by the Madonna, John, Mary Magdalene, and John the Baptist. Like many Germanic Medieval artists, Grünewald preferred harsh, jagged, and twisted forms that are powerfully expressive. His sense of deep space and natural light, however, link him with the Renaissance.

JAN. U. & S.

Albrecht Dürer (Germany, 1471–1528).   Dürer began training as a goldsmith in Nuremberg but turned to painting and studied under Michael Wohlgemuth, a painter of altarpieces in the late Gothic style. Yet Dürer's fame spread more because of his engravings and woodcuts than because of his paintings. The woodcut of *The Four Horsemen of the Apocalypse* (PLATE 49) rivals wood engraving in its detail and demonstrates Dürer's love of intricate, boiling line. In an eruption of seething activity, the Four Horsemen—War, Sickness, Famine, and Death—ride down their helpless victims. This print is part of Dürer's *Apocalypse* series, based on the revelations of St. John. The artist also designed a series on the *Life of Mary* (1504–05) and others on the *Passion of Christ*: the *Great Passion* in woodcuts (1500–10), the *Little Passion* in woodcuts (1509–10), and a *Passion* in prints from metal engravings (1508–12). For the woodcuts, Dürer did the drawings, and expert cutters prepared the wood blocks. The best-known of Dürer's single metal engravings are *Adam and Eve*, *Knight, Death, and the Devil*, and *Melencolia I*, all done between 1504 and 1514 (prints in the Metropolitan Museum of Art in New York and

PLATE 49 JAN. U. & S.

in the Museum of Fine Arts in Boston). Although he traveled to Italy and to the Netherlands, most of Dürer's work retained the gnarled forms and intricate line characteristic of German Medieval art; but his landscape and anatomical studies, his observation of textures and of light effects, his use of aerial and linear perspective, and his interest in portraiture all link him to the Renaissance. In paintings like the *Madonna of the Rose-Garlands* (1506, Prague Museum), Dürer used the chiaroscuro and sfumato that had been developed in Italy; and in the *Four Apostles* (1526, Alte Pinakothek, Munich), he employed simplified massive cascades of drapery that are reminiscent of Italian art.

PLATE 50
JAN.
U. & S.

Hans Holbein the Younger (Switzerland and England, 1497–1543). Holbein grew up in Augsburg and established himself in Basel as a wall painter, woodcut designer, and portraitist, but he found his greatest success as a portrait painter in England at the court of Henry VIII. In *The Ambassadors* (PLATE 50), Renaissance interests are apparent in the depiction of individual facial character and in the array of different forms and textures carefully situated in space and rendered in natural light. Like many Italian painters of the preceding century, he was not above using some illusionistic trickery to display his conquest of the physical world: when the long bony form in the foreground is viewed from the proper angle (hold the page against your face and sight along the length of the object), it becomes a skull. Like many of his contemporaries, Holbein was intrigued by the idea of death, and he designed woodcuts portraying the figure of death coming to claim men of various social levels. His portrait of *Henry VIII* (1540, National Gallery, Rome) is a remarkably frank expression of luxury and crafty cupidity, yet underlying the bulk of the head and costume is the Medieval preference for silhouetted shapes and flat backgrounds. The portrait of *Erasmus* (1523, Louvre, Paris) silhouettes the profile of cap and face against a close background of restrained textile pattern; the quiet concentration of the scholar's personality is expressed along with his individual physical traits.

BLUNT
JAN.
U. & S.

François Clouet (France, 1500?–72). François was trained by his father, Jean Clouet, and succeeded him as painter to Francis I. François Clouet's earliest known portrait, *Pierre Quthe* (1562, Louvre, Paris) shows Italian influence in pose, setting, and massiveness. Later portraits, like *Charles IX* (1570, Kunsthistorisches Museum,

Vienna), belong to an international portrait style of the second half of the sixteenth century, a style that owes much to Holbein as well as to Italian painting. Standard poses and accessories are combined with elaborate costume detail, which is treated rather flatly. Clouet's chalk portraits achieve some of Holbein's conciseness of characterization, and his portrait of *Elizabeth of Austria* (1571, Louvre, Paris) reflects Holbein's ability to depict an orchestral range of textures.

Pieter Bruegel the Elder (Flanders, 1525–69). Although Bruegel may have had a Dutch birthplace, his career is part of Flemish art. After registering with the painters' guild in Antwerp in 1551, he traveled in Italy and then returned to Antwerp to work as an engraver. After 1563, Bruegel lived in Brussels. An intellectual, he was a friend of leading humanists in his region. His paintings suggest a considered philosphical position and often make subtle satirical comment. *The Wedding Feast* (PLATE 51) exemplifies his leadership in genre painting. The rounded, knobby forms, small scale, and jerky movements of the countless little people are in jolting contrast to sixteenth-century Italian style, but they are not an illogical outgrowth of fifteenth-century Flemish art. Although the individual figures are rounded and the space deep, the contrast of local colors and values gives the effect of a complex, richly varied patchwork of flat shapes. Bruegel's best-known works include the *Way to Calvary* (1563, Kunsthistorisches Museum, Vienna) and a series done in 1565 representing the seasons: *The Harvest* (Metropolitan Museum of Art, New York), the *Hunters in the Snow*, the *Dark Day*, and *The Return of the Cattle* (all in the Kunsthistorisches Museum, Vienna).

PLATE 51
JAN.
U. & S.

ARCHITECTURE IN THE NORTH

In northwestern Europe, the Gothic style lingered into the fifteenth and sixteenth centuries. Renaissance details slowly infiltrated Gothic detail until at last the basic structure changed and an integrated Renaissance style was formed. The change occurred first in France, the Renaissance influence coming from northern Italy in the early sixteenth century because of French military campaigns there. The importation of Roman moldings, pilasters, columns, arches, and floral ornament is evident in churches such as *St. Eustache* in Paris and in the châteaux of the Loire Valley, where Medieval forms are given Renaissance decorative details. The Palace of Francis I at *Fontainebleau* demonstrates various phases of Renaissance architecture during his reign and afterward. Of considerable influence were the writings of the Italian Serlio, who was called to France by Francis I in 1540. Typical sixteenth-century northern features are steeply pitched roofs and ornate gables. As in painting, the northerners often applied Italian Renaissance motifs in a spirit of fantasy and profusion that suggests the Middle Ages.

BLUNT
JAN.
U. & S.

Pierre Lescot (France, 1510/15–78).   Lescot came from a family of means and received a broad education. His architectural style was formed before he traveled to Italy, although he undoubtedly knew the standard sourcebooks for Renaissance and antique architecture. Most of Lescot's work has been changed or destroyed. The most complete remaining structure is the façade of the *Square Court of the Louvre* (begun in 1546), in which the major horizontal and vertical dividing lines are broken at intervals, and the smallness of columns and pilasters, along with the ornamental breakup of the surfaces, creates richness rather than the monumental grandeur of Italian design.

BLUNT
JAN.

Philibert de l'Orme (France, 1510/15–70).   De l'Orme worked in Lyons and then studied in Rome for three years before going to Paris, where he eventually became Superintendent of Buildings for Henry II. His two writings on the theory and practice of architecture warn against slavish copying of the Italians and urge the development of French versions of the Doric, Ionic, and Corinthian orders. De l'Orme's solution was a column shaft with bands or ornament to hide the joints of the drums (sections) that were necessary with French stone. Of the few remaining buildings by De l'Orme, one of the most significant is the *frontispiece* (center section consisting of a main entrance with framing elements) for the *Château of Anet* (1547–52). The Roman sequence of Doric, Ionic, and Corinthian orders is used from bottom to top, and the restraint of ornament and largeness of proportions produce somewhat more monumentality than is found in most northern work of the time. The originality of De l'Orme's ornament is evident in the shields at the top of the frontispiece and also in the geometric openwork of the balustrades on top of the entrance gate at Anet.

SCULPTURE IN THE NORTH

In the North, sculpture, like painting and architecture, clung to the Gothic style until well into the sixteenth century. The fifteenth century had nurtured increasing portraiture in tomb sculpture, the use of standard types in faces portrayed in religious and mythological scenes, and both the smoothly flowing drapery common to late Gothic French art and the crackling angular drapery of the Lowlands and the Germanic areas. Sixteenth-century sculpture produced more portraiture, more anatomical detail, and more interest in landscape and deep space in relief compositions. Countries with the tradition of angular drapery and thin figures turned to fuller masses and curving forms. French sculpture was strongly affected by the Italian Manneristic sculptors serving Francis I, and Renaissance concepts were introduced to England after 1512 by the Italian sculptor Pietro Torrigiano.

Peter Vischer the Elder (Germany, about 1460–1529).   Vischer the Elder was one of a large family of Nuremberg sculptors and bronze casters. Of his many tomb reliefs, tomb statues, religious and mythological statues, and portraits, the masterpieces are considered to be the *Tomb of St. Sebald* in Nuremberg and the *Tomb of Maximilian* in Innsbruck. The *Tomb of St. Sebald* (1507–12) is a casket with a complex bronze architectural enclosure decorated with sculpture. The profusion of forms seems Gothic, but individual figures show Renaissance qualities in anatomy and drapery. Although Peter Vischer the Elder did not travel to Italy, he would have known Italian art from drawings and engravings. The life-size bronzes of *Theodoric* and *King Arthur* (1513) from the *Tomb of Maximilian* are extraordinary displays of realistic armor. Vischer the Elder was helped by his five sons, and there is uncertainty about the roles of father and sons in the design of the two tombs.

JAN.

Jean Goujon (France, ?–1567).   Although Goujon was one of the major sculptors of his day, little is known of his life. By 1540, he had developed a Renaissance style based on a knowledge of both Italian and antique art. His *Pietà* from St. Germain l'Auxerrois (1544–45) reveals Manneristic poses and proportions. Both the *Pietà* and the relief panels of nymphs from the *Fontaine des Innocents* (Paris, 1548–49) have a delicate flowing harmony in the thin linear drapery folds which seems peculiar to Goujon's style.

BLUNT
JAN.
U. & S.

References for representative artists

Blunt, Anthony. *Art and Architecture in France: 1500–1700* (Pelican History of Art). Baltimore: Penguin Books, 1953.

BLUNT

DE W.   DeWald, Ernest T. *Italian Painting: 1200–1600*. New York: Holt, Rinehart and Winston, 1961.

GOULD   Gould, Cecil. *An Introduction to Italian Renaissance Painting*. London: Phaidon Press, 1957.

JAN.   Janson, H. W., and D. J. Janson, eds. *Key Monuments of the History of Art: A Visual Survey*. Englewood Cliffs, N.J.: Prentice-Hall; New York: Harry N. Abrams, 1959.

P.-H.   Pope-Hennessy, John. *An Introduction to Italian Sculpture*. New York and London: Phaidon Publishers, 1955–62. 3 vols.

U. & S.   Upjohn, Everard M., and J. P. Sedgwick, Jr. *Highlights: An Illustrated History of Art*. New York: Holt, Rinehart and Winston, 1963.

Suggestions for further study

Anderson, William J. *The Architecture of the Renaissance in Italy*. 4th ed. rev. and enl. London: B. T. Batsford, 1909.

Blunt, Anthony. *Artistic Theory in Italy: 1450–1600*. New York: Oxford University Press, 1956.

Clements, Robert J. *Michelangelo's Theory of Art*. New York: New York University Press, 1961.

DeTolnay, Charles. *Michelangelo*. Princeton, N.J.: Princeton University Press, 1943–1960. 5 vols.

Fischel, Oskar. *Raphael*. Trans. by Bernard Rackham. London: Kegan Paul, Trench, Trubner & Co., 1948. 2 vols.

Freedberg, Sydney J. *Painting of the High Renaissance in Rome and Florence*. Cambridge, Mass.: Harvard University Press, 1961. 2 vols.

Krautheimer, R., and Trude Krautheimer-Hess. *Lorenzo Ghiberti*. Princeton, N.J.: Princeton University Press, 1956.

Lowry, Bates. *Renaissance Architecture* (Great Ages of World Architecture). New York: George Braziller, 1962.

Panofsky, Erwin. *Albrecht Dürer*. 3rd ed. Princeton, N.J.: Princeton University Press, 1948. 2 vols.

———. *Early Netherlandish Painting: Its Origins and Character*. Cambridge, Mass.: Harvard University Press, 1953. 2 vols.

———. *Renaissance and Renascences in Western Art*. Stockholm: Almqvist and Wiksell, 1960.

Vasari, Giorgio. *The Lives of the Painters, Sculptors, and Architects*. Ed. by Betty Burroughs. New York: Simon and Schuster, 1959.

Wittkower, Rudolf. *Architectural Principles in the Age of Humanism*. 3rd rev. ed. London: Alec Tiranti, 1962

Chapter Twelve # BAROQUE AND NEO-CLASSIC ART: 1600-1800

The term Baroque has dual sources and has been used with varied meanings. The Italian word *barocco* grew out of the language of Medieval logic and by the seventeenth and eighteenth centuries had come to mean any system of thought that was contorted, irrational, or untrue; in Portugal, the word *barroco* referred to a rough, imperfect pearl. Both words seem to have been sources for the French word *baroque*, which meant originally an imperfect pearl and by extension something irregular or bizarre, and hence was applied to an artistic style that did not conform to accepted rules of proportions but rather to individual whim. *Baroque* was used by eighteenth-century writers as a disparaging term for such artists as Giovanni Lorenzo Bernini, Francesco Borromini, and Pietro da Cortona and writers who showed an appetite for novelty or untraditional forms. In the nineteenth century, *Baroque* was used more objectively to denote a historical period and certain stylistic characteristics. In the narrowest sense, the period was the seventeenth century, but many writers today prefer the broader dates of 1600 to 1750. Since Baroque qualities persevere in many important works until the end of the eighteenth century, however, we will use the even broader dating of 1600 to 1800.

The art of this period developed a wider variety of styles than we have seen in earlier centuries, and it is necessary to consider a wide range of characteristics under the concept of a Baroque style. Much art of the period dramatized sensory experience. Complexity, contrasts, bold effects of gradation and climax, overwhelming vastness or unexpected intimacy in scale, deliberate lack of clarity, illusionistic effects, and calculated surprise were used together or in various combinations. The roots of such art are found in the work of Michelangelo, in Mannerism, and especially in the Proto-Baroque.

Some art of the Baroque period is distinct enough to merit subsidiary labels. *Rococo* art was an eighteenth-century phase that retained the complexity of the Baroque but sacrificed power for refined elegance and a delicate, light profusion of forms. Within the Baroque period, there was also a major stylistic development that cannot be considered Baroque, but rather a reaction against Baroque and Rococo characteristics—*Neo-Classicism.* Neo-Classic theory, promulgated as early as 1755 by the German writer Johann J. Winckelmann, was stimulated by the discovery and excavation of two Roman cities which had been buried by a volcanic eruption in 79 A.D.: Herculaneum and Pompeii. The increasing importance of Neo-Classic art after 1750 has led some scholars to consider that date as the end of the Baroque period.

The Baroque period was one of bold contrasts within and between ideological systems: a rising bourgeoisie challenged the old aristocracy, Catholicism struggled with Protestantism, and religious truth had to be reconciled with newly discovered scientific truths. Seventeenth-century science replaced the old concept of a finite and fixed universe with a more awesome vision of infinite space and ceaseless motion. The new view was paralleled in art by a preference for vast spaces and the effect of constant movement in much of the architecture, painting, and sculpture of the seventeenth and early eighteenth centuries.

In art, the prevailing system of values was promulgated by the French Royal Academy, established in the seventeenth century to provide acceptable forms and standards. Effective at first, the Academy later acquired a dogmatism and authoritarian control that restricted creativity; consequently, artists rebelled against it many times during the eighteenth and nineteenth centuries. During the eighteenth century, the Academy's preference for Baroque styles was modified to accommodate an increasing enthusiasm for Greco-Roman culture and Neo-Classic art that was encouraged by the growth of archaeology as a science. One aspect of the Baroque which developed during the eighteenth century was an aesthetic concept called the *sublime.* This is articulated in works like Edmund Burke's essay on *The Sublime and Beautiful* (1756), which distinguished between the beautiful and the sublime in that the latter could include the ugly. While the Enlightenment sought to unravel the systematic order of nature and bring it under man's control, the lovers of the sublime gloried in the mysterious power of nature over man. The sublime could be frightening, painful, or astonishing; it stimulated the emotions and the imagination. The concept of the sublime was fostered by Goethe and the *Storm and Stress* movement, which emphasized the struggle of the individual against the world. It was the interest in the sublime that provided a basis for the broad nineteenth-century attitude called *Romanticism*.

The seventeenth century

PAINTING IN ITALY AND SPAIN

Rome was the international center where the major stylistic tendencies of seventeenth-century painting were formed. Early seventeenth-century Italian painting reveals three major currents: a continuation of sixteenth-century Mannerism, a reappraisal, led by Annibale Carracci, of High Renaissance styles, and a pioneering trend led by Michelangelo da Caravaggio. The attitude of Carracci and his followers was conservative in that it sought to incorporate chosen qualities from certain High Renaissance and Late Renaissance paintings. Clarity in parts, in expressive gestures, and in focus was joined to sturdy compositional structure and massively solid, ideal human form. The Carracci group was the strongest camp in Rome at the beginning of the century, and its stylistic character—sometimes called *Restrained Baroque* or *Baroque Classicism*—was influential during the remainder of the century. The Caravaggio trend sacrificed clarity for dramatic light effects and a rich complexity of natural detail. As the seventeenth century unfolded, all three trends contributed to full Baroque painting, which exploited illusionistic perspective, dramatic value contrasts, active, irregular forms suggesting constant change rather than stability, compositions with a minimum of stabilizing vertical and horizontal lines and a maximum of diagonals or undulating curves, and ideal figures of heroic proportions. It attempted to break through the limits of the frame, making the painted scene a more overwhelming experience because it appears to be a part of the spectator's real world.

The seventeenth century saw a more distinct division of painting into different types of subject matter with greater specialization by many artists. During the early seventeenth century, landscape painting in Rome was led by German and Flemish painters and tended to ally itself with either the Carracci or the Caravaggio groups. Later, it was dominated by the French expatriates, Nicolas Poussin and Claude Lorrain, both in the Carracci camp. Genre painting gained popularity with private patrons. The genre painters, called *Bamboccianti*, were led by Dutchmen living in Rome and were scorned by the critics of the Carracci persuasion, partly because of the commonness of genre subjects and partly because many genre painters rejected ideal form for the realistic detail and bold lighting of Caravaggio. Still-life painting was indebted to Dutch and Flemish art for its intense study of details and textures and to Caravaggio for its lighting.

Several other cities in addition to Rome were important for seventeenth-century painting. Venice continued in the tradition of its sixteenth-century masters, and Venetian color was a significant influence throughout the century. In Milan, a tradition of sixteenth-century Mannerism was modified by influences from the art of the Flemish painters Rubens and Van Dyck, both of whom, in turn, owed much to the art of Caravaggio. Genoa enjoyed the stimulus of numerous foreign visitors; the Flemish, especially Rubens, were leaders, and both the Caravaggio and the Carracci trends were represented. Bologna was the stronghold of the Carracci Academy, established before Annibale Carracci went to Rome. Florence, however, played a relatively minor role in seventeenth-century Italian painting.

In Spain, Seville and Madrid were the important centers. Early seventeenth-century painting there shows a strong Caravaggesque influence, and painting from the latter part of the century is marked by the soft fleshiness, undulating forms, and dramatic light of Rubens and Van Dyck.

PLATE 52
JAN.
U. & S.
Domenikos Theotocopoulos, called El Greco (Spain, 1541–1614). El Greco came from Crete to Spain by way of Italy, working first in Venice, where he was impressed by the chiaroscuro of Titian and the active compositions of Tintoretto, and then briefly in Rome, where he became acquainted with the art of Michelangelo. He settled in Toledo in 1576 or 1577. There he received numerous commissions for portraits and religious subjects. The Prado *Crucifixion* (PLATE 52) is typical in the bold value contrasts, the jagged shapes of the highlights, and the elongated figures with undulating contours. The crackling, flamelike energy of the stormy sky, the billowing garments, and the hovering weightless figures all express ecstatic religious experience. His famous landscape, the *View of*

Toledo (1604–14, Metropolitan Museum of Art, New York), acquires the same electric intensity and the same tendency of forms to glow as though illuminated from within. Even El Greco's portraits seem to transcend the physical world; the bodies, the garments, and the large eyes seem to shimmer like a mirage. In style as in actual chronology, El Greco holds a position between Late Renaissance Mannerism and the seventeenth-century Baroque.

Annibale Carracci (Bologna and Rome, 1560–1609). Carracci began his career as a Mannerist but turned more and more to High Renaissance and Proto-Baroque characteristics. His famous frescoes in the *Farnese Gallery* in Rome (1597–1604) depict the loves of the classical gods and employ the heavy muscular figures seen in the art of Michelangelo and in the late work of Raphael. Carracci used an ideal facial type with full cheeks, straight, flat-planed nose, and broad forehead; his work often has strong value contrasts and compressed compositional activity. For color, his idols were first Correggio and later Titian. Annibale Carracci, his brother Agostino, and their cousin Ludovico opened an art school in Bologna before Annibale went to Rome in the 1590's. The teaching was eclectic, urging a combination of the best qualities from various masters. JAN. WITT.

Michelangelo da Caravaggio (Rome and Naples, 1573–1610). While Annibale Carracci and his followers led the conservative tendency in early Baroque painting, Caravaggio represented the more pioneering spirit. He went from Milan to Rome about 1590 and, at first, earned a precarious living by painting still lifes with one or two half-length figures, such as the *Bacchus* (Uffizi Gallery, Florence). These works have remarkably precise details and distinct local colors. About 1597, he received his first commission for a church (Contarelli Chapel, S. Luigi de' Francesi) and from then on his subjects were usually religious. The style that made Caravaggio known is evident in his *Conversion of St. Paul* (1601–02, S. Maria del Populo, Rome). All the traditional accessory figures have been omitted. We see an armored man lying on his back with arms outstretched, while his nervous horse and mystified companion look on. The scene is pushed into the immediate foreground so that we have a startlingly close view. A flesh-and-blood reality is stressed by precise physical detail, yet there seems to be something extraordinary about the event. The strong spotlight that illuminates the objects against the dark back- JAN. U. & S. WITT.

ground can hardly be natural light. Its source is outside the picture
and remains a mystery to us, but its effect is to dramatize rather than
to clarify. The few forms are broken into many parts by the light
and shadow, making the composition complex and hard to comprehend immediately. This use of chiaroscuro to transcend physical
reality is typical of Caravaggio's mature style and forecasts later
Baroque painting. Caravaggio was forced to flee Rome in 1606 after
he had killed a man, and he sojourned in Naples, Malta, Syracuse,
and Messina before his tempestuous career was cut short by malaria.

JAN.
WITT.

Guido Reni (Bologna, Rome, and Naples, 1575–1642).   Reni studied
in Bologna, visited Rome in 1600, and moved to Rome in 1605. He
became a leader among the many painters executing commissions
for Pope Paul V. Reni's conservative style was influenced by the
Carracci, Raphael, Titian, and Correggio. His *Aurora* (1613) in the
Casino Rospigliosi is a processional arrangement with precisely
contoured, clearly spaced, ideal figures and smoothly flowing,
rhythmic drapery lines. After considerable success in Rome, Reni
went to Naples in 1620, where the jealousy of local painters forced
him to flee to Bologna. There, the last period of his life was burdened
by gambling debts, and he was driven to the extensive use of assistants to increase his output. His late work tends toward a superficial
sentimentality.

WITT.

Domenico Zampiere, called Domenichino (Bologna, Rome, and Naples,
1581–1641).   Domenichino was one of the Bolognese artists who
came to join Annibale Carracci in Rome. After the departure of
Caravaggio in 1606, Domenichino became for a time the leading
painter in Rome. His early work is characterized by clearly organized poses and gestures that tend to move back and forth across the
foreground of the composition. Later, he turned to more complex
intertwined forms, as in the paintings for S. Andrea della Valle in
Rome.

JAN.
U. & S.
WITT.

Pietro da Cortona (Florence and Rome, 1596–1669).   Pietro was one
of the major seventeenth-century artists in both painting and architecture. He represented the full Baroque rather than the conservatism of the Carracci school. His best-known painting, the *Glorification of Pope Urban VIII's Reign* (1633–39), in the Barbarini Palace in
Rome, contains boiling masses of clouds and figures soaring up
through an illusionistically painted architectural frame that seems

to surround an opening into the sky. Light and shadow play over the forms, breaking them into complex parts. There is a strong focus upon the central figure, Divine Providence, who points to a group of bees, a symbol taken from the Barbarini coat of arms. The allegorical-mythological scenes at the sides refer to the piety, justice, and prudence of the Barbarini Pope. The elaborate program of symbolism was worked out not by Pietro but by a poet in the Pope's circle. Pietro's dazzling production included frescoes in the Pitti Palace in Florence, in S. Maria in Vallicella in Rome, and in the Palazzo Pamphili in the Piazza Navona in Rome. Unlike some of his contemporaries, Pietro restrained his illusionism to the extent of maintaining a clear division between painted areas and the stucco architectural framework. In his late easel paintings, he stabilized the compositions with firmer vertical and horizontal lines and contained the figures in more rigid groupings, thus rejecting his earlier dynamism.

Diego Velázquez (Seville and Madrid, 1599–1660).   Seville was a center of Caravaggesque influence in Spain. Velázquez's early work, such as *The Water Carrier of Seville* (c. 1619, Wellington Museum, London), sparkles with the brilliant detail and bold value contrasts loved by Caravaggio. At the age of twenty-three, Velázquez was appointed painter to the court, and he painted mainly for the royal family for the remainder of his life. His mature style exploits glazing and impasto to produce rich color and textural effects. *The Maids of Honor* (1656, Prado, Madrid) demonstrates his interest in the play of direct and reflected light on a variety of textures. Close observation reveals that details have been softened by brushwork that is much freer than in his early painting, and the light bathes the forms like a palpable liquid, suggesting a source of nineteenth-century Impressionism. *The Maids of Honor* presents an enigma in compositional arrangement. Velázquez and the Infanta look out toward the spectator, who can see the faces of the king and queen in a mirror on the back wall. Either the spectator is placed in the position of the royal couple or the mirror is reflecting part of the picture the artist is painting.

JAN. U. & S.

SCULPTURE IN ITALY
At the beginning of the seventeenth century, sculpture in Italy was dominated by the style of Giovanni da Bologna, with its Mannerist poses and its Proto-Baroque irregularity and openness of form. Full

Baroque sculpture developed after 1618, when the expression of greatest vitality was sought in poses, multiple and overlapping planes were employed, and deep undercutting produced dramatic shadows planned to provide gradation and climax from a principal point of view. The sculpture of this period often breaks through the boundaries of its architectural frame or extends beyond the private spatial environment suggested by the base, so that the composition seems to inhabit the spectator's world of space and action. Such efforts to overwhelm the spectator or to draw him into the work of art are analogous to the illusionistic perspective or the intimate views employed by the painting of the period. Full Baroque sculpture, like painting, used realistic details, complexity of parts, and lavish color. Varieties of colored stone were combined with bronze, but the leading sculptors did not use colored materials merely to counterfeit nature. Polychrome backgrounds and frames were used for contrast with figures in white stone or bronze. Special lighting, sometimes from hidden windows of colored glass, often intensified dramatic effects. As in painting, there were both full Baroque and conservative trends in sculpture, but the distinction is less clear because the influence of Bernini's full Baroque was so pervasive. After Bernini's death in 1680, the many French sculptors who had come to Rome after the founding of the French Academy in Rome in 1666 made French leadership a significant force in Roman sculpture.

P.-H.
WITT.

Alessandro Algardi (Mantua and Rome, 1595–1654). Algardi studied at the Bologna Academy run by Ludovico Carracci, spent several years in Mantua, and finally settled in Rome, where Domenichino helped him obtain commissions. In portraiture, Algardi's style varies from statically rendered sharp detail, as in the *Bust of Francesco Bracciolini* (shortly after 1630, Victoria and Albert Museum, London), to the equally static but much simplified features and textures in the *Bust of Panfilo* (?) *Pamphili* (after 1644, Palazzo Doria, Rome). In spite of his conservative Bolognese background, Algardi was influenced by the full Baroque art of Bernini. The *Tomb of Innocent XI* (1634–44, St. Peter's) recalls Bernini in the shadows created by deep undercutting, the activity of the drapery, and the twisting poses. Unlike Bernini, Algardi used simple architectural backgrounds and eschewed lavish combinations of materials. One of Algardi's most Baroque compositions is the large relief of *The Meeting of Pope Leo I and Attila* (1646–53, St. Peter's). Here, the violent activity is reinforced by contrasts in values and in diagonal forces;

and the foreground figures extend beyond the architectural frame, invading the space of the spectator and partially effacing the distinction between art and actual life. Nevertheless, Algardi's sculpture generally shows less action, more restrained color, and a clearer distinction between the parts than does the art of Bernini. Algardi's style represents the conservative side of Baroque sculpture.

Giovanni Lorenzo Bernini (Rome, 1598–1680).   Bernini, the greatest genius of the Italian Baroque, considered himself to be primarily a sculptor, although he was also architect, painter, and poet. His prodigious abilities as sculptor were demonstrated by an early series of statues done for Cardinal Scipione Borghese between 1618 and 1625. The series included the *Rape of Proserpina, David*, and *Apollo and Daphne*, all in the Borghese Gallery in Rome. The open twisting poses, the complex silhouettes, and the realistic detail make the works intensely alive. Although the Baroque is the antithesis of the serenity of much Greek sculpture, Bernini's admiration for Greek art is evident in such features as the modified Greek profiles used for Apollo and Daphne. From Bernini's middle years came the *Tomb of Urban VIII* (1628–47, St. Peter's), with its exuberant forms in various marbles and in bronze. In the same period, he did the *Cornaro Chapel*, which includes *The Ecstasy of St. Teresa* in S. Maria della Vittoria (PLATE 57). The members of the Cornaro family are sculpted as spectators in boxes on the side walls, and the space between the walls belongs both to the world of the spectator and to the architectural-sculptural composition, deliberately blurring the limits of the work of art. Multicolored marble and lavish architectural details lead to the climactic group within an undulating, concave-convex frame. White marble figures with rippling garments and lively open silhouettes are suspended in space behind the frame and in front of a dark background. A hidden yellow glass window lights the group from above. Bernini's abilities as an organizer enabled him to assemble a large studio with many helpers to develop his ideas for the commissions that showered upon him, and it is often hard to distinguish between works executed by Bernini and those executed by assistants.

PLATE 57
JAN.
P.-H.
U. & S.
WITT.

ARCHITECTURE IN ITALY AND SPAIN

Baroque architecture ran the gamut from restrained composition to dynamic complexity. Full Baroque architecture tended to exploit painting and sculpture as well as materials of different colors for a compelling total effect with strong focal emphasis. Masses were composed in complex parts and in many layers of depth; the effect of movement was obtained not only by receding and projecting parts, with their concomitant value contrasts, but also by wall surfaces of concave-convex alternations and by rhythmic variations of spaces, walls, piers, columns, and pilasters. Each layer of a multi-layered wall may have a rhythmic scheme of its own, giving a fugue-like complexity to the total effect. Accordingly, architectural space was molded to express dynamic rather than static form. Converging streets, façades, or walls focus upon the façade of a major building. Interiors reveal a preference for oval plans rather than the more static circular plan, and alternations of expanding and contracting spaces urge the spectator to change position constantly in order to experience the architecture completely. Characteristically, neither the masses nor the spaces have easily or simply perceived limits. Light was manipulated for focus; it often alternates with darkened areas or spaces to create movement or gradation and climax.

In Spain, a special style called the *Churrigueresque*, after a family of designers, developed in the second half of the seventeenth century; it is characterized by an extraordinary richness of decoration.

JAN.
U. & S.
WITT.

Pietro da Cortona. Pietro's art exemplifies the Baroque tendency to fuse painting, sculpture, and architecture for a powerful total effect. His first major commission in architecture was the church of *SS. Martina e Luca*, which came in 1634 while he was working on the Barbarini frescoes. He gave movement to the façade in two ways: first, by using a convex center that seems to bulge out in response to the pressure of projecting wings at the sides; and secondly, by creating an elaborate play of light and shadow through the use of many layers of pilasters, engaged columns, and panels. While the exterior uses the Ionic order below and Corinthian above, the interior is restricted to the Ionic. The Greek cross plan is opened up and given flexibility by the interior walls, which are built up in layers of panels, pilasters, and columns that create a rhythm of projecting and receding elements; the wall is transformed into undulating systems of supports. In the vaults and dome, Pietro used quantities of exuberant architectural ornament. A strong unifying feature of the interior is the unusual restriction of color to white. His other church designs include *S. Maria della Pace* and *S. Maria in Via Lata*, both of which exploit deep porches or balconies for

dramatic shadows and bold focus. Broken pediments—pediments
whose frames have been opened up or cut into projecting and receding parts—are important features of Pietro's architecture and of the
Baroque period in general.

Giovanni Lorenzo Bernini.   Bernini's activity as an architect began   JAN.
U. & S.
WITT.
earlier than Pietro da Cortona's. In 1624, Bernini designed the
façade of *S. Bibiana* in Rome. He opened the ground floor with a
three-arched porch and gave climactic emphasis to the upper story
with a deep niche and broken pediment. Although the façade is
composed of simple elements and many plain surfaces, it is developed
in layers of superimposed pilasters which add to the sculptural effect
and to the deep shadows of the porch. Soon Bernini turned to more
complex composition. His *Baldachino for St. Peter's*, the canopy
shelter over the tomb of St. Peter, done between 1624 and 1633,
fuses architecture and sculpture to produce a focal center for the vast
interior. Over twisted, vine-covered columns, he placed a canopy of
sweeping scroll curves flanked by restless angels and topped by an
active receding and projecting entablature. Bernini also designed the
keyhole-shaped piazza in front of St. Peter's. The enclosing colonnades shape the piazza into an expanding and contracting space that
demonstrates the preference for active spaces in Baroque art. Between
1658 and 1670, Bernini designed the small church of *S. Andrea al
Quirinale* in Rome. Concave walls focus upon the convex porch with
its rounded broken pediment and ornate coat of arms. Behind the
porch, actively curving scroll buttresses support the drum, which,
in turn, supports the dome. From the entrance, one looks across the
width of the oval interior to the high altar set deeply within an
architectural frame with a concave, rounded, and broken pediment.
In the opening of the pediment, the twisting figure of S. Andrea is
shown ascending into heaven, the irregular white shape of the saint
contrasting boldly with its surroundings and creating a powerful
focal point. Below, the inset altar receives dramatic illumination
from a hidden window. Elsewhere, the walls are opened to form
deep niches and secondary altar spaces that enrich the lighting and
the spatial effect of the interior. Exuberant architectural ornament
and multicolored marble complicate the wall surfaces, while the
dome depends for its effect upon a contrast of white and gold.
Bernini's fame led to an invitation from Louis XIV in 1665 to come
to Paris to suggest plans for the completion of the Louvre Palace,

but the more restrained taste of the French and the jealousy of French architects led to the rejection of all of Bernini's proposals. His architecture did, however, influence that of French architects.

PLATES
54–56
JAN.
U. & S.
WITT.

Francesco Borromini (Rome, 1599–1667).   From a carver of architectural ornament, he moved to the position of architectural draftsman for Maderna and Bernini and finally became an architect after 1633. His first major work was the dormitory, refectory, and cloisters for the monastery of *S. Carlo alle Quattro Fontane* (PLATES 54–56). He planned the church itself, using undulating walls and a complex rhythmic spacing of wall panels, niches, and engaged columns for the interior. The entablature has projecting and receding parts that accentuate the active design of the wall and tie together the various parts. Overhead, pendentives support an oval dome cut into deep hexagonal, octagonal, and cross shapes. The exterior façade was added by Borromini much later (1665–82) and presents an undulating multilayered composition. In the bottom half, engaged columns connect two floors, divide the façade into concave and convex areas, and support an entablature that unifies the verticals and emphasizes the movement of the whole. Above, the third floor and attic are grouped by columns, the center area becomes an oval *pavilion* (part of a building projecting from the main part and often emphasized with ornament) to provide a transition from the convex area below, and the entablature is broken to embrace a medallion that becomes the climax of the upper section. The moldings, balustrades, sculpture, and niches with small framing columns all add richness and value contrast. The tower and the lantern over the dome repeat the in-and-out movements of the façade. Borromini's other works include *S. Ivo della Sapienza* (begun in 1642, Rome) and much of *S. Agnese in Piazza Navona* (1653–63, Rome), a church that had been started by Girolamo Rainaldi and his son Carlo. Borromini frequently used surprising combinations of curves and angles to produce directional forces. His inventive and unorthodox approach led him to squeeze proportions and thus produce tensions, to create sudden contrasts in shapes and directions, and to provide rapid variations on thematic forms. The source of some of these qualities is found in Mannerist architecture of the preceding century. Bernini and his followers felt that Borromini went too far, and there was antagonism between these two leaders in full Baroque architecture.

PAINTING IN THE NORTH

Seventeenth-century painting in the North was influenced by Italian art, since many northern artists studied in Italy. For French painting, Caravaggesque lighting and the realism of Bamboccianti subject matter were important during the first half of the century. A restrained style, derived from the Carracci, but emboldened by Caravaggesque lighting, was brought to France when the Frenchman Simon Vouet returned to Paris from Rome in 1627 and acquired a large following. One of his pupils, Charles Lebrun, became director of the French Royal Academy of Painting and Sculpture in 1663. The records of the Academy meetings reveal a conflict between advocates of the restrained Baroque and those of the full Baroque; as in Italy, the hero of the conservative attitude was Poussin, while the idol of the full Baroque was Rubens.

In Holland, the prevalence of Protestantism limited the demand for religious subjects, but the merchant class provided a market for portraits, landscapes, cityscapes, interiors, genre painting, and still life. A number of Dutchmen returned from Rome to Utrecht and created a center of Caravaggesque painting that reached a height about 1620. In the 1640's, more Caravaggesque influence in the form of Bamboccianti painting emanated from Haarlem. There were both Italianate and Flemish strains in seventeenth-century Dutch landscape painting; the first stemmed from Annibale Carracci, Claude Lorrain, and the German Adam Elsheimer, and the second came from the tradition of the Flemish painters Joachim Patinir and Pieter Bruegel. Low horizons and vast cloudy skies are typical of Dutch landscape painting. Still life tends toward lavish displays of colors, textures, and detail in foods and utensils or toward prodigious bouquets of flowers. Sensory experience is dramatized in such work by the intensity and luxury of shapes, colors, textures, and light effects. Flanders also developed outstanding still-life and genre painting, but the prevailing Roman Catholic religion encouraged religious subjects. In Holland, the major painter of the century was Rembrandt; in Flanders, Rubens dominated.

English seventeenth-century painting was dominated by foreigners, particularly Rubens and his pupil, Van Dyck. German and Austrian painting of the period reveals no school of real national character; there was considerable dependence upon Italy and Flanders.

PLATE 53
JAN.
U. & S. *Peter Paul Rubens* (Flanders, 1577–1640). Rubens, the leading Flemish painter of the seventeenth century, received a broad classical education and was accepted as master painter by the Antwerp Guild in 1598. In 1600, he traveled to Italy and for eight years served the Duke of Mantua as both painter and diplomat. In this capacity, he brought gifts—including many of his own paintings—to King Philip III in Spain. Spanish painting was widely influenced by the Rubens paintings that became part of the royal collections. Rubens was active also in Florence and in Rome, where he copied works by Michelangelo, Caravaggio, and others. By 1608, he was reestablished in Antwerp and was soon appointed court painter to Archduke Albert and the Archduchess Isabella. Rubens' early painting, particularly before 1620, included some relatively quiet compositions, but the majority of his work shows a remarkable assimilation of the violent action and dazzling light of Tintoretto, the massive figures of Michelangelo, the spotlighting of Caravaggio, and the warm color of Venetian painting. The *Coup de Lance* (PLATE 53) employs the heroic proportions, the fleshy figures, the dynamic opposition of diagonal forces, the activity, and the intimate view that are characteristic of his Baroque style. Contours tend to twist and undulate; faces tend to have large eyes, delicate flaring nostrils, and small Cupid's-bow mouths; hands and feet are small and tapering. As his style developed, Rubens used loose, fluid brushwork and paint textures ranging from heavy impasto to delicate transparent glazes. His international renown brought him many students and a number of large commissions, including the series of allegorical compositions depicting the *Life of Marie de' Medici* (1620's, Louvre, Paris). Many assistants were necessary, but Rubens' letters to patrons indicate clearly which paintings of a given group were done by his own hand and which were done mainly by helpers. His well-organized workshop made possible an enormous productivity in spite of Rubens' time-consuming but historically important diplomatic missions to England and to Spain.

Frans Hals (Holland, 1580–1666). Hals was born in Antwerp but is considered to be Dutch because he made his career as a portrait painter in Haarlem. His Bohemian life and huge family made him the subject of constant law suits for debt and, in his later years, a recipient of assistance from the paupers' fund. His many commissions commanded low prices, partly because there was a limited appreciation of his increasingly loose brushwork, which suggested rather than delineated details. Hals painted directly without preliminary drawings, and the effortless spontaneity of his brush adds liveliness to many of his subjects. The *Banquet of the Officers of St. George* (1616, Frans Hals Museum, Haarlem) exemplifies the bold color of his early work. Its casual grouping, active poses, and sweeping diagonal forms helped to loosen up the traditionally rigid compositions in Dutch group portraits and prepare the way for Rembrandt's *Night Watch*. Unlike Rembrandt, Hals was careful in giving almost equal illumination to each face in his group portraits. In spite of his bold modeling, Hals's impasto bravura seems flat compared with the deep glazes and luminous color in the art of Rembrandt. Hals's famous *Laughing Cavalier* (1624, Wallace Collection, London) is painted with considerable detail; his later paintings, such as the *Women Guardians of the Haarlem Almshouse* (1664, Frans Hals Museum, Haarlem), use more and more of the shorthand brushwork but become more reserved in color and more contemplative in mood. These characteristics are partly due to the changing taste of the time, but they may also reflect the changing attitude of Hals, for whom old age brought increasing troubles and fewer commissions.

Nicolas Poussin (France and Rome, 1593/4–1665). From a peasant village in Normandy, Poussin traveled to Rouen and then to Paris, seeking instruction in art. In 1624, he carried a Mannerist style with him to Rome, where he worked in the studio of Domenichino. Poussin apparently disliked the large scale required by most major commissions; his paintings are relatively small, and he depended upon a small group of private patrons. His subjects are usually religious, allegorical, or mythological, but the landscape settings often dwarf such subject matter. His early works, such as *The Inspiration of the Poet* (c. 1628–29, Louvre, Paris), reveal the influence of Titian and Veronese. Later, his composition became more formal, with a stable structure of vertical and horizontal elements and an alignment of the main objects with the picture plane. For example, in his *Orpheus and Eurydice* (PLATE 58), the groups of trees, the hills, the buildings, and the river are all parallel to each other and to the surface of the painting. Gradation and climax are provided by lighting and by bright color in the foreground figures. Poussin believed that the spectator should read the gestures and symbols in the painting and that the content should be expressed logically and clearly by effective gestures and composition. Painting was to appeal to the mind more than to the senses. Poussin's method consisted in making a

PLATE 58
BLUNT
JAN.
U. & S.

rough sketch of the subject and then setting up the composition with little wax figures and linen drapery in a stagelike box in which lighting could easily be controlled. Changes were made with the figures and lighting until the composition was decided upon. Poussin said that he did not paint directly from live models because he wanted to preserve idealism in the forms. The sources for his concepts of ideal form were Raphael, Raphael's follower Giulio Romano, Annibale Carracci, and Greek and Roman sculpture. With the exception of a sojourn in Paris between 1640 and 1642, Poussin made his career in Rome. His work exemplifies the conservative Baroque that started with the Carracci School. His painting was an important source for artistic theory as taught in the French Royal Academy from the mid-seventeenth century until the French Revolution.

BLUNT
JAN.
U. & S.
WITT.

Claude Lorrain (France and Rome, 1600–82).   Claude of Lorraine or Claude Gellée is often linked with Poussin, not only because they were contemporary French expatriates in Italy but also because they both represent the conservative Baroque. By 1627, Claude had established himself permanently in Rome. His style owed much to German and Flemish landscape painters who had settled there. Landscapes and seascapes provided the real subjects for his paintings; their Christian or mythological subjects were, even more than in Poussin's painting, merely *staffage*—that is, an intellectual or literary excuse for the landscape and a means of giving scale or providing nostalgia for the past. Claude's major interest was in the poetic qualities of landscapes or seaports seen in late afternoon light. Unlike Poussin's horizontally anchored planes with sharp edges and clear spatial relations, Claude's landscapes suggest no such flat stage-platform base but glide easily along rolling hills and meadows, while the trees shimmer in the breeze and present soft lacy silhouettes against the light. A composition like his *Ermina and the Shepherds* (1666, Collection of the Earl of Leicester, Holkham, Norfolk) is less closed in depth than those of Poussin; the vistas give the effect of infinite space. The seaport scenes, such as *The Embarkation of St. Ursula* (1641, National Gallery, London), often have the spectator looking directly into a setting sun that dissolves the details of architecture and ships on either side. The great demand for Claude's work encouraged forgery, and he was obliged to make a book of drawings, the *Liber Veritatis*, that recorded all his authentic paintings.

Rembrandt van Rijn (Holland, 1606-69).   Rembrandt, the son of a   COLOR
Leiden miller, studied in Leiden and Amsterdam with minor masters.   PLATE 2
Although he admired Italian art and eventually collected a number   JAN.
of Italian works, he never traveled to Italy. His early style, exempli-   U. & S.
fied in *The Blinding of Samson* (1636, Staedel Institute, Frankfort),
reveals the influence of Caravaggio's lighting, perhaps by way of the
Utrecht painters. He broke with the conventionally even lighting
and formal grouping of Dutch group portraits; his celebrated *Night
Watch* (1642, Rijksmuseum, Amsterdam) subordinates some of the
company of Captain Frans Banning Cocq to shadowed areas. The
dramatic value contrasts, the glowing color, the subtle organization
of the active figures into the form of an "M" extending into depth,
and the rich variety of personality all help make this painting the
outstanding Baroque group portrait in the North. From the 1640's
on, Rembrandt's art acquired a deeper gentleness; the drama became
less physical and more psychological. The *Supper at Emmaus* (COLOR
PLATE 2) has the deeper chiaroscuro, the softer light, the suppression
of local color, the reduction of physical movement, and the intensely felt human relationships that characterize his later work.
Detail has been sacrificed to the fluidity of heavy impasto in the
lighted areas and deep glazes in the shadows. The period from 1650
until 1669 produced many of Rembrandt's major etchings. The
velvet-rich blacks—often reinforced with drypoint—and the quick,
telling characterization of the lines have made these works masterpieces in the history of printmaking. Although portraits were an
important source of income for him, he painted an unusually large
number of religious subjects, many of them done, like his self-
portraits, for his own satisfaction. Like Caravaggio, but unlike
Rubens, Rembrandt visualized Biblical events in terms of common
people with unheroic proportions and individual features, although
he did occasionally use exotic costumes for accessories. Rembrandt's
landscape paintings make striking use of stormy skies, luminous
areas of foliage, dramatic cloud shadows, and ruined architecture.
Rembrandt had acquired several students and some wealth, but the
death of his wife in 1642 was the beginning of a period of poor
financial management that finally drove him to bankruptcy. His last
years were probably unhappy ones, for his fame had been eclipsed in
his own country by the successes of younger men.

Jan Vermeer (Holland, 1632-75).   Little is known about the life of   JAN.
the greatest of the Dutch painters of interiors. He made a precarious   U. & S.

living as painter and picture dealer and left his widow with a large family and numerous debts. Only thirty-six paintings are now attributed to him, but his limited output seems to have found a ready market. Although Vermeer was a genre painter, he is more readily thought of as a painter of interiors because the quiet human activity in his pictures is usually subordinated to the structure of the composition and to the play of light on colors and textures. As in a landscape by Poussin, most of the larger objects in a Vermeer interior are parallel to the picture plane, and we experience the picture space in a measured progression from one parallel to another. Occasionally, diagonal forms accelerate the transitions between the parts. The shapes also build a system of interlocking rectangles whose sides are often aligned with the sides of the painting, further emphasizing the static serenity of an all-pervasive order. In such works as *The Artist in His Studio* (c. 1666, Kunsthistorisches Museum, Vienna), the underlying geometry is given relief by the curves and irregular forms of people and drapery. Light and shadow are used to group objects and to subordinate large areas of a composition in order to focus upon others; light seems to wash the spaces and reveal textures and colors with gentle softness. This effect comes from the pearl-like globules of paint and from the softening of the shadow areas with reflected light.

SCULPTURE IN THE NORTH

France was the major center of seventeenth-century sculpture in the North. During the first half of the century, however, France was represented by men of competence rather than genius. Style in portraiture tended toward much heavy detail, while allegorical, mythological, and religious subjects received some idealization of form. Objects were clearly defined, and drapery was simpler and less active than in Italian full Baroque work. Essentially, the French sculptors were conservative. The second half of the century saw more inspired sculpture, much of it done under the auspices of the French Royal Academy for the enormous *Palace* at Versailles. Bernini was a major influence, but the restraint of French sculptors tempered their borrowings from Italy.

BLUNT
JAN.
U. & S.

Pierre Puget (France, 1620–94).   Puget worked under Pietro da Cortona on the rooms of the Pitti Palace in Florence and then did paintings and designed decorations for warships in Marseilles and

Toulon. His statues of *St. Sebastian* (c. 1661–65, S. Maria di Cari-
gnano, Genoa) and *Milo of Cortona* (1671–83, Louvre, Paris) display
the torsion and opposition of diagonals seen in Bernini's work.
Puget's relief depicting *Alexander and Diogenes* (1671–93, Louvre,
Paris) crackles with abrupt changes of direction, and the directional
forces are emphasized by deep undercutting that produces strong
shadows. Although Puget's sculpture is more restrained than much
Italian work, he was too violent in his compositions and in his
personality to suit the French leaders of taste. Animosity between
Puget and the powerful minister Colbert kept the sculptor from
obtaining commissions for the *Palace* at Versailles.

François Girardon (France, 1628–1715).   In contrast to Puget, BLUNT
Girardon subscribed to the taste and theory of the French Academy, JAN.
worked closely with the director Lebrun, and established his career
with the commissions for Versailles. Girardon was very interested
in ancient sculpture; his famous *Apollo Tended by the Nymphs* (1666,
Versailles) shows the influence of Greek art in the profiles of the
faces, the serene poses, and the relatively calm drapery. The original
arrangement of the statues was more symmetrical than the present
one. Similarly quiet contours and smooth transitions from part to
part can be seen in Girardon's *Tomb of Richelieu* (1675–77, Sorbonne,
Paris). Girardon represents the restrained Baroque attitude that
was shared by such artists as Poussin.

ARCHITECTURE IN THE NORTH

France, like Italy, developed city planning as an adjunct to seventeenth-century architecture. Parisian squares and circular places
utilized converging avenues for focal emphasis upon a special building. The triumph of the age was Versailles, the court palace of
Louis XIV, where vast gardens and enormous buildings collaborate
in an all-encompassing geometric plan. French churches of the period
show the restraint, as well as the Italian influence, seen in French
sculpture. A special French species of town house evolved in the
hôtel particulier, a central structure which had side wings embracing
a court with an entry gate facing the street.

   English architecture had imported Renaissance details in the sixteenth century, but not until the seventeenth century did the total
effect of plan, structure, and detail become Renaissance in attitude,
largely through the influence of the sixteenth-century Italian

Andrea Palladio. The great fire of London in 1666 allowed a fresh start to city planning and architecture. More squares were created, helping to open up the dense city. The rebuilding of churches provided England's first Baroque architecture; the style was influenced mainly by Italy but showed considerable restraint.

In the Low Countries, Holland was inspired by Palladio, but Flanders produced an architecture of strident Italianate Baroque with a special Flemish insistence upon fantastically ornate gables.

In German and Austrian architecture, Italy provided the models for churches, while Versailles was the model for palaces. Italian architects were frequently employed, and on several occasions German and Austrian architects were sent to Paris to have their plans approved by leading French architects.

JAN.
SUM.
U. & S.

Inigo Jones (England, 1573-1652). We know little of Jones's background, but he traveled in Italy, made a reputation in England as a designer of stage sets, accompanied the Earl of Arundel on a European trip, and was appointed to the highest architectural office in England—Surveyor of the King's Works. It was Jones who finally brought to England a classical attitude in the total design of a building. The austere formality of his *Queen's House* (1616-35, Greenwich) depends upon stark simplicity of plan and elevation, precise symmetry, and a crystalline clarity in all the parts. The rigid equilibrium of quiet, unbroken lines and plain wall surfaces suggests the work of Palladio, Jones's major source. Jones's best-known building, the *Banqueting Hall* at Whitehall Palace (1619-22, London), has slightly more activity in its three-dimensional variation and in decorative elements. His first ecclesiastical building was the *Queen's Chapel*, St. James Palace (1623-27, London), where the flat wall surfaces of a rectangular box are broken only by severely simple window frames and limited by sharply defined *quoins* (especially bold stonework used to emphasize the corners of a building), corbeled cornices, and a corbeled pediment. A Palladian window is used at the east end. Jones's architecture inspired a number of followers and was the major source for the eighteenth-century architectural trend in England called the Palladian movement.

PLATES
60-62
BLUNT
U. & S.

François Mansart (France, 1598-1666). Mansart was one of the most competent French architects of the seventeenth century, but his independence and his difficult disposition apparently limited the number of his commissions. Just as Inigo Jones set the key for the general conservatism of English architecture, so Mansart represents the restraint of French designers. His *new wing* for the *Château at Blois* (1635–38) has a court façade with very restricted decoration and modest variation in depth, but the powerful focus on the entrance is typical of the Baroque. Curving colonnades fill in the corners and lead our attention to the pavilion, where pilasters, engaged columns, a decorated pediment, a shield, and breaks in the cornice and in the roof levels all provide an effect of gradation and climax for the entrance. He used the classic succession of orders, from Doric below to Corinthian above. The most complete surviving work by Mansart is the *Château of Maisons* (1642–51), which consists of a rectangular main structure flanked by two freestanding wings at the sides. The main building, like the wing at Blois, has very clear vertical and horizontal lines and a relatively shallow buildup of layered masses around the frontispiece. As at Blois, the classic succession of orders was used. Inside, the crisply carved ornament is unified by the exclusive use of white stone, without color or gilt paint. Mansart also planned the *Val-de-Grâce* (PLATES 60–62) in Paris and was responsible for construction up to the second story of the façade and up to the vaults of the nave. The second story, the vaults, and the dome were completed by Jacques Lemercier. The plan is that of a Latin cross basilica with a chapel added to the rear of the apse, all quite simple and stable compared to plans by an Italian like Borromini. The nave is divided from the side aisles by Roman arches and piers with Corinthian pilasters; the entablature is simple, and the richest ornamentation is saved for the vaulting. On the exterior, the façade employs the Corinthian order. On the first level, the façade moves from corner pilasters to engaged columns and then to the freestanding columns of the porch. Above, Lemercier reversed the effect by making the engaged columns at the sides come forward while the center pulls back, taking the horizontal molding of the upper pediment with it. The large scroll buttresses at the sides of the upper level are indebted to Italian architecture.

Louis Le Vau (France, 1612–70).   Little is known of Le Vau's life. He was probably trained by his father, who was a master mason. Le Vau began with commissions for wealthy financiers and was brought to the attention of the court by the château *Vaux-le-Vicomte* (1657–61), which he built for Fouquet, the minister of finance. Com-

BLUNT
U. & S.

pared with Italian architecture of the period, Vaux-le-Vicomte reveals the restraint common to much seventeenth-century French art. Le Vau used strong contrasts on the exterior and ornate decor—including murals by Lebrun—within. The magnificence of Vaux-le-Vicomte is said to have aroused the jealousy of the king, hastened the fall of Fouquet, and gained royal favor for Le Vau. Louis XIV chose Le Vau to design the Palace of Versailles, while André Le Nôtre planned the gardens, which extend the orderly geometry of the architecture into the vastness of nature. The exterior of Le Vau's building has clearly defined masses, restricted sculptural decoration, and vast scale; the interior was lavishly decorated with stucco and paintings designed by Lebrun and executed by a small army of craftsmen. The grandeur of Versailles inspired imitations in other European monarchies and even influenced the original street plan for Washington, D.C.

JAN.
SUM.
U. & S.

Sir Christopher Wren (England, 1632–1723). Wren started his remarkable career as an astronomer and inventer of practical devices of all kinds. His first architectural work of significance was the *Sheldonian Theater at Oxford* (1662–63), a design inspired by the Roman *Theater of Marcellus* as described in one of Serlio's books. In 1665, Wren traveled in France and visited many major works of architecture. His great opportunity came the following year when the London fire destroyed eighty-seven parish churches. As one of the Commissioners for Rebuilding the City of London, and as Surveyor-General of the Royal Works, Wren designed many of the new churches. Like many of the architects of his day, Wren learned much from the designs of the ancient Roman Vitruvius and was aware of seventeenth-century Italian architecture. Nevertheless, the London churches show considerable originality. Their most Baroque qualities are found in the steeples. The best-known example of Wren's work is *St. Paul's Cathedral* (1666–1717), which developed from an early design in central form to a Latin cross basilica with Baroque complexity in the many-layered façades. The west façade employs deep porches for dramatic shadow and lavishly ornamented towers that recall Borromini's *S. Agnese in Piazza Navona.* A deep colonnade provides sharp value contrasts at the base of the drum from which springs the great dome. Inside, colors and materials are varied, but the basic form of the interior space is relatively simple. This most Baroque of Wren's churches seems conservative in comparison with full Baroque design in Italy. Wren's *Royal Hospital at Chelsea* (1682–89) and his designs for *Hampton Court Palace* (1682–89) reveal even more clearly his essential reserve.

The eighteenth century

PAINTING IN THE NORTH

French painting continued to be dominated by the Royal Academy until the time of the Revolution. The older Academy of St. Luke, which had grown out of the guild system, was held down to a secondary role. No painter could paint and sell pictures unless he was a member of one of these academies. The Royal Academy maintained a monopoly on exhibitions; its *Salon*, a periodic exhibition named for its location (after 1725) in the Salon Carré of the Louvre, had royal sanction. Until 1748, all members could exhibit in the Salon; after that time, a jury of academicians screened submitted works. With the aid of the government, the Academy suppressed attempts by other organizations to sponsor painting exhibitions. Academic teaching used various methods, from apprenticeship under a master to copying accepted masterpieces from sixteenth-, seventeenth-, and eighteenth-century painters, drawing from plaster casts of Greek and Roman sculpture, and drawing from live models. Prizes were given for the best work in anatomy, perspective, facial expression, and other categories. The most important prize was the *Prix de Rome*, which since its establishment in the seventeenth century has given selected students the opportunity to study at the French Academy in Rome. Leading academicians gave periodic discourses on theory and principle. A hierarchy was established for subject matter; history painting—religious, historical, allegorical, or mythological subjects—was the highest category, and only painters of history could become professors. Following history painting came portraiture, genre painting, landscape (including seascapes and city views), animal painting, and still life. Early in the century, another category, that of the *fête champêtre* (an elegant outdoor entertainment), was added to sanction the popularity of Watteau's work. The style of history painting owed much to Rubens and to sixteenth- and seventeenth-century Italian masters. The conflict between *Poussinistes* and *Rubénistes* in the Academy was won by the *Rubénistes* early in the century, but the full Baroque style gave way increasingly to the lighter colors and playful intricacy of the Rococo. Mythological subjects became more intimate than heroic, more gay than dignified. Genre painting gained in popularity during the period of Louis XV and often shows Rococo characteristics. Portraiture became more casual and livelier in pose and expression. Pastel portraits enjoyed great vogue. Landscape was often combined with battle scenes or with ruins, the style varying from repetitive formulas to the freshness of direct observation from nature. The major source for landscape, animal painting, and still life was seventeenth-century painting in Holland and Flanders. The reign of Louis XVI and the revolutionary period that followed reemphasized history painting and Neo-Classic style. Simplicity in accessories, clarity of contours, and rigid organization supplanted the billowing power of the Baroque and the tinkling delicacy of the Rococo.

In England, a royal academy was not founded until 1768. Although its first president, Sir Joshua Reynolds, stressed in his famous discourses the superiority of history painting, he and other English painters found portraiture to be more rewarding financially. The glory of eighteenth-century English painting is its portraiture, ranging from heroic poses, idealized faces, and pompous settings to casual poses, candidly recorded faces, and unassuming environments. Genre painting and satire were also significant in England, and style ran the gamut from caricature to tentative and humble faithfulness to natural detail. Although seventeenth-century Dutch landscape and seventeenth- and eighteenth-century Italian landscape were popular with English collectors, English painters of landscape were not given great encouragement at home. Despite this situation, Englishmen produced some outstanding landscape painting that varied from the delicate detail of John Crome's watercolors to the broadly brushed, sparkling watercolors of Alexander Cozens, and from the deliberate rendering of Richard Wilson's ideal landscape to the dazzling brushwork of the early Constable. In the realm of animal painting, George Stubb's carefully rendered horses appealed to a major interest of the aristocracy. Neither Rococo nor Neo-Classic stylistic qualities were developed in England as fully as on the Continent.

In German regions during the eighteenth century, the northern areas reveal a dependence upon Holland and France; southern areas were inspired by Italy. Imported painters strengthened such influence, but a vigorous native Rococo style developed in the religious paintings of the German C. D. Asam and in the work of the Austrian

Franz Anton Maulbertsch. German painters living abroad, such as Anton Raffael Mengs and Asmus Carstens, were leaders in developing Neo-Classic art.

Antoine Watteau (France, 1684–1721).   Of the three major eighteenth-century French painters whose art represents the Rococo style, Watteau is the earliest. He came from the Franco-Flemish city of Valenciennes to Paris, where he found an international market for his work, partly through the help of several wealthy patrons. His painting was so successful that, in order to accommodate it, the French Academy created a new category of subject matter: the *fête champêtre*. Although Watteau painted religious works, portraits, and scenes with soldiers, the majority of his works depict characters or scenes from theatrical comedy or from the French aristocracy at leisure. His procedure was to paint directly on the canvas without elaborate preparatory drawings, but he composed by selecting figures from a large collection of sketches made from life. Thus his compositions are not so much records of a particular event as they are imaginative constructions. The famous *Embarkation for Cythera* (PLATE 59) is derived from a play and depicts a gay company about to sail for the legendary island of love. The painting is typical of Watteau in its soft, dreamlike landscape, luxurious costumes, dainty slender figures, and rich silvery colors. Its seeming casualness in composition and its softness in form contrast sharply with the paintings of Poussin. Indeed, Watteau's acceptance in the French Academy represents one of the triumphs of the *Rubénistes*. Watteau's idol was Rubens; the delicate pointed noses, small mouths, and tapering hands of Rubens' people reappear with slender bodies and more restrained sensuality in the art of the Frenchman. Watteau also learned from the Rubenesque painters in Paris and from the art of sixteenth-century Venice. He chose not to portray important historical actions; instead he depended upon the spectator's associations or emotional responses to lyrical variations on the themes of theatrical entertainment and a leisurely aristocracy in friendly natural settings. Sometimes it is difficult to draw a distinction between the actor and the aristocrat, between the theater and the *fête champêtre*.

PLATE 59
FOSCA
JAN.
U. & S.

William Hogarth (England, 1697–1764).   The famous eighteenth-century satirist began as an apprentice to a silver-plate engraver but soon turned to painting and produced a number of *conversation pieces*—group portraits posed as an informal gathering with a sug-

FOSCA
JAN.
U. & S.
WAT.

gestion of typical activity or anecdote. In 1731, Hogarth painted six works that were engraved and distributed the following year under the general title of *The Harlot's Progress*. This moralizing story of the downfall of a young woman in the big city was immediately successful and inspired a number of unauthorized copies. Hogarth then promoted the Copyright Act for Engravers (1735) to secure his market and proceeded to make engravings of a similar series, *The Rake's Progress*, eight scenes portraying the dissolution of a young man. Such work was far more lucrative than the history painting that was Hogarth's ambition; yet the artist did occasional history paintings and continued with portraiture while he produced paintings for the engravings that were both moralizing and satirical. His satire aimed at all classes, striking sometimes at topical events, sometimes at specific facets of British society, and sometimes at universal human weaknesses. His remarkable visual memory was aided by a mnemonic system that he had devised for remembering the positions and gestures of principal characters in a witnessed event. Hogarth formed his own St. Martin's Lane Academy for teaching art and became a governor of the Foundling Hospital, where he arranged for picture exhibitions; he also found time to write a theoretical treatise, *The Analysis of Beauty* (1753), urging the aesthetic values of asymmetry, intricacy, and the serpentine line. Although the proportions, intricacy, and frequent intimacy of his paintings link him with the Rococo, he was indebted to seventeenth-century Dutch genre painting and to the fifteenth- and sixteenth-century art of Bosch and of Bruegel the Elder. Hogarth was the predecessor of such satirical artists as Goya and Daumier.

FOSCA
JAN.

Jean-Baptiste Siméon Chardin (France, 1699–1779).   After working as an assistant to the painter Noël Coypel, Chardin was accepted by the Royal Academy in 1728 as a "genre painter of animals and fruit." In the tradition of Dutch seventeenth-century genre and still life, he painted works such as *The Mother's Advice* (1739, Collection of the Prince of Liechtenstein) and *Clay Pipes and Earthenware Jug* (undated, Louvre, Paris). His art is outstanding in its subtlety of color, light, and texture. By 1740, Chardin enjoyed critical acclaim and an international demand for his paintings as well as for the engravings done after them. He spent considerable time copying his own works to satisfy collectors. By 1755, he was treasurer of the Academy and in charge of hanging exhibits. In his later years, when public favor had shifted from his still-life painting to the more moralizing and anecdotal art of others, Chardin turned to portraiture in pastels, where the cross-hatching of color used in his oils is amplified.

François Boucher (France, 1703–70).   Boucher was the second major representative of French Rococo art. He was admitted to the Academy in 1734 and became first painter to King Louis XV in 1765. As a favorite of Madame de Pompadour, the mistress of the king, Boucher received many commissions, was made director of the Gobelins Tapestry Works, and designed tapestries as well as figures for the Royal Porcelain Factory at Sèvres. Boucher's subjects ranged from the religious to landscape, but the most frequent are allegory and mythology presented with dainty sensual figures in powder-puff landscapes that suggest stage settings. A typical example is the *Captive Cupid* (1754, Wallace Collection, London). The pretty faces, coy poses, sweet colors, delicate accessories, and lilting lines all relate Boucher to the Rococo decorations of his early master, François Lemoyne. To appreciate such art, we must not demand depth or monumentality; Boucher's graceful facility was employed to create a pleasant, carefree world that ignores the problems of a more physically real existence.

FOSCA
U. & S.

Thomas Gainsborough (England, 1727–88).   Gainsborough started as an assistant to an engraver who had studied under Boucher. As a restorer of seventeenth-century Dutch landscape paintings, Gainsborough acquired a love for landscape but found portraiture more profitable. His landscapes vary from the earthy Dutch details of *Gainsborough's Forest* (c. 1748, National Gallery, London) to the soft, airy forms of *Mountain Landscape with Sheep* (c. 1783, Collection of the Duke of Sutherland, Sutton Place, Surrey). Gainsborough's portraiture moved from the solid detailed style of *Mr. and Mrs. Andrews* (c. 1749, Collection of G. W. Andrews, Redhill, Surrey) to light, freely brushed backgrounds, rather insubstantial bodies, and fairly solid heads, as in *The Morning Walk* (1785, on loan by Lord Rothschild to the Birmingham Gallery). The gauzelike background and the fluffy forms suggest Watteau, whose works Gainsborough had copied. Although the full-blown Rococo never found a footing in England, Gainsborough began what has been called English Rococo portraiture. Late in life, he also developed what

FOSCA
JAN.
U. & S.
WAT.

BAROQUE AND NEO-CLASSIC ART: 1600-1800

he called "fancy pictures," genre scenes combining pretty, unsophisticated children and rustic nature. From 1761 on, Gainsborough exhibited with the London Society of Artists, and he was one of the original members of the British Royal Academy at its founding in 1768.

FOSCA
JAN.
U. & S. *Jean-Honoré Fragonard* (France, 1732–1806).   The third major representative of the Rococo lived through the French Revolution and beyond his own era. Fragonard left Chardin's instruction for the studio of Boucher, where the student copied the master so skillfully that it is sometimes difficult to distinguish between their works. In 1752, Fragonard won the *Prix de Rome* and was deeply impressed, during his stay in Italy, by the work of Pietro da Cortona and Giovanni Battista Tiepolo. His other idols were Rubens and Rembrandt. Although Fragonard offered a history painting as his acceptance work for the Academy, he chose as his role the development of the subjects and the Rococo style of Watteau and Boucher. Fragonard's dazzling technical facility is evident in *The Marionettes* (c. 1770, A. Veil-Picard Collection, Paris), in which the *fête champêtre* has acquired glowing pools of light and color and contrasts of impasto with glazes. One thinks of Rembrandt, but Fragonard's lightness of touch, the dainty proportions of the figures, the breaking up of the forms, and the fluttery, rippling line are all thoroughly Rococo. Like Boucher, Fragonard often painted panels to be used as part of wall decorations in Louis XV interiors. Well-known examples are the panels on the theme of love (1770–73, Frick Collection, New York) which Fragonard executed for Madame du Barry, the lady who succeeded Madame de Pompadour in the affections of Louis XV.

PLATE 68
FOSCA
JAN.
U. & S. *Jacques Louis David* (France, 1748–1825).   David lived through some of the most violent periods in French history, and his art spearheads several of the most drastic stylistic changes in French painting. As a student in the Paris Academy, David won a *Prix de Rome* in 1774 with a history painting done in the Baroque manner. During his sojourn at the French Academy in Rome, he changed his style to such an extent that the *Oath of the Horatii* (1784, Louvre, Paris; a small version, done later, in the Toledo, Ohio, Museum of Art) and other works caused great excitement in Rome and Paris. The stylistic change is also demonstrated in *The Death of Socrates*

(PLATE 68). This composition is starkly simple; the figures form triangular or rectangular groupings, and the main elements are aligned with stable verticals and horizontals as well as with the picture plane. While the light is dramatic, it does not obscure the rigid structure of the painting. There is no softening effect of sfumato in the sharp contours of the forms. David's inspiration came from certain Greek and Roman works, from his teacher Joseph Vien, and from the theories of Johann J. Winckelmann, who praised the noble simplicity and calm grandeur of ancient Greek art. David's style, in its simplicity and strength, seemed the very antithesis of the aristocratic art of the Rococo, and David was adopted as the artist of the developing Revolution. Not only the style but also the subject of *The Death of Socrates* easily acquired political meaning. Socrates gave his life for the principles of reason and truth, principles that the antiroyalists were citing in 1787 as arguments for liberty, equality, and fraternity. After the Revolution, David became a veritable dictator of the arts. His style, called Neo-Classicism, was the order of the day, and he was powerful enough to have the Royal Academy abolished.

SCULPTURE IN THE NORTH

As in painting, the three general trends in sculpture were (1) a continuation of the seventeenth-century Baroque, ranging from stereotyped forms to a robust naturalism; (2) a Rococo style, emphasizing lilting, playful curves, intricate details in accessories, and slender proportions; and (3) a Neo-Classic tendency toward simplification, quiet equilibrium, and long sweeping curves. Neo-Classicism was especially important in the second half of the century. France was the most prolific producer of sculpture, but after the death of Louis XIV in 1715 the number of commissions for Versailles declined. The nobles were less attached to the court; they built town houses in Paris and furnished them with small sculptures in the Rococo style. Statuettes of porcelain and terra cotta were produced at the Sèvres workshops, a special interest of Louis XV's favorite, Madame de Pompadour. Baroque and Neo-Classic styles were preferred for public monuments or other large works. Some sculptors modified their styles to suit the commission.

In German areas, demand was greater for small sculpture than for monumental works. Meissen porcelain inspired the manufacture of France's Sèvres; but north Germany imported French sculptors

and French influence, while south Germany and Austria were influenced by Italian sculpture, particularly in the stucco sculpture for
their fantastically ornate Rococo churches.

Sculpture was meager in eighteenth-century England. French
Baroque influence was brought to England by the sculptor Louis
François Roubillac. Italian influence came from several leading
Englishmen who studied in Italy. John Flaxman, for example, sent
designs and sculpture from Italy to Wedgwood in England. The
resulting Wedgwood ware is Neo-Classic in the manner of Robert
Adam decoration, that is, with a touch of Rococo delicacy. Other-
wise, the Rococo did not take root in English sculpture.

PLATE 63
JAN.
Cosmas Damian and Egid Quirin Asam (Bavaria, 1686–1739 and 1692–
1750).   The Asam brothers were trained by their father, Hans G.
Asam, and had the benefit of a year in Rome (1712), where they were
impressed by the works of Giovanni Lorenzo Bernini, Giovanni
Battista Gaulli, Andrea dal Pozzo, and Pietro da Cortona. The
brothers formed a partnership but also worked separately. Cosmas
Damian specialized in fresco painting and Egid Quirin in stucco
ornament and sculpture. Their early collaborations include the
Assumption of the Virgin (PLATE 63) above the high altar in the monastery church at Rohr, near Regensburg. In this overwhelming
demonstration of Baroque dramatics, the sculpted figures of the
Apostles, gesticulating violently, are gathered around the sarcophagus, while Mary ascends toward sculpted clouds and metallic rays
that partially eclipse the architecture. The highly colored sculpture
of the Madonna and supporting angels presents a light, active, and
irregular group contrasted with a darker curtain in the background
and suspended in the actual space of the church. The avoidance of
framing and the concentrated lighting from above and from the sides
are typically Baroque. The complexity, activity, and richness of the
forms indicate a continuation of seventeenth-century sculptural-
architectural combinations. The more delicate forms of the Rococo
had not yet sapped the boisterous strength of Baroque composition.
The later work of the brothers, however, became more Rococo.

JAN.
U. & S.
Claude Michel, called Clodion (France, 1738–1814).   Clodion came
from a family of sculptors; he studied first with his uncle, L. S.
Adam, and then with Jean-Baptiste Pigalle, a leading Rococo sculp-
tor. Clodion won a *Prix de Rome* and stayed in Italy from 1761 to

1771, where he found a ready market for small terra cotta statuettes in the Rococo style. In France, he continued to produce the popular Rococo works, such as the *Satyr and Bacchante* (c. 1775, Metropolitan Museum of Art, New York). He neither sought nor executed many official commissions; in fact, he never bothered to present an acceptance work for membership in the Academy. He was quite capable of more conventional academic sculpture, however, as his *S. Cecilia*, done for the Cathedral of Rouen, indicates. After the Revolution, Clodion adopted a more Neo-Classic style and was allowed to do reliefs for the *Vendôme Column* in Paris.

Jean Antoine Houdon (France, 1741–1828).   Houdon studied under the Baroque sculptors Jean-Baptiste Pigalle and Michel-Ange Slodtz, won prizes as a youth at the Academy, and spent the years from 1764 to 1768 at the French Academy in Rome. His thorough study of anatomy was demonstrated in the *Ecorché* (c. 1766, École des Beaux Arts, Paris), a statue of a man without skin. Copies of this work served as study aids for anatomy classes in art schools. However, Houdon decided early upon portraiture as a specialty and received many commissions from the nobility. His portrait style was one of keen characterization and precise detail. He used neither the delicate forms of the Rococo nor the generalization of the Neo-Classic. Between 1771 and 1789, Houdon undertook a series of portraits of great men, including the *Voltaire* (1781, Comédie Française, Paris). His fame spread, and the esteem of Benjamin Franklin and Thomas Jefferson led to the commission for the full-length statue of *George Washington* (1785) in the State Capitol of Virginia, at Richmond. Houdon adopted a more Neo-Classic style in a number of lesser-known works with mythological or allegorical subjects. He lived beyond the Revolution and continued to receive commissions, although he did not enjoy the favor of the leader David or the patronage of Napoleon.

JAN.
U. & S.

ARCHITECTURE IN THE NORTH

Eighteenth-century French architecture displayed a strong trend of the chastened Baroque that continued through most of the century and received the official sanction of the Academy. During the reign of Louis XV, the Rococo style was popular for interiors; bold projections were reduced to flatter surfaces, and pilasters and engaged columns were replaced by encrustations of dainty floral ornament and fluttering ribbons that break through any restraining geometric frames. Curves obscure, soften, and complicate the straight structural lines. Large halls gave way to small apartments and intimate rooms. Occasionally the Rococo was used for an exterior. The discovery of the buried Roman cities of Herculaneum (found in 1719) and Pompeii (found in 1748) provided inspiration for Neo-Classicism, which developed in several directions after 1750. Simpler interiors with uninterrupted lines, rectangular rigidity, and more dependence upon Roman ornament appeared in the work of Jacques-Germain Soufflot. With architects like Charles Nicolas Ledoux, however, simplicity and Greco-Roman elements were combined with jolting contrasts, grandiose scale, and surprisingly imaginative forms. The Revolution slowed building but strengthened the preference for the Neo-Classic, partly because it was associated with the republican governments of certain periods in Greek and Roman history.

German eighteenth-century architecture developed a variety of styles within the general trends of Baroque, Rococo, and Neo-Classicism. Some of the leading architects studied in Italy and France, and designers from these countries were imported. Churches of the early eighteenth century show the influence of the Italian Baroque. By mid-century, southern Germany and Austria were creating churches with interiors of amazingly rich Rococo design. Palaces were inspired by both Italian and French examples. Exteriors are often quite reserved, with decoration in low relief that does not obscure the basic masses; interiors could be lavishly Rococo. Winckelmann's influence was important in the second half of the century, and Neo-Classicism waxed strong, particularly in Berlin. Neo-Classic interiors often recall those by Adam in England and suggest faint echoes of the delicacy of the Rococo.

The eighteenth century in England opened with the reserved Baroque that had developed in the previous century. After 1710, this tendency was challenged by the *Palladian Revival*, a movement espousing a return to the simpler Roman forms of the sixteenth-century Italian Palladio. A third tendency is evidenced by the occasional designs in Romanesque or Gothic styles. The ruins of medieval architecture could be appreciated, as could Roman ruins, for *picturesque* qualities, a combination of subject matter and style which evolved nostalgic enjoyment of man's smallness and of the transitory character of his achievements in the face of nature's vastness and power. Furthermore, Gothic ornament could be enjoyed for some of the qualities of the Rococo. Neo-Classic architecture developed in the second half of the century under the leadership of Robert Adam, Sir William Chambers, and Sir John Soane. It is notable that a given architect might work in several of these four trends.

Johann Bernhard Fischer von Erlach (Austria, 1656–1723). After JAN. training in Rome, Fischer von Erlach returned to Vienna, where he became a leader in seventeenth- and eighteenth-century Austrian architecture. His church of *St. Charles Borromaeus* (1716–37) in Vienna provides a strong focus upon the main altar, which is placed in an extension at one end of an elliptical interior space. At the opposite end, a wide narthex is placed at a right angle to the elliptical center section. The exterior façade of this narthex consists of a Corinthian porch connected by two concave wings to towers at the sides. Within the concave areas at each side of the porch stand two tall columns with spiral reliefs in the manner of the ancient *Column of Trajan* in Rome. Above the impressive façade looms a high dome which is set over the elliptical interior. The total effect both inside and out is one of dramatic contrasts between parts, but there is greater restraint in ornament than in many Italian Baroque churches.

Balthasar Neumann (Germany, 1687–1753). Neumann was trained PLATES by the Würzburg bronze caster Sebald Kopp, and in addition gained 64–66 considerable experience as a military engineer-architect. In 1720, JAN. he was given responsibility for the building of the *Episcopal Residence at Würzburg* and, in 1723, was sent to Paris to study French architecture. The Residence, like so many other eighteenth-century palaces, owes much to Versailles. French influences were important in the development of Neumann's Rococo style, one which left a wide imprint upon the architecture of southern Germany. Of his many buildings, the most celebrated church is that of *Vierzehnheiligen* (*The Fourteen Saints*, PLATES 64–66). Here, the façade pushes forward in a convex center framed by engaged columns and broken pediments; the twin towers become more complex and bolder in value contrasts as they rise. Rococo touches can be seen in the lilting curves of pediments and window frames, but the real drama is reserved for the interior. Neumann's basilica plan was based on ovals and circles, producing even more restless wall planes than those of Borromini's *S. Carlo alle Quattro Fontane*. The activity of the walls is intensified by the profusion of vinelike, irregular ornament which seems to crawl over the surfaces. The lavish colors, the delicate details, and the amazing effervescence of the interior make it an outstanding example of German Rococo.

JAN.
U. & S.

Anges-Jacques Gabriel (France, 1699–1782).   Gabriel came from a family of architects and studied under his father. As architect for Louis XV, he produced both independent buildings and large building groups. His *Military School* (1751) in Paris presents an elevation that is simple at the sides but strongly focused on the center, where a bold colonnaded pavilion is surmounted by a pediment, a four-sided dome, and extensive sculpture. Gabriel's typical reserve is better demonstrated in the pair of palaces (1761–1771) in the *Place de la Concorde*, formerly the Place Louis XV. Rusticated and arcaded bases support colossal Corinthian orders that carry an entablature, balustrades, and corner pediments. Although the seventeenth-century east front of the Louvre inspired Gabriel's design, he used more three-dimensional variation and value contrast in the base. The simplest of his buildings is the small *Petit Trianon* (1762–68) at Versailles, an almost square structure with a symmetrical arrangement of interior spaces. While the interior has some traces of Rococo decoration, the exterior is remarkably austere. Three façades use slightly projecting pavilions marked by columns or pilasters framing the tall windows of the main floor and the square windows of the attic. The blocky form is topped by an entablature and a balustrade. It has been claimed that Gabriel was influenced by the publication, in 1758, of J. D. LeRoy's *Ruins of the Most Beautiful Monuments of Greece*, but the natural reserve of Gabriel's style came basically from the traditional restraint of French architecture in the preceding two centuries.

JAN.
SUM.
U. & S.

Robert Adam (England, 1728–92).   Robert Adam was born in Scotland and attended the University of Edinburgh. From 1754 to 1758 he toured Italy, joined the artist's Academy of St. Luke in Rome, became a friend of Piranesi, and measured and drew the ruins of the *Palace of the Roman Emperor Diocletian at Spalato*. Upon his return to England, he formed an architectural office with his brothers James and William. In 1761, Robert Adam was appointed one of the two Architects of the King's Works. He and his brothers designed whole houses, reconstructions, interiors, and furnishings. Their work was one of the most significant styles in the England of the 1760's and 1770's, and their influence was international. The Adam style may be called, with qualification, Neo-Classical. Floor plans such as that of *Syon House*, Middlesex, have balanced symmetry and were inspired by particular Roman or Greek buildings. Façades range from the massive stately *South Front of Kedleston Hall*, Derbyshire, with its Roman triumphal arch motif, to the delicate, crisp, minia-ture character of the *Adelphi Houses* in London. The Adams' greatest influence was on interiors. Their preference was for slender pilasters, Grecian urns, and architectural moldings borrowed from Rome and Greece and used with rich profusion in very slight relief with sharp contrasts in value or color. The result has some of the delicacy of the Rococo but much more rigid geometric structure. In speaking of architecture, Robert Adam stressed "movement," the rise and fall, the advance and recession of parts that is a facet of the Baroque love of strong gradation and climax.

Carl Gotthard Langhans (Germany, 1732–1808). Langhans' career demonstrates the development and overlapping of various interests in late eighteenth-century German architecture. His first important work, the *Hatzfeld Palace* (1766–74)—later the *Oberpräsidium*—in Breslau had an exterior influenced by the Italian Baroque and a slightly later interior that was Rococo. Langhans moved increas-ingly toward simpler cubic masses and wall surfaces, in keeping with the growing interest in ancient Greek architecture. In 1788, he went to Berlin to become the Director of Architecture for Fried-rich Wilhelm II. His best-known work there is the *Brandenburg Gate* (1789–94), a Doric structure inspired by the *Propylaea* in Athens but indebted to Roman architecture in the use of a base with a Doric shaft. Langhans' taste for rich decoration did not disappear as his Neo-Classicism grew; the interiors of his *Palace of the Netherlands* in Berlin have an ornate elegance and carefully framed delicate detail that relate them to Adam's design in England.

JAN. U. & S.

PAINTING IN ITALY

Major centers for eighteenth-century Italian painting were Naples, Bologna, Rome, and Venice; many Italian painters also found em-ployment in other countries. As elsewhere, there was increased specialization in subject matter. Style in history painting was based on the work of the Carracci, Pietro da Cortona, Rubens, Titian,

Tintoretto, and Veronese. The lighter shimmering color of Veronese can be seen as one source for the Italian Rococo, which was developed independently by Giovanni Battista Tiepolo. Loose brushwork and ragged, fluttering shapes created light, spacious compositions that maintain more breadth and grandeur of scale than the Rococo in France. Foreign painters were responsible for Neo-Classic work in Italy. Portraiture was abundant in both the Baroque and in the Rococo styles. The painting of city views, ruins, landscapes, and imaginative combinations of all three found a wide international market. Not only were many north Italian palaces decorated with such subjects, but travelers collected them as souvenirs. Style varied from precise, dry detail, natural light, and documentary accuracy to fluid brushwork, dramatic lighting, and exaggerated scale. Genre painting followed the traditions of the Bamboccianti and that of the upper-class interiors from seventeenth-century Dutch painting.

FOSCA
JAN.
U. & S.
WITT.

Giovanni Battista Tiepolo (Venice, Lombardy, Würzburg, and Madrid, 1696-1770).   Tiepolo's rise to fame began even during his study under a secondary master in Venice. Commissions for wall and ceiling frescoes eventually led him from one city to another. The heavy forms and powerful value contrasts of his early work, like the *Sacrifice of Abraham* (1715-16, Church of the Ospedaletto, Venice), show the influence of Titian and of Tintoretto, but Tiepolo then turned to lighter and more open composition. In the Church of the Gesuati in Venice, he did the ceiling painting of *St. Dominic Instituting the Rosary* (1737-39), a composition that recalls the illusionistic architecture in Veronese's *Triumph of Venice*. Yet Tiepolo reduced the proportion of heavy solids and increased the proportion of sky. The thin, fluffy clouds, the fluttering airborne figures, and the light colors and shadow areas produce an effect of happy buoyancy. Between 1750 and 1753, he decorated the *Episcopal Residence in Würzburg*. The ceiling painting of the throne room depicts *Apollo Conducting Beatrice of Burgundy to Barbarossa* and goes further than earlier work in lightening and opening the composition. Architecture is reduced to a small structure in the lower left, and the figure groups present fluttering irregular shapes like leaves blown in the wind. The sweeping clouds are thin overlapping veils with delicately scalloped edges. Around the painting, a gilded stucco frame assumes a complex shape of compound curves and lacy edges, broken in several places by painted forms that seem to spill over it in typical Baroque illusionistic fashion. From 1762 until 1770, Tiepolo worked in Spain, decorating the Royal Palace at Madrid. The jealousy of rivals and the growing preference for Neo-Classicism led to a decline in his popularity and may have hastened his death. Tiepolo's painting presents the fullest expression of the Rococo in Italian art.

Giovanni Antonio Canal, called Canaletto (Venice, Rome, and London, 1697–1768). Canaletto learned first from his father, a painter of theatrical scenery. In 1719, the young artist traveled to Rome, where he saw Giovanni Paolo Pannini's paintings of ruins and the Bamboccianti paintings of everyday life in the city. After his return to Venice, Canaletto became a specialist in painting views of the city and obtained numerous commissions from Englishmen making the grand tour of the continent and wishing to take home souvenirs. Canaletto painted Venice in sharp linear detail, sweeping spaces, and vast gentle skies, as in the *Piazza S. Marco* (c. 1760, National Gallery, London). The popularity of his art led to a series of engravings of his paintings that was used as a catalogue by his clients and an aid by his imitators. It is probable that he visited Rome again in 1740. Between 1742 and 1743, he painted a series of scenes with Roman ruins. Canaletto did not always restrain himself to documenting particular spots; he occasionally created imaginary scenes, sometimes containing well-known buildings. Much of the period from 1745 to 1755 was spent in England, where his reputation had preceded him. The visit was a great success, although, at first, the English collectors were disconcerted by the *caprices*—imaginary scenes that the painter produced along with many views of London. Commissions were so plentiful that Canaletto employed assistants. Cityscapes and landscapes were considered inferior subject matter by academic standards, however, and in spite of his international success Canaletto was not accepted into the Venetian Academy until 1763.

FOSCA
U. & S.
WITT.

Giovanni Battista Piranesi (Rome, 1720–78). Piranesi's engravings and etchings demonstrate the growing eighteenth-century interest in Greco-Roman art and the appreciation of the picturesque. Piranesi began his career in Venice as a student of architecture but established himself in Rome in 1740. There he turned to engraving and etching prints of the ruins of Roman architecture. His etching of *The Great Hall of the Baths of Caracalla* indicates his love of grand scale, often

JAN.
U. & S.
WITT.

exaggerated by reducing the size of the figures, and ragged, crumbling architecture eaten away by time and vegetation. Etching needles of different sizes made for rich diversity of line. Piranesi's best prints have a wide variation of grays and deep blacks. He documented and interpreted ancient Rome in his views of that city, but the range of his imagination is shown in his *Carceri*, imaginary interiors of prisons in fantastic scale and structural elaboration based vaguely on Roman architecture. A comparison of the art of Piranesi with that of David indicates the wide range of style that could be inspired by intense interest in ancient Greco-Roman art. In an effort to describe Piranesi's particular attitude and style, some writers have turned to the rather awkward term *Romantic Classicism*.

References for representative artists

BLUNT Blunt, Anthony. *Art and Architecture in France: 1500–1700* (Pelican History of Art). Baltimore: Penguin Books, 1953.

FOSCA Fosca, François (pseudonym for Georges de Traz). *The Eighteenth Century: Watteau to Tiepolo* (Great Centuries of Painting). Trans. by Stuart Gilbert. Geneva: Skira, 1952.

JAN. Janson, H. W., and D. J. Janson, eds. *Key Monuments of the History of Art: A Visual Survey*. Englewood Cliffs, N.J.: Prentice-Hall; New York: Harry N. Abrams, 1959.

P.-H. Pope-Hennessy, John. *An Introduction to Italian Sculpture*. New York and London: Phaidon, 1955–62. Vol. 3.

SUM. Summerson, John. *Architecture in Britain: 1530–1830* (Pelican History of Art). Baltimore: Penguin Books, 1953.

U. & S. Upjohn, Everard M., and J. P. Sedgwick, Jr. *Highlights: An Illustrated History of Art*. New York: Holt, Rinehart and Winston, 1963.

WAT. Waterhouse, Ellis. *Painting in Britain, 1530–1790* (Pelican History of Art). Baltimore: Penguin Books, 1953.

WITT. Wittkower, Rudolf. *Art and Architecture in Italy, 1600–1750* (Pelican History of Art). Baltimore: Penguin Books, 1958.

Suggestions for further study

Bazin, Germain. *Baroque and Rococo Art* (Praeger World of Art Series). Trans. by Jonathan Griffin. New York: Frederick A. Praeger, 1964.

Bergström, Ingvar. *Dutch Still-life Painting in the Seventeenth Century*. Trans. by Christina Hedström and Gerald Taylor. New York: Thomas Yoseloff, Publisher, 1956.

Dowd, David L. *Pageant-Master of the Republic: Jacques Louis David and the French Revolution*. Lincoln, Neb.: University of Nebraska Press, 1948.

Gerson, Horst, and Engelbert H. ter Kuile. *Art and Architecture in Belgium: 1600–1800* (Pelican History of Art). Trans. by Olive Renier. Baltimore: Penguin Books, 1960.

Mayor, Alpheus H. *Giovanni Battista Piranesi*. New York: H. H. Bittner & Company, 1952.

Morassi, Antonio. *Tiepolo: His Life and Work*. New York: Phaidon, 1955.

Powell, Nicolas. *From Baroque to Rococo: An Introduction to Austrian and German Architecture from 1580 to 1790*. New York: Frederick A. Praeger, 1959.

Redgrave, Samuel, and Richard Redgrave. *A Century of British Painters*. Rev. ed. New York: Oxford University Press; London: Phaidon Press, 1947.

Rosenberg, Jakob. *Rembrandt*. Cambridge, Mass.: Harvard University Press, 1948. 2 vols.

Rothlisberger, Marcel. *Claude Lorrain: The Paintings*. New Haven, Conn.: Yale University Press, 1961. 2 vols.

Swillens, P. *Johannes Vermeer: Painter of Delft, 1632–1675*. Trans. by C. M. Breuning-Williamson. Utrecht: Spectrum, 1950.

Trapier, Elizabeth du Gué. *Velázquez*. New York: Hispanic Society of America, 1948.

Wittkower, Rudolf. *Gian Lorenzo Bernini: The Sculptor of the Roman Baroque*. London: Phaidon Press, 1955.

Chapter Thirteen

MODERN ART: 1800 TO THE PRESENT

Modern art is often dated from David's rebellion against the French Academy in the late eighteenth century, because rebellion against tradition and the search for new forms to express new content are important characteristics of the new art, but the nineteenth century constitutes the first major period in the history of modern art. The development of archaeology, history, and art history as disciplines seems to have led to greater self-consciousness about individual style and to an increased awareness of stylistic movements and group identities. For some artists, however, the interest in these disciplines led to more precise borrowing from the art of the past. These diverging tendencies, along with changing ideas in philosophy and science, help to explain why different concepts of artistic "truth" are implicit in the different styles in art and in the writings of art critics during the nineteenth century.

The most important geographical area for developments in painting and sculpture was France. In architecture, England played a significant role, especially since her leadership in the Industrial Revolution encouraged pioneering in structures of iron and glass.

During the first half of the nineteenth century, the various styles tended to express one of two major attitudes, *Neo-Classicism* or *Romanticism*. The distinction between the two is not always sharp since there were considerable overlapping and mutual influence. Nineteenth-century Neo-Classicists borrowed more specifically from Greek and Roman art than did their eighteenth-century predecessors. Underlying the many Neo-Classic styles is the search for an absolute beauty based on the perfection of nature, in accord with preconceived ideal types. Clarity of parts, stable equilibrium, and proportions inspired by Greek and Roman art are basic to Neo-Classic work. The attitude called Romanticism produced such a wide range of styles that it is more difficult to characterize; generally there is an insistence upon the freedom of the individual and the importance of individual experience. Individual characteristics—the unique form rather than the ideal type—are stressed, and restrictive traditions are rejected. In the famous preface to his play *Cromwell* (1827), Victor Hugo provided a manifesto for Romanticism. He attacked academic dogma and argued that the Christian concept of the worth of the individual makes possible a new kind of pity, *melancholy*. He stated that the individual, indeed all of nature, contains the ugly as well as the beautiful, evil as well as good. Art should therefore dramatize the dual nature of reality, stress the worth of the individual, and evoke the profound sentiment of melancholy. Romantic artists found subject matter in the works of Lord Byron and Sir Walter Scott and inspiration in the appeal to emotional and mystical experience by writers like François René de Chateaubriand and Wilhelm H. Wackenroder. Christian pietism frequently reinforced the Romantic attitude and created an interest in the Middle Ages; the Romantic could turn to any period in the past, however, since he appreciated the exotic and the remote in time or place.

After the middle of the nineteenth century, the Neo-Classic and Romantic attitudes gave way to tendencies that have been described as a *positivistic reaction* and that are reflected in some of the pioneering literature, painting, and sculpture of the period. The continuing desire to upset conventional ideas was joined by an interest in treating all aspects of everyday life in styles that were labeled *realistic* or *naturalistic*. Such art was linked with the growing enthusiasm for science, and artists began to investigate even the chaotic incidental nature of human events and the impressionistic character of our experience of the physical world. Toward the end of the century, however, the realization grew that science and progress would not solve all the ills and mysteries of the world. The *Symbolist movement* in literature and art emphasized the enigma of existence and the subjective nature of reality.

The twentieth century, even more than the nineteenth, has been characterized by international and individual rather than regional styles and by a diversity that makes generalization difficult. Not only new materials and techniques but a rapidly changing world view have influenced art. The increasing importance of the machine seems to be reflected in some styles and reacted against in others, while psychology and physics have reshaped the artist's conceptions of man and the physical world; the complex interaction of factors that go to form the artist's style, however, does not encourage simple or easy explanations. Although several twentieth-century stylistic trends have attempted to devaluate individual style, the prevailing tendency has been to stress originality. The individual's reaction to his world, his exploration of the realm of fantasy, and his creation of new worlds, without familiar objects, have all become significant features of twentieth-century painting and sculpture, as has the interest in and influence of the art of primitive cultures.

Geographically, the United States has become much more important since the Second World War; New York now rivals Paris as a creative center.

The nineteenth century

PAINTING

In France, the early years of the century saw Neo-Classic stylistic qualities supplanted temporarily, in the work of many artists, by more irregular masses, deliberate merging and obscuring of some compositional parts, more individualistic details in anatomy, and more specific and contemporary details in accessories. These features, some of which recall seventeenth-century Baroque art, were particularly evident in the painting of Napoleonic history and were further developed, during the years after the fall of Napoleon, in much of the painting that has been called Romantic. The immediate ancestry of Romantic art can be traced in the eighteenth-century enjoyment of the picturesque and in the moralizing sentimentality of such eighteenth-century painters as the Frenchman Jean Baptiste Greuze. Delacroix was considered to be the leader of Romanticism, while Ingres led academic art in the search for the ideal truth of Neo-Classicism. The Salon of 1824 provided a confrontation of works by the two leaders, and it is from this date that the conflicting and overlapping attitudes of Neo-Classicism and Romanticism assume major importance in French art.

Academically approved "classic landscape" painting, exemplified by Poussin's work, was superseded during the first half of the century by the art of certain French painters who turned to more direct experiences of nature. These so-called *Barbizon painters* did much painting outdoors, in the forest of Fontainebleau near the village of Barbizon; although the works were usually finished in the studio, they retained the freshness of firsthand experience in more casual, varied, and free compositions than those of academic landscape. The Barbizon painters made their debuts around 1830 but were not widely accepted until the second half of the century. Their delight in sensitive interpretation of the moods of nature, ranging from lyrical reverie to dramatic storm, links them with Romanticism, while their ancestry may be found in seventeenth-century Dutch landscape painting.

The mid-century was marked not only by political revolution but also by a new movement in French painting, *Realism*, which treated all facets of daily life in a style that showed frank enjoyment of the natural shapes, textures, and colors of things and a delight in the manipulation of the paint texture itself. In comparison with Realist work, the painting of the Barbizon artists and the exotic subjects, grand passions, glowing colors, and dashing brushwork of Delacroix became much more acceptable to conservative critics, and Realism succeeded Romanticism as the renegade of the period. The leader of Realism, Gustave Courbet, was rebuked for vulgarity in form and subject matter and for lack of finish.

The hegemony of the French Academy suffered a blow in 1863 when the outcry against the severity of the Salon jury caused the emperor to order an exhibition of rejected works that was called the *Salon des Refusés*. Although the public tended to agree with the jury's decisions, the artist's right to exhibit outside the Salon was taken more seriously than before.

After mid-century, certain French artists, notably Edouard Manet, began to intensify their pictorial images by using patches of color relatively unbroken by internal modeling. An important inspiration for this trend was the Japanese woodblock print. The intensification of vision assumed another form in the stylistic movement called *Impressionism*, which made its formal debut in the exhibit of the Association of Artist-painters, Sculptors, Engravers, etc. in 1874. The momentary visual impression of a world of light and color in constant change became the major interest of Impressionist leaders like Claude Monet and Auguste Renoir, who went one step further than the Barbizon painters by finishing their paintings outdoors, working directly from the subject. Their patient study of the effects of light on color has been linked with the scientific study of optical phenomena, but they intensified the effects of shimmering light, reflected colors, and simultaneous contrasts, re-forming the visual world into a luminous matrix of small strokes of rich color. Their scientific objectivity seems to have been qualified by sensual enjoyment of visual experience. By the 1890's, Impressionist work was grudgingly accepted by academic juries and even awarded occasional prizes.

Meanwhile, attitudes in academic painting had undergone changes. The fall of Napoleon had not stopped Napoleonic history painting, and the taste for specific details and local color that had been inspired by Napoleonic history was strengthened by an interest in developing scientific methods in archaeology and history and by the exactitude of photography. Neo-Classic painting was continued by some painters, but after mid-century, academic painters turned increasingly to precise, carefully researched details, and the truth of Neo-Classic ideal form was supplanted in academic work by this documentary or archaeological truth.

In the 1880's and 1890's, a number of pioneering young painters, who had tried Impressionistic painting early in their careers, came to feel that Impressionism sacrificed too much solidity of form and compositional structure for the sake of color and light. They therefore turned to very different styles in their mature painting. The most important of these men were Seurat, Van Gogh, Cézanne, and Gauguin. They have been called *Post-Impressionists*, and their styles forecast significant directions in the painting of the twentieth century.

German painting at the beginning of the nineteenth century was molded by the doctrines of Winckelmann and the influence of the Frenchman David. Rome was the training ground for many of the leading German painters, just as it had been for David. A group calling itself the *Nazarenes* joined religious fervor with a self-consciously simple, linear, Neo-Classic style that was softened by flowing harmonies derived from Raphael's painting. Members of the Nazarene group later obtained positions of leadership in German academies in Düsseldorf, Munich, and Berlin. German Romanticism was expressed in styles that incorporated more precise detail than did those in France; evocations of nostalgia about the brevity of man's existence, the mysterious forces of nature, and the secret life of the individual are frequent in paintings by Philipp O. Runge and by Caspar David Friedrich. A Courbet-inspired Realism developed in the work of Germans like Wilhelm Leibl, and the concept of documentary truth formed the styles of Max Klinger and Karl von

Piloty. Impressionism had a belated emergence in Germany after a promising forecast in the early work of Adolf Menzel.

In Italy, as in France and Germany, the major academies were dedicated to Neo-Classicism in the early part of the century. A Romanticism that rejected Neo-Classic ideal form for individualistic details made its appearance with the work of Francesco Hayez in Milan in 1820. By mid-century, a group of Roman painters called the *Macchiaiuoli* were employing bold patterns of color patches that forecast the style of Manet in France several years later. Documentary history painting became important in the second half of the century.

In England, the opening years of the nineteenth century were dominated by several of the great eighteenth-century portrait painters. As the century unfolded, genre painting found a wide market. Landscape painting was led by Constable, whose free brushwork influenced Delacroix, and by Turner, who exploited dramatic effects of light and color in both real and imaginary landscapes. In 1848, the *Brotherhood of Pre-Raphaelites* united several precocious young painters whose moralizing zeal was combined with a yearning for mystical experience, a love of involved literary symbolism and feverishly bright detail, and a desire to return to the style of art before Raphael. Carefully staged and minutely rendered history painting came from the brushes of academicians like Alma Tadema and Frederick Leighton. Impressionism did not develop in England as it did in France. The American expatriate James McNeill Whistler was fascinated by oriental art, and his muted, misty riverscapes of scenes along the Thames combine the broad patterns of Manet's art with Impressionistic interest in atmospheric effects. Whistler's English student, Walter Sickert, used more broken color, but his heavy, earthy style is quite unlike French Impressionism.

During the nineteenth century in the United States, patrons became increasingly more sophisticated and developed interests in a wider range of subject matter and style. Portraiture remained the type of painting in greatest demand, and style ranged from the facile brushwork of Thomas Sully to the sparkling detail of Thomas Eakins. Genre and landscape painting expressed a patriotic enthusiasm for the local customs and natural beauty of a rapidly growing America. The so-called *Hudson River School*, a group of landscape painters dedicated to arcadian river views, might be compared with the Barbizon painters in France. During the second half of the century, a romantic nostalgia for grandeur and overpowering scale is evident in the landscapes of Albert Bierstadt, Thomas Moran, and others. The mystery of nature was expressed in the glowing somber landscapes and seascapes of Albert P. Ryder, and the Impressionistic interest in natural light and color came only in the last decade of the century.

Francisco Goya (Spain, 1746–1828).   While Goya's fantasy has led some historians to consider him a Romantic, his expository portrayal of human personality has inspired the term *Realist*. The latter designation seems more accurate in that even his imaginative work stresses the realistic acceptance of the role of the irrational in human experience; yet Goya's art is far different from that of the French Realists in the mid-nineteenth century. Goya's teachers were minor masters, who had less influence on his art than did the paintings of Tiepolo and Velázquez. In his mature work, Goya used a dazzling variety of texture in paint; his style ranges from harsh light and simplification of forms to soft light and the effect of mass and detail seen through dense air. In *May Third, 1808* (PLATE 67), which shows Spanish citizens being shot by French soldiers, a harsh style underscores the painting's social comment. The grouping of shapes into simple areas of light and dark intensifies the gestures of the subjects and the total impact of the composition; Goya seems to forecast the art of Manet. Social commentary is implicit in some of Goya's portraits as well. *The Family of Charles IV* (1800, Prado Museum, Madrid) candidly reveals the homeliness or viciousness of the different personalities and contrasts these with the costumes. Goya's frankness makes his official success surprising, for he became painter to the king and president of the Spanish Royal Academy. His strongest social commentary and his most unrestrained fantasy are found in his prints. *The Caprices*, a series of eighty-two aquatint etchings, depict man as unreasonable, petty, self-indulgent, and sadistic. The *Disparates*, a set of twenty-two aquatint etchings, reveal Goya's extraordinary imagination in a sequence of grotesque visions; they are frequently ambiguous in meaning, but the total effect is one of fascination and horror in the observation of man. Inhumanity and viciousness are the essence of *The Disasters of War*, a series of eighty-three aquatint etchings presenting a catalog of barbaric cruelties.

PLATE 67
CAN.
JAN.
U. & S.

Jacques Louis David.   David's painting, which we have already considered as part of late eighteenth-century art, changed in the

CAN.
JAN.
U. & S.

early years of the nineteenth century. David and others were inspired
by Napoleonic history, and Greco-Roman subjects gave way to
dramatic contemporary events. The austere rigidity of David's early
style softened to suggest more dramatic movement and more detailed accessories. For example, the *Bonaparte Crossing the Alps* (1800,
Kunsthistorisches Museum, Vienna) employs unsupported contrasting diagonal forms quite unlike the stable triangular arrangements in David's earlier works. The search for timeless ideal human
form changed to an interest in topical detail, as demonstrated by
The Coronation of Napoleon (1805, Louvre, Paris). After the fall of
Napoleon, David went into exile in Belgium, where he continued
to produce portraits and also painted mythological subjects which
he treated in a lighter, less dramatic manner than that of his earlier
style.

PLATE 70
CAN.
JAN.
U. & S.

Joseph Turner (England, 1775–1851).   Turner was first a water-
colorist, adding color washes to drawings by Thomas Girtin, but
in the 1790's he began painting landscapes in oil, his major sources
of influence being seventeenth-century Dutch landscape, Claude
Lorrain, and Nicolas Poussin. During walking trips in England and
France, he made thousands of drawings which were the bases for
his paintings. Turner worked in two styles: one recorded nature in
faithful detail and was the basis for his acceptance by a part of his
public; the other, thought of today as the typical Turner, intensified
the vast scale of nature and the effects of light and atmosphere. Solid
forms dissolve in a shimmer of mist, glowing light, and irridescent
color. *Rain, Steam, and Speed* (PLATE 70) exploits a combination of
rain and the steam of a locomotive for these effects. Sunrise, sunset,
storm, and the clearing after a storm were favorite moments for
Turner. He frequently added mythological staffage, or sentimental
subject matter, as in *Ulysses Deriding Polyphemus* (1829, National
Gallery, London) and *The Fighting Téméraire* (1838–39, National
Gallery, London). Because many of his works sacrifice detail for
effects of light and color, Turner has been considered a source of
French Impressionism, which developed in the latter half of the
century. But Turner modulated color in a more traditional manner;
he did not use the small brush strokes of colors juxtaposed in complementary contrast and often broken into their constituent parts.
Turner's more imaginative paintings are visions that magnify the
mystery and grandeur of nature; in this respect, they reflect the
attitude of Romanticism.

Caspar David Friedrich (Germany, 1774–1840).   Friedrich studied at the Academy of Copenhagen and moved to Dresden in 1798, where he joined a circle that included the Romantic writers Ludwig Tieck and Novalis and the painters Philipp Runge and Ferdinand von Olivier. In 1805, Friedrich's sepia drawings earned a prize in a competition judged by Goethe. Friedrich's subjects tend to show a single person or a small group dwarfed by the vastness of nature. He loved grand scale, sweeping vistas, effects of sunrise or moonlight, and a mood of solitude, meditation, or melancholy. He is identified with Romanticism in Germany as was Delacroix in France, yet there are wide differences in the styles of the two men. Friedrich loved precise detail and patterns formed by delicate silhouettes. His *Cloister Graveyard in the Snow* (1810, now lost) is typical. It depicts the jagged but lacy silhouettes of huge trees against an ancient, snow-covered graveyard. In the background, a solemn procession of hooded monks moves into the tall ruins of a Gothic chapel. The painting evokes a powerful mood of melancholy. Although it has none of the vigorous brushwork and apparent spontaneity of Delacroix's art, it contains a similar suggestion of man's tragic and ephemeral existence.

CAN.
JAN.

John Constable (England, 1776–1837).   Constable began life as the son of a country miller but in 1799 was admitted as a student at the Royal Academy in London. His mature style was considered to be crude and unfinished by some critics. *The Hay Wain* (PLATE 69), one of his best-known landscapes, was exhibited in 1821. Although considerably more detailed than a full-sized oil sketch of the subject (Victoria and Albert Museum, London), the final work has sparkling color and buttery paint application that create an effect of dewy freshness. The middle-ground grouping of mill and trees acts as a foil for the deep meadows and towering clouds on the right, while foreground interest is held by a wagon fording the stream. The composition reflects the influence of Constable's idols, Claude Lorrain and Thomas Gainsborough, as well as of seventeenth-century Dutch landscape painting. *The Hay Wain* was purchased by a Parisian dealer and exhibited in 1824. French critics, like the English, had mixed responses, but painters were impressed by the vigor and freedom of the execution. Delacroix is said to have repainted the background of his *Massacre de Scio* after having seen Constable's painting. Along with Turner, Constable helped to open the way for the freer interpretation of landscape later in the nineteenth century.

PLATE 69
CAN.
JAN.
U. & S.

PLATE 76
CAN.
JAN.
U. & S.

Jean Auguste Dominique Ingres (France, 1780–1867). David's replacement as leader of academic Neo-Classicism did not appear immediately. Ingres, a pupil of David, had his early work criticized for the distortions of anatomy and complexities of drapery which the young artist created in the interests of rhythmic line. Ingres was happy, therefore, to spend eighteen years in Rome after winning the *Prix de Rome* with a carefully constructed academic exercise. In 1824, however, his Salon contribution *The Vow of Louis XIII* was so successful that he returned to Paris as the leader of academic painting and became president of the School of Fine Arts. *The Apotheosis of Homer* (PLATE 76), done three years later, exemplifies the most official, rather than the most personal, aspects of his style. Severe symmetry, precise contours, simplified anatomy, and clean, sweeping drapery lines make for a more abstract classicism than that of David; yet Ingres was hailed as his successor. The tendency toward rounded contours and ovoid forms reveals the influence of Ingres' idol, Raphael. Under Ingres' leadership, academic teaching was very dogmatic; he insisted that drawing was the basis of art, and he stressed sharply defined contours and smooth finish. He was considered to be the leader of Neo-Classicism and the foe of Romanticism; at the Paris International Exposition of 1855, the most lavish representation in the exhibit of French painting was accorded the paintings of Ingres and Delacroix.

PLATE 78
CAN.
JAN.
U. & S.

Camille Corot (France, 1796–1875). Corot was born in Paris and trained by painters of classic landscape in the tradition of Poussin. During a sojourn in Italy in the 1820's, Corot painted landscapes with bold masses and simplified areas of light and dark, usually grouped around a horizontal or vertical axis. In his later landscape painting he developed the silvery, cloudlike foliage and poetic delicacy typified by *Souvenir de Mortefontaine* (PLATE 78). Small flecks of light-colored flowers float against deep shadows; light filters through the leaves, and hazy banks of foliage step back into space. Occasionally, forest nymphs dance in a clearing. While these scenes are more earthbound than those of Turner, Corot's landscapes are often imaginary visions based on a lifetime of drawing and painting out of doors; he was associated with the Barbizon painters. Corot's figure paintings were appreciated less than his landscapes until the present century. Most are portraits of anonymous people whom Corot painted in subtle colors and solid forms and with quiet dignity, using some of the broad simple areas of value and color that are typical of his early work. Corot was awarded the Legion of Honor in 1846 and lived to see his works forged to meet a growing demand by collectors.

Eugène Delacroix (France, 1798–1863).   For Delacroix, the most important qualities in painting were vitality and the sensuous appeal of color. Although his teacher was the academic painter Guerin, his real inspiration was the art of Michelangelo and Rubens; Delacroix belongs to the posterity of the *Rubénistes*. While his subjects usually came from literature, as did those of Ingres, Delacroix's painting seemed violent, crude, and unfinished to Ingres and his followers. *The Lion Hunt* (PLATE 75) recalls similar subjects by Rubens and reveals Delacroix's love of dramatic action and exotic settings; a trip to Morocco in 1832 and the reading of Byron's *Childe Harold* had fired his enthusiasm for the Near East. The writhing entanglement of hunters, horses, and lions suggests the eternal struggle between man and his environment, a theme dear to Delacroix and to Romantic art and literature.   The explosive energy of the composition is organized within an oval of light. The blurred edges, the *lost and found* (discontinuous) outlines, rapid brush strokes, vigorous paint texture, and touches of bold color all make the action more convincing.   Delacroix did not seek the timeless ideal form and precise sleek finish of Ingres' painting, nor did he employ the heroic proportions of Rubens' figures. The sense of immediate, everyday reality in Delacroix's treatment of literary themes comes in part from his use of ordinary human proportions, like those of the little people—with whom we sympathize so readily—in the painting of Rembrandt. It is not surprising that Delacroix's painting is often described as emotional and that of Ingres as intellectual; yet Delacroix's *Journals* indicate a calculating nature, while Ingres' emotional nature was well known. The freedom and spontaneity of Delacroix's canvases were achieved with deliberation and method. His use of complementary colors to obtain liveliness within shadow areas forecasts the practices of the Impressionists. Delacroix learned much from the dynamic compositions of his fellow student Théodore Géricault and from the English painter Constable, who often placed colors side by side rather than blending them smoothly together. In spite of official opposition to his work, Delacroix received a number of important mural commissions and was finally granted membership in the Academy in 1857.

PLATE 75
CAN.
JAN.
U. & S.

CAN.
JAN.
U. & S.

Honoré Daumier (Paris, 1808–79).   Daumier's keen observation and remarkable ability as a draftsman made up for his lack of formal training. He earned a meager living as a cartoonist, using woodcuts for book illustrations and lithography for political journals like *La Caricature* and *Le Charivari*. The bourgeoisie, the law courts, and the government all provided material for Daumier, but his basic protests were against the shortcomings of human nature on all social levels. His work ranges from brutal caricature to gentle humor and warm appreciation of life. Daumier was essentially an optimist endowed with the grace of liking people in spite of their failings. Unlike Goya, he was a realist without bitterness. Daumier's oil paintings were relatively unknown until his first exhibition, which was in 1878, the year before his death. While the prints rely upon line reduced to its most essential and expressive gesture, the paintings depend upon starkly simple masses modeled in strong chiaroscuro; yet in all his works, whether the subject is a third-class carriage, a print collector, or a scene from *Don Quixote*, we are compelled to share some of Daumier's compassion for people.

CAN.
JAN.
U. & S.

Gustave Courbet (France, 1819–77).   While various aspects of realism are basic to the art of Goya and of Daumier, the artist who chose the term Realism for his battle standard was Courbet. Museum study was the major source of Courbet's training. He came from the farm to Paris and had several of his early works accepted by the Salon. His notoriety and his leadership in French painting began with the Salon of 1850, where his *Rock Breakers* (destroyed in 1945) and *The Funeral at Ornans* (Louvre, Paris) were attacked as unartistic, crude, and socialistic. His early works had been admitted to the Salon because their moody chiaroscuro fitted the now acceptable qualities of much Romantic painting. His mature work stresses the physical reality of the everyday world and the artist's enjoyment of paint textures. Neither the polite veil of acceptable ideal form of Ingres nor the exotic dramatic subject matter of Delacroix appealed to Courbet, who preferred subjects from his own experience and painted them with an obvious enjoyment of the texture of the paint itself, which he applied with brush and palette knife. The epithet "socialistic" came partly from the combination of style and subject that made the *Rock Breakers* look like ragged workers doing a miserable task—the wrong kind of content for a bourgeoisie still frightened by the socialist uprising that occurred after the Revolution of 1848—and partly from the perennial tendency of some critics to ascribe any deviation from conventional standards in the arts to the latest unpopular political movement. Courbet was adopted as a standard-bearer by the socialist philosopher Proudhon, but his painting continued to be a fresh appreciation of the people and the landscape around him. During the International Expositions of 1855 and 1867 in Paris, Courbet built his own pavilions of Realism and held private showings of his work, thus helping to establish the artist's right to have privately organized exhibitions.

Edouard Manet (France, 1832–83).   The most shocking painting in the Salon des Refusés in 1863 was *The Luncheon on the Grass* (Le Déjeuner sur l'herbe, PLATE 77) by Manet. Earlier work by the painter had been accepted; Manet had come from a wealthy family and had studied under the academic painter Couture. His *Spanish Guitar Player* (Metropolitan Museum, New York) had even won an honorable mention in the Salon of 1861, probably because of the popularity of Spanish culture at that moment. Neither subject nor style of *The Luncheon on the Grass*, however, was considered proper by the public or by many critics. Manet had borrowed the poses of the main figure group from an engraving of a Raphael painting of the *Judgment of Paris*, but Manet had omitted the mythological explanation and shown a nude woman in the company of two well-dressed contemporary Frenchmen. Further, the forms are reduced to large simple areas of color and value; few highlights or shadows break up the shapes. The brushwork is bold and rejoices in the texture of paint. Frans Hals and Rembrandt, not to mention Delacroix, had used bold brushwork but without such drastic simplification of form. Although many of the young painters adopted Manet as their idol, his aristocratic background and his earlier promise of official success kept him from full association with the younger pioneering artists. After 1874, Manet's style changed under the influence of the Impressionists; the large forms were broken more and more into small areas of bright color, and he increasingly depicted outdoor scenes and effects of light. His late work is represented by *The Bar at the Folies-Bergères* (Courtauld Collection, London) of 1881. Here the intensity of vision is of another kind than that in the early work. The shimmer of color and light partially fuses the forms and suggests a momentary glimpse during an ebb and flow of constant change. Manet owed this vision to the young Impressionists.

PLATE 77
CAN.
JAN.
U. & S.

PLATE 79
CAN.
JAN.
U. & S.
Edgar Degas (France, 1834–1917).   Manet's friend Degas also came from a family of means. Degas admired Delacroix but idolized Ingres and studied under one of Ingres' pupils. Line was the most natural medium of expression for Degas, but he was not interested in adopting the ideal forms of Neo-Classicism. He found his favorite subjects in the streets of Paris, the cafes, race tracks, and theaters. *The Glass of Absinthe* (PLATE 79) is typical. Almost-empty table tops lead our attention to a couple in the upper right-hand corner. The figures, architecture, and tables form a bold arrangement of shapes that creates a firm equilibrium within the frame yet retains the effect of a random glance. The attention of the man and part of his body extend beyond the frame and suggest that this is part of a much wider scene. Unlike Manet, Degas often chose to depict the marginal event, the wings of the stage, as though the essential meaning could be seen best in those watching or waiting to perform. Main figures often seem to be almost missed by the view, and large simple spaces may be balanced by more detailed shapes almost out of the picture. Such composition owes much to Japanese prints, and it is this "keyhole" vision that gives the impression of a momentary glimpse in Degas' particular kind of Impressionism, which differed sharply from that of the Impressionist leader Claude Monet. Degas did not subscribe to the soft form and vague edges in Monet's work until late in his career. While Monet saw human forms merely as objects reflecting light and color, Degas evidenced strong interest in the character of individuals. In *The Glass of Absinthe*, the isolated loneliness of the couple and the preoccupied stare of the woman make an unforgettable statement about human experience. In his later work, Degas abandoned oil for pastels and found many of his subjects in the ballet theater. Soft light and glowing, broken colors are combined with firm anatomical structure and the softened but ever present contour. His more traditional use of line enabled Degas to exhibit frequently at the Salon. Although he disliked the term Impressionism, he also participated in most of the eight Impressionist exhibits.

CAN.
JAN.
U. & S.
Winslow Homer (United States, 1836–1910).   Homer's early training was in lithography, but his work in magazine illustration involved the use of woodcuts, which encouraged bold massing of values and incisive characterization. Homer made a sensational debut as an oil painter with his *Prisoners from the Front* (1866, Metropolitan

Museum of Art, New York). For a time after the Civil War, he continued his illustration and did paintings of genre scenes with a keen interest in outdoor light and atmospheric effects. Trips to France and a two-year sojourn in England were followed by residence in Maine. He turned increasingly to elemental subjects of man and nature: the lone hunter, the struggle of boats in rapids, and the violence of the sea. He traveled in the Adirondacks, the Canadian woods, and the islands of the Caribbean, doing quantities of watercolors that range in technique from broad sweeping brush strokes with sparkling transparent washes to small areas of overlapping washes and careful detail. All have the conviction of firsthand experience. Both in watercolors and oils Homer subordinated detail to large areas of contrasting values that strengthen the visual impact of the composition. His method of working was apparently instinctive, for he denied that he modified nature for the sake of art.

Paul Cézanne (France, 1839–1906). One of the most celebrated of the Post-Impressionist painters was Cézanne, who came from Aix-en-Provence to Paris and studied at the Académie Suisse, an unusual institution that provided models and working space but no instruction. The young artist admired Delacroix and Courbet but also several of the academic painters. Cézanne's early work is characterized by dark values, bold awkward forms, and thick paint handled in such a way as to suggest powerful feelings. In the 1870's, he turned to Impressionistic painting and exhibited the *House of the Hanged Man* (1873, Louvre, Paris) in the first Impressionist show in 1874. He came to feel, however, that Impressionism sacrificed too much solidity and structure in the composition, and in the 1880's he changed to the style for which he is well known today. Cézanne's portraits, still lifes, and landscapes all reduce objects to basic planes and masses which are brought into subtle complementary relationships on the canvas. The *Mt. S. Victoire from Bibemus Quarry* (PLATE 83) is typical in the small groups of parallel brush strokes that suggest massive form in mountain and foliage and even in sky. Lost and found outlines define the masses but allow them to flow into each other at various points, and the planes and angles of one form are echoed and modulated elsewhere. All the forms acquire a structural unity—a family resemblance—in this way. Roundness is achieved not only with light and shadow but also with advancing and receding colors. Yet all forms are obviously

PLATE 83
CAN.
JAN.
REW.
U. & S.

constructed with paint, and there is a paradoxical suggestion of mass and depth and at the same time of a flat painted surface. In contrast to Impressionist work, Cézanne's mature painting emphasizes a static structure that largely excludes motion or the changing effects of light and weather. Cézanne said that he wanted "to make of Impressionism something solid and durable like the art of the museums." His link with the past can be found in the art of Poussin. Cézanne's importance for the future was summed up in his advice to a young painter to paint nature in terms of the cylinder, the sphere, and the cone—i.e., the basic geometric forms. This is literally what was done in Cubist art which began in 1907, one year after Cézanne's death and the same year as his first large retrospective exhibition.

COLOR
PLATE 3
CAN.
JAN.
U. & S.

Claude Monet (France, 1840–1926).   Monet came from Le Havre to Paris and studied at the Académie Suisse and in the studio of the academic painter Gleyre, where he met Renoir and several other young men who would later participate in the Impressionist movement. Monet early acquired a love of painting outdoors, partly through the example of his older friends Eugene Boudin and Johan Jongkind. His early style was bold in color and vigorous in brushwork. Large unbroken areas recall the art of Manet; yet the Salons of 1865 and 1866 accepted some marines and a portrait by Monet and praised him as a "naturalist." However, as he went further in his studies of the effects of light on color and as his forms became less clearly defined, Monet was continually rejected by juries. In 1874, his *Impression: Sunrise* (1872, Musée Marmottan, Paris) caused the label "Impressionism" to be attached to the group by critics. The smoldering light of the rising sun coming through mist and shimmering on the surface of the water is rendered in loose brush strokes and vague forms, a technique meant to distill the total visual impression of a particular moment. For many critics this appeared to be sheer incompetence. Seeking more subtle distinctions in changing light and color, Monet sometimes worked in series, painting the same subject—a haystack, a railway station, or the Cathedral of Rouen—in various kinds of light. The *Rouen Cathedral* (COLOR PLATE 3) employs the complementary colors blue and orange in separate brushstrokes to create a vibrating mirage-like image that sacrifices solid form for intensity of visual experience. Had the blues and oranges been blended by the brush, they would have neutralized rather than intensified each other. Where the brush strokes are small enough to allow the spectator's eyes to "mix" the complementary colors when viewing the painting at a distance (*optical mixing*), the effects range from intense color to lively grays. The Impressionist process of applying colors separately in order to exploit their effect upon each other is called the technique of *broken color*. By the 1890's, Monet's series paintings had met with considerable success; his approach could be appreciated as scientific, although scientific interest is not a satisfactory explanation of his work. There is an intensification or exaggeration of natural color and light effects—typified in Color Plate 3—that comes from the artist's sensual enjoyment of such phenomena. Monet's last great series, spread over the latter years of his life, was dedicated to a pond with water lilies. Here the imaginative quality of his art grew more evident, and the paintings became increasingly abstract.

Auguste Renoir (France, 1841–1919).   Renoir, Monet's friend and fellow Impressionist, began as an apprentice to a porcelain decorator. He then studied with the academic painter Gleyre and supported himself with commercial art. His early work consists of rather tightly detailed landscapes and earthy, solidly painted nudes that show the influence of Courbet. Renoir was accepted by the Salon in the 1860's and occasionally thereafter. With Monet, he turned increasingly to broken color and the evanescent effects of light. *The Swing* (PLATE 80) treats human forms as objects dappled by light and color reflections. Man is seen not as an individual but as a moving, light-reflecting object in a constantly changing environment. Renoir employed somewhat more detailed forms in portraiture and managed to obtain a number of commissions. One, *Madame Charpentier and Her Daughters* (1878, Metropolitan Museum of Art, New York), was a success in the Salon of 1879. During Renoir's travels in the 1880's, his encounter with Raphael's paintings in Italy led him to return temporarily to sharper outlines and curved forms in flowing, rhythmical relationships. The major example of this Raphaelesque phase is *The Bathers* (1884–87, Tyson Collection, Chestnut Hill, Pennsylvania). In the work which followed, the interest in curving forms remained, but contours were softened. Woman is the main subject, and Renoir gave her his personal concept of ideal form: soft, ponderous masses of flesh in delicate, luminous colors. The impersonal treatment of the human figure in earlier work

PLATE 80
CAN.
JAN.
U. & S.

here gives way to a mystical reverence for woman as a symbol for the fecundity and glory of nature.

CAN.
JAN.
U. & S.

Thomas Eakins (United States, 1844–1916).   Eakins first studied at the Pennsylvania Academy of Fine Arts in Philadelphia and then went to Paris in 1866, right after the stormy Salon des Refusés and during Manet's notoriety. Yet Eakins studied with the French academic painter Jean L. Gérôme, and his art shows little influence of the young French painters of the day. He seems to have been more sympathetic to the art of Velázquez and Ribera, which he saw during a trip to Spain. Upon his return, Eakins settled in Philadelphia and spent the rest of his career painting the people and the life around him. His major interest was in the individual character of a human face, the anatomical structure of the body, and the rich variety of textures and details in all things. The portrait of *Miss Van Buren* (c. 1891, Phillips Collection, Washington, D.C.) is typical in its unflinching presentation of the strong but hardly ideal features of the face, in the distinction of textures, and in the powerful illusion of space. *Max Schmitt in a Single Shell* (1871, Metropolitan Museum of Art, New York) shows the principal figure looking over his shoulder as he pauses in his rowing. The diamond-bright detail suggests a photograph with equally sharp focus from foreground to infinity. As the focal point of the composition, Schmitt's figure is framed by the dark area in the foreground water, the reflection of trees on the left, and the arches of a bridge in the background. He is centrally located along the diagonal of the shell, a diagonal that is echoed by the marks of the oars in the water and by the cloud above. This careful compositional structure keeps the details from weakening the whole and provides a satisfying unity of parts.

CAN.
JAN.
REW.
U. & S.

Paul Gauguin (France, 1848–1903).   As a young man, Gauguin developed a promising career in a brokerage firm, a collection of Impressionist paintings, and a hobby of painting. The latter eventually led him to leave his secure situation and become a painter. Partly for cheaper living, partly because he was fascinated by primitive societies, he went to Brittany (first to Pont-Aven and then to Le Pouldu). His early work there was Impressionistic, and he exhibited in some of the Impressionist exhibits in Paris. Under the influence of Cézanne, Manet, Japanese prints, and the young painter Bernard, Gauguin slowly turned away from broken color and began to use parallel brush strokes and outlines around areas of closely modulated color. The color areas became more closed, suggesting flat textile patterns, and color contrasts became bolder. Several young men joined Gauguin in Brittany and accepted him as their leader. These Pont-Aven artists chose the word *synthesism* to describe their painting. Later the term *symbolist-synthesist* was used frequently as Gauguin became acquainted with some of the symbolist writers. Two of the Pont-Aven painters joined the *Nabis* (Hebrew word for prophets), a group which derived some of its symbolism from the mysticism of Theosophy, but Gauguin maintained an independent attitude. His symbolism expresses the mystery and the imaginative life of primitive peoples. In 1891 he traveled to Tahiti, where he produced such works as *The Spirit of the Dead Watching* (1892, Good-year Collection, New York). Here resonant harmonies of yellows, purples, oranges, and blues join the flat patterns which set off the ponderously solid body of the frightened girl lying on a bed. The spirits of the dead, represented by small flashes of light, and a ghost, represented by a woman in profile, watch from above and behind. Gauguin returned to Paris for a short time (1893–95) and rapidly went through a small inheritance. He was soon back in Tahiti, where his health began to fail. His last two years were spent in the Marquesas Islands.

Vincent Van Gogh (Holland, 1853–90). Van Gogh was a Dutchman, but most of his painting was done in France during the last four years of a short but intense life. After abortive attempts at working for art dealers (in The Hague, London, and Paris), studying theology, and preaching Evangelism among coal miners, Van Gogh turned to painting in 1880. Millet, Daumier, and Rembrandt were the idols of his early period; in works like *The Potato Eaters* (1885, Collection of V. W. Van Gogh, Laren, Holland), poverty-stricken workers are portrayed compassionately with heavy blunt forms and dark brownish color. In 1886, Van Gogh settled in Paris with his brother Theo, who directed a small gallery. Study with the academic painter Cormon soon gave way to enthusiasm for the Impressionists. Under the encouragement of Camille Pissarro, Van Gogh's color became brighter and lighter, and he began to use broken color; yet his brush strokes have a writhing liveliness unlike those in most Impressionist work. While in Paris, Van Gogh became acquainted with Japanese prints, such as those shown in the back-

PLATE 82
CAN.
JAN.
REW.
U. & S.

ground of his portrait of *Père Tanguy* (1887–88, Collection of Stavros Niarchos, Athens). In 1888, Van Gogh left Paris for Arles in southern France. His compositions began to employ more powerful colors, often clashing complementaries; thick paint textures that seem to be sculpted with the brush or the palette knife; and shapes whose abruptly changing contours express a convulsive energy. Van Gogh was subject to occasional epileptoid seizures, and these led to a year's residence in the asylum at Saint-Rémy. *Wheat Field with Cypresses* (PLATE 82) is typical of this period in its glowing colors and in the dancing, twitching rhythm that activates earth and sky. Paint is applied in short, choppy strokes that seem to sculpt edges and surfaces. From Saint-Rémy, Van Gogh went to Auvers, near Paris, to receive treatment from Dr. Gachet, a friend of Pissarro, and it was at the small village of Auvers that he died of a self-inflicted wound. Van Gogh is usually considered as one of the Post-Impressionists because he painted as an Impressionist for a short period before developing his mature work. His imaginative use of color, his expressive distortion of natural forms, and the total emotional force of his art made him an important source for many trends in twentieth-century painting, particularly French Fauvism and German Expressionism.

PLATE 81
CAN.
JAN.
REW.
U. & S.

Georges Seurat (France, 1859–81).   The last exhibition of the Impressionist group, in 1886, was marked by dissension; Monet and Renoir were both absent. A central problem was the new approach represented by Seurat and his followers. Their works were displayed in a separate room and their style came to be called *Neo-Impressionism*, one of the terms subsumed under the label of *Post-Impressionism*. The intensity of light and color in Impressionist work appealed to Seurat, but he felt—as did Cézanne—that mass and compositional structure had been sacrificed; so he set out to systematize the broken color of Impressionism and to clarify its forms. On the basis of color theories which had been published by Michel Chevreul and by Charles Henry, Seurat applied colors in uniformly small dots in specific quantities to create particular effects when the spectator experienced optical mixing. Seurat's technique was called *pointillism* in regard to the paint application and *divisionism* in regard to the systematically broken color. The suggestion of constant change and movement in much Impressionist work was replaced, in Seurat's painting, by more rigid organization and static form. In his *Sunday*

Afternoon on the Island of La Grande Jatte (PLATE 81), the shadows, trees, and figures form a horizontal and vertical gridwork in three dimensions; the clearly edged and simplified forms become standard rather than individual objects, and there is a quality of geometric order, of inflexible balance, and of calculated method. In 1884, the Post-Impressionist Seurat was one of the founders of the *Salon des Indépendants*, which provided exhibition opportunities without jury selection and thus answered one of the basic needs that had inspired the Impressionist exhibitions between 1874 and 1886.

Henri de Toulouse-Lautrec (France, 1864–1901).   The spectacular dissoluteness of Toulouse-Lautrec's life, his aristocratic ancestry, and his dwarfed and crippled body have made dramatic material for biographies. In spite of the dissolute life he led, however, his short career was remarkably productive. After training in the studio of Cormon and working in an Impressionistic vein, Toulouse-Lautrec formed a style that is closely related to that of Degas. His *Au Moulin Rouge* (1892, Art Institute of Chicago) is a casual passing glimpse of the cabaret life that provided many of his subjects. The large areas of color function as bold patterns and reveal the influence of Japanese prints and the paintings of Degas. As in Degas' work, movement is expressed by the contours of active shapes, the sweeping asymmetrical diagonals, and the extension of major figures beyond the edges of the composition. Like Degas, but unlike many of the other Impressionists, Toulouse-Lautrec was interested in human personality. His depictions of Paris dandies and prostitutes show a sensitivity that neither condones nor criticizes but mercilessly reveals the monotony, the frantic efforts to live fully, the cynicism, the lust, and the gaiety of a certain stratum of international society. His famous posters for several of the cabarets are brilliant demonstrations of lithography applied to advertising art. Toulouse-Lautrec never became a member of the Impressionist group and belongs more properly to the Post-Impressionists.

CAN.
JAN.
U. & S.

SCULPTURE

Nineteenth-century sculpture was less inventive than painting, and stylistic trends are less distinct. France had given preference to the clear sweeping lines and ideal forms of Neo-Classic sculpture after the Revolution. Napoleon supported this preference and commissioned portraits from the Italian Neo-Classicist Antonio Canova. The Romantic attitude in sculpture became apparent in the Salons of 1833 and 1834, when rough surfaces, individualistic features, and entangled forms were used to accentuate active subjects. Antoine Barye, François Rude, and Antoine Préault were considered the leaders. The second half of the century saw more precise anatomical and costume detail, ranging from the sensual fleshiness of Jean-Baptiste Carpeaux's sculpture to the dry precision of Emmanuel Frémiet's work. The major figure in French sculpture of the late nineteenth and early twentieth centuries was Rodin, who combined an interest in lively, rippling surfaces with expressions of man's aspirations and of conflicts between mind and body.

During the first half of the century Italy was the center of Neo-Classic sculpture, which was led by Antonio Canova and Bertel Thorvaldsen. In Germany and Austria, the Neo-Classic sculpture of Johann G. Schadow, Johann von Dannecker, and Christian D. Rauch was indebted to the Italians. Germanic Neo-Classic sculpture occasionally became sentimental, but no clearly Romantic trend developed. American sculptors, such as Hiram Powers and Horatio Greenough, were also influenced by Italian Neo-Classicism. During the second half of the nineteenth century, the tendency toward increasingly naturalistic detail was international.

PLATE 71
JAN.
U. & S.
Antonio Canova (Italy, 1757–1822).   This famous Neo-Classic sculptor was trained in Venice and developed an early style that combined naturalistic detail with late Baroque composition. When he moved to Rome in 1779, however, and studied Roman ruins and ancient sculpture, his style changed to the simplified anatomy, long sweeping curves, and quiet compositions that became representative of the Neo-Classic aesthetic. Canova's international reputation as a portraitist led to a commission for a full length statue of *Napoleon* (1802, Brera Gallery, Milan), in which he portrayed the French leader as a nude Greco-Roman warrior in a pose like that of the *Hellenistic Ruler* (second century B.C., National Museum, Rome). A better-known portrait is that of *Pauline Borghese as Venus* (PLATE 71), which presents an idealized figure in a serene pose with clear stately contours in a static alignment of vertical and horizontal elements. The composition seeks an absolute beauty outside the reach of motion, change, or time. Canova is also noted as a major influence in forcing the Congress of Paris to return works of art taken from Italy by Napoleon.

Antoine Barye (France, 1795–1875).   Barye studied with the Neo-Classic sculptor Bosio and worked for some years as a goldsmith. He sketched constantly in the Paris Zoological Museum and became a specialist in animal sculpture. A preference for scenes of violent action, showing the strong devouring the weak, links Barye with Romanticism, although his work has more detail and less freedom of form than that of Delacroix. In the Salon of 1831, Barye's *Tiger Devouring a Gavial* was praised by some critics, and by 1833, when he exhibited the *Lion Crushing a Serpent,* he was hailed as a leader of Romanticism in sculpture. The anatomical accuracy in his animals made the rough surfaces and violent action easier for conservative critics to accept. Barye became interested in Greek art, however, and some of his later works, such as the *Theseus and the Centaur Bianor* (1850, Museum of Puy, France), are characterized by slightly simplified anatomy and idealized form. Some of his late pieces are calm and even static in composition. Barye became a member of the French Academy in 1868.

JAN.
U. & S.

Jean-Baptiste Carpeaux (France, 1827–75).   Carpeaux, one of the major French sculptors of the second half of the nineteenth century, won a *Prix de Rome* after studying under François Rude. While in Italy, he produced the *Neapolitan Fisherboy with a Shell* (1858, Louvre, Paris), a subject appealing for its liveliness and humble humanity rather than for any ideal form. The *Ugolino and His Starving Sons* (1857–61, Tuileries Gardens, Paris) draws its subject from Dante and, like the work of Barye, is Romantic in its emotional intensity and its restless, complex composition. Carpeaux's most important commissions included the *Triumph of Flora* (1863–66) for the Tuileries Gardens and *The Dance* (1867–69) for the Paris Opera. Both compositions have a rippling, delicate complexity that recalls the Rococo, but they reveal the nineteenth century in their voluptuous fleshiness combined with realistic anatomical detail that is not made to echo the larger rhythms of the forms. They are clear examples of the tendency of some art in the second half of the nineteenth century to take inspiration from science and photography and to *document* nature. *The Dance* created a great scandal because of the unidealized nakedness of its nude figures, but eventually it was accepted as one of the major works of its time.

JAN.
U. & S.

Constantin Meunier (Belgium, 1831–1905).   After thirty years as a painter, Meunier turned to sculpture in 1885 and achieved an inter-

JAN.
U. & S.

national reputation as the portrayer of man at labor. He generally avoided the limitations of a topical social message, expressing rather the universal dignity of physical work. His interest was not in ideal physical form but in the earthy reality of ordinary bodies and relaxed or straining muscles, often revealed by clinging work clothes. Yet many of his figures have an aura of power and self-confidence that comes partly from pose and partly from Meunier's ability to subordinate anatomical and costume details to the larger forms and to suggest monumental scale. His workers in repose sometimes echo the strength and poise of fifth-century B.C. Greek sculpture. An obvious source for Meunier's style is the painting of the Frenchman Millet, while the expressive force of his art anticipates the sculpture of the German Barlach.

PLATE 73
JAN.
SEU.
U. & S.
Auguste Rodin (France, 1840–1917). The Frenchman Rodin dominated western sculpture in the late nineteenth and early twentieth centuries. He was trained as a sculptor's helper and as a carver of architectural ornament. In his spare time, he listened to the lectures of Barye and prepared himself to be a sculptor. A voyage to Italy in 1875 opened his eyes to the expressive power of Donatello and Michelangelo; he was particularly impressed by the pulsating life suggested in the undulating rough surfaces of Michelangelo's unfinished work. For his first Salon offering in 1875, Rodin chose *The Man with a Broken Nose* (Rodin Museum, Paris), a head that preserves in the bronze cast something of the rough, flowing, easily shaped quality of clay, Rodin's favorite material. *The Age of Bronze* (1877, Rodin Museum, Paris) has the same breakup of surfaces into soft undulating musculature that produces a flickering complexity of highlights. In 1879, Rodin began planning *The Gates of Hell* for the Museum of Decorative Arts in Paris. Although the project, which took its theme from Dante, was never finished, the constantly evolving plan for the great work served as a source from which Rodin took figures for other sculptures. *The Thinker* (PLATE 73) was first conceived as part of the reliefs for *The Gates of Hell* but gained fame as a single figure. The bronze presents a convincing muscular and skeletal structure, but details have been omitted or softened, and the surfaces are both rougher and more lively than those of Carpeaux's *Dance*. Like many of Michelangelo's figures, *The Thinker* implies that physical power does not hold the solution for man's most challenging problems. *The Burghers of Calais* (1884, Calais) is

one of the most powerful emotional expressions in Rodin's work. Rough surfaces, distortions in proportion, and conflicting directional forces express the fear and the strength of will required of these citizens who gave themselves up to the enemy in order to save their city. Because of such expressive distortions, Rodin's *Monument to Balzac* (1891, Rodin Museum, Paris) was refused by the society which had commissioned it. But in 1898, his famous *Kiss* (1886, stone version in the Rodin Museum, Philadelphia) was purchased by the French government. Rodin's style is best seen in his bronzes, which catch the essence of the artist's work in clay; assistants did much of the stone carving. The effect of moving surfaces in Rodin's work has caused him to be called an Impressionist in sculpture. Such a designation ignores the powerful emotional expression in his work, a quality not basic to Impressionism in painting but most important to French Fauvism and to German Expressionism.

ARCHITECTURE

Nineteenth-century architecture has been described as the "Battle of the Styles" because of the prevailing tendency to borrow forms from various periods in the past. This eclecticism had begun in the eighteenth century, especially in England, where the work of a single architect would frequently include buildings in the Greek, Roman, Romanesque, Gothic, and Renaissance styles. Eclecticism became international during the nineteenth century, and the word *revival* is often used to indicate the close dependence of a particular style upon its historical prototype. Iron could be cast into different kinds of ornamental details, but it could also be used inventively for strikingly new architectural forms such as those of the *Crystal Palace*, built as an exhibition hall for the London International Exhibition of 1851. During the second half of the century, England developed the so-called *Victorian Gothic* (Italianate Gothic with polychrome stripes) and imported the Second Empire Style from France.

France had begun the century with dreams of creating an empire rivaling that of ancient Rome. Napoleonic plans provided for vast Greco-Roman monuments, like the *Arch of Triumph* and the *Church of the Madeleine*, many of which were finished long after the Battle of Waterloo. Renaissance revival designs were also popular. The *Second Empire Style*, named after the empire of Napoleon III, is characterized by *mansard* roofs (steeply pitched roofs with a flat or almost flat platform at the top) and highly decorated dormer windows. Walls were treated with ornate sculptural richness, in a style often described as *Neo-Baroque*. French and Belgian architecture of the 1890's led in the international style called *Art Nouveau*, which turned away from eclecticism and exulted in a profusion of irregular, curving, linear ornament inspired by plant life.

German architecture during the nineteenth century was strongly influenced by that of France. Greek and Roman revival styles competed with variations on Italian Renaissance features, usually including simple blocky masses and round-arched windows. After the middle of the century, German architecture often displayed features of the Second Empire Style.

In Italy, classic revival designs found increasing competition from the Renaissance and the Baroque revivals, especially in the second half of the century. Huge scale and ponderous proportions are typical.

In the United States, various builder's guides served as pattern books for carpenters and spread eclecticism in buildings of modest budget or in provincial locations. The invention of the jigsaw made possible cheap ornament in wood. Listings of styles for private houses included such labels as *Suburban Greek*, *Moorish*, *Lombard Italian*, *Ancient Etruscan*, and *Collegiate Gothic*. For large buildings, Greek, Roman, and Gothic were the most common styles in the first half of the century; later, Renaissance revival, Romanesque revival, and Second Empire were widely used. The reaction against eclecticism began with the work of Louis Sullivan and Frank Lloyd Wright. The steel-framed skyscraper developed first in the United States, partly because of the high cost of land but especially because of the availability and relative cheapness of steel.

PLATE 72
JAN.
U. & S.

Thomas Jefferson (United States, 1743–1826).   One of the stylistic phases of post-colonial architecture in the eastern United States is often called the *Federal Style*. Thomas Jefferson's home *Monticello* (PLATE 72) is a fine example of this Roman phase of the Neo-Classic. Of the many amateur architects of his day, Jefferson produced some of the most influential buildings, even while he was engaged in a variety of other activities. Jefferson felt that most architecture of his time was poor in its proportions and details because it strayed from the example of ancient Roman buildings. Monticello is based on Palladio's Renaissance interpretation of Roman architecture. Jefferson used strict symmetry, a pedimented porch with a semicircular Roman window, Roman-inspired Tuscan columns, a low Roman dome on an octagonal base, severely simple ornament, and the single story effect of a Roman temple. His designs for the *Capital of Virginia* at Richmond (1785–89) were based on the *Maison Carrée* (PLATE 19) and drawn up with the help of the French architect Clérisseau. The Corinthian order of the Roman temple was changed to the simpler Ionic, and necessary windows were added to the cella. For the *University of Virginia*, Jefferson's favorite architectural project, he used the example of the *Pantheon* (PLATE 15) for the library. Jefferson's architecture, however, shows a flexibility and inventiveness in the application of Roman forms that is a refreshing contrast to the more imitative pedantry of many Neo-Classic designers.

Sir John Soane (England, 1753–1837). One of England's most original Neo-Classicists was Sir John Soane. During a visit to Italy, he studied the imaginative antique world of Piranesi's prints, actual Roman ruins, and Renaissance buildings. In 1788, he was appointed architect for the Bank of England. He used Roman domes and Roman arches for the building, but in place of the usual columns and pilasters he employed inscribed linear ornament. The total effect is one of crisp precision, with thin sturdy surfaces rather than the ponderous mass of Roman work. His own house in London— No. 12, Lincoln's Inn Fields—provided more opportunity for experiment. Canopy-like cross-vaulted ceilings cover spaces that continue over screening walls which stop short of the ceiling. From low dark spaces, one is drawn toward high, brightly lighted areas. Mirrors help to convey light and to emphasize the continuity of space. The variety of spaces and light effects and the variety of Soane's collection of art objects lead one to expect surprises around every corner. It is here, rather than in the austerely simple surfaces and restrained linear ornament of his larger buildings, that we see Soane's kinship with the imaginative Piranesi.

Karl Friedrich von Schinkel (Germany, 1781–1841). Germany's leading architect in the first half of the nineteenth century began, like Inigo Jones, as a designer of stage sets. He was a painter of moody landscapes with Gothic buildings, but his architecture began as Greek revival and eventually employed Roman domes and arches. A good example of his early work is the *Neue Wache* (1816–18) in Berlin, built after his appointment as State Architect of Prussia. A severe block with corner towers is faced with a Doric porch. The authentic proportions of the Doric order, the avoidance of round arches, and the simplicity of the parts are characteristic of the purest Greek revival architecture. Schinkel's *Berlin Theater* (1819–21) has greater complexity of parts but the same severe blockiness, post and lintel structure, and restrained decoration. His *Old Berlin Museum* (1824–28) masks the two-story interior with a huge Ionic stoa and hides the interior Roman dome behind a simple rectangular attic.

PLATE 74
HIT.
JAN.
U. & S.

Sir Charles Barry (England, 1795–1860). Barry's career demonstrates the various enthusiasms of nineteenth-century architects and their patrons. Barry began by designing Gothic revival churches but turned to Renaissance revival as his major interest. His *Travelers' Club* in London (1829–31) takes its form from Italian Renaissance palaces. In 1836, however, he won the competition for the new *Houses of Parliament* (PLATE 74) with a Gothic design, forecasting the wide popularity of Gothic in the Victorian period. In the same year, A. Welby Pugin's book *Contrasts* appeared, arguing that the Gothic style was the most Christian style and should be used exclusively. It was Pugin who designed the details for the *Houses of Parliament*; late Gothic was used because its more complex ornament was considered to be richer and more picturesque for a skyline as prominent as that of Parliament. In keeping with the increasing use of iron in architecture, Barry placed iron roofs on the building.

HIT.
JAN.
U. & S.

Henri Labrouste (France, 1801–75). After winning a *Prix de Rome* and studying ancient and Renaissance architecture in Italy, Labrouste returned to Paris and established a studio where he taught architecture. His insistence that the climate should be considered in the design and choice of materials was unusual in his day and prophetic of the future. Labrouste's masterpiece is the *Bibliothèque Sainte Geneviève* in Paris (1843–50), a design based on the form of Italian Renaissance palaces but handled with sensitivity in proportions and inventiveness in the application of iron in the interior. The reading room gains spaciousness from the slender iron columns, which support a ceiling of plaster panels between round arches of perforated iron. Labrouste added a reading room to the *Bibliothèque Nationale* in Paris (1862–68) where he again used thin iron columns, this time supporting light terra cotta domes. The book stack areas that he designed for the same building are of iron and glass. Both in design and materials, Labrouste was an important leader in French architecture in the mid-nineteenth century.

Louis Sullivan (United States, 1856–1924). America's most pioneering architect in the late nineteenth century was Louis Sullivan, who was trained at the Massachusetts Institute of Technology and the École des Beaux Arts of the French Academy. At a time when architecture was deriving inspiration from the past, Sullivan insisted upon a fresh approach to form and decoration. His concept that *form follows function* (suggested earlier in the century by Horatio Greenough) argued that design should express the use, structure, and materials of a building. The Bostonian Sullivan came to Chicago in 1873 and eventually became partner to Dankmar Adler for the period from 1881 to 1895. Sullivan's early work is represented by the *Chicago Auditorium Building* (1886–89). In the lower floors, the granite masonry is handled with bold roughness and deep shadows, emphasizing the base and creating an effect of vast scale and strength. Above, the smooth stone façade is unified by tall arches with groups of windows that decrease in size as they approach the final cornice. Sullivan here shows the influence of Henry Hobson Richardson, an older architect noted for his sensitive interpretation of Romanesque forms. Other Chicago architects were more advanced than Sullivan in exploring new structural methods and materials, particularly the steel frame, but the new technique was hidden behind a facing of columns and pilasters. It was only in 1890 and 1891 in St. Louis that Sullivan used the steel frame in a design independent of the past. In his *Wainwright Building*, the idea of form following function resulted in large-windowed shops at the base, a central section of offices treated as a framed area, and a crowning band of floral ornament beneath the projecting cornice. The steel frame is expressed in the large windows and slender brick-covered piers; it is obvious that the steel skeleton, not the wall, supports the building. Sullivan believed that a tall building should look tall, so he made the vertical piers rise through the contrasting horizontal floors with their panels of rich ornament. The ornament, which emphasizes rather than hides the structure, is composed of geometric and plant forms in intricate profusion. There is no direct reference to past styles, although the total effect recalls Celtic art or the looser, more

HIT.
JAN.
U. & S.

asymmetrical *Art Nouveau* in Europe. Sullivan's commissions for large buildings fell off as eclecticism increased in commercial archi-tecture during the late nineteenth and early twentieth centuries. He spent the last part of his career designing small buildings for towns in the Midwest. His ideals gained fuller acceptance after his death when they were carried on in the work of his former em-ployee, Frank Lloyd Wright.

The twentieth century

PAINTING

The first major event in twentieth-century painting occurred at the Paris Salon d'Automne in 1905, when a number of French painters, including Derain, Vlaminck, Marquet, Rouault, and Matisse, ex-hibited paintings with such intense color, free brushwork, and expansive shapes that a critic called the painters *fauves* (wild beasts). *Fauvism* was a short-lived movement, lasting only about three years and never formally organized; while its influence was widespread in later twentieth-century painting, only a few of its members, notably Matisse, continued to paint in the style. The immediate sources of Fauvism were Van Gogh and Gauguin, and its bursting vitality and instinctive spontaneity give it the pre-dominant quality of expressionism.

The year 1905 also marked the first exhibition of an organized group of German painters that called itself *Die Brücke* (The Bridge). The group, centered about Karl Schmidt-Rottluff, Emile Nolde, Ernst Ludwig Kirchner, Erich Heckel, and Max Peckstein, lasted from 1905 until 1913. These men, whose headquarters were in Dresden, were inspired by the paintings of the Fauves and the Norwegian painter Munch and by medieval German woodcuts. They used harsh, brutally simplified forms and strong, often clash-ing colors in a heavy expressionistic manner. Some of the Bridge group were absorbed by *Der Blaue Reiter* (The Blue Rider), a group formed in Munich in 1911 by Vassily Kandinsky that encompassed a variety of styles ranging from Kandinsky's gay, buoyant, non-objective paintings to the angular, geometric abstractions of Franz Marc. The Bridge and the Blue Rider groups provided the basis for the broad trend known as *German Expressionism*, which is still evident today.

Meanwhile, *Cubism* developed in France during the period from 1907 to 1914 under the leadership of Pablo Picasso and Georges

Braque. Its early phase, often called *Analytical Cubism*, sought to reduce nature to its basic geometric shapes while viewing objects from several sides simultaneously. This simultaneity of vision implies a summation of visual experience from different moments and different positions in space and suggests an intriguing parallel to the concepts of relativity that Einstein was proposing in the same period. Analytic Cubism employed very restrained colors, limited space, and a limited repertoire of geometric shapes; it may be understood partly as a reaction to the spontaneous freedom and lively color of Fauvism. The second phase of Cubism has been called *Synthetic* because it is a more imaginative reconstruction of or improvisation on the forms of natural objects. Color and space are less limited, and shapes are less restricted to basic geometry. Synthetic Cubism employed *collage*, the pasting of actual objects, such as pieces of newspaper, to the surface of the painting.

French Cubism inspired the Russian painter Kazimir Malevich, who started a movement called *Suprematism* in 1913. Malevich's geometric compositions evolved from Cubism to nonobjectivity. A broader movement, which concerned both painting and sculpture, was *Constructivism*, the manifesto of which was drawn up in Moscow in 1920 by the brothers Antoine Pevsner and Naum Gabo. Constructivist painting employed precise geometric forms in compositions that were generally nonobjective. French Cubism also inspired the Dutchman Mondrian to seek even greater austerity in compositions of rectangles and primary colors. In Holland, Mondrian founded a group in 1917 that is generally known by the name of its magazine, *De Stijl*. The wide influence of Cubism may be seen in the Italian movement called *Futurism* (c. 1909–15), which used multiple contours, diagonal lines, and swirling curves to express the dynamism of the machine age.

The tendency to apply a severe geometric system of order to an objective or a nonobjective world has been widespread in twentieth-century painting and has produced a wide variety of styles. A very different tendency has developed concurrently since 1916 when *Dada* was founded in Zurich, Switzerland. Dadaism was a nihilistic rejection of rationality and order. Arising from the disillusionment of the First World War, Dada sought to destroy through ridicule the old ideas about the character, aims, and standards of art in order to build a new standard with an appreciation of fantasy and the irrational. Dadaists used sculpture, painting, and photomontage to present extraordinary combinations of ordinary objects, thereby destroying the conventional meaning of the objects and opening the way for new interpretations by the spectator. Dadaism reflected the growing appreciation of the role of the irrational as revealed by psychiatry. It spread quickly to Cologne, Berlin, Paris, and New York. Its organized life was short (1916–22), but its influence can be traced in much contemporary painting and sculpture. Many Dadaists joined the *Surrealist* movement, which announced its aims in a Paris manifesto in 1924 and which continues as one aspect of painting today. Some Surrealist work, like that of Salvador Dali, attempts to depict hallucinatory or dream experiences, where recognizable and unrecognizable forms appear in surprising combinations and vast scale. Other Surrealists, like Joan Miró, produce compositions with lighter, more humorous fantasies. A major source of both Dada and Surrealism was the Italian Giorgio de Chirico, who was painting haunting, dreamlike landscapes as early as 1913.

In the 1920's and 1930's, while Surrealism, Expressionism, and various kinds of geometric abstraction developed, there was also much painting with social commentary being done in Europe and the Americas. The cynicism that grew out of the First World War encouraged not only the Dada movement but also a trend which in Germany was called *The New Objectivity* (Die Neue Sachlichkeit). Here realistic detail was used more specifically than in Dadaism to point out the horrors and corruption of men and society. There were counterparts to the New Objectivity in other countries. In the United States, the vigorous life of crowded cities, particularly that of the slum areas, provided subject matter for the so-called *Ash Can School* or *The Eight*, led by John Sloan from 1904 until 1930. After the 1913 New York Armory Show, which provided a rude awakening to advanced trends in European art, American patrons were more sympathetic to abstract art. A generation of American artists, many of whom had studied in Paris during the crucial years of Fauvism and Cubism, had become pioneers in American abstract painting. However, the late 1920's produced a tendency away from abstraction and toward painting the American scene. The Depression during the 1930's encouraged such art to depict not only the face of America but also the tragedy and suffering caused by economic crisis. In Russia after 1922, the Communist government forced into exile those artists who would not turn to a propagandistic realism in support of its political ideas. Mexico produced two of the most powerful artists of social commentary in the 1920's and 1930's, Orozco and

Rivera, whose mural paintings protest the viciousness of humanity and the oppression of the weak by the strong.

Since the Second World War an international trend toward abstract and nonobjective art has been dominant. Many European artists were driven by the war to the United States, bringing with them quantities of talent and new ideas. It was in New York, under the leadership of Jackson Pollock, Franz Kline, and Willem de Kooning, that the first major movement developed in postwar painting—*Abstract Expressionism.* This painting is sometimes abstract and sometimes nonobjective, but it is always explosive in the activity of its forms. The quality of expressed activity—often cathartic in its violence—led American critics to speak of much Abstract Expressionist art as *Action Painting.* It has its ancestry in Fauvism, German Expressionism, and the Surrealist emphasis upon instinct and fantasy. Although the term Abstract Expressionism was applied first to American painting of this type during the 1940's, similar work has been done in other countries.

In the 1960's, the dominance of Abstract Expressionism has been challenged by variations of two international trends: *Pop Art* and *Op (Optical) Art.* Pop Art developed first in England and then in America and France. The images made popular by mass media advertising and comic strips are presented in bizarre combinations, distortions, or exaggerated size, blurring the distinctions between commercial art, fine art, and real life. Although the term *Neo-Dada* has been used in connection with Pop Art, satirical intent is often less evident than enthusiasm for the daily images and objects of our urban culture. Optical Art is a development within the broad category of geometric abstraction; it employs precise shapes and optical illusion for effects of movement and ceaseless change.

Vassily Kandinsky (Russia, Germany, and France, 1866–1944). Kandinsky was born in Moscow but settled in Munich to become the leader of the Blue Rider group in 1911. Earlier he had abandoned a career in law and had turned to Fauvist painting and increasingly abstract forms. It may have been as early as 1910, depending on the disputed date of a watercolor, that he developed nonobjective art. His treatise *Concerning the Spiritual in Art*, published in 1912, urged that painting can approach the state of pure music—that is, that line, color, and form may be used like sounds to evoke emotional response without the help of subject matter. He often used titles

PLATE 86
CAN.
JAN.
U. & S.

such as "fugue" or "improvisation" to stress the correspondence with music. The *Improvisation* in Plate 86 is typical of his early non-objective paintings. Cloudlike forms, angular and wavy lines, and rainbow colors expand spirally from a nucleus of smaller, brighter, denser, and more sharply contrasting parts. The activity is buoyant and spontaneous in effect but carefully controlled within the limits of the picture. From the 1920's on, Kandinsky also composed with rigid, precise, geometric shapes or combinations of geometric and freer forms. Occasionally, recognizable objects appear in his work. In 1934, Kandinsky settled in Paris, where he spent much of the remainder of his life. His art has been a major influence in twentieth-century painting.

COLOR
PLATE 4
CAN.
JAN.
U. & S.

Henri Matisse (France, 1869–1954). The study of law failed to satisfy the young Matisse, and his brief study with the academic painter Adolphe Bouguereau was equally frustrating. After this, he studied with the lenient Gustave Moreau and copied works of the masters in the Museum of the Louvre. Early encouragement came when the Salon of the Société Nationale accepted four of his paintings done in a competent bold brushwork recalling the style of Manet. Soon, however, Matisse discovered Impressionism. His Impressionistic *La Desserte* (1897, Collection of Stavros Niarchos, Athens) created a furor among the conservatives of the Société Nationale. Matisse then became enthusiastic about the work of Cézanne and Gauguin, acquiring a painting by each. By 1905, Matisse's art had developed large areas of relatively unbroken colors, often chosen quite independently of nature, and shapes manipulated to intensify their directional forces. In the Salon d'Automne of 1905, Matisse was seen as the leader of the Fauve group. *The Green Line* (1905, State Museum, Copenhagen), a portrait of Madame Matisse, indicates by its title the artist's concern with color. Vibrating complementaries—greens and reds, yellows and violets—achieve a dynamic equilibrium and a life of their own. Such gymnastics with color continued to be typical of Matisse's style, but in his later works he tended to use thinner paint and to create looser forms. *Decorative Figure on an Ornamental Background* (COLOR PLATE 4) is one of the more tightly constructed works from the 1920's, yet the solid rigidity of the figure contrasts with the exuberance of the patterns and colors. The exhilarating effect of ease and spontaneity masks the continual repainting and the deliberation that went into Matisse's painting. In *Notes of a Painter*, published in 1908, Matisse describes his dream of an art of balance, purity, and serenity devoid of troubling or depressing subject matter—art that would serve as an armchair in which to rest. No elaborate theories guided him; he relied on his instinctive reactions as he worked and reworked a composition according to his conviction that everything—shapes, spaces between shapes, colors, and lines—should contribute to the total expression.

Georges Rouault (France, 1871–1958).   Rouault's training consisted of an apprenticeship to a maker of stained glass and the study of painting with Gustave Moreau. By 1905, Rouault was painting with the slashing brushwork and urgent scumblings seen in *The Head of Christ* (Collection of Walter P. Chrysler, Jr., New York). Although his works were not exhibited in the same room with those of the Fauves during the Salon of 1905, he was Fauvist in the expressive violence of his forms. Rouault's content, however, which deals more with the pathos, tragedy, and corruption of man, links him with German Expressionism. Frequent subjects are prostitutes, sorrowing clowns, evil judges, and heads of Christ. His deep religious convictions owed much to the writings of Léon Bloy; his sense of social justice recalls the art of Daumier. As Rouault's style matured, the contours became rigid containers for islands of thick glowing color. *The Old King* (1937, Carnegie Institute, Pittsburgh) has the radiance of a stained glass window or a Byzantine icon. His genius as a printmaker is revealed in the lithography and intaglio prints which he executed as book illustrations under the patronage of his dealer, Ambrose Vollard, during the period from 1916 to 1927 and which he eventually published as the *Miserere*.

CAN.
JAN.
U. & S.

Piet Mondrian (Holland, 1872–1944).   Mondrian, even more than Kandinsky, was the exponent of nonobjective painting. Mondrian studied at the Amsterdam Academy and began as a painter of landscapes in bright Fauve colors, exemplified by *The Woods near Œle* (1907, City Museum, The Hague). After moving to Paris in 1912, his style was strongly influenced by Cubism and became increasingly abstract. The *Composition No. 7 (Façade)* (Nieuwenhuizen Segaar Gallery, The Hague) indicates that by 1914 he was reducing subject matter to intricate flat rectangular systems limited to a few colors. Mondrian returned to Holland in 1914 and remained there during

PLATE 90
CAN.
JAN.
U. & S.

the First World War. In 1917, he and a circle of friends founded the magazine *De Stijl*, whose name would subsequently be attached to their group in spite of Mondrian's choice of the term *Neo-Plasticism*. He remained the major spokesman for the group and the only faithful follower of the strict principles he enunciated. He stated that the new plastic idea would find its expression in the universal elements of straight lines and primary colors. He saw subject matter as an impurity that limited the universality of the painting by tying it to a particular time and place. Neo-Plasticism sought a balanced relationship of pure forms. *Composition with Blue and Yellow* (PLATE 90) exemplifies Mondrian's mature style; a certain intensity of warm yellow and a certain intensity of cool blue are adjusted in quantity to form an equilibrium within the simple gridwork of black lines. This search for absolute order makes an interesting parallel with the Neo-Classic artist's effort to find an absolute beauty that would last through the changes of time and place. In 1919, Mondrian returned to Paris and stayed there until 1938, when the Second World War forced him to move to London for two years and then to New York. His art has had a wide influence on painting, sculpture, architecture, and product design.

CAN.
JAN.
U. & S.

Paul Klee (Switzerland and Germany, 1879–1940).   Klee grew up in Bern, Switzerland, but studied in the Academy at Munich. After traveling in Italy, he painted and did etchings in Bern until 1906, when he moved back to Munich. In 1912, he participated in the second Blue Rider exhibit there. Although his studies included a firm academic grounding in life drawing and perspective, Klee early developed a preference for abstractions done in small scale with subtle color and delicate line. His intellectual attitude was very sophisticated, but his writings show a desire to join adult understanding and experience with the freshness of vision and the delightful fantasy usually left behind with childhood. *The Landscape with Blue Birds* (1919, Philadelphia Museum of Art) is typical of many of his landscapes of the 1920's in its delicate rectangles of color and the softly emerging shapes of trees and birds. The quality of intimate personal fantasy is all-pervasive. Klee's sly sense of humor and sensitivity of line are evident in works like the *Twittering Machine* (1922, Museum of Modern Art, New York). During the 1930's, the shapes tend to become bolder, the line heavier, and the colors more opaque, as in the *Diana* (1931, Bernoudy Collection, St. Louis) and the *Park near L[ucerne]* (1938, Klee Foundation, Bern). From 1925 to 1930, Klee taught at the Bauhaus, the pioneering German school of design. During these years, he published many of his ideas in the *Pedagogical Sketchbook*. After teaching at the Dusseldorf Academy from 1931 to 1933, Klee was dismissed by the Nazi government; he returned to Bern, where he worked until his death.

Pablo Picasso (Spain, 1881–   ).   After a triumph as a precocious academic student, Picasso came from Spain to Paris and quickly tried the revolutionary styles of the recent past. From early attempts at Impressionism, he moved to the first of many personal stylistic developments: a Blue Period (1901–04), when he used blues and grays to depict people who seem spiritually and physically exhausted, as in *The Old Guitarist* (1903, Art Institute of Chicago). The Blue Period changed to a period of circus subjects (1905) with warm delicate color and then to the Rose Period, in 1905 and 1906, when sensitive contours were combined with nuances of red. Slowly the forms stiffened to become masklike in works like the *Portrait of Gertrude Stein* (1906, Metropolitan Museum of Art, New York); Picasso had become interested in the primitive formal power of African Negro and ancient Spanish sculpture. A major milestone is the *Demoiselles d'Avignon* (1907, Museum of Modern Art, New York), in which five female figures with masklike faces and flat angular body forms become part of a sequence of splintered planes with lost and found edges. The painting is often seen as the starting point for Cubism. An example of Analytic Cubism is Picasso's *Girl with a Mandolin* (1910, Penrose Collection, London), while Synthetic Cubism is exemplified by *The Three Musicians* (PLATE 92). Here, the effect of collage is produced in paint, and the liveliness of the composition is achieved within a more severe discipline than is the vitality of Fauve work. The drawing of *Dr. Claribel Cone* (PLATE 84), done in the same period, presents an entirely different stylistic discipline. It employs the massive simplified forms seen in many of Picasso's paintings during the 1920's. These works have been called Neo-Classical because they have some of the qualities of Greek sculpture. From the next decade, the best known work is the *Guernica* mural, done for the Spanish government building at the Paris World's Fair of 1937. The painting is a violent but controlled expression of the horror evoked by the bombing of the town of Guernica during the Civil War. Interest in dissonant forms—shapes

PLATES 84
and 92
CAN.
JAN.
U. & S.

with much internal conflict in their directional forces—had been building in his work before *Guernica* and has since been prevalent in his art. The stylistic variety continues, however, and ranges from precise portraits to ebullient patterns in strident colors. Even in his advanced age, Picasso continues to maintain a position of world leadership with an inexhaustibly fresh vision.

CAN.
JAN.
U. & S.

Georges Braque (France, 1882–1963).   After doing freely brushed, colorful student work, Braque began a short liaison with Fauvism by turning, in 1906, to highly saturated colors and freely expanding forms. In the following year, he became enthusiastic about the art of Cézanne, and some of Braque's offerings to the Salon d'Automne of 1908 were refused because of his startling use of lively geometric form applied to landscape subjects. The critic Louis Vauxcelles wrote of "Cubism" in describing Braque's work, thus naming one of the most important movements in twentieth-century art. Picasso had already initiated this trend in 1907, and he continued to provide the inventiveness and drive for Cubism, while Braque went through fewer drastic changes of style and worked more methodically in exploring stylistic possibilities within a limited range. The shallow depth, restrained color, and many-faceted order of Analytical Cubism are evident in Braque's *Young Girl with Mandolin* (1910, Collection of Walter P. Chrysler, Jr., New York). After his service in the First World War, Braque worked in the realm of Synthetic Cubism but employed rather unique, low-keyed, sonorous color harmonies like those of *Café-Bar* (1919, Basel Kunstmuseum). In the 1920's, he painted a number of nudes with delicate wavering outlines, thin washes of paint, and monumental proportions like those in some of Picasso's figure compositions from this period. At the same time, Braque continued to work out the sensitive modulations of shape, texture, and color in still-life paintings such as *The Round Table* (1929, Phillips Gallery, Washington, D.C.). More playful arabesque curves and lighter colors appear in some of the work during the 1930's, while the 1940's saw a series of compositions on the theme of the *Atelier* (studio). These paintings reach a new height in complexity and control; textures, textile patterns, and transparent and opaque shapes move back and forth within labyrinthine spatial relationships. To the end of his life, Braque's colors tended to be rich, subtle, and relatively quiet, setting a special mood for each composition.

Edward Hopper (United States, 1882–). Commercial art provided Hopper's living for years while he studied painting with Robert Henri and absorbed European art in museums and on trips abroad. Since 1908, he has lived in New York and spent summers in Maine. Hopper's subjects include New England houses and coast scenes, but he is best known for paintings of the city. Works like *Early Sunday Morning* (1930, Whitney Museum of American Art, New York) and *Night Hawks* (1942, Art Institute of Chicago) utilize bold patterns of light, shadow, and color to distill the character of buildings and to express the monotony and the drama of daily life. A poignant loneliness frequently haunts the mute façades. As Hopper paints the American scene, he helps us find significance in the commonplace; we sense the isolation of the individual within the group, the ageless cycle of life and death, and the ever present witness of man's buildings.

CAN.
U. & S.

José Orozco (Mexico, 1883–1949). Orozco was brought by his family to Mexico City in 1888. After training in the Academy of San Carlos, he turned to painting with social commentary, at first depicting city prostitutes and scenes from college life. From 1923 to 1926, his style became more powerful in the murals for the National Preparatory School in Mexico City. Themes of revolution, pillage, suffering, and cruelty were expressed in huge massive forms. In 1926, he went to New York, where his scenes of revolution were interspersed with views of the city. Orozco's first mural commission in the United States was for the wall of a dining area in Frary Hall at Pomona College (1930). In huge scale, raw angular anatomy, and harshly opposed forms, he depicted *Prometheus Bringing the Gift of Fire to Man*. Next came murals for the New School for Social Research in New York, depicting the revolution of the proletariat in various parts of the world, and the Baker Library murals at Dartmouth College showing the history of America. The Dartmouth paintings include one of the most overwhelming of Orozco's compositions: *Christ Destroying His Cross* (1932–34). Having lost patience with man, Christ has repudiated his sacrifice, chopped down the Cross, and stands facing us with the ax in one hand and the other hand raised in a clenched fist. Behind him are a statue of Buddha, a broken Greco-Roman column, and a mountain of tanks, cannons, and other weapons. Christ's wrath is awesome as he stands with enlarged eyes, blue-shadowed face, reddish beard and hair, a torso

CAN.
JAN.
U. & S.

of blue, orange, green, gray, and purple, and legs that are partially flayed. In 1934, Orozco returned to Mexico to paint his most furious condemnations of warring society in murals for the Palace of Fine Arts in Mexico City and for the University, the Government Palace, and the Hospicio Cabañas in Guadalajara.

PLATE 85
CAN.
JAN.
U. & S.

Max Beckmann (Germany, 1884–1950).   The Weimar Art School provided training for the young Beckmann, whose early style was a boldly brushed Impressionism. During military service in the ambulance corps, he developed compositions of greater dissonance and intensity, like that of his *Self-Portrait with Graver* (PLATE 85). As a leader in the German New Objectivity movement, he depicted the poverty, corruption, and hopelessness of his era. *The Dream* (1921, Collection of Benno Elkan, London) jams into a cramped vertical space an organ grinder, a woman holding a doll, a woman with a cello, a crippled man, and a man with bandaged stumps for hands leaning against a ladder and holding a fish. The twisted, angular, wooden bodies are thrust forward by the upended floor plane, compacting the space and intensifying the conflicts in the forms. Although Beckmann's symbolism does not lend itself to precise interpretation—and was not meant to do so, according to the artist— the composition seems to be a statement of the human situation as Beckmann felt it. The woman suggests the female domination of man, who is left mutilated; the fish may stand for sexuality; and the organ grinder might reflect the monotony and commercialism of human relationships. Beckmann left Germany for Amsterdam during the Second World War. In 1947, he moved to the United States, where he taught painting in St. Louis and in New York. His art is one of the most powerful expressions of concern for the anguish and suffering of twentieth-century man.

CAN.
JAN.
U. & S.

Marcel Duchamp (France and the United States, 1887–   ).   Duchamp has been one of the most publicized exponents of the irrational in art. He studied at the Académie Julian in Paris and painted under the influence first of Cézanne and then of Fauvism. By 1912, he had formed a personal style and painted the *Nude Descending a Staircase* (Arensberg Collection, Philadelphia Museum of Art) that became the focus of attention in the New York Armory Show of 1913. The concern with motion and its expression through multiple contours or repeated shapes suggests the influence of Cubism, photography, and the Italian Futurist movement. In 1912, Marcel and his brothers Jacques Villon and Raymond Duchamp-Villon helped organize the Salon of the Section d'Or (Golden Section), a varied exhibition of trends growing out of Cubist painting. In the following year, Marcel Duchamp proposed a new system of aesthetics based on chance. He dropped three pieces of thread one meter long from a one-meter height onto a flat surface, fixed the accidental positions of the threads on sheets of glass, and then transferred the curves of each piece of thread to the contour of a flat piece of wood. The resulting sheets of glass and pieces of wood were called *Three Standard Stoppages*. Here, Duchamp projects the attitude basic to his art, a celebration of freedom from logic. He exhibited common machine-made articles, such as the *Bottlerack* (1914, original lost), as art objects and called them "ready-mades." In 1915, he came to the United States, where he has spent most of his time since. Duchamp was the center of the New York Dada group by 1921, the year when he filled a metal cage with blocks of marble, a piece of cuttlebone, and a thermometer and called it *Why Not Sneeze, Rose Sélavy?* (Arensberg Collection, Philadelphia Museum of Art). Duchamp's activity as an artist slowly gave way to his interest in chess, although he did help organize the 1942 Surrealist exhibition in New York.

Giorgio de Chirico (Italy and France, 1888–   ).   The well-known precursor of Surrealism was trained in Athens and in the Munich Academy, where he grew to admire the art of the Swiss painter Böcklin, the German painter Klinger, and the German philosopher Nietzsche. For De Chirico, Böcklin's rather literary fantasies, painted with realistic detail, may have expressed the reality underlying the physical world. After a period of Böcklinesque painting, De Chirico returned to Italy in 1909 and developed his own style, though the brooding figure of Odysseus in Böcklin's *Odysseus and Calypso* (1881–83, Museum of Basel) continued to haunt many of his compositions. *The Nostalgia of the Infinite* (Museum of Modern Art, New York), dated 1911 but probably painted in 1913 and 1914, exemplifies the style that made De Chirico famous during his stay in Paris from 1911 to 1915. From the shadow of a foreground arch, we look out upon a huge tower of indeterminate architectural style. Long late-afternoon shadows stretch across the barren landscape, and two small middle-ground figures give enormous scale to the architecture. Colors are somber and the paint is applied thinly. There is an almost hypnotic effect of loneliness and quiet. De

CAN.
JAN.
U. & S.

Chirico's deserted cities, echoing arcades, and vast spaces suggest the world of dreams, and he was properly appreciated by the Surrealists in Paris. After being called into the Italian army in 1915 and stationed in Ferrara, De Chirico found time to paint. He and Carlo Carra, a former Futurist, established the *Scuola Metaphysica*, a small group of painters who were influenced by De Chirico's style. In 1918 De Chirico returned to Rome, became interested in technical procedures and traditional painting, and changed his style slowly toward more conventional work in a Neo-Classic vein. The Surrealists attacked him for having deserted their camp; the critics lost interest in his work, and the unfortunate De Chirico was reduced, upon occasion, to copying or imitating works in his earlier style.

CAN.
JAN.
U. & S.

Joan Miró (Spain and France, 1893–   ).   Miró was born in Barcelona and trained in the La Lonja School of Fine Arts. His early work consisted of landscapes and portraits, which were done in lively colors, patterns of repeated shapes, and occasional delicate detail. After 1919, Miró spent much of his time in Paris, and in 1924 he associated himself with the Surrealist group. By that time, his work had developed a combination of reality and fantasy that evoked the quality of dream experience so interesting to the Surrealists. *The Harlequin Carnival* (1924–25, Albright-Knox Art Gallery, Buffalo, New York) presents a preposterous collection of brightly colored objects. Balloon faces, butterfly-like insects, snake forms with hands, musical notes, dolls, and fish all wriggle buoyantly in the space of an interior. Many of Miró's works are more abstract than this, but some identifiable objects are usually present. Frequently, the soft, undulating, amoeba-like shapes change color where they overlap. Miró often dribbles or splashes paint onto a new canvas, employing accident to suggest the start of a composition. Renown has brought him a number of important mural commissions, such as that for the graduate center at Harvard University (1950–51). After devoting much time to ceramics between 1955 and 1959, he produced two ceramic murals for the UNESCO Building in Paris, compositions for which he was awarded the Guggenheim Prize.

PLATE 91
CAN.
JAN.
U. & S.

Stuart Davis (United States, 1894–1964).   Davis started in the New York school of Robert Henri, the painter of the American scene, and his early work includes street scenes done with Henri's vigorous brushwork. The famous Armory Show of 1913 introduced Davis to Cubist and Fauve painting. After some tentative work in a style like that of Van Gogh, Davis turned to more geometric forms and real or simulated collage effects. During a year in Paris (1928–29), he produced a number of street scenes with delicate line and rectangular patterns of simplified façades. After returning to New York, his compositions were still lifes, bustling city street scenes with garish advertising, or harbor scenes—all done with the aggressive shapes, jangling colors, and bits of letters or words that have come to characterize his mature style. *Something on the Eight Ball* (PLATE 91) is typical in the jerky curves and angles that weave a loose dynamic structure. Shapes are stretched, compressed, or contrasted to intensify their directional forces. Blues, oranges, reds, yellows, and blacks produce a vibrating accompaniment to the dancing forms. It is no surprise to learn that Davis enjoyed jazz music, for his painting has some of the same condensed vitality.

Salvador Dali (Spain and the United States, 1904–   ).   Dali's studies at the School of Fine Arts in Madrid began in 1921 and were interrupted by one suspension in 1924 and a final suspension in 1926; his behavior was too extraordinary to be acceptable to the School. His early interests included Impressionism, Futurism, the art of Vermeer, and that of De Chirico. Between 1925 and 1927, Dali painted in several styles, exploring Cubism, precise realism, and monumental figure painting influenced by Picasso's Neo-Classicism of the 1920's. By 1927, Dali's mature style began to emerge in works that combined recognizable and unrecognizable forms in vast spaces. In 1929, he settled in Paris and became a member of the Surrealist group. *The Persistence of Memory* (PLATE 87) introduced the motif of limp watches hanging over a dead tree, a block, and an organic form. The barren beach, sea, and rocky headland in late-afternoon light have the infinite space and silent loneliness of De Chirico's painting. Dali has written that he wishes to discredit the world of daily reality and give concrete form to irrationality by painting paranoiac hallucinations. Like the other Surrealists, Dali is inspired by the ideas of Freud, and his combinations or metamorphoses of objects evoke the realm of dream experience. Since 1948, he has painted major works using transformations of traditional religious subjects. Great technical skill in illusionistic realism, an extraordinary imagination, and a deliberate effort to arouse

PLATE 87
CAN.
JAN.
U. & S.

public curiosity in his personal appearances have all contributed to Dali's international reputation.

PLATE 88
JAN.
U. & S.

Willem de Kooning (Holland and the United States, 1904–   ).   De Kooning worked at commercial art during the day and studied art in night classes, first at the Academy in Rotterdam, later in Belgium, and after 1926 in New York. Finally, in 1935, he became a full-time painter, and during the 1940's he made his reputation in New York. His early style, in the 1920's and 1930's, often combined recognizable objects with geometric shapes. Forms are solidly modeled in some parts and flattened in others, and there is a constant shifting from mass to plane and from flatness to depth. Colors develop around pinks, yellows, and light blue, sometimes in vibrating contrasts. In the 1940's, he produced a series of abstract and nonobjective works in black and white, with sprightly curving planes and active lines. Such painting composed the major part of his first one-man show in 1948, one which immediately established his reputation. During the 1950's, color was added to the slashing brushwork and explosive energy of these works, as is evident in the series on *Woman*. Plate 88 is typical of this group; the work seems to have emerged from a violent encounter of artist and materials to become a record of action and spontaneous decision.

PLATE 89
U. & S.

Franz Kline (United States, 1910–62).   Kline, one of the leaders in Abstract Expressionism, was born in Pennsylvania. He established himself in New York in 1938, teaching at Pratt Institute and doing commercial art to earn a living. During the 1930's and 1940's, he painted portraits, landscapes, and cityscapes. In 1950, the year of his first one-man show, he saw some of his small drawings enlarged by an opaque projector. The power of the forms thus magnified inspired Kline to turn to broad sweeping strokes in nonobjective compositions. For several years, he used only black and white, but in the mid 1950's he began to employ color again. Kline did brush drawings on newspapers and the pages of telephone books. These sketches were then framed with different-sized rectangles or cut into fragments to find the desired strength, spontaneity, and equilibrium. Once the plan was established in this way, the sketch fragment was enlarged on canvas and painted with large brushes. Kline thus combined chance and selectivity. Although his painting has been compared to Japanese calligraphy, he obtained a sense of urgency unlike the suave, flowing oriental characters. *Le Gros* (PLATE

89) is typical in the slashing power of the black strokes, which establish a horizontal shape poised upon a vertical one. Prolonged observation, however, calls into question the relationship between the black figure and the white background, for the artist dragged white paint over the black in certain areas to keep the white from being simply emptiness. It takes little effort to reverse the figure-ground relationship and see the white shapes as positive forms in black space.

Jackson Pollock (United States, 1912–56).   Pollock studied in Los Angeles and New York and eventually settled on Long Island. His painting became increasingly abstract after 1940. From convulsive linear shapes that sometimes acquire the character of humans, animals, or cryptic symbols, as in the *Pasiphaë* (1943, Collection of Lee Krasner Pollock, Long Island), he turned by 1948 to intricate, non-objective networks of swirling, colored line. The *Blue Poles* (1952, Sidney Janis Gallery, New York) is typical of the late works, sometimes called drip paintings because they were done by dripping paints of different thicknesses from cans onto a canvas stretched flat on the floor. Pollock's rise to fame was cut short by his death in a car accident, but he has had a wide influence as a leader of Abstract Expressionism and Action Painting. CAN. JAN. U. & S.

Andy Warhol (United States, 1931–   ).   Warhol, one of the leaders of Pop Art, was born in Philadelphia and trained at the Carnegie Institute of Technology. He began a career of advertising art and window display and then employed the images of advertising in his paintings. Since 1961, his subjects have included cola bottles, soup cans, Brillo boxes, and the actress Marilyn Monroe. The Brillo boxes are plywood boxes on which labels have been silk-screened; they belong more to the realm of sculpture than do the other subjects, which are depicted on flat surfaces. Repetition is an important characteristic of Warhol's art. Frequently his compositions consist of one subject repeated many times, sometimes with slight variations. Warhol has verbally expressed a conviction that men's individual characteristics are on the wane; his art celebrates the impersonal nature of a machine-oriented culture. RUB.

SCULPTURE

During the first half of the twentieth century, sculpture often reflected movements that occurred first in painting; since about 1950, however, sculpture has shown increasing vitality and inventiveness, greatly increasing its importance in western culture. As the twentieth century has unfolded, especially notable characteristics of sculpture have been: (1) a tendency to find inspiration in primitive art, (2) the rejection of mass by many sculptors, (3) the consideration of space as a positive compositional element, (4) the use of actual movement in sculptural compositions (kinetic sculpture), (5) the increasing use of welded metal, and (6) the tendency to create sculpture by assembling objects that have been worn out or cast aside by our culture.

In the early years of the century, the mobile surfaces of Rodin's art were countered by the stable massivity of Maillol's work. Revolutionary portents emerged in the simplified forms and aggressive three-dimensionality of sculpture done by the Fauve painter Matisse. Cubist sculpture, like Cubist painting, practiced disciplined analysis and free improvisation on natural forms. The Russian-instigated movement of Constructivism produced much nonobjective sculpture, created a pioneering example of kinetic sculpture, and provided a significant statement in the form of the *Realist Manifesto* (1920), which asserted the essential reality of space and time, rather than mass, as elements from which art should be built. The few pieces of sculpture created by Futurists are important three-dimensional expressions of their obsession with speed and constant change. The Dada movement carried further the technique of *assemblage* that had been initiated by Cubist collage and first realized in sculpture by Picasso, with his *Glass of Absinthe* (1914, Daniel-Henry Kahnweiler Collection, Paris). Dada sculptures, sometimes called objects of non-art by their creators, were efforts to ridicule the world of convention and reason. Portentous for later art was the Dada blurring of distinctions between painting, sculpture, and commercially manufactured objects. Surrealist sculpture has been more methodical in the effort to investigate the realm of the non-rational and to stimulate fantasy and free association by surprising combinations. Pop sculpture has ranged from garishly colored depictions of ice cream cones and other foodstuffs, sometimes enormous in scale, to plaster molds of human figures combined with actual furniture. In recent years, kinetic sculpture has become international in scope and combines movement with forms ranging from crisp geometry to bristling assemblages of cast-off objects. The Swiss sculptor Tinguely has even designed kinetic sculpture that destroys itself through fire and explosion in a predetermined sequence; the sculpture becomes not only a unique temporary thing but also a dramatic performance within time and space. Today, sculpture presents a fascinating array of styles; some express spontaneity, freedom, and strong feeling, some glory in the calculated precision of a machine age, and others employ machine-like forms which slyly suggest the character of cult-images.

Aristide Maillol (France, 1861–1944).   Maillol and Rodin were major sources of influence in early twentieth-century sculpture. In the 1890's, Maillol turned from painting and tapestry design to sculpture, and he quickly developed a mature style that remained essentially unchanged throughout his career. Unlike Rodin, Maillol preferred ponderous masses and broad simple surfaces; his poses are usually static. In the *Mediterranean* (PLATE 93), the back and the raised knee and arm create a large stable triangle that is reinforced by the smaller triangular forms of the raised leg and the arm supporting the head. The geometric stability is strengthened by the simple, massive body forms, but the stony monumentality of the work is softened by slight undulations in contour. Throughout Maillol's work, this sturdy female body appears, acquiring the blocky hardness of the *War Memorial at Port-Vendres* (c. 1923) or the more active musculature of *Action in Chains* (c. 1906, Metropolitan Museum of Art but on extended loan to Museum of Modern Art, New York). Although the quiet equilibrium and the ideal form in Maillol's art relate him to the Neo-Classic attitude, he derived his proportions less from ancient Greco-Roman art than from the painting of Gauguin. While appreciation of Gauguin's symbolism, unusual color, and figure distortions was limited during his lifetime, Maillol's symbolism and form received wider public acceptance, in part because of his place later in the twentieth century, and he received many commissions for public monuments.

PLATE 93
JAN.
SEU.
U. & S.

Ernst Barlach (Germany, 1870–1938).   The key to Barlach's style may be found not so much in his studies in Hamburg and Dresden but in an early trip to Paris in 1895, where he saw and admired the massive peasants in Jean François Millet's painting, the expressive force of Van Gogh's art, and the enduring strength of the workers sculpted by Constantin Meunier. From early work in clay, Barlach turned to wood as a favorite material. He reduced the human body

CAN.
JAN.
SEU.
U. & S.

and its costume to large simple masses, often unified by a common texture of gouge marks, emphasizing lines of force that express powerful feeling. His *Man Drawing a Sword* (1911, Cranbrook Academy of Art, Bloomfield Hills, Michigan) rises from the lines of tension in the skirt to the sweeping flare and bold shadows of the cape which focus on the hands drawing the sword. Tense urgency and vitality emanate from the simple forms. Likewise, in *The Avenger* (1923, Wallraf-Richartz Museum, Cologne), the body and clothing are simplified to strengthen the expressive gesture of the form: the projectile-like momentum of the sword-bearing figure and its intense concentration of attention and energy. Barlach illustrated his own plays as well as the writings of Schiller and Goethe. His lithographs, woodcuts, and drawings belong to the general attitude of German Expressionism. Barlach's work was proscribed by the Nazi government, and he died as an outcast in his own land.

CAN.
JAN.
SEU.
U. & S.

Constantin Brancusi (Rumania and France, 1876–1957).   Brancusi studied at the Academy of Fine Arts in Bucharest and, after settling in Paris in 1904, at the École des Beaux Arts. His first exhibit in 1906 revealed the influence of Rodin. Brancusi was even offered a chance to work for Rodin but refused for fear that he would become subservient to Rodin's style. By 1908, Brancusi was finding his way toward greatly simplified forms with slight but important surface variations. The *Girl's Head* (1907–08, Arensberg Collection, Philadelphia Museum of Art) gains monumentality from sweeping planes and the reduction of facial features to grooves and ridges. Such heads indicate Brancusi's debt to African sculpture and his influence on the sculpture of Amedeo Modigliani. By 1910, Brancusi had pushed simplification still further in the *Sleeping Muse* (Solomon R. Guggenheim Museum, New York). The head is reduced to an egg shape with slight ridges for nose, lips, and ear. This reduction to geometric forms must be distinguished from that of Cubism; Brancusi was not interested in a multiplicity of views or a plane-by-plane analysis. He sought form that would be both visually exhilarating in its absolute simplicity and significant in its symbolism. *The New-Born* (1915, Museum of Modern Art, New York) is a sleek bronze egg form that is sliced by a plane and interrupted by a ridge. Where flat surface meets curved surface, the resulting edge gives a more precise idea of the nature of the curved surface. In addition to satisfying formal elegance, the work has subject matter that can be discerned with the help of its title. The egg not only refers to the beginning of life but also suggests the head of an infant, the anonymous face of a child whose personality is yet to be shaped by experience. Brancusi's preference for ovoid form is evident in the series of heads entitled *Mlle Pogany,* done in many versions over a period of years, or in the versions of the *Fish* (one in Museum of Modern Art, New York, done 1918–28), where the sleek, blade-shaped form is poised over a flat surface. Brancusi remained aloof from the various groups or movements in twentieth-century art, yet the influence and appreciation of his sculpture have been international.

Naum Gabo (Russia, Germany, France, England, and the United States, 1890–   ).   Gabo's Russian parents sent him to study medicine in Munich, but his interests turned toward science and sculpture. Acquaintance with Kandinsky, travels in Italy, and visits with his brother Antoine Pevsner, then a painter in Paris, all strengthened Gabo's interest in art. He began to use wood, metal, and celluloid to create forms that were open spatial volumes rather than masses. In 1917, Gabo returned with his brother to Russia, and in 1920 they spoke for the *Constructivist Group* in publishing the *Realist Manifesto,* which called upon art to express the new realities of space, time, and motion. Soon the Soviet government became hostile to abstract art, and Gabo and Pevsner were among the many artists to leave Russia. His *Linear Construction* (PLATE 95) is typical of his mature style. Nylon string and plastic sheets form gracefully curving planes that are subtly adjusted to the square edges of the composition and frame a central opening. Light and space permeate the transparent composition, and space participates as a positive element, providing the major theme in the form of the central opening. Gabo's work continues to embody most of the principles of the 1920 *Manifesto.* Using transparent planes, he imposes order upon space. Time is organized by motion, but motion is expressed by flowing rhythmic continuity rather than actual movement. Since his first experiment with motorized kinetic sculpture in 1920, Gabo has felt that expressed movement, rather than actual move-ment, is more effective for his sculpture.

PLATE 95
CAN.
JAN.
SEU.
U. & S.

Jacques Lipchitz (Lithuania, France, and the United States, 1891–   ).   Lipchitz left his Russian section of Lithuania in 1909 and came to Paris, where he studied at the École des Beaux Arts and the Académie Julian. His early work, such as *Woman and Gazelles* (1912,

CAN.
JAN.
SEU.
U. & S.

owned by the artist), shows a tendency toward stolid equilibrium and heavy simplified anatomy similar to that in the art of Maillol. Soon, however, Lipchitz became involved with the concepts of Cubism. The *Sailor with Guitar* (1914, Philadelphia Museum of Art) has the cascading sequences of planes found in Cubist painting, and the *Man with Guitar* (1916, Museum of Modern Art, New York) develops a more abstract construction of geometric shapes with a hole through the center; Lipchitz' art was to become still more open in form. After a series of relief plaques in a Cubist style, he moved toward freer flowing curves. A series of *transparencies*, as he called them, abandoned the traditional mass of sculpture for thin perforated planes, straps, and wiry forms. During the 1930's, the forms regained some of their mass and became knotted and muscular. *The Song of the Vowels* (1931–32, The Rockefeller Collection, New York) absorbs both harp and harpist in an active heavy cluster of organic forms embracing space. In *Prometheus Strangling the Vulture II* (1944–53, Philadelphia Museum of Art), done after Lipchitz' arrival in the United States, the forms become more convulsive in their energy. Primarily a modeler, Lipchitz makes the malleable clay burst with a life force. He has attempted to exploit the spontaneity of accident by forming blindly a mass of clay and then improvising with the result. He calls such works *semi-automatics*. Although most of his subjects can be recognized, their expressive and symbolic character is not always easy to define; the forms seem laden with suggestions of fecund plant and animal life, of male and female elements, and of the mystery of creation.

PLATE 97
CAN.
JAN.
SEU.
U. & S.

Alexander Calder (United States and France, 1898–   ).   Although Gabo experimented with moving motor-driven sculpture, Calder is acknowledged internationally as the most important pioneer in kinetic sculpture. Calder was born in Philadelphia; he studied engineering before he became a student at the Art Students' League in New York. In Paris, in 1926 and 1927, he used wire to create toy circus performers and caricatures. From this, he turned to more abstract compositions of wire, metal shapes, or wood forms that were activated by electric motors or hand cranks. His acquaintance with the work of Mondrian led him to use color on some parts. Since 1932, he has felt that natural air currents are the best means of activating kinetic sculptures. *Under the White Sickle Moon* (PLATE 97) is typical in the lively curved metal shapes attached to the ends of wires that are delicately hinged and balanced. The flat metal pieces, like those of a weather vane, react to air currents, and the composition bobs and turns. Such sculpture renounces the traditional importance of mass; the open compositions participate actively in time and space. Calder has also done many *stabiles*, in which the motionless forms acquire liveliness from the directional forces within the cut-out sheet metal pieces. It is not surprising that he is also interested in fountains designed as mobile sculpture; he made his debut in this area with a mercury fountain for the Spanish Pavilion at the Paris World's Fair of 1937.

Henry Moore (England, 1898–   ).   England's most renowned twentieth-century sculptor studied sculpture at the Leeds School of Art in London and had his first one-man show in 1928. His early work is simple, massive, and blocky, reflecting an enthusiasm for ancient Mexican sculpture. *The Reclining Woman* (1929, Leeds Gallery, London) has ponderous monumentality in repose. By 1935, he was piercing the masses with openings treated as shaped spaces. The *Reclining Figure* in Plate 94 has such positive spaces; the female figure acquires the broad undulating hills and valleys of a landscape. As in so many of Moore's reclining figures, there is the suggested symbolism of the great earth mother, source of all life. During the 1930's, he did a number of string figures, in which string is threaded through the masses to form groups of lines that define spaces. Meanwhile, the reclining figures became increasingly open. During the bombings of London in the Second World War, Moore made drawings of Londoners sleeping in subway tunnels; war had driven men back into the womb of the earth. The cavernous openings within the figures suggest a relationship with their cavernous environment. It was also during the war that Moore began his series of *Helmet Heads*, helmet-like metal shells into which one of a number of bony core forms could be fitted. Although very abstract, the results produce the uncanny effect of a frightened being looking out of a sheltering helmet. In the 1950's, Moore was chosen to do a large reclining figure for the UNESCO Building in Paris. He also produced a number of sparse skeletal figures, with a regal if occult bearing, and several mutilated warriors, timeless expressions of man's self-destruction. Moore's sculptures, like those of Lipchitz, rely not on precise conventional symbols but on forms that suggest partly hidden truths about the nature of man and his relation to his universe.

PLATE 94
CAN.
JAN.
SEU.
U. & S.

JAN.
SEU.
U. & S.

Alberto Giacometti (Switzerland and France, 1901–1966). Giacometti settled in Paris in 1922. His early work was inspired by Cubism, but from 1929 until 1934 he was a member of the Surrealist group and produced such sculpture as *The Palace at 4* A.M. (1932–33, Museum of Modern Art, New York), a cagelike structure inhabited by skeletal forms. After 1934, he turned to more definite human figures, employing drastically elongated proportions. *The Chariot* (1950, Museum of Modern Art, New York) depicts a corroded set of chariot wheels with an axle upon which stands a female figure so thin that she threatens to dissolve into nothingness. Giacometti's work continued to employ fragile, isolated, phantom figures. Not only the forms but the titles express a concern with man's alienation from his fellows, his loneliness, and his helplessness.

PLATE 96
SEU.
U. & S.

Theodore Roszak (United States, 1907–). Roszak was born in Poland and came to Chicago in 1909. He settled in New York in 1931 and created geometric nonobjective sculpture in the manner of the Constructivists. In 1945 came the style change that led to his mature style, a bristling explosive combination of jagged torn forms and rough textures. The *Whaler of Nantucket* (PLATE 96) has the elusive symbolism of *Moby-Dick*. The welded steel assumes threateningly violent forms that refer obliquely to the snout of a whale, the thrust of a harpoon, or the prow of a boat. Such active, powerful form links Roszak's art to the painting of Abstract Expressionism and Action Painting.

SEU.

Giacomo Manzu (Italy, 1908–). Manzu was trained in the Fine Arts Academy at Verona; his mature style developed in the 1930's. The influence of Medardo Rosso and Auguste Rodin might be seen in the softly flowing wax surfaces of *Susanna* (1937, National Gallery of Modern Art, Rome), but Manzu prefers more quiet contours, more serene poses, and clearer distinctions between the parts. His many statues of girl dancers employ simplified anatomy and sharply defined contours to express the delicate curves of a young body. Unlike Degas, Manzu seeks not action but poise, both relaxed and alert. Manzu's many statues of seated and standing cardinals present an isolated figure frozen within the bold contours of a great stiff cloak. The facial expressions range from fleshy somnolence to tense skeletal asceticism. One finds a jolting stylistic contrast between these works and the reliefs on the Crucifixion theme, done

in the 1940's. The ephemeral forms of the low relief detach themselves only partially from the background by means of inscribed
outlines that frequently fade away.

ARCHITECTURE

Twentieth-century architecture has lost almost all vestiges of regional style and has been characterized by broad international
trends. Eclecticism and Art Nouveau continued as rival stylistic
tendencies in the early years of the century. The relatively new
materials—steel and reinforced concrete—were usually disguised by
traditional forms in eclectic work; their structural potential was
demonstrated more clearly in the organic curves of Art Nouveau.
An architectural style that exploited the advantages of reinforced
concrete had its beginnings in buildings by the Frenchman Auguste
Perret. The simplicity of Perret's work provided refreshing contrast
to the crowded surfaces and self-conscious ornament of both eclecticism and Art Nouveau. Simplification was carried further by several Viennese architects, notably Adolf Loos. After 1910, the severe
cubic forms of Loos's work were echoed in other countries and came
to be known as the *International Modern Style*. Such austere geometric
buildings were produced by Gropius, Mies van der Rohe, and other
architects who worked at the *Bauhaus*, Germany's famous school of
design during the 1920's, and by Le Corbusier in France. A secondary
trend developed between 1910 and 1925 in Holland and Germany,
where certain architects designed buildings with sudden curves or
exaggerated streamlining. Effects ranged from playful fancy to overpowering animated or machine-like forms. This architecture has
been described as expressionistic.

In the United States, Frank Lloyd Wright followed his master
Sullivan in rejecting eclecticism, and Wright's use of uninterrupted
interior spaces, asymmetrically expanding plans, long horizontal
lines, and interlocking masses influenced the early work of Gropius,
Mies van der Rohe, and several of the Dutch architects, all of whom
learned of Wright's work through German publications. In place of
severe geometric simplicity, however, Wright preferred proliferation
of masses and the enrichment of surfaces with contrasting textures
and colors. Wright has had great influence in house design, while
Gropius and Mies van der Rohe have shaped the prevailing styles in
skyscraper design. Except for these tall buildings, the architecture
of the 1950's and 1960's has revealed a general tendency away from

simple cubic forms toward more variety and complexity in mass and surface. Bold contrasts of projecting and receding parts create dramatic light and shadow, and different materials vary texture and color, while reinforced concrete and glass provide hovering masses and exhilarating spatial vistas.

PLATES 98
and 99
HIT.
JAN.
U. & S.

Frank Lloyd Wright (United States, 1867–1959).   America's leading architect in the first half of the twentieth century had two years of engineering training at the University of Wisconsin before going to Chicago and joining the firm of Adler and Sullivan. Wright became a lifelong disciple of Sullivan, although their business relationship was broken off after Wright executed commissions outside the auspices of the firm. Unlike Sullivan, Wright designed few large public buildings. From Sullivan, he acquired a love of mass, a hatred of imitation, and the conviction that form should be determined by function and that decoration should emphasize structure. The low, widespread, asymmetrical ranch house has its ancestry in Wright's early *prairie houses*, of which the best-known is the *Robie House* (PLATES 98 and 99). Here the ground floor contains recreation and utility rooms, the first floor provides the main living areas, and the small third floor contains bedrooms. The asymmetrically arranged spaces are interrupted as little as possible and flow around the central chimney mass. Wright believed that walls should be opened up by large groups of windows to achieve the greatest sense of spaciousness, but he loved to contrast large window areas with unbroken masses of wall. He felt that the exterior should seem to be part of the building's site. The long low lines of the Robie House echo the flat earth plane and were originally punctuated by greenery in planters, so that the house seemed to be a part of nature. The wide overhanging eaves are typical of Wright's conviction that the sheltering function of a roof should be emphasized. Concrete, brick, stone, and natural wood were used for contrasts of color and texture. Wright enjoyed elaborating on interlocking structures; throughout his work, the masses, spaces, and the smallest details interpenetrate to express the unity of the whole. Wright's favorite term for such unity of site, structure, and decoration was *organic architecture*. His designs are remarkably original, though he learned much from Japanese architecture and though some of his more massive buildings have a similarity to ancient Mayan architecture. His greatest technical triumph was the design of the *Imperial Hotel* in Tokyo

(1915–22), which was planned to be earthquake-proof and was un-damaged by the terrible earthquake of 1923. In the 1930's and 1940's, he produced an outstanding design for the growing *Johnson Wax Factory* in Racine, Wisconsin. The houses of his later years sometimes employ a polygonal, circular, or triangular thematic shape as a unifying module for floor plans, for built-in furniture, and even for gardens. A circular module was the basis for the most controversial large building of his career, New York's Guggenheim Museum.

Adolf Loos (Austria and France, 1870–1933). Loos was one of the architects who rebelled against both eclecticism and ornament. He attended a technical high school in Dresden, spent three years (1893–96) in the United States, and returned to Vienna for a career as architect, teacher, and writer. The *Gustav Scheu House* (1912, Vienna) illustrates his preference for starkly simple, boxlike geo-metric forms that rely completely on proportions for aesthetic effect. Loos acquired an international reputation first by his writing, which was published in Vienna and then republished in Berlin and Paris. His most controversial essay was *Ornament and Crime* (1908), in which he equated ornament with crime and argued that culture advances as ornament decreases. Loos, like many of the International Style architects, was an avid admirer of engineers and machines. After 1923, he was active in Paris.

Auguste Perret (France, 1874–1954). Perret was trained as an archi-tect in the École des Beaux Arts and then joined the family building firm. He is especially important as a pioneer in the use of reinforced concrete. In 1902 and 1903, his *Rue Franklin Apartments* used a ferro-concrete framework protected on the exterior by tile. The soaring vertical shafts of superimposed bays give the eight-story building impressive dignity. The thin members of the ferroconcrete frame are evident on the exterior; inside, large spaces are made possible by the widely spaced supports. Even more dramatic openness was arranged in the *Garage Ponthieu* (1905–06, Paris), where the stark concrete frame is filled in with glass. Perret's basilica church of *Notre Dame Le Raincy* (1922–23), near Paris, has canopies of ferro-concrete vaults supported by slender columns. Since the walls are not needed to support the vaulting, they consist of concrete blocks perforated with designs and filled with stained glass. The buoyant,

HIT.

HIT.
JAN.
U. & S.

light-filled interior thus uses new means to achieve some of the qualities of Gothic architecture. Perret often mixed color aggregates with concrete in order to vary the color and minimize weather staining. His later works include the buildings of the *Place de l'Hôtel de Ville* at Le Havre (1948–54), whose carefully proportioned masses and openings are precisely framed with simple moldings and balconies. The effect of discipline and reserved dignity is typical of Perret's designs.

HIT.
JAN.
U. & S.
Walter Gropius (Germany and the United States, 1883–   ).   Mies van der Rohe, Le Corbusier, and Gropius were the major leaders in the trend toward austere simplicity from about 1920 until 1940. Of these, Gropius is the one whose theories have been most influential, through his architecture, his teaching, and his writing. In 1918, after several years of private practice as a Berlin architect, he was appointed Director of the Grand Ducal Saxon School of Applied Arts and the Grand Ducal Academy of Arts in Weimar. He united the two schools under the name *Staatliches Bauhaus* with the aim of joining the creative energies of artists and product designers. Like Loos, Gropius was enthusiastic about the possibilities of the Machine Age and deplored the use of applied ornament as a kind of cultural cake frosting. Gropius' buildings have been consistent with his theory. His first major work (in collaboration with Adolf Meyer), the *Fagus Factory* (1911, Alfeld an der Leine), employed steel supports, concrete floor slabs, and screen walls of glass. He used glass curtain walls again with dramatic effect in an *Office Building for the Cologne Werkbund Exhibition* in 1914 and in the new Bauhaus buildings at Dessau in 1926. In the *Stuttgart Werkbund Housing Exhibition* of 1927, where Le Corbusier and others demonstrated their advanced ideas, Gropius submitted a prefabricated house using a metal frame with asbestos and cork walls. In 1934, Gropius was forced by Nazi policies to leave Germany. He first went to England and then came to the United States. He has often worked with groups on large projects such as the *Pan Am Building* in New York.

PLATE
103
HIT.
JAN.
U. & S.
Ludwig Mies van der Rohe (Germany and the United States, 1886–   ).   Like Gropius, Mies worked with the architect Behrens before starting independent practice in Berlin. The extent of his vision was evidenced in this project for an *Office Building for Friedrichstrasse* in 1919. He proposed a steel frame with cantilevered floors and curtain walls of glass. His design for a *Brick Country House* (1923) has low

spreading lines, grouped windows, and asymmetrical spaces suggesting the influence of Frank Lloyd Wright. Mies directed the Werkbund Exhibition of 1927 in Stuttgart; his apartments built for that occasion exploit the patterns of windows, balcony railings, and drainpipes to create a design with visual interest. Two years later, for the *German Pavilion* at the International Exhibition at Barcelona, Mies produced one of the landmarks of twentieth-century architecture. The small building consisted of marble panels, steel supports, and glass walls. Spaces were defined without being isolated from each other or from the exterior. The spaciousness, the long low lines, the reflecting pools, and the steel, glass, and marble materials all created an effect of serene elegance. The German Pavilion was dismantled after the exhibition, but its stylistic features were incorporated in the famous *Tugendhat House* (1930, Brno, Czechoslovakia). The exterior of the house is starkly simple, employing blank walls and translucent glass on the street side and curtain walls of transparent glass on the garden side. Within, slender steel columns support the roof, and the minimum number of dividing walls creates a maximum sense of space. In 1933, Mies, who was then its director, closed the Bauhaus because of political pressure, and in 1938 he came to Chicago to direct the Armour Institute, which later became the Illinois Institute of Technology. The buildings that he designed for I.I.T. became Mies's manifesto in America. The simple rectangular forms were made of steel cages constructed on a twenty-four-foot module and filled in with brick or glass. The *Seagram Building* (PLATE 103) was planned in 1958. The interior floor space gained by the height of the building enabled the architect to leave a large open area at the base for outdoor pools and gardens set into a pink granite platform, thus relieving the congestion at street level. The amber-gray glass and bronze tower that forms the main part of the building extends beyond the steel piers upon which it is raised, emphasizing its lightness and openness. The vertical bronze beams, partly structural and partly decorative, stress the soaring height and provide a delicate linear pattern in relief. The top is planned to give a strong feeling of culmination without suppressing the vertical emphasis.

Charles Edouard Jeanneret, called Le Corbusier (Switzerland and France, 1888–1965). Charles Edouard Jeanneret, who took the name Le Corbusier to avoid confusion with his cousin, the architect Pierre Jeanneret, was born in Switzerland but made his career in France. For two years he studied with Perret, learning about ferroconcrete

PLATES 100–102 HIT. JAN. U. & S.

and inheriting Perret's admiration for engineering and the efficiency
of machines. Le Corbusier's interests extended from city planning to
low-cost multiple housing. His *Dom-ino* multiple housing project,
planned in 1914 and 1915 but never built, used ferroconcrete frames
that reduced walls to weather screens having no weight-bearing
function. The projects for the *Citrohan House* (1919–22) were a
fuller exposition of his aims. Standardized parts were used wherever
possible, and the severely simple boxlike form was of plain ferroconcrete, with no effort to vary texture. A wall of windows at one
end illuminated a two-story-high living room; bedrooms were on a
balcony and a third floor, and a recreation area was provided on the
flat roof. A second version raised the whole house on concrete piers.
Like Frank Lloyd Wright, Le Corbusier was a leader in opening up
interior space with grouped windows and a minimum of partition
walls. Although his houses were criticized as bleak machines, Le
Corbusier often sacrificed the practical for the aesthetic—the huge
window areas and two-story living rooms, for example, are very
costly to heat. Le Corbusier's sense of the beautiful was inspired by
machines, and his buildings have the look of machine-like efficiency,
but they are designed to satisfy his love of spaciousness and light.
Many of his projects were never built, but the *Citrohan* idea was
realized in a special group of houses built for the Stuttgart Werkbund
Exhibition of 1927. His debut in city planning was made in the
Salon d'Automne of 1922. His project for a contemporary city of
three million inhabitants used mammoth high-rise apartments to
handle population density and to allow vast areas of public parks
on the ground level. Only in recent years, however, did Le Corbusier
have the opportunity to realize his planning theories. The most
notable design is that for Chandigarh, the new capital of Punjab.
After 1940, Le Corbusier's architecture developed a very different
character. The rigid boxlike forms gave way to irregular curves and
deep openings in wall surfaces, producing a more sculptural effect.
Notre-Dame-du-Haut at Ronchamp (PLATES 100–102) is an outstanding
example and one of the most controversial church designs of our
time. The billowing vitality of the roof, the sweeping curves of the
walls punctuated by deep irregular windows, and the spotlighting
effects on the interior dramatize the experience of worship.

HIT.
U. & S.
Eero Saarinen (Finland and the United States, 1910–61).   After
moving with his family to the United States in 1923, Eero studied

in Paris and at Yale before joining the architectural firm of his father, Eliel Saarinen. The son's developing concept of architecture led to a separation from his father in 1948. Eero's firm designed the huge *General Motors Technological Center* near Detroit (1951–57), using a severely rectangular architecture influenced by Mies van der Rohe. Saarinen, unlike Mies, enlivened the forms with red, blue, yellow, and orange walls. From this colorful outgrowth of the International Modern Style, Saarinen turned, like Le Corbusier, to a more complex, animated style. In his *Vassar College Dormitory* (1954–58) and in the *University of Chicago Law School* (1956–60), he employed glass in vertical accordian pleats as deliberate embellishment. Although his former restraint occasionally returned, as in the *IBM Building* in Yorktown, New York (1956), his late trend is strikingly exemplified in the *TWA Terminal* at Kennedy Airport (1956). Here, the convoluted ferroconcrete forms are notable for their absence of stabilizing horizontal and vertical lines. The interior space is restlessly enveloped by ebbing and flowing masses; the exterior suggests a giant bird with lifted wings.

References for representative artists

Canaday, John. *Mainstreams of Modern Art*. New York: Henry Holt and Company, 1959.   CAN.

Hitchcock, Henry Russell. *Architecture: Nineteenth and Twentieth Centuries* (Pelican History of Art). Baltimore: Penguin Books, 1958.   HIT.

Janson, H. W., and D. J. Janson, eds. *Key Monuments of the History of Art: A Visual Survey*. Englewood Cliffs, N.J.: Prentice-Hall; New York: Harry N. Abrams, 1959.   JAN.

Rewald, John. *Post-Impressionism from Van Gogh to Gauguin*. New York: The Museum of Modern Art, 1956.   REW.

Rublowsky, John, and Ken Heyman. *Pop Art*. New York: Basic Books, 1965.   RUB.

Seuphor, Michel (Ferdinand Louis Berckelaers). *The Sculpture of This Century*. Trans. by Haakon Chevalier. New York: George Braziller, 1960.   SEU.

Summerson, John. *Architecture in Britain: 1530–1830* (Pelican History of Art). Baltimore: Penguin Books, 1953.   SUM.

Upjohn, Everard M., and J. P. Sedgwick, Jr. *Highlights: An Illustrated History of Art*. New York: Holt, Rinehart and Winston, 1963.   U. & S.

Suggestions for further study

Crespelle, Jean Paul. *The Fauves*. Trans. by Anita Brookner. Greenwich, Conn.: New York Graphic Society, 1962.

Gropius, Walter. *Scope of Total Architecture* (World Perspectives). Ed. by Ruth N. Anshen. New York: Harper & Brothers, 1955.

Haftmann, Werner. *Painting in the Twentieth Century*. Trans. by Ralph Manheim. New York: Frederick A Praeger, 1960. 2 vols.

Huyghe, René. *Delacroix*. Trans. by Jonathan Griffan. New York: Harry N. Abrams, 1963.

Jean, Marcel. *The History of Surrealist Painting*. Trans. by Simon Watson Taylor. New York: Grove Press, 1960.

Neumann, Erich. *The Archetypal World of Henry Moore*. Trans. by R. F. C. Hull. New York: Pantheon Books, 1957.

Read, Herbert, and Leslie Martin. *Gabo: Constructions, Sculpture, Paintings, Drawings, and Engravings*. Cambridge, Mass.: Harvard University Press, 1957.

Rewald, John. *The History of Impressionism*. New York: The Museum of Modern Art, 1946.

———. *Paul Cézanne: A Biography*. Trans. by Margaret H. Liebman. New York: Simon and Schuster, 1948.

Rosenblum, Robert. *Cubism and Twentieth-Century Art*. New York: Harry N. Abrams, 1960.

Selz, Peter. *German Expressionist Painting*. Berkeley: University of California Press, 1957.

Sloan, Joseph C. *French Painting Between the Past and the Present*. Princeton: Princeton University Press, 1951.

Sullivan, Louis. *Kindergarten Chats and Other Writings*. Ed. by Isabella Athey. Rev. 1918. New York: Wittenborn, Schultz, 1947.

Verkauf, Willy, Marcel Janco, and Hans Bollinger, eds. *Dada: Monograph of a Movement*. Teufen, Switz.: A. Niggli, 1957.

Wright, Frank Lloyd. *An American Architecture*. Ed. by Edgar Kaufmann. New York: Horizon Press, 1955.

PLATE 1   *Menkure and his queen*, from Giza. Dyn. IV. Museum of Fine
Arts, Boston.

PLATE 2 *Temple of Horus*, Edfu. Largely 237–212 B.C. (Photo: Alinari—
Art Reference Bureau)

PLATE 3 *Temple of Horus*, hypostyle hall from the court.

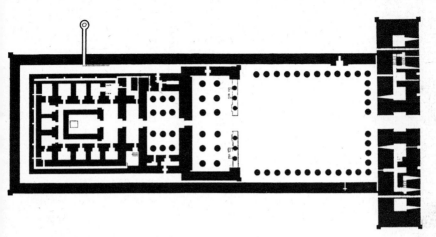

PLATE 4 *Temple of Horus.*

PLATE 5 *Fowling scene from the tomb of Amenemheb, Thebes.* Dyn. XVIII.
British Museum, London. (Photo: Oriental Institute of the University of
Chicago)

PLATE 6   *Parthenon*, Athens. 447–432 B.C.

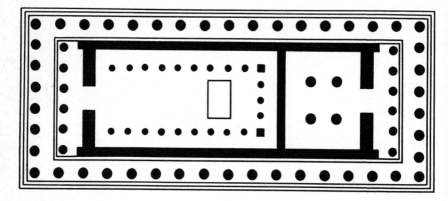

PLATE 7   *Parthenon*.

PLATE 8   *Artemision statue*. About 460–450 B.C. National Museum,
Athens. (Photo: Alison Frantz, Athens)

PLATE 9   *Lapith fighting with centaur,* metope from the Parthenon. 447–432 B.C. British Museum, London.

PLATE 10   EXEKIAS. *Ajax and Achilles playing draughts,* vase painting. 550–525 B.C. Vatican Museum, Rome. (Photo: Furtwängler-Reichhold)

PLATE 11 PRAXITELES. *Hermes with the infant Dionysus.* About 350 B.C. Olympia Museum. (Photo: Alinari—Art Reference Bureau)

PLATE 14 *Colosseum*, Rome. 71–80 A.D. (Photo: Alinari—Art Reference Bureau)

PLATE 15   *Pantheon*, Rome.   Mainly built 118–126 A.D.

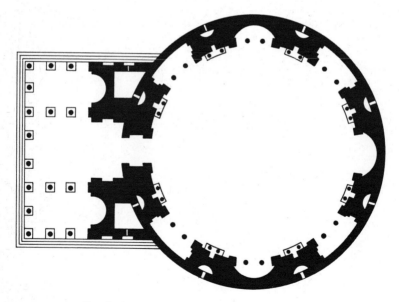

PLATE 16   *Pantheon*.

PLATE 17   *Pantheon*, interior as shown in an 18th-century painting by
Pannini. National Gallery of Art, Washington, D.C., Samuel Kress
Collection.

PLATE 18 *Triumphal Arch of Constantine*, Rome. About 312 A.D. (Photo: Alinari—Art Reference Bureau)

PLATE 19 *Maison Carrée*, Nîmes, France. Completed in 16 B.C. (Photo: French Embassy Press and Information Division)

PLATE 20   *Mosaic showing street musicians.*   Probably first century B.C.
National Museum, Naples.   (Photo: Alinari—Art Reference Bureau)

PLATE 21   *S. Apollinare in Classe.* (Photo: Anderson—Art Reference Bureau)

PLATE 22   *S. Apollinare in Classe*, Ravenna. Interior toward apse, 530–549. (Photo: Alinari—Art Reference Bureau)

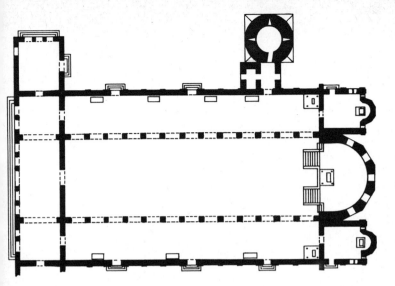

PLATE 23   *S. Apollinare in Classe.*

PLATE 24   *The Apocalyptic Christ*, tympanum, Moissac. Twelfth century.
(Photo: Marburg—Art Reference Bureau)

PLATE 25   *St. Sernin*,
Toulouse. Eleventh and
twelfth centuries.
(Photo: Marburg—Art
Reference Bureau)

PLATE 26   *St. Sernin*,
interior toward apse.
(Photo: Marburg—Art
Reference Bureau)

PLATE 27 *Amiens Cathedral.* Thirteenth century, with later additions.
(Photo: Herschel Levit)

PLATE 28   *Amiens Cathedral*, nave. (Photo: Clarence Ward)

PLATE 29   *Amiens Cathedral*, choir vaults.
(Photo:Clarence Ward)

PLATE 31   Golden Virgin (Vièrge Dorée), from south
transept trumeau of Amiens Cathedral. 1250–70.
(Photo: Marburg—Art Reference Bureau)

PLATE 30   Last Judgment, from central portal of west
façade of Amiens Cathedral. About 1220–30. (Photo:
French Embassy Press and Information Division)

PLATE 32 JAN VAN EYCK. *Arnolfini and His Bride*. 1434. Panel.
33″ x 22½″. Courtesy of the Trustees of the National Gallery, London.

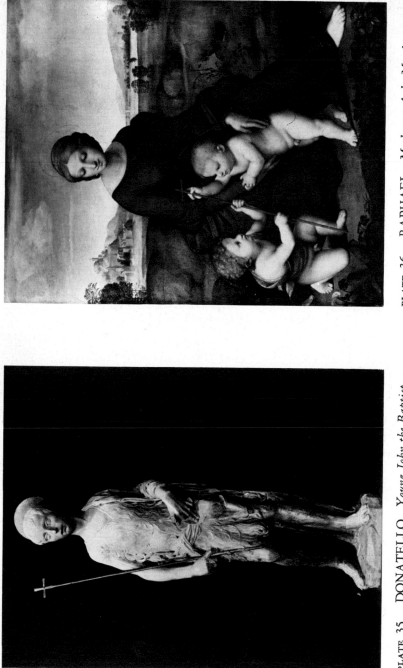

PLATE 36   RAPHAEL.   *Madonna of the Meadow.*
1505.   Panel.   About 4' x 3'.   Kunsthistorisches

PLATE 35   DONATELLO.   *Young John the Baptist.*
About 1455.   Marble.   About 6'.   National Museum,

PLATE 37   MICHELANGELO. *Tomb of Giuliano de' Medici*, New
Sacristy, S. Lorenzo, Florence. 1524–34. Marble. Height of central figure:
about 6'. (Photo: Alinari—Art Reference Bureau)

PLATE 38   MASACCIO. *The Tribute Money*, Brancacci Chapel, S. Maria del Carmine, Florence.   About 1425.   Fresco.   About 20' x 8'.   (Photo: Alinari—Art Reference Bureau)

PLATE 39 LEONARDO DA VINCI. *The Madonna of the Rocks*. About
1485. Panel. About 6′ x 4′. Louvre Museum, Paris. (Photo: Alinari—
Art Reference Bureau)

PLATE 41   TITIAN. *Danaë.* About 1545. Oil on canvas. About 4' x 6'. Capodimonte Museum, Naples. (Soprintendenza alle Gallerie della Campania, Naples.)

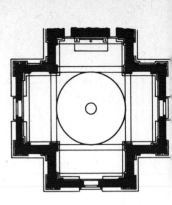

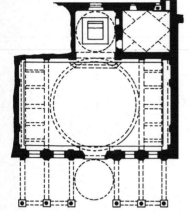

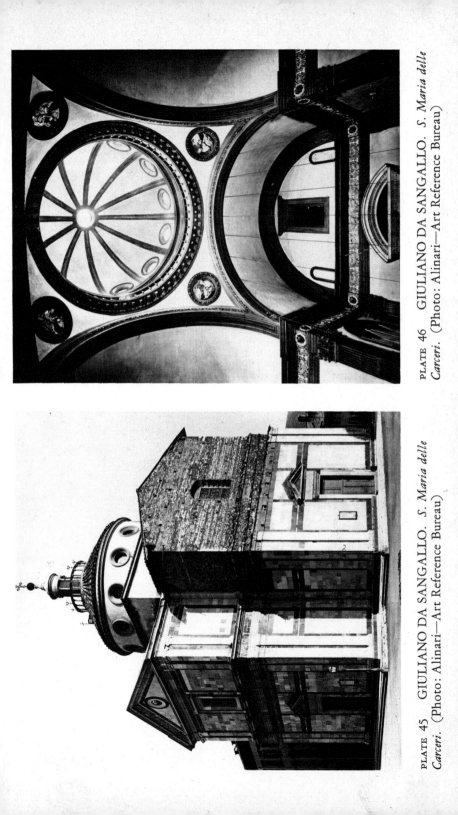

PLATE 46 GIULIANO DA SANGALLO. *S. Maria delle Carceri*. (Photo: Alinari—Art Reference Bureau)

PLATE 45 GIULIANO DA SANGALLO. *S. Maria delle Carceri*. (Photo: Alinari—Art Reference Bureau)

PLATE 47   PALLADIO. *Villa Rotonda*, Vicenza. Begun 1550. (Photo: Alinari—Art Reference Bureau)

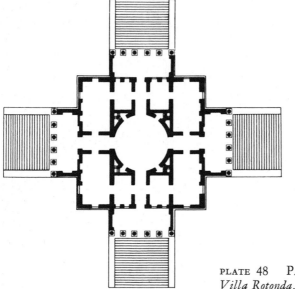

PLATE 48   PALLADIO.
Villa Rotonda.

PLATE 49   DÜRER. *The Four Horsemen of the Apocalypse.* 1497–98.
Woodcut, 15½″ x 11″. Metropolitan Museum of Art, New York, gift of
Junius S. Morgan, 1919.

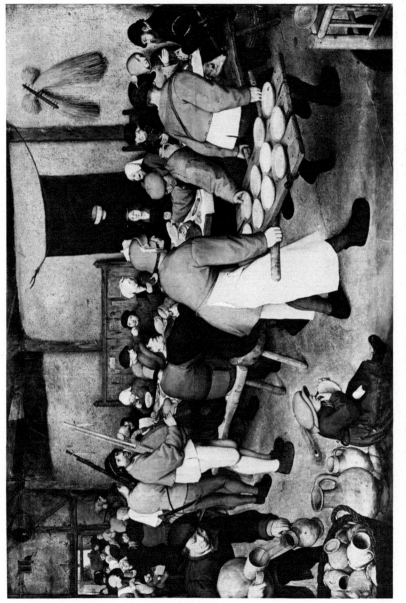

PLATE 51 BRUEGEL THE ELDER. *The Wedding Feast.* About 1565. Panel. About 4' x 5'. Kunsthistorisches Museum, Vienna.

PLATE 53   RUBENS.   *Coup de Lance (The Crucifixion)*

PLATE 52   EL GRECO.   *Crucifixion.*

PLATE 56 BORROMINI. *S. Carlo alle Quattro Fontane*, interior toward altar. Interior: about 53' x 34'. (Photo: Alinari —Art Reference Bureau)

PLATE 55 BORROMINI. *S. Carlo alle Quattro Fontane.*

PLATE 54 BORROMINI. *S. Carlo alle Quattro Fontane*, Rome. 1635–67. (Photo: Anderson—Art Reference Bureau)

PLATE 57   BERNINI. *The Ecstasy of St. Teresa, Cornaro Chapel*, S. Maria
della Vittoria, Rome. 1645–52. Marble. Life-size. (Photo: Alinari—Art
Reference Bureau)

PLATE 58   POUSSIN. *Orpheus and Eurydice*. 1659. Oil on canvas. About
4' x 7'. Louvre Museum, Paris. (Photo: Giraudon, Paris)

PLATE 59   WATTEAU. *Embarkation for Cythera*. 1717. Oil on canvas.
About 4' x 6'. Louvre Museum, Paris. (Photo: Alinari—Art Reference
Bureau)

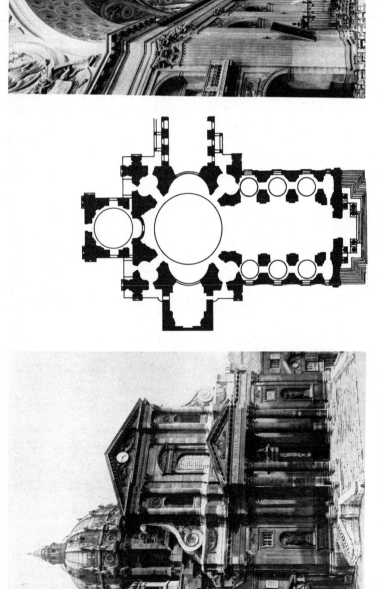

PLATE 62 MANSART AND LEMERCIER. *Val-de-Grâce*, interior toward entrance. Photo: Marburg—Art Reference Bureau)

PLATE 61 MANSART AND LEMERCIER. *Val-de-Grâce.*

PLATE 60 MANSART AND LEMERCIER. *Val-de-Grâce*, Paris. 1645–66. 133' high. (Photo: Marburg —Art Reference Bureau)

PLATE 63   COSMAS AND EGID QUIRIN ASAM. *Assumption of the Virgin*, high altar, monastery church at Rohr. 1718–25. (Photo: Marburg—Art Reference Bureau)

PLATE 64   NEUMANN.
*The Church of the Fourteen
Saints (Vierzehnheiligen),*
near Banz. 1743–72.
(Photo: Marburg—Art
Reference Bureau)

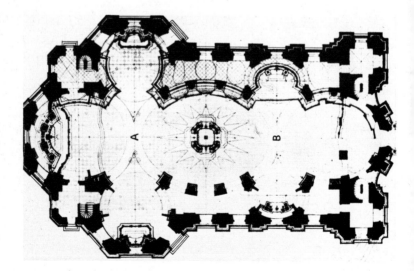

PLATE 65   NEUMANN. *The Church of the Fourteen Saints.*

PLATE 67   GOYA. *May Third, 1808.* 1814–15. Oil on canvas. About
9′ x 13′. The Prado, Madrid.

PLATE 68   DAVID. *The Death of Socrates.* 1787. Oil on canvas. About
5′ x 7′. Metropolitan Museum of Art, New York, Wolfe Fund, 1931.

PLATE 69   CONSTABLE. *The Hay Wain*. 1821. Oil on canvas. About
4' x 6'. Courtesy of the Trustees of the National Gallery, London.

PLATE 70   TURNER. *Rain, Steam, and Speed*. 1844. Oil on canvas.
3' x 4'. Courtesy of the Trustees of the National Gallery, London.

PLATE 71   CANOVA. *Pauline Borghese as Venus*. 1805–08. Marble.
Life-size. Borghese Gallery, Rome. (Photo: Alinari—Art Reference Bureau)

PLATE 72   JEFFERSON. *Monticello*. Charlottesville, Virginia. 1796–1808.
(Photo: Thomas Jefferson Memorial Foundation)

PLATE 73   RODIN. *The Thinker*. 1889. Bronze. 27½″ high. Metropolitan Museum of Art, New York. Gift of Thomas F. Ryan, 1910.

PLATE 74   BARRY AND PUGIN. *Houses of Parliament*, London. Begun 1835. (Photo: Louis H. Frohman)

PLATE 75   DELACROIX.   *The Lion Hunt*.   1861.   Oil on canvas.   30½″ x 38¾″.   Art
Institute of Chicago.   *Potter Palmer Collection*.

PLATE 76   INGRES. *The Apotheosis of Homer*. 1827. Oil on canvas. About 13′ x 17′.
Louvre Museum, Paris. (Photo: Giraudon, Paris)

PLATE 77   MANET. *The Luncheon on the Grass.* 1863. Oil on canvas. About 7' x 9'.
Louvre Museum, Paris. (Permission: SPADEM, © 1963 by French Reproduction Rights,

PLATE 78   COROT.   *Souvenir de Mortefontaine*.   1864.   Oil on canvas.   25¼″ x 34½″.
Louvre Museum, Paris.   (Photo: Giraudon, Paris)

PLATE 80   RENOIR. *The Swing*. 1876. Oil on canvas. 36½" x 28½". Louvre Museum, Paris. (Photo: Giraudon, Paris)

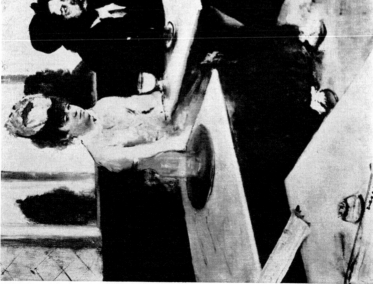

PLATE 79   DEGAS. *The Glass of Absinthe*. 1876. Oil on canvas. 36" x 27". Louvre Museum, Paris. (Permission: SPADEM, © 1963 by French

PLATE 81   SEURAT. *Sunday Afternoon on the Island of La Grande Jatte.* 1884–86. Oil on canvas. About 7′ x 11′. Art Institute of Chicago.

PLATE 82   VAN GOGH.   *Wheat Field with Cypresses.*   1889.   Oil on canvas. $28\frac{1}{2}''$ x $36''$.
Courtesy of the Trustees of the National Gallery, London.

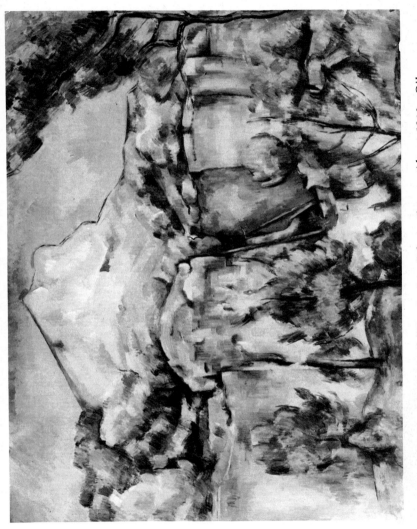

PLATE 83 CEZANNE. *Mt. S. Victoire from Bibemus Quarry.* About 1898. Oil on canvas. 25½″ x 32″. Baltimore Museum of Art, Cone Collection.

PLATE 84   PICASSO.
Dr. Claribel Cone. 1922.
Pencil on paper.
$25\frac{3}{16}''$ x $19\frac{1}{2}''$. Baltimore
Museum of Art, Cone
Collection.

PLATE 85
BECKMANN. *Self-
Portrait with Graver.*
1917. Drypoint.
$11\frac{3}{4}''$ x $9\frac{3}{8}''$. Museum
of Modern Art, New
York, gift of Edgar
Kaufmann, Jr.

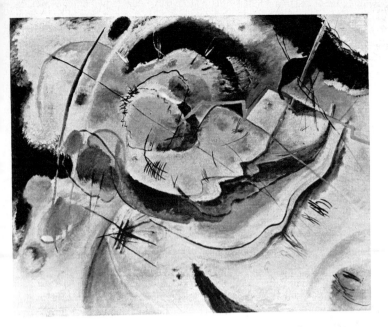

PLATE 86   KANDINSKY. *Improvisation*. 1914. Oil on canvas.
30¾″ x 39⅞″. Philadelphia Museum of Art, Louise and Walter
Arensburg Collection.

PLATE 87   DALI. *The Persistence of Memory*. 1931. Oil on canvas.
9½″ x 13″. Museum of Modern Art, New York.

PLATE 88   DE KOONING.
Woman. 1953-54. Oil on
paper. $34\frac{7}{8}''$ x $23\frac{5}{8}''$.
Brooklyn Museum, New
York.

PLATE 89   KLINE. *Le
Gros*. 1961. Oil on canvas.
About 3' x 4'. Sidney Janis
Gallery, New York.

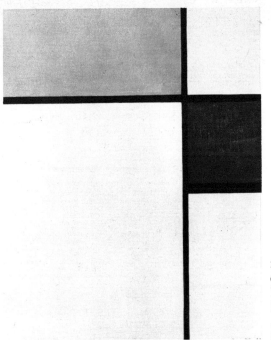

PLATE 90 MONDRIAN.
*Composition with Blue and
Yellow*. 1932. Oil on canvas.
Philadelphia Museum of
Art, A. E. Gallatin
Collection.

PLATE 91 DAVIS.
*Something on the Eight
Ball*. 1954. Oil on
canvas. About 5′ x 4′.
Philadelphia Museum
of Art, A. E. Gallatin
Collection

PLATE 92   PICASSO. *The Three Musicians*. 1921. Oil
on canvas. About 7′ x 6′. Philadelphia Museum of Art.

PLATE 93   MAILLOL. *Mediterranean*. About 1901. Stone. About 3′
high. Collection of Dr. Oskar Reinhart, Winterthur, Switzerland.

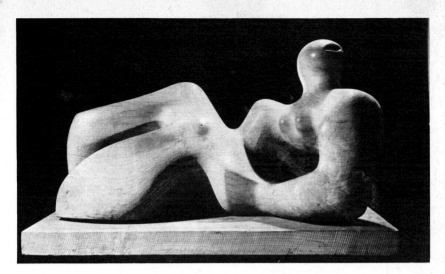

PLATE 94   MOORE. *Reclining Figure*. 1935. Wood. 19″ x 35″.
Albright-Knox Art Gallery, Buffalo.

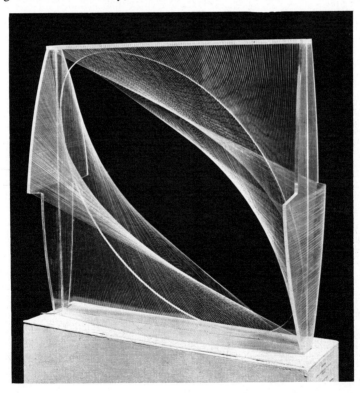

PLATE 95   GABO. *Linear Construction*. 1942–43. Plexiglass.
24¼″ x 24¼″. Phillips Gallery, Washington, D.C.

PLATE 96   ROSZAK. *Whaler of Nantucket*. 1952. Steel. About 3′ x 4′.
Art Institute of Chicago, Edward A. Ayer Fund.

PLATE 97   CALDER. *Under the White Sickle Moon*. 1963. Steel. About
4′ x 5′. Perls Galleries, New York.

PLATE 98   WRIGHT. *Robie House*. Chicago. 1909. (Photo: Chicago Architectural Photo Co.)

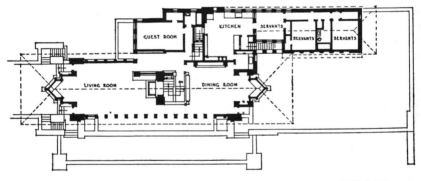

UPPER FLOOR

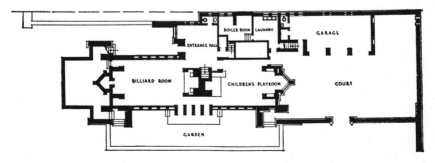

LOWER FLOOR

PLATE 99   WRIGHT. *Robie House*.

PLATE 100
LE CORBUSIER.
Notre-Dame-du-Haut,
Ronchamp, France. 1955.
(Photo: George Holton
from Photo Researchers)

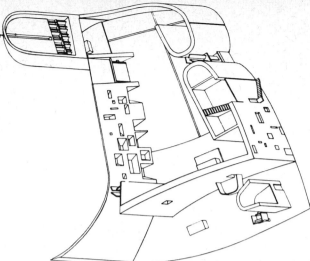

PLATE 102   LE CORBUSIER.
Notre-Dame-du-Haut.

PLATE 101   LE CORBUSIER.   *Notre-Dame-du-Haut,* interior toward altar.
(Photo: G. E. Kidder Smith)

PLATE 103   MIES VAN DER ROHE. *Seagram Building*, New York.
1958. 520' high. (Photo: Ezra Stoller Associates)

Index

Italicized numbers refer to illustrations.

Abbey Church of Moissac, 24, 26
Abstract Expressionism, 249, 260, 261, 268
Action Painting, 249, 261, 268
Adam, L. S., 206
Adam, Robert, 206, 210–11
Adler, Dankmar, 245
Adoration of the Magi, The (Botticelli), 149
aerial perspective, 15
aesthetics, 58–59: concept of sublime in, 178–79
Age of Bronze, The (Rodin), 240
agoras, 92
Ajax and Achilles playing draughts (Exekias), 82
Akhenaten, 76
Alberti, Leon, 154, 155
Alexander and Diogenes (Puget), 195
Alexander mosaic, 100
Algardi, Alessandro, 184–85
alla prima, 40
Allegri, Antonio. *See* Correggio
Altar of Peace, 98–99
Altar of Zeus and Athena, 92
altars, 110
Amarna style painting, 77
Ambassadors, The (Holbein), 14, 15, 172, PLATE 50
ambulatory, 124
Amenhotep IV, 76
American art. *See* Mexican painting; United States architecture; United States painting; United States sculpture

Amiens Cathedral, 4, 16, 25, 26, 50, 51, 134–35, 137, PLATES 27–29
amphitheaters, 101
amphora, 82
Analysis of Beauty, The, 202
Analytical Cubism, 247, 253, 254
anatomy: Egyptian, 69, 76; Greek, 80, 81–82, 87–88, 89; Italian Renaissance, 157; Roman, 100, 104
Antelami, Benedetto, 130, 131
Antwerp Mannerism, 170
Aphrodite from Melos, 93
Apocalyptic Christ, The, 131
Apollo, 81
Apollo and Daphne (Bernini), 185
Apollo Tended by the Nymphs (Girardon), 195
Apollodorus of Damascus, 102
Apotheosis of Homer (Ingres), 23, 25, 226, PLATE 76
Apoxyomenos (Lysippos), 93
apses, 92, 124
aquatint etching, 39
aqueducts, 97, 102
Ara Pacis, 98–99
arch: Greek, 46, 47, 48; Roman, 96
Arch of Titus, 104
Archaic period: Egypt, 63, 64–71; Greece, 80–83
architectural design, 44–55
architectural materials, 44–45. *See also* reinforced concrete
architrave, broken, 154
Arena Chapel (Padua), 139

armature, 42, *43*
Armory Show of 1913, 248, 256, 259
Arnolfini and His Bride (J. van Eyck), 29, 143–44, PLATE 32
Art Nouveau, 242, 246, 269
Artemision Statue, 6, 8, 88, PLATE 8
Artist in His Studio, The (Vermeer), 194
artistic truth, 217, 221
artist's proofs, 36–37
Asam, Cosmas D., 3, 200, 206
Asam, Egid Q., 3, 206
Ash Can School, 248
assemblage, 262
Assumption of the Virgin (Asam), 3, 206, PLATE 63
asymmetrical balance, 21, 22
Athenian grave vase, 82
atmospheric perspective, 15
atrium, 96
Au Moulin Rouge (Toulouse-Lautrec), 237
authentication, 62
Avenger, The (Barlach), 264
axial balance, 21, 22

Bacchus (Caravaggio), 181
balance, 21, 22
Bamboccianti, 180, 189, 212
Banquet of the Officers of St. George (Hals), 191
Bar at the Folies-Bergères (Manet), 229
Barbarian architecture, 124–25
Barbarian metalwork, 122
Barbarian painting, 122–23
Barbizon painters, 219–20
Barlach, Ernst, 263–64
barrel vault, 47
Barry, Sir Charles, 244
barocco, 177
Baroque architecture, 185–88, 195–99
Baroque Classicism, 179
Baroque painting, 179–83, 189–94
Baroque sculpture, 183–85, 194–95
Barye, Antoine, 239
basilica, 96: domed, 116; double-ender, 124; Gothic, 133
Basilica of Constantine, 103
Bathers, The (Renoir), 233–34

Battle of the Centaurs (Michelangelo), 163
Bauhaus, 269, 272
bays, 47
Beatus Commentary on the Apocalypse, 131
Beckmann, Max, 3, 256
Bellini, Giovanni, 148
Bellini, Jacopo, 148
Belvedere Court, 166
Berlin Museum, 244
Berlin Theater, 244
Bernini, Giovanni, 8, 15, 166, 185, 187–88
Bertoldo, Giovanni, 157
Bibliothèque Nationale, 244–45
Bibliothèque Sainte Geneviève, 244
binder, 39, 40, 41
Birth of Spring (Botticelli), 149
Birth of Venus (Botticelli), 149
black-figure painting, 81
Blaue Reiter, Der, 246, 249, 252
blind arcades, 125
Blue Poles (Pollock), 261
Blue Rider group, 246, 249, 252
Böcklin, 257
Bologna, Giovanni da, 165, 183
Bonaparte Crossing the Alps (David), 224
Book of Hours of Étienne Chevalier, 144
Book of Kells, 123
Book of Pericopes of Henry II, 132
Borromini, Francesco, 188
Bosch, Hieronymus, 145
Botticelli, Sandro, 149
Bottlerack (Duchamp), 257
Boucher, François, 203
Bramante, Donato, 166, 168, 169
Brancusi, Constantin, 264–65
Brandenburg Gate, 211
Braque, Georges, 254
Bridge group, 246
broken color, 233, 234
bronze casting, 42, 130
Brücke, Die, 246
Bruegel, Pieter the Elder, 173
Brunelleschi, Filippo, 147, 152, 154
brush drawing, 36
buon fresco, 41
Burghers of Calais, The (Rodin), 240–41

burins, 37
Burke, Edmund, 178
buttressing, 47
Byzantine architecture, 115–16
Byzantine mosaics, 117–18
Byzantine painting, 116–18
Byzantine sculpture, 118–19

Café-Bar (Braque), 254
Calder, Alexander, 266–67
Callicrates, 86
campanili, 116
Campidoglio, 167–68
Campin, Robert, 143, 144
Canaletto, 213
Cancelleria, 154
Canova, Antonio, 3, 238
cantilever, 45
cantoria, 151
Capitol of Virginia, 243
caprices, 213
Caprices, The (Goya), 223
Captive Cupid (Boucher), 203
Caravaggesque lighting, 189
Caravaggio, Michelangelo da, 179, 180,
    181–82
carbon 14 measurement, 62
Carceri (Piranesi), 214
caricature, 228
Carolingian architecture, 124–25
Carolingian painting, 123–24
Carpeaux, Jean-Baptiste, 239
Carra, Carlo, 258
Carracci, Annibale, 179, 181
Carracci Academy, 180
cartoon, 35
carving, 44
caryatids, 86
casein paints, 41
cast stone, 44
Castiglione, Baldassare, 142
casting, 42–44
catacomb paintings, 109, 111, 113–14
Cathedral of Notre Dame, 134
cave paintings, 61
cellae, 83
Cellini, Benvenuto, 164–65

Celtic art, 122–23
centering, 47
central balance, 21, 23
ceramic glazes, 42
Cézanne, Paul, 231–32
chalk, 36
Chapel of Charlemagne, 124–25
charcoal drawing, 36
Chardin, Jean-Baptiste, 202–03
Chariot, The (Giacometti), 268
Charles VII (Fouquet), 144
Chartres Cathedral, 131, 136
Château at Blois, 197
Château of Anet, 174
Château of Maisons, 197
chevet, 127
Chevreul, Michel, 236
chiaroscuro, 14
Chicago Auditorium Building, 245
choir, 124
Choragic monument of Lysicrates, 90
Christ Destroying His Cross (Orozco),
    255–56
Church of St. Michael, 126–27
Churrigueresque architecture, 186
cire perdue method, 43
Citrohan House, 274
classic landscape painting, 219
Claude of Lorraine, 180, 192
clerestory windows, 96
climax, 25
Clodion, 206–07
Cloister Graveyard in the Snow (Friedrich),
    225
closed form, 11
Clouet, François, 172–73
codex manuscript form, 111
coffering, 102
collage, 247, 262
Cologne Werkbund Exhibition, 272
color, 16–17: broken, 233, 234; effects of,
    18; nature of, 17–18; theories, 236;
    value, 17, 18; wheel, 17
Colossal Head of Constantine, 105
colossal orders, 168
Colosseum, 102
Column of Trajan, 104–05

Commentaries, 152
complementary colors, 17–18
composite capital, 101
composition, 1
Composition with Blue and Yellow (Mondrian), 252, PLATE 90
compound piers, 127
Concerning the Spiritual in Art, 249
Constable, John, 225, 227
constructed sculpture, 44
Constructivism, 247, 262, 265
consular diptychs, 115
contrapposto pose, 87
contrast, 25
Contrasts, 244
conversation pieces, 201–02
Conversion of St. Paul (Caravaggio), 181–82
cool colors, 18
Copyright Act for Engravers, 202
corbel tables, 125, *126*
corbeled arch, 47, *48*
Corinthian order, 85
Coronation of the Virgin (Fra Angelico), 146
Corot, Camille, 9, 14, 226–27
Correggio, 160–61
Cortona, Pietro da, 182–83
Coup de Lance (Rubens), 9, 14, 58, 190, PLATE 53
Courbet, Gustave, 228–29
Courtier, The, 142
courtyard, 74
crayons, 36
Creation of Adam (Michelangelo), 158, PLATE 40
Cromwell, 218
Cross vault, 47, *50*, 96
cross-hatching, 3
crossing, 124
Crucifixion, The (El Greco), 180, PLATE 52
crypt, 124
Cubism, 232, 246–47, 253, 254, 262

Dada, 247–48, 257, 262
Dali, Salvador, 15, 32, 259–60
Danaë (Titian), 158, PLATE 41
Dance, The (Carpeaux), 239

Danube style, 170
Daumier, Honoré, 228
David, Jacques Louis, 204–05, 221, 223–24
David (Bernini), 185
David (Donatello), 152
Da Vinci, Leonardo, 142, 149–50, 157
Davis, Stuart, 9, 258–59
Dead Christ, The (Mantegna), 148
Death of Socrates, The (David), 204–05, PLATE 68
De Chirico, Giorgio, 257–58
Decorative Figure on an Ornamental Background (Matisse), 6, 16, 23, 250, COLOR PLATE 4
Degas, Edgar, 6, 230
Déjeuner sur l'herbe (Manet), 229, PLATE 77
De Kooning, Willem, 260
Delacroix, Eugène, 3, 4, 15, 227
Della Robbia, Luca. *See* Robbia, Luca della
De l'Orme, Philibert, 174
Demoiselles d'Avignon (Picasso), 253
Descent from the Cross, The (Van der Weyden), 144
De Stijl group, 247, 252
Dionysiac Mysteries, 100, 145
Dioskourides of Samos, 100–01
dipteral plan, 92
diptych of Anastasius, 119
direct sand casting, 43
Discus-thrower (Myron), 88
Disparates, The (Goya), 223
divisionism, 236
Domenichino, 182
domes, 53, *54*, *55*, 115–16
Dom-ino housing project, 274
Donatello, 152
Doric order, 83, 85, *86*
Dr. Claribel Cone (Picasso), 3, 9, 35, 253, PLATE 84
drapery effects, 93, 131
drawing, 35–36
Dream, The (Beckmann), 256
dry brush drawing, 36
drypoint process, 38
Duccio de Buoninsegna, 138, 139

Duchamp, Marcel, 256–57
Dürer, Albrecht, 171–72
Durham Cathedral, 125, 128–29, *129*
Dutch painting: Baroque, 189, 190–91, 193–94; Renaissance, 145; twentieth century, 247, 251–52, 260

Eakins, Thomas, 234
Early Christian architecture, 110–11
Early Christian mosaic, 114
Early Christian painting, 111, 113–14
Early Christian sculpture, 114
eclecticism, 241, 246, 269
Ecorché (Houdon), 207
Ecstasy of St. Teresa, The (Bernini), 8, 14, 15, 185, PLATE 57
edition, 36
Egyptian architecture: Archaic period, 64–69; Middle Kingdom, 72; New Kingdom, 74–75; Old Kingdom, 64–69
Egyptian painting: Amarna style, 77; Archaic period, 71; Middle Kingdom, 73; New Kingdom, 76–77; Old Kingdom, 71
Egyptian sculpture: Archaic period, 69–70; Middle Kingdom, 72–73; New Kingdom, 75–76; Old Kingdom, 69–70
Eight, The, 248
El Greco, 180–81
elevations, 44
Embarkation for Cythera (Watteau), 201, PLATE 59
empathy, 21
encaustic painting, 41
engaged columns, 47, 96
English architecture: Baroque, 195–96, 198–99; eighteenth century, 208–09, 210–11; Gothic, 133–34, 135; nineteenth century, 241, 243, 244; Romanesque, 128–29
English painting: Baroque, 189; eighteenth century, 200, 201–02, 203–04; nineteenth century, 222, 224–25; Renaissance, 171
English Perpendicular style, 133, 135
English sculpture, 267
engraving, 213
Enlightenment, the, 178

entablature, 83
entasis, 85
Erasmus (Holbein), 172
Erechtheum, 86
etching, 38–39, 213–14, 223
Exekias, 82
Expressionism. *See* Abstract Expressionism; German Expressionism

Fagus Factory, 272
Family of Charles IV (Goya), 223
Farnese Gallery, 181
Fauve, 236, 241, 246
Federal Style, 242
ferroconcrete. *See* reinforced concrete
fête champêtre, 199, 201, 204
Fidenza Cathedral, 131–32
fired clay, 42
Fischer von Erlach, Johann, 209
fixative, 36
flamboyant Gothic, 133
flask, 42
flat masonry arch, 47, *48*
Flaxman, John, 206
Flemish painting: Baroque, 189, 190; Renaissance, 143–44, 145, 170, 173
floodlighting, 14
Florence Cathedral, 152
Florentine architecture, 154–56
Florentine Baptistery doors, 151
Florentine painting, 157–58, 160
Florentine sculpture, 150–53
flying buttresses, *53*
foliated openings, 25
Fontaine des Innocents, 175
foreshortening, 89, 90, 148
form, 1–2, 6, 11. *See also* ideal form; unique form
"form follows function" concept, 245
formal analysis, 2
Forum of Trajan, 102, *103*
forums, 101
fountain, 163
Fouquet, Jean, 144
Four Books of Architecture, 169
Four Horsemen of the Apocalypse, The (Dürer), 171, PLATE 49
Fourteen Saints, The, 209, PLATES 64–66

Fra Angelico, 146–47

Fragonard, Jean-Honoré, 204

Francesca, Piero della, 147–48

freestanding sculpture, 42, 69, 72

French architecture: Gothic, 133, 134; nineteenth century, 241–42, 244–45; Renaissance, 173–74; Rococo, 207–08, 210; Romanesque, 127; seventeenth century, 195, 196–98; twentieth century, 269, 271–72, 273–74

French painting: Baroque, 179–80, 189, 191–92; eighteenth century, 199–200, 201, 202–03, 204–05; Gothic, 138, 139; nineteenth century, 219–21, 226–30, 231–34, 234–35, 236–37; Renaissance, 144, 171, 172–73; Romanesque, 132; twentieth century, 246–47, 250–51, 254, 256–58

French Royal Academy, 178, 199

French sand, 42

French sculpture: eighteenth century, 205, 206–07; Gothic, 136–37, 138; nineteenth century, 237–38, 239–41; Renaissance, 175; Romanesque, 130–31; seventeenth century, 194–95; twentieth century, 263, 264, 268

fresco painting, 41

fresco-secco, 41, 111

fret pattern, 82

Friedrich, Caspar David, 225

Futurism, 247, 256, 262

Gabo, Naum, 11, 15, 44, 265

Gabriel, Anges-Jacques, 210

Gainsborough, Thomas, 203–04

Garage Ponthieu, 271

Gates of Paradise (Ghiberti), 151

Gattamelata (Donatello), 152

Gauguin, Paul, 234–35

Gayrard, Raymond, 127

General Motors Technological Center, 275

genre painting, 170, 173, 180, 189, 200, 212

genre subjects, 93

geodesic dome, *54*, 55

Geometric period, 80–83

Géricault, Théodore, 227

German architecture: Gothic, 134, 135; nineteenth century, 242, 243–44; Rococo, 208, 209–10, 211; Romanesque, 125, 126–27; twentieth century, 269, 272–73

German Expressionism, 236, 241, 246, 248, 251, 264

German painting: nineteenth century, 221–22, 225; Renaissance, 170, 171–72; Rococo, 200–01; Romanesque, 132; twentieth century, 246, 248, 252–53, 256. *See also* German Expressionism

German sculpture: eighteenth century, 205–06; Gothic, 137; Renaissance, 175; Romanesque, 130; twentieth century, 263–64

Ghent altarpiece, 144

Ghiberti, Lorenzo, 42, 151–52

Ghirlandaio, Domenico, 157

Giacometti, Alberto, 268

Giorgione da Castelfranco, 15, 16, 18, 159

Giotto di Bondone, 138, 139, 146

Girardon, François, 195

Girl with a Mandolin (Picasso), 253

Girl's Head (Brancusi), 264

Gislebertus, 130

Glass of Absinthe, The (Degas), 6, 230, PLATE 79

Glass of Absinthe (Picasso), 262

glazes, 40

Glorification of Pope Urban VIII's Reign (Cortona), 182–83

Gloucester Cathedral, 135

Goethe Johann Wolfgang von, 179

Golden Mean, the, 22, *24*

Gospel Book of Ebbo of Reims, 123–24

Gothic architecture, 133–35

Gothic cathedral, *53*

Gothic painting, 138–39

Gothic sculpture, 136–38

gouache, 40

Goujon, Jean, 175

Goya, Francisco, 223

gradation, 25–26

Grand Manner, the, 156, 162

Great Hall of the Baths of Caracalla, The (Piranesi), 213–14

Greek architecture: Archaic period, 82–83; fifth century B.C., 83–86; fourth century B.C., 90; Geometric period, 82–83; Hellenistic, 92
Greek key pattern, 82
Greek painting: Archaic period, 81–82; fifth century B.C., 89–90; Geometric period, 81–82
Greek sculpture: Archaic period, 80–81; fifth century B.C., 86–89; fourth century B.C., 91; Geometric period, 80–81; Hellenistic, 93–94
Green Line, The (Matisse), 250
Greenough, Horatio, 245
groin vault, 47, 50
Gropius, Walter, 272
Gros, Le (Kline), 260–61, PLATE 89
ground: in etching, 38; for paint, 40
Grünewald, 171
Guernica (Picasso), 253–54
Guggenheim Museum, 271
Gustav Scheu House, 271

Hagia Sophia, 116
half-timber construction, 124
hall churches, 126
Hals, Frans, 190–91
Harlequin Carnival, The (Miró), 258
Harlot's Progress, The (Hogarth), 202
Hay Wain, The (Constable), 225, PLATE 69
Head of Christ, The (Rouault), 251
Helmet Heads (Moore), 267
Henri, Robert, 258
Henry, Charles, 236
Henry VIII (Holbein), 172
Hiberno-Saxon art, 122–23
Hildesheim Cathedral, 130
history painting, 211–12
Hogarth, William, 201–02
Holbein, Hans the Younger, 14, 15, 172
Homer, Winslow, 230–31
Hopper, Edward, 255
hôtel particulier, 195
Houdon, Jean Antoine, 207
House of Menander, 97
Houses of Parliament, 244, PLATE 74

Hudson River School, 222
hue, 17
Hugo, Victor, 218
hyperbolic paraboloid, 55
hypostyle hall, 74

IBM Building, 275
iconoclasm, 109–10, 117
iconoclasts, 109–10
iconography, 30, 133
iconology, 32
iconophiles, 109–10
Ictinos, 86
ideal form, 156, 162, 221, 224
illuminated manuscripts. See manuscript illumination
impasto, 40
Imperial Hotel, 270–71
Impression: Sunrise (Monet), 232
Impressionism: French, 220–21, 229–30, 231–34, 234–35, 250; German, 222
Improvisation (Kandinsky), 250, PLATE 86
individual style, 62
Ingres, Jean Auguste, 3, 23, 25, 226
ink drawing, 35
inner sanctum, 74
intaglio processes, 37–39
International Modern Style, 269, 271, 275
Ionic columns, 83, 85
Ionic volutes, 101
Isenheim Altarpiece, 171
Italian architecture: Baroque, 185–88; Early Renaissance, 153–56; High Renaissance, 165–69; Late Renaissance, 165, 169; Romanesque, 127–28
Italian painting: Baroque, 179, 180, 181–83; Early Renaissance, 145–50; eighteenth century, 211–14; Gothic, 138, 139; High Renaissance, 156–62; Late Renaissance, 157; nineteenth century, 222
Italian sculpture: Baroque, 183–85; Early Renaissance, 150–53; High Renaissance, 162–65; nineteenth century, 238; Romanesque, 131–32; twentieth century, 268–69
ivory carvings, 114, 115, 119

jambs, 130
Japanese prints, 220, 235–36, 237
Jeanneret, Charles Edouard. *See* Le Corbusier
Jefferson, Thomas, 242–43
Johnson Wax Factory, 271
Jones, Inigo, 196, 243
Julia Domna, 105
Justinian and Attendants, 6, PLATE 13

Kandinsky, Vassily, 32, 249–50
Karnak temple, 75
keyhole vision, 230
kiln, 42
kinetic sculpture, 44, 262, 265, 266
King Mentuhotep, 73
Kiss, The (Rodin), 241
Klee, Paul, 252–53
Kline, Franz, 260–61
Kopp, Sebald, 209
kouroi, 80–81

Labrouste, Henri, 244–45
lancets, 135
landscape painting, 179, 200, 222–23; classic, 219; Dutch Baroque, 189; Flemish sixteenth century, 170; Roman monochrome, 105, 106
Landscape with Blue Birds (Klee), 252
Langhans, Carl Gotthard, 211
Laocoön and His Sons, 93–94
Last Judgment, The (Van der Weyden), 144
Last Supper, The (Da Vinci), 150
Last Supper, The (Tintoretto), 161
Laughing Cavalier (Hals), 191
Laurentian Library, 166–67
Lebrun, Charles, 189
Le Corbusier, 269, 273–74
Ledoux, Charles Nicolas, 208
Legend of the Holy Cross (Della Francesca), 148
Le Mans Cathedral, 132
Lemercier, Jacques, 197
Le Nôtre, André, 198
Leonardo da Vinci. *See* Da Vinci, Leonardo

Le Roy, J. D., 210
Lescot, Pierre, 174
Le Vau, Louis, 197–98
Liber Veritatis, 192
Liebfrauenkirche, 135
line: definition of, 3; motion in, 4, 5; space and, 4, 6
Linear Construction (Gabo), 11, 15, 44, 265, PLATE 95
linear perspective, 4, 6, 7
linoleum cuts, 37
lintel. *See* post and lintel
Lion Hunt, The (Delacroix), 15, 227, PLATE 75
Lipchitz, Jacques, 265–66
Lippi, Fra Filippo, 147
lithography, 39, 237
local color, 17
Loggia del Capitanio, 169
Lombard pilaster strips, 125
Lombard porch, 125–26
Loos, Adolf, 269, 271
Lorrain, Claude. *See* Claude of Lorraine
lost and found outlines, 227
lost wax method, 43
Louvre Palace, 187–88
Luncheon on the Grass, The (Manet), 229, PLATE 77
Luzarches, Robert de, 134
Lysippos, 93

macchiaiuoli, 222
Maderna, Carlo, 166
Madonna Enthroned, 118
Madonna of the Meadow (Raphael), 29, 58, 160, PLATE 36
Madonna of the Rocks (Da Vinci), 149, 150, PLATE 39
Maestà Altar, 139
Maids of Honor, The (Velázquez), 183
Maillol, Aristide, 263
Maison Carrée, 97, 243, PLATE 19
Man Drawing a Sword (Barlach), 264
Man with a Broken Nose, The (Rodin), 240
Man with Guitar (Lipchitz), 266
mandorla, 130
Manet, Edouard, 229

Mannerism, 150, 157, 160, 161, 162, 165, 167, 169, 170, 177, 179, 181

mansard roofs, 241–42

Mansart, François, 196–97

Mantegna, Andrea, 148

manuscript illumination, 111, 113, 117, 122–23, 132: Gothic, 138; Reims school of, 123–24; Renaissance, 144

Manzu, Giocomo, 268–69

Marionettes, The (Fragonard), 204

martyria, 110

Mary Magdalene (Donatello), 152

Masaccio, 4, 6, 9, 15, 147

mass, 6, 9, 11, *12–13*

mast construction, 124

mastaba, 65, *66*

Mastaba of Itet, 71

Mastaba of Ti, 69

Master of Flémalle, 143

Matisse, Henri, 6, 16, 17, 23, 24, 58, 250–51

mausoleum, 90

Max Schmitt in a Single Shell (Eakins), 234

May Third, 1808 (Goya), 223, PLATE 67

Mazzola, Francesco. *See* Parmigianino

Medici-Riccardi Palace, 155

Medieval art, 121, 122

Mediterranean (Maillol), 263, PLATE 93

medium of expression, 35

Meeting of Pope Leo I and Attila, The (Algardi), 184–85

Meissen porcelain, 205

melancholy, concept of, 218

Menkure and His Queen, 11, 70, PLATE 1

Menzel, Adolf, 222

metal cut, 37

metal engraving, 38

metalwork, Barbarian, 122

Meunier, Constantin, 239–40

Mexican painting, 248–49, 255

Meyer, Adolf, 272

Michel, Claude. *See* Clodion

Michelangelo Buonarroti, 24, 142, 157–58, 163–64, 166–68, 177

Michelozzo di Bartolommeo, 154–55

Middle Ages, 121

Middle Kingdom, 63, 72–73

Mies van der Rohe, Ludwig, 272–73

Military School, 210

Miró, Joan, 258

Miserere, 251

Miss Van Buren (Eakins), 234

Mnesicles, 86

mobile sculpture. *See* kinetic sculpture

modeling, 42

modern art. *See* Abstract Expressionism; Action Painting; Analytic Cubism; Cubism; Futurism; German Expressionism; Op Art; Pop Art; Surrealism

Modigliani, Amedeo, 264

modulation, 24

molds, 42–44

Mona Lisa (Da Vinci), 150

Monaco, Lorenzo, 146

Monastery of the Chartreuse de Champmol, 139

Mondrian, Piet, 32, 251–52

Monet, Claude, 10, 16, 230, 232–33

monotype process, 39

Monticello, 242, PLATE 72

Moore, Henry, 267

Moreau, Gustave, 250, 251

mosaics, 6: Byzantine, 117–18; Early Christian, 114; Roman, 99–101, 105–06

motion: in architecture, 211; in line, 4, *5*; in sculpture (*see* kinetic sculpture); in shapes, *8*–9, *10*

Mt. S. Victoire from Bibemus Quarry (Cézanne), 231, PLATE 83

multiple-point perspective system, 6, 7

mummies, 105, 106

Myron, 87, 88

Nabis, 235

narthex, 110

naturalism, 218

Nazarenes, 221

Nefertiti, 76

Neo-Baroque, 242

Neo-Classicism, 58–59, 178, 205–07, 208–09, 217, 221, 237–41

Neo-Dadaism, 249

Neo-Impressionism, 236

Neo-Plasticism, 252

Neue Sachlichkeit, Die, 248, 256

Neue Wache, 244
Neumann, Balthasar, 209–10
New-Born, The (Brancusi), 264–65
New Kingdom, 63, 74–77
New Objectivity, 248, 256
Night Watch (Rembrandt), 193
nimbus, 161
nonobjective art, 33
Nostalgia of the Infinite (De Chirico), 257–58
Notes of a Painter, 251
Notre-Dame-du-Haut, 13, 16, 274, PLATES 100–102
Notre Dame Le Raincy, 271–72
Nude Descending a Staircase (Duchamp), 256

obelisks, 75
objectivism, 58–59
oculus, 103
Odo of Metz, 124
Odyssey landscapes, 100
oil painting technique, 41, 157
Old Basilica of St. Peter, 110–11
Old Berlin Museum, 244
Old Guitarist, The (Picasso), 253
Old King, The (Rouault), 251
Old Kingdom, 63, 64–71
Old Stone Age, 61
Olympic Theater, 169
one-point perspective system, 6, 7
Op Art, 249
open form, 11
optical mixing, 233
order, 21, 23–25
orders: Greek, 83, *86*; Roman, 101; Tuscan, 101
organic architecture, 270
Ornament and Crime, 271
Orozco, José, 255–56
Orpheus and Eurydice (Poussin), 191, PLATE 58
Osiris cult, 72
Ottonian art, 130

painting techniques, 39–41
paints, 39–40
Palace at 4 A. M., The (Giacometti), 268

Palazzo Massimi, 168
Palazzo Thiene, 169
Paleolithic Age, 61
palette, 41
palisades, 124
Palladian motive, 169, *170*
Palladian movement, 196
Palladian Revival, 208
Palladio, Andrea, 168, 169, 196
Pan Am Building, 272
Pannini, Giovanni Paolo, 213
Pantheon, 102–03, 243, PLATE 15
papyrus, 71
parchment, 111, 123
Paris Psalter, 118
Parmigianino, 150, 161
Parthenon, 25, 45, 86, PLATE 6
Parthenon metopes, 89
Pasiphaë (Pollock), 261
Passion of Christ (Dürer), 171
pastel, 36
Pastoral Concert, The (Giorgione), 15, 16, 159, COLOR PLATE 1
patina, 43
patinières, 43
Pauline Borghese as Venus (Canova), 3, 238, PLATE 71
pavilion, 188
Pazzi Chapel, 153, 154, PLATES 42 & 43
Pedagogical Sketchbook, 253
pediment sculptures, 88
pediments, 85
pencil drawing, 35
pendentive, *54*, 55, 115
Pericles, 85
period style, 62
peripteral buildings, 92
peristyle, 83
Perpendicular period, 133
Perret, Auguste, 269, 271–72
Perseus (Cellini), 164–65
Persistence of Memory, The (Dali), 15, 259, PLATE 87
perspective, *7*: aerial, 15; linear, 4, 6, 7; multiple-point system, 6, 7; one-point system, 6, 7; view, 44
Perugino, 149
Peruzzi, Baldassare, 168

Petit Trianon, 210
Phidias, 87, 89
Picasso, Pablo, 3, 6, 9, 13, 25, 35, 58, 253–54, 262
picturesque qualities, 208–09
Pietà (Botticelli), 149
Pietà (Giotto), 139
Pietà (Goujon), 175
Pietà (Michelangelo), 163
Pietà (Titian), 159
Pietà of Nouans (Fouquet), 144
Pigalle, Jean-Baptiste, 206, 207
pilasters, 101
Piranesi, Giovanni, 213–14
Pisano, Nicola, 136
Place de l'Hôtel de Ville, 272
planographic processes, 39
plans, 44
plaster casting, 42
plate drapery, 131
plate mark, 38
podium, 103
pointillism, 236
pointing machine, 44
Pollock, Jackson, 261
Polyclitus, 87, 89
Polygnotus, 89
Pont-Aven artists, 235
Pont du Gard, 102
Pop Art, 249, 261
Pop sculpture, 262
Portinari Altarpiece, 145
Portrait of a Roman, 99
Portrait of Gertrude Stein (Picasso), 253
portrait sculpture, 162
portraiture, 200, 222: English, 171, 203; Roman, 98
positivistic reaction, 218
post and lintel, 45, 47
posters, 237
Post-Impressionism, 221, 231–32, 235–37
Potato Eaters, The (Van Gogh), 235
Poussin, Nicolas, 179, 189, 191–92
Poussinistes, 199
Praxiteles, 91
Pre-Raphaelites, 222
primary colors, 17
Primaticcio, Francesco, 164

Prince Rahotep and His Wife Nofret, 70
print, 36–37
Prix de Rome, 199
Prometheus Bringing the Gift of Fire to Man (Orozco), 255
proportion, 22, 24
Proto-Baroque, 157, 162, 165, 177, 181
Proto-Doric columns, 72
Psalter of St. Louis, 139
pseudo-dipteral plan, 92
Pucelle, Jean, 138
Puget, Pierre, 194–95
Pugin, A. Welby, 244
putti, 151
pylon, 74
Pyramid of Khafre, 67
Pyramid of Khufu, 66, 67
Pyramid of Menkure, 67
pyramid tomb, 65, 66, 67

quadriga, 90
quadripartite vault, 50
Queen's Chapel, 196
Queen's House, 196
quoins, 196

Rain, Steam, and Speed (Turner), 224, PLATE 70
Rake's Progress, The (Hogarth), 202
Rape of Proserpina (Bernini), 185
Rape of the Sabine Women, The (Bologna), 165
Raphael Sanzio, 29, 58, 157, 160, 168–69
ready-mades, 257
realism, 218: French, 220, 228–29; German, 221–22; Spanish, 223
Realist Manifesto, 262, 265
Reclining Figure (Moore), 267, PLATE 94
red-figure painting, 81, 89
regional style, 62
registers, 71
registration, 37
Reichenau, 132
reinforced concrete, 44, 269, 271, 273–74
relativism, 59
relief processes, 37
relief sculpture, 42, 69
religion: Egyptian, 64; Greek, 79–80

reliquaries, 114
Rembrandt van Rijn, 9, 14, 17, 25, 58, 193
Renaissance architecture, 153–56, 165–69, 173–74
Renaissance painting, 142–50, 156–62, 169–73
Renaissance sculpture, 150–53, 162–65, 174–75
Reni, Guido, 182
Renier of Huy, 130
Renoir, Auguste, 233–34
repetition, 23–25
representational art, 33
Restrained Baroque, 179
Resurrection (Della Francesca), 148
revival, 241
rhythm, 21, 22
ribbed cross vaults, 50, 52, 127, 128, 129
ribs, 50
Richardson, Henry Hobson, 245
rinceau, 97
Robbia, Andrea della, 153
Robbia, Luca della, 152–53
Robie House, 14, 25, 270, PLATES 98 & 99
Robusti, Jacopo. *See* Tintoretto
Rock Breakers (Courbet), 228
Rococo architecture, 207–11
Rococo painting, 200, 201, 213
Rococo style, 178
Rodin, Auguste, 240–41
Roman arch, 96, 101
Roman architecture, 95–97, 101–04
Roman baths, 102
Roman mosaics, 105–06
Roman painting, 99–101, 105–06
Roman sculpture, 98–99, 104–05
Romanesque architecture, 125–29
Romanesque painting, 132
Romanesque sculpture, 129–32
Romanticism, 179, 217–18: French, 219–20; German, 221; Italian, 222; in sculpture, 239; Spanish, 223
Roszak, Theodore, 11, 25, 44, 268
rotulus manuscript form, 111
Rouault, Georges, 251
Roubillac, Louis, 206
Rouen Cathedral (Monet), 16, 232–33, COLOR PLATE 3

round arch, 47, *48*
Rubénistes, 199, 201, 227
Rubens, Peter Paul, 9, 58, 189, 190
Rucellai Palace, 155
Rue Franklin Apartments, 271
Ruins of the Most Beautiful Monuments of Greece, 210
Russian painting, 247, 249–50
rustication, 155

Saarinen, Eero, 274–75
Sacrifice of Abraham (Tiepolo), 212
Sacrifice of Isaac (Ghiberti), 42, 151, PLATE 34
St. Charles Borromaeus, 209
St. Étienne, 125, 127
St. Francis Receiving the Stigmata (Bellini), 148
St. George mosaics, 114
St. James (Jacopo), 164
St. Maclou, 133
St. Marie im Kapitol, 137
St. Matthew (Ghiberti), 151–52
St. Paul's Cathedral, 198
St. Peter's, 110–11, 166, *167*, 168, 187
St. Sernin, 47, 127, *128*, 130–31, PLATE 26
SS. Martina e Luca, 186
Salisbury Cathedral, 135
Salon des Indépendants, 237
Salon des Refusés, 220, 229
Salon exhibitions, 199, 219, 228. *See also* Salon des Indépendants; Salon des Refusés; Salon of the Section d'Or
Salon of the Section d'Or, 257
Samnite House, 100
S. Ambrogio, 125, 127–28
S. Andrea al Quirinale, 187
S. Apollinare in Classe, 116, 117–18, 119
S. Bibiana, 187
San Carlo alle Quattro Fontane, 188, PLATES 54–56
S. Maria delle Carceri, 4, 8, 153, 156, PLATES 44–46
S. Vitale, 116, 118
sand mold process, 42
Sangallo, Giuliano da, 155–56
Sansovino, Jacopo, 164
Sta. Costanza, 111, *112*

sarcophagi, 114, 115, 119
saturation, 17, 18
schiacciato, 152
Schinkel, Karl von, 243–44
School of Athens, The (Raphael), 160
sculpture techniques, 42–44
scumbling, 40
Scuola Metaphysica group, 258
Seagram Building, 13, 273, PLATE 103
Seated King Khafre, 70
Second Empire Style, 241–42
secondary colors, 17
Self-Portrait with Graver (Beckmann), 3, 256, PLATE 85
semi-automatics, 266
serigraphy, 39
Serlio, 174, 198
Seurat, Georges, 236–37
Sèvres porcelain, 203, 205
sexpartite vault, 50, *51*
sfumato effect, 156, 160
shades, 18
shape, 6, 8: motion in, 8–9, *10*; and space, 9, *11*
Sickert, Walter, 222
Siena Cathedral, 139
silk-screen process, 39
simultaneous contrast, 14
Sistine Chapel, 158
sketch, 35
Sleeping Muse (Brancusi), 264
Slodtz, Michel-Ange, 207
Sluter, Claus, 138
Soane, Sir John, 243
soft ground etching, 38
Something on the Eight Ball (Davis), 9, 259, PLATE 91
Soufflot, Jacques-Germain, 208
Souvenir de Mortefontaine (Corot), 9, 226, PLATE 78
space: line and, 4, 6; shape and, 9, *11*; value contrast and, 14–15
Spanish architecture, 186
Spanish painting: Baroque, 180–81, 183; twentieth century, 253–54, 258, 259–60
spans, 45
Spear-bearer (Polyclitus), 89
splayed openings, 125

springing, 47
Squarcione, Francesco, 148
squinch, *54*, 55, 115
Staatliches Bauhaus, 272
stabiles, 267
staffage, 192
stained glass, 132, 133, 138, 251
Standing Youth from Attica, 81
states, 37
Statue of Augustus, 98
steel frame design, 245
stele, 69
stencil processes, 39
step-pyramid of King Zoser, 65, *66*
stoas, 90
Storm and Stress movement, 179
strapwork, 123
stratigraphy, 62
stringcourse, 125
stucco, 152
study, 35
Stuttgart Werkbund Exhibition, 272, 273, 274
style, 62
subject matter: conventional meaning in, 29–32; definition of, 29; degree of, 33; subjective meaning in, 32; symbolism in, 30–32. *See also* symbolism
subjectivism, 59
sublime, the, 178–79
Sublime and Beautiful, The, 178
Sullivan, Louis, 242, 245–46, 270
Sunday Afternoon on the Island of La Grande Jatte (Seurat), 237, PLATE 81
sunken relief, 72, 73, 75, 76
Supper at Emmaus (Rembrandt), 9, 14, 17, 25, 193, COLOR PLATE 2
support, 40
Suprematism, 247
Surrealism, 145, 248, 257, 259
Surrealist sculpture, 262
Susanna (Manzu), 268
Sutton Hoo ship-burial, 122
Swing, The (Renoir), 233, PLATE 80
Swiss painting, 172, 247–48
Swiss sculpture, 262–63, 268
symbolism, 30–32: anthropomorphic, 117; Christian, 114; Gothic, 133; Medieval,

143; in modern art, 256; Renaissance, 145

Symbolist movement, 218

symbolist-synthesist, 235

symmetrical balance, 21, 22

synthesism, 235

Synthetic Cubism, 247, 253, 254

Syon House, 211

tabernacles, 151

tablinium, 96

tempera painting, 40

Tempietto (Bramante), 166

Temple of Bacchus, 103

Temple of Ceres, 83

Temple of Zeus Olympios, 92

temples: Egyptian mortuary, 74–75; Greek, 83, *84–85*, 90; Roman, 96

terra cotta, 42

tesserae, 100

texture, 15–16

theaters, Greek, 90

thematic colors, 24

Theotocopoulos, Domenikos. *See* El Greco

Thinker, The (Rodin), 240, PLATE 73

tholos, 83, 90

three-dimensional solidity, 9, 11, *12–13*

Three Musicians (Picasso), 6, 9, 13, 25, 58, 253, PLATE 92

Three Standard Stoppages (Duchamp), 257

Tiepolo, Giovanni Battista, 212–13

Tintoretto, 161

tints, 18

Titian, 158–59

Tomb of Amenemhat, 72

Tomb of Amenemheb, 77

Tomb of Guiliano de' Medici (Michelangelo), 24, 162, 163, PLATE 37

Tomb of Innocent XI (Algardi), 184

tomb statues, 75

tombs: Egyptian, 65–69, 72, 73, 74; German Renaissance, 175; Italian Renaissance, 162

Torrigiano, Pietro, 175

Toulouse-Lautrec, Henri de, 237

tracery, 133

transparencies, 266

transverse arches, 47

Travelers' Club, 244

Tribute Money (Masaccio), 4, 9, 15, 147

Trinité, La, 129

triptych, 145

Triumphal Arch of Constantine, 104

true arch, 47, *48*

trumeau, 130

truss, 45, *46*, 47

Tugendhat House, 273

tunnel vaults, 47, *49*, 50, 96

Turner, Joseph, 224

Tuscan order, 101

TWA Terminal, 275

Twittering Machine (Klee), 252

tympanum, 24

Under the White Sickle Moon (Calder), 266–67, PLATE 97

unique form, 218

United States architecture: nineteenth century, 242–43, 245; twentieth century, 269–71, 272–73, 274–75

United States painting: nineteenth century, 222–23, 230–31, 234; twentieth century, 249, 256–57, 258–61

United States sculpture, 265–67, 268

University of Chicago Law School Building, 275

Val-de-Grâce, 197, PLATES 60–62

Valley of the Tombs of the Kings, 74

value: changes, 13–14; of color, 17, 18; contrast, 14–15; relations, 14, *15*

Van der Goes, Hugo, 145

Van der Weyden, Roger, 144

Van Eyck, Hubert, 144

Van Eyck, Jan, 29, 143–44

Van Gogh, Vincent, 235–36

vanishing point, 4, 7

Vannucci, Pietro. *See* Perugino

variation, 23–25

vase painting, 81–82, 89–90

Vassar College Dormitory, 275

vaulting, 47, *49*, 50, *51*, *52*, *53*

Vaux-le-Vicomte, 197–98

Vauxcelles, Louis, 254

Vecelli, Tiziano. *See* Titian

Velázquez, Diego, 183

vellum, 123
Venetian painting, 158–59, 161–62
Venus de Milo, 93
Vermeer, Jan, 193–94
Veronese, Paolo, 162, 212
Verrocchio, Andrea del, 149, 153
Versailles, Palace of, 198, 205
Vicchio, Guido da, 146–47
Victorian Gothic, 241
Victory Palette of Narmer, 70
Vien, Joseph, 205
Vierzehnheiligen, 209, PLATES 64–66
View of Toledo (El Greco), 180–81
Villa Madama, 169
Villa of the Mysteries, 100
Villa Rotonda, 13, 169, PLATES 47 & 48
Virgin and Child, The (Van der Weyden), 144
Virgin and Child before a Fire Screen (Campin), 143
Virgin and Child from Melun (Fouquet), 144
Virgin and Child with St. Sebastian (Correggio), 160–61
Vischer, Peter the Elder, 175
Vitruvius, Pollio, 154, 198
votive statues, 75
Vouet, Simon, 189

wagon vault, 47
Wainwright Building, 245
wall paintings: Byzantine, 117; First Style, 99, 100; Fourth Style, 105, 106; Greek, 89; Second Style, 99, 100–01; Third Style, 105, 106; in tomb of Nakht, 77

Warhol, Andy, 261
warm colors, 18
wash drawing, 36
washes, 40
waste mold, 42
watercolor painting, 40
Watteau, Antoine, 199, 201
wattle and daub construction, 124
Wedding Feast, The (Bruegel), 173, PLATE 51
Wedgwood ware, 206
westwork, 124
wet drapery effect, 93
Whaler of Nantucket (Roszak), 25, 44, 268, PLATE 96
Wheat Field with Cypresses (Van Gogh), 236
wheel windows, 125
Whistler, James McNeill, 222
Why Not Sneeze, Rose Sélavy? (Duchamp), 257
Winckelmann, Johann J., 178, 205, 208, 221
Winged Victory from Samothrace, 93
Woman (De Kooning), 260, PLATE 88
wood engraving, 37
woodcuts, 37, 171
Wren, Sir Christopher, 198–99
Wright, Frank Lloyd, 242, 246, 269, 270–71

Young Girl with Mandolin (Braque), 254
Young John the Baptist (Donatello), 152, PLATE 35

Zeuxis, 89

VALUE

WHITE

Each hue may be changed in value (lightness or darkness) and in saturation (purity of color). Red is shown here in different degrees of saturation at one point on a value scale.
[MUNSELL SYSTEM OF COLOR NOTATION]

SATURATION

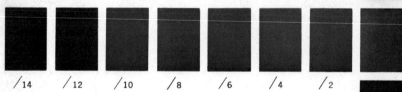

/14   /12   /10   /8   /6   /4   /2

BLACK